Perforating the Iron Curtain

Perforating the Iron Curtain

European Détente, Transatlantic Relations,
and the Cold War, 1965-1985

Edited by

Poul Villaume and Odd Arne Westad

Museum Tusculanum Press
University of Copenhagen
2010

Poul Villaume and Odd Arne Westad (eds.).
Perforating the Iron Curtain: European Détente, Transatlantic Relations, and the Cold War, 1965-1985

© Museum Tusculanum Press and the authors, 2010
Copy editor: Jordy Findanis
Cover design: Signe Schmidt-Jørgensen
Set and printed by Narayana Press, www.narayanapress.dk
ISBN 978 87 635 2588 6

Cover photo: President Gerald Ford standing between Soviet Secretary General Leonid Brezhnev and Soviet Foreign Minister Andrei Gromyko following the conclusion of the European Security Conference Summit in Helsinki on 2 August 1975. American Secretary of State Henry Kissinger can be seen to the left of the group. Polfoto/Corbis.

This book is published with financial support from
Satsningsområdet Europa i Forandring, University of Copenhagen
The Saxo Institute, University of Copenhagen

Museum Tusculanum Press
126 Njalsgade
DK-2300 Copenhagen S
Denmark

www.mtp.dk

Contents

7   Introduction:
    The Secrets of European Détente
    Poul Villaume and Odd Arne Westad

19 The Cold War:
    What It Was About and Why It Ended
    Wilfried Loth

35 Polish Reactions to the West German Ostpolitik and
    East-West Détente, 1966-1978
    Wanda Jarzabek

57 The GDR in the Era of Détente:
    Conflicting Perceptions and Strategies, 1965-1975
    Oliver Bange

79 Forced to Cooperate: The Brandt Government and the
    Nixon Administration on the Road to Helsinki
    Giovanni Bernardini

101 Transformation versus Status Quo: The Survival of the
    Transformation Strategy during the Nixon Years
    Stephan Kieninger

123 The Main Task of the European Political Cooperation:
    Fostering Détente in Europe
    Angela Romano

143 Bridging the Gap between East and West:
    The N+N as Catalysts of the CSCE Process, 1972-1983
    Thomas Fischer

179 The Rise of the Helsinki Network:
    "A Sort of Lifeline" for Eastern Europe
    Sarah B. Snyder

195 Transatlantic Relations, Human Rights, and Power Politics
Gregory F. Domber

215 French Support for Eastern European Dissidence, 1968-1989: Approaches and Controversies
Bent Boel

243 Appendix:
From Helsinki to Belgrade
Skjold G. Mellbin

253 Contributors

257 Select Bibliography

265 Index

Introduction

The Secrets of European Détente

Poul Villaume and Odd Arne Westad

The period from the mid-1960s to the mid-1980s was a time in which the stalemate in the superpower confrontation was gradually superseded, in terms of global importance, by the intensification of peaceful interaction between European states. As an international system, it was generally recognized that the Cold War had had its origins in Europe and would also have its end there, either by a breakdown of the ideological lines of division that split the continent in two, or by cataclysmic war. By 1965 Europe was growing out of the straightjacket that World War II had imposed on it. The post-war period, dominated by rebuilding, austerity, and fear, was over both East and West, and in western Europe the processes of integration were taking hold. While Europe in the first twenty years of the Cold War, from the mid-1940s onwards, had been a main creator of conflict, there seemed to be a possibility that a resurgent Europe could help ease the Cold War. But such a new role required that the politics and policies of the main western European states catch up with the new economic status of their countries. The chapters in this volume help to explain why and how this happened, and why the process of pan-European détente that emerged from the revitalization of France and West Germany was able both to flourish as superpower tension relaxed and to survive the deep freeze that followed up to 1985.

In overall terms, there are three reasons why the global repositioning of Europe led to a lasting détente. All of them are products of changes in Western Europe rather than in the continent's eastern half, even though the eastern response to the changes was important. As Wilfried Loth explains, Europe could only begin to overcome its Cold War when the policies of its major countries began to change, so the emphasis is on Germany and France, and to a lesser extent Britain and Italy. But building bridges is also, as we will see below, dependent on processes of integration, adjustment, and expiation. These were continent-wide phenomena, created both by need and by desire, and as difficult to stop as the more extensive political projects.

The first reason for the durability of détente in Europe was the attraction that Western Europe's increasing affluence, openness, and democracy had on the peoples of Eastern Europe. Despite its monetary problems and energy crises, during the 1960s and 1970s all of Western Europe did not only become richer, but also more equal and offered real opportunities to more of its citizens than ever before. While much of the growth was due to the implementation of American technologies, systems of manufacturing, and business methods, the social model included safety nets that the United States did not possess. It made Europe appear more egalitarian and more preoccupied with workers' welfare, and signalled – not least to many East Europeans – that the choice was no longer between capitalist exploitation and Communist oppression. The Social Democratic and Christian Democratic versions of western politics were seen as having implemented a social contract that was also highly productive in industrial terms. In countries like Czechoslovakia, where the Soviet invasion in 1968 had destroyed the last vestiges of Communist legitimacy, and in Poland, where the workers in 1970 rebelled against the workers' state (and forced the resignation of Wladyslaw Gomulka and the party leadership), the western European model seemed increasingly attractive.

As we discover more about the inner workings of the East European regimes, it becomes clearer that by the 1970s most of them had become dependent, in one form or another, on cooperation with Western Europe. Poland, Hungary and the GDR had received major loans from western banks, without which none of them could import the capital goods they needed for their development. Czechoslovakia and Romania, which – for different reasons – had received fewer loans from the West, saw Western European markets as the only source for the increased trade they depended on. Western consumer products were in vogue throughout this entire region, and a parallel economy, in which the Deutschmark ruled supreme, had, by the late 1970s, become almost as big in terms of value as the state sanctioned economy. In addition, listening to and watching the western part of the continent through radio and television became a significant part of daily life in some areas, and a form of contact – in addition to travel and literature – that the regimes simply did not dare cut off for fear of massive protest.

The second reason why détente in Europe proved to be lasting was the willingness of the new German leadership to accept the historical and territorial boundaries that had been imposed on Germany after World War II – that Germany alone were to blame for the war and that its loss of territory had been just retribution for its aggression. As we see from some of the chapters in this book, this crucial readjustment started even before the coming to power of the *Großkoalition* in 1966, and had been prepared as an intellectual project well prior to Willy Brandt becoming federal chancellor in 1969. For most West Germans, World War II was fading into history, and they failed to see why the FRG – now safely integrated both into the EEC and NATO – could not begin a limited cooperation with the eastern European countries and even the Soviet Union, especially if such a policy could help build contacts with Germans living in the other German state. As Brandt's Ostpolitik got going, many people in eastern Europe – including some of the state leaders – saw the new West German policies as the signs they had waited for to move closer to what was by far the most successful European economy. Brandt's symbolic atonement was of great importance to the public in countries that had suffered from German aggression in World War II, but in terms of the willingness to cooperate financially and economically the new *Bundeskanzler* was walking through open doors.

West Germany's remarkable turnabout was based on the successes of European integration, which, throughout the period, anchored West Germany in western Europe, assimilated authoritarian states (Spain, Portugal, and Greece), and showcased how voluntary forms of cooperation could assist everyone involved. The latter was particularly meaningful to people living in states that relied on the dysfunctional and unproductive forms of integration that the Soviet Union had tried to create, such as CMEA. In détente terms, the close West German cooperation with other countries – indeed, the way in which the new generation of German leaders made their country's future *dependent* on the advances of their partners – painted a new picture of Germany: no longer autarchic, it had become a champion of genuine cooperation both within the West and across the blocs. That it was a German state that became the foremost messenger of European détente was deeply significant to a great number of people in both East and West, even though a minority of stalwarts (especially in Britain) kept fearing a Cold War Rapallo.

The final reason why European détente outlasted that between the superpowers was the durability of the alliance relationships between western Europe and the United States. Many Realist scholars had expected that as economic interests began to differ between the two sides of the Atlantic and as conflicts within the Alliance proliferated (France's withdrawal from NATO's military wing, the direction of Germany's *Ostpolitik*, Communist influence in Italy), then the alliance itself would be weakened. In effect, the opposite happened. As the western Europeans gained more influence within the alliance, the cohesion on key strategic aims improved. And even though the collapse of superpower détente created major strains in the transatlantic political relationship during the last part of Jimmy Carter's presidency and the first part of Ronald Reagan's, neither the military effectiveness nor the political cohesion of NATO was ever in serious doubt, at least not where it mattered: with the leaders in the Kremlin.

In a curious way, the strong alliance between the United States and western Europe made détente more attractive to eastern European elites. It signalled that at least on some issues one could have *both* the power and productivity of America *and* the social inclusiveness of France or Germany. By the 1980s some emerging leaders within the Communist parties wanted to be part of that Europe, and not of the one to which they had belonged since 1945. While Reagan's rhetoric of combating evil appealed to some of the dissidents in the East, many more (at least in the four northernmost Warsaw Pact states) had seen enough of the eroding faith in Communism among party members to believe that negotiations for compromises could succeed. With the Soviet Union on the defensive, many Europeans – East and West – had already prior to 1985 started thinking that change in eastern Europe was underway.

The collection of articles in this book are all revised versions of papers delivered at the "Copenhagen Cold War Conference 2007" at the University of Copenhagen from 30 November–1 December 2007, subtitled "European and Transatlantic Strategies to Overcome the East-West Division of Europe", and chronologically focused on the period from the mid-1960s to the mid-1980s.[1] In his contribution as keynote speaker at the conference "The Cold War: What It Was About and Why It Ended", Wilfried Loth ponders some of the many metaphors of the Cold War as a way of spelling out the inner nature of the Cold War conflict in general, and why it ended the way it did in particular. Noting that the very term "Cold War" is a *contradictio in adjectio*, Loth admits that this metaphor does express essential points of the conflict, mainly that of mutual life-and-death nuclear threats and deterrence. Yet he emphasizes the significance of the institutional and judicial framework of the conflict, from the Yalta and Potsdam agreements in 1945, via the United Nations as a "forum of de-escalation", to the Conference on Security and Cooperation in Europe (CSCE) in the 1970s. According to Loth, the détente and CSCE process favoured the reform forces of the East bloc, thus contributing to the overcoming of the East-West conflict defined as "a competition of the notions of order in coincidence with bipolar tensions". Thus, the Soviet bloc was undermined by ideas of Western think tanks and NGOs, which contributed to what Loth terms the self-liberalization of its people; accordingly, Loth deems it misleading to talk of a defeat of the Eastern side in the sense of the "Cold War" metaphor.

In her chapter "Polish Reactions to the West German Ostpolitik and the East-West Détente", Wanda Jarzabek examines the détente process from the perspective of the Polish leadership, which followed what she terms the Gomulka Doctrine: an endeavour to influence the Warsaw Pact's policies towards Germany in ways favourable to Polish national interests. Polish concerns were that the West German Ostpolitik might leave Poland isolated within the Eastern bloc in yet another "Rapallo", where the Soviet Union and other Pact countries would establish relations with West Germany. In its attempt to coordinate Soviet and Pact détente policies towards the West, and in order to give Poland more room to manoeuvre, Polish leaders suggested, as early as 1969, that even disarmament and economic cooperation be included in the process for a pan-European security conference. Moscow did not give up its resistance against allowing other Warsaw Pact countries to participate in such an extended agenda of a security conference until 1972. Hence, Polish leaders viewed the CSCE agreements in 1975 as a victory, although they were not blind to the Helsinki Final Act's potential to undermine the legitimacy of the Eastern regimes. Even as human rights began to be used as an instrument in international relations in 1977-78, Warsaw did not regret its support of the CSCE process, which also entailed Western transfer of hard currency and modern technology to Poland.

The East German party leadership also realized the danger of ideological challenges and of Social Democratic penetration of the German Democratic Republic, as Oliver Bange's contribution "The GDR in the Era of Détente: Conflicting Perceptions and Strategies, 1965-1975" shows. Yet GDR officials, including party leaders Walter Ulbricht and Erich Honecker, were confident around 1970 that time was on the side of the East German Communists, and that they could use the CSCE process to promote their policies of containing NATO cooperation in western Europe and stem West European integration. However, as Bange notes, this kind of self-deception was, ironically, a significant psychological background for the acceptance of the CSCE process by the East German leadership. By 1974 the Secret Police, Stasi, had realized the imminent dangers of an ideological subversion of the GDR that could follow from the CSCE. While the critical economic, financial and technological needs of the GDR could only be met by cooperating with the West, the GDR leadership was locked in a delicate balancing act between pressure from the Soviet "peace offensive" and demands for a strict political delimitation (*Abgrenzung*) from the West. The increased internal surveillance and repression, which was seen by the regime in East Berlin as the only way out, ultimately led to the popular uprisings of 1989.

The following two chapters focus, from different points of departure, on the attitude of the Nixon-Kissinger administration towards the European détente process. Giovanni Bernardini's article "Forced to Cooperate: The Brandt Government and the Nixon Administration on the Road to Helsinki" points out that although Washington for a long time remained opposed to a specific European role in the détente process between East and West, and explicitly warned West Germany and other western European countries against potential dangers of the CSCE process, Nixon and Kissinger ended up being forced to cooperate with their European allies on détente. The main reasons for this change were, according to Bernardini, the need for closer transatlantic relations after years of inter-allied tensions and the fact that western Europe had become a serious commercial and economic rival to the United States. Furthermore, the US needed West European cooperation on the common defence effort and on reorganizing the capitalist world economy after the crises of the early 1970s. On the West German side, the Bonn government supported the CSCE idea both as a completion of its Ostpolitik and in order to render full international status to the FRG. Yet Bonn failed in its efforts to have East-West talks on Mutual and Balanced Force Reductions (MBFR) included in the CSCE agenda; Bonn feared, with good reason as it turned out, that isolated MBFR talks would be buried in fruitless negotiations on technical details.

In his contribution "Transformation versus Status Quo: The Survival of the Transformation Strategy during the Nixon Years", Stephan Kieninger explains how the US State Department also considered the MBFR talks an important element of the détente process because they served as a mechanism or lever for inducing change in the Soviet system by strengthening the détente-minded elements of the Party top leadership. The State Department tried to persuade Kissinger and Nixon to integrate the MBFR talks into what Kieninger terms the State Department's *transformation strategy* towards the East bloc (including bridge building and freer movement of goods, people and ideas). However, Nixon-Kissinger gained and kept the upper hand on isolating the MBFR issue with their – in Kieninger's wording – Realpolitik-based *status quo* strategy towards the Pact. This strategy was meant to stabilize US political and economic power in the wake of the debacle in Vietnam, widespread social unrest, and the weakening of the dollar. Nixon's and Kissinger's view on Communism in Europe was based on perceptions from the 1950s, in which future risks of domino effects and disintegration of NATO as a consequence of the CSCE process loomed large. The conceptual dualism in Washington's détente policies appears to have weakened the US negotiation position at the CSCE.

The European Community and its newly institutionalized foreign policy cooperation, EPC, on the other hand, clearly came out of the CSCE process as a successful and vigorous negotiator, according to Angela Romano's chapter "The Main Task of the European Political Cooperation: Fostering Détente in Europe". While the United States showed little interest in playing a leading role in pushing for increased mobility and contacts between the blocs or for a more active human rights agenda, the EPC made these issues a key part of its agenda in the so-called Basket III of the CSCE. Remarkably, the EPC countries declined formal coordination with NATO on these and other CSCE issues, arguing that anything more than consultation between EPC and NATO might alienate the participating non-aligned and neutral countries and provoke a more united discipline among the Communist countries involved. Although the West Europeans shared much of the US criticism of Soviet human rights abuses at the 1977 Belgrade CSCE meeting, the EPC joined with neutral and Communist countries in their criticism of the United States for hampering the chances for East-West dialogue on these issues. Similarly, the EPC did not participate in the US led trade embargo against the Soviet Union after the Soviet invasion of Afghanistan in 1979-80. The EC/EPC efforts contributed, Romano concludes, to the continuation of the European détente process in the late 1970s and early 1980s, despite the breakdown of superpower détente during this period.

In addition to the EC/EPC, the European neutral and non-aligned states contributed to the CSCE process on three distinct levels, according to Thomas Fischer's analysis in "Bridging the Gap between East and West: The N+N as Catalysts of the CSCE Process, 1972-1983". They worked as catalysts by performing administrative tasks for the CSCE; they acted as intermediaries between East and West during negotiations; and they were strong advocates of the so-called Basket IV, i.e. clarification of the terms of follow-up mechanisms of the CSCE after Helsinki. Although the position and influence of the N–N states were largely determined, and limited, by the state of relations between NATO and the Warsaw Pact, this group of states did perform significant services as bridge-builders for new ideas and as mediators of compromises that would bring talks forward and save the follow-up process, Fischer concludes. The N+N states were far from a homogeneous group, and with its internal contradictions it was a rather loose coalition; however, it had similar overall interests in various respects, and in particular during the late 1970s and the early 1980s countries such as Austria (mainly reflecting Western positions), Finland (reflecting Soviet/Eastern positions), and Austria and Sweden (acting as arbiters) played important long-term roles in keeping negotiating contacts open until the mid-1980s when the de-escalation of the Cold War took hold.

The following two chapters focus on the impact of the increased United States interest in the CSCE and Helsinki processes from the late 1970s to the mid-1980s. As Sarah B. Snyder points out in her chapter, "The Rise of the Helsinki Network: 'A Sort of Lifeline' for Eastern Europe", the Helsinki Final Act's human rights principles and human contact provisions spurred a flurry of transnational and international responses in support of dissident activism in the Eastern bloc. Snyder attaches particular importance to the increasing American role in the CSCE follow-up meetings, and not least the role played by the lawyer Arthur Goldberg, President Jimmy Carter's head of delegation to the CSCE at the Belgrade meeting 1977-78. Goldberg helped to found the Helsinki Watch Group, the US based monitoring group of private citizens which became the most prominent Western NGO devoted to following the implementation of the Helsinki Act provisions. Helsinki Watch also initiated the International Helsinki Federation for Human Rights, a more formal Helsinki coalition of NGOs. Although there were several contributing factors, Snyder concludes that such transnational activism in support of the Helsinki Final Act played a demonstrably important role in the ultimate release, by the end of 1988, of 600 political prisoners in the Soviet Union, and the return of 80,000 emigrants from East bloc countries. This, in turn, consolidated Western support for Gorbachev's policies of internal and external reform.

In "Transatlantic Relations, Human Rights, and Power Politics", Gregory F. Domber offers a somewhat different analytical perspective, suggesting that the Reagan administration pursued far more flexible and pragmatic policies than often assumed on sanctions and actions against Poland after the imposition of martial law in late 1981. Bilateral and multilateral US diplomatic activities on various levels in western Europe and in NATO were aimed at creating a greater degree of allied consensus, at least on the rhetorical level, on sanctions against Poland. These activities included US use of the Helsinki Final Act provisions to induce the West European governments to take a harder position on Poland. According to Domber, US application of power policies, including the threat of specific economic sanctions against Poland, did unite the West by 1986, thus paving the way for Polish human rights improvements. On this basis, Domber questions some of the conclusions reached by political scientist Daniel Thomas, according to which punitive Western action, including sanctions, did not matter so much to Eastern Communist leaders who, according to Thomas, voluntarily tended to adopt more liberal international norms.[2] This happened only, Domber argues, because Communist leaders entrapped by CSCE regulations modified their behaviour when confronted with a unified US and West European posture.

If détente and an increased focus on human rights in the East in general and in Poland in particular was dependent to some degree on Western top-level pressure, Bent Boel, in his contribution "French Support for Eastern European Dissidence, 1968-1989: Approaches and Controversies", provides evidence from French source materials that the process was at least supplemented significantly by "détente from below", which was particularly alive in France after 1973, and even more so after 1980. Especially the Trotskyites, traditionally a relatively strong left-wing fringe in France, were active in support of dissidents and critics in the Eastern bloc from 1973 and onwards, stimulated by the Helsinki Final Act and by the repressive measures in eastern Europe against Czech and Polish human rights activists. But especially after the Gdansk strikes and the formation of Solidarnosc in Poland in 1980, widespread French sympathy for the dissidents translated into a more proactive strategy. Without confronting directly the east European Communist leaderships, concern for human rights and increased direct personal contacts with Eastern dissidents involved much broader circles in France – including trade unionists and some intellectuals, thus consolidating the "détente from below" perspective.

The Danish top CSCE diplomat in the 1970s, Skjold G. Mellbin, offers his personal "détente from above" perspectives as an appendix to the volume. Mellbin gives some insight into the sometimes haphazard ways in which small states such as Denmark may play significant roles at certain junctures of major historical events. Mellbin's brief eyewitness accounts confirm several of the points of the preceding chapters, including the at times central role of the EC/EPC countries in the CSCE process, the initial reluctance of the US government to engage in the preparation of the CSCE, and the high-profiled yet flexible stance of US representative Goldberg at and after Belgrade.

While historical failures are all orphans, historical successes have many parents. As the present collection indicates, the pan-European détente and

CSCE processes in the 1970s contributed in significant ways to the developments that led to the end of the Cold War in the 1980s, and may thus be called successes. Denmark is among the countries that can claim a share in the process from the beginning, since the Danish Foreign Minister Per Hækkerup – as the first representative of a NATO country – in 1966 proposed that NATO respond favourably to the Warsaw Pact's call for the convening of a pan-European security conference. Although the Danish proposal was rejected out-of-hand by the NATO allies as premature or naïve, or both, the idea was formulated, and three years later it was unanimously accepted by the NATO Council. This was perhaps what Helmut Sonnenfeldt, councellor at the US State Department and Henry Kissinger's closest adviser on European affairs, had in mind when the Danish ambassador to the US, during a conversation in 1974, stated that Denmark supported détente. Sonnenfeldt immediately responded, courteously, that Denmark "not only supports détente. You blazed the trail. The U.S. came to it later".[3]

This volume shows some of the diversity of the origins and the development of détente in Europe. Still, much historical research based on multinational and comparative archival studies in the eastern and western parts of the continent needs to be done before we can determine with even greater accuracy how and under what circumstances the multinational and multiform European détente process came into being, and to what extent it contributed to the demise of the East-West conflict.[4] It seems safe to predict that even more secrets of European détente remain to be revealed.

Notes

1. The editors wish to thank Esben Birk Mortensen for preparing the index of the volume and Kirsten Bruun for assistance with proofreading and preparation of the index.
2. Daniel C. Thomas, *The Helsinki Effect: International Norms, Human rights, and the Demise of Communism* (Princeton 2001).
3. U.S. National Archives & Records Administration, College Park, MD, RG 59, Records of the Office of the Counsellor, 1955-1977, Lot #81 D286 (Records of Helmut Sonnenfeldt), Box 3: Fld. May-July 1974: MemCon July 18, 1974, Bartels & Sonnenfeldt. See also Thorsten Borring Olesen and Poul Villaume, *I blokopdelingens tegn 1945-1972. Dansk Udenrigspolitiks historie, bd. 5* [*By the Sign of the Bloc Division, 1945-1972. History of Danish Foreign Relations, vol. 5*] (Copenhagen 2005), 575-594 and 648-665.
4. For further recent scholarship on European détente, published after 2007, see in

particular Andreas Wenger, Vojtech Mastny and Christian Nuenlist (eds), *Origins of the European Security System. The Helsinki Process Revisited, 1965-75* (Oxford and New York 2008); Frédéric Bozo, Marie-Pierre Rey, N. Piers Ludlow and Leopoldo Nuti (eds), *Europe and the End of the Cold War: A Reappraisal* (London 2008); Oliver Bange and Gottfried Niedhart (eds), *Helsinki 1975 and the Transformation of Europe* (New York and Oxford 2008); Vladislav M. Zubok, "The Soviet Union and Détente of the 1970s", *Cold War History*, vol. 8, no. 4 (November 2008) (Special Issue: Détente and its Legacy), 427–447; Wanda Jarzabek, "Hope and Reality: Poland and the CSCE, 1964-1989", *CWIHP Working Paper*, no. 56 (May 2008); Richard Davy, "Helsinki Myths: Setting the Record Straight on the Final Act of the CSCE, 1975", *Cold War History*, vol. 9, no. 1 (February 2009), 1–22.Thomas Fischer, "'A mustard seed grew into a bushy tree': The Finnish CSCE Initiative of 5 May 1969", *Cold War History*, vol. 9, no. 2 (May 2009), 177-201; Thomas Fischer, *Neutral Power in the CSCE: The N+N and the Making of the Helsinki Accords 1975* (Vienna 2009); Angela Romano, "Détente, Entente, or Linkage? The Helsinki Conference on Security and Cooperation in Europe in U.S. Relations with the Soviet Union", *Diplomatic History*, vol. 33, no. 4 (September 2009), 703-722.

The Cold War

What It Was About and Why It Ended

Wilfried Loth

The "events of 1989" have changed the study of the Cold War in two ways: while historians previously studied a period of contemporary history with an unknown outcome, they have been dealing with a closed subject since 1989. Furthermore, it is roughly known how this story ended. This allows for a more precise approach to the subject, a more precise definition of the terms, and a more secure weighing of the factors. On the other hand, the opening up of archives in the former sphere of influence of the Soviet Empire has reduced the previous one-sidedness of the approach to the sources on the history of the Cold War. Even if much source material still is not available, it has become possible in principle to study decision-making processes in the Soviet sphere of influence.

The study of the new sources, of course, has not only met practical difficulties. The necessity to justify one's previous positions and behaviour, that many have felt, and the hope for spectacular finds and the fame that might be won, have obstructed possible findings. Almost two decades after the radical changes of 1989/1990 it should have become possible to soberly take stock. The question to be dealt with here is how to interpret the history of the Cold War in Europe in the light of the new information.[1]

A Complex Conflict

First, some things have to be said about the terms. Those who deal with Cold War history often speak in metaphors. The term "Cold War" itself is a metaphor, for the first time used by Bernard M. Baruch in a speech of April 1947 and popularized by Walter Lippmann in a booklet published in the autumn of 1947, in order to sum up a new phenomenon for which, up until that time, no term had existed.[2] But "Iron Curtain" also belongs to this category, as do "Thaw", "Détente", the "Prague Spring", the "Velvet Revolution" and "Reunification". Compared to the real events to which they refer, even the terms "building of the wall" and the "fall of the wall" contain metaphorical dimensions. Historians who have dealt with the history of the Cold War to some degree made up their own metaphors in order to express what they thought relevant. In the mid-80s, the American historian John Lewis Gaddis, for example, spoke of the "long peace", which marked the History of the Cold War,[3] and in 2001 the French historian Georges-Henri Soutou named his comprehensive history of the Cold War "The Fifty Year War."[4]

Two things can be gathered from the use of these metaphors, and more precisely from the fact that a variety of metaphors is applied: first, the facts with which the study of the Cold War deals are complex; and, second, the studies oftentimes do not do justice to this complexity. Metaphors are never really precise; they express the facts more or less well, and over time the facts often change and the metaphors once chosen fail to apply any longer. Thus, in analyzing the Cold War it is regularly misleading to primarily hang on to the images we have of the conflict. Rather, it is inevitable to question the sources for how they correspond to the conventional metaphors and to correct them, if necessary. Considering the suggestiveness of the images to which many dealing with the Cold War fall, this, unfortunately, has to be done over and over again.

The metaphor "Cold War" is problematic insofar as it is a *contradictio in adjectio* with the essential point – at least according to Walter Lippmann's intention – being expressed in the adjective. Lippmann meant tensions, tough conflicts, a confrontation between the USA and the Soviet Union, which, however, remained beneath the threshold of a military conflict. In other words: for him, the Cold War was not really a war and neither did it serve the preparation of a war.

In looking back on the epoch of the Cold War one has to agree that he chose the term well. In the world of the Cold War, wars only took place on the periphery, influenced more or less by the tension between the two parts of the Cold War. The extension of power and the pushing through of notions of order without a military confrontation were at the centre of the conflict, and even these objectives were not constantly pursued with equal intensity. Security and prosperity in one's own sphere were more important than successes over the opponent, and there are long stretches in which the history of the Cold War also is a history of reciprocal war prevention.

Georges-Henri Soutou, who introduced the term of "The Fifty Year War", argues along the same lines: "It was not about destroying the enemy in order to take away his territory and resources, he was rather to be pushed to change

internally, to take on a new conception of political and social organisation."[5]
In choosing his terms, Soutou indeed thought about the forming functions of such long conflicts as the Hundred Years' War and the Thirty Years' War, and thus chose a rather unlucky metaphor for an otherwise successful comprehensive study of the Cold War.

The Cold War is such a complex phenomenon because it essentially was made up of two conflicts, which were inseparably linked; but neither were they complementary nor did they follow the same rules.[6] One was the conflict between two notions of order and ideological patterns: liberal democracy, on the one hand, and the voluntaristic dictatorship of a self-appointed avantgarde of historic progress on the other. It was about convictions, social and political conflicts primarily within the existing, constitutional societies. The other conflict's dynamics derived from the polarity of two superpowers that after the Second World War had emerged as the two most important factors of order in world politics. It was about rivalry and common responsibility for world peace, about trust and distrust, about deterrence and cooperation.

On another level of complexity, both sides took up formally equal roles in this double conflict, but which were structured completely differently in material terms. On the one hand, we dealt with developed pluralist societies, which constantly had difficulties in agreeing on common positions, but at the same time always reacted productively to new challenges. On the other hand, there was a centralist despotic system which brought about industrialization without the preliminary bourgeois stage and allowed for developing imperialist power, but at the same time moved towards an ever larger drop in productivity. On the one hand, there was a voluntary alliance of security partners which, besides a few problems among its members, was also a community of values. On the other hand, there was a pact system showing Soviet hegemony which, while bolstering the strategic interests of the Soviet Union, also served the maintenance of power of the Communist apparatus; military force in the Warsaw Pact was indeed only utilized for that purpose.

Thirdly, both sides were subject to considerable processes of change, which altered the conflict's constellation. It was only in the initial post-war period that the Communist model of order had a certain fascination in the West, when the failure of the liberal systems was still well-remembered, while the Soviet Union had left a good impression with its victory over Hitler-Fascism. However, as a result of the Stalinist terror in the Eastern bloc and the stabilization of the Western democracies that took place at the same time, it soon lost appeal in the West. In contrast to the official Soviet self-assurance, the Western model, on the other hand, continuously became more attractive in the Eastern bloc. The Eastern system, thus, depended on bulk-heading itself; the West only gained from the opening of its borders, the exchange of people, information and opinions.

Further changes resulted from the development of atomic weaponry: at first, caution and efforts to secure peace became the inevitable need of the moment for both sides; ever since the second half of the 1970s, the perfection of technology and the arsenals made it ever harder to come to an agreement on how to prevent a nuclear catastrophe. Under the surface of the immobility of the Brezhnev-era, far-reaching changes of an industrial society were taking place which could no longer be controlled by the methods of the command economy and ideological spoon-feeding. Finally, the miniaturizing of computer technology, digitalization and networking as well as the extension of telecommunication via satellite and also the Internet led to a qualitative shift in the conflict situation: now the strengths of the West emerged more clearly, as well as the Eastern weaknesses.

Of course, it does not follow from the complexity of events that the history of the Cold War did not show any distinctive traits of development and structures. However, it can only be identified with an unusual methodical caution. Considering that the Cold War is a highly political and emotional issue, it is hardly surprising that this caution is occasionally missing. Yet, one should not allow oneself to be led astray by it.

Eastern Ambivalences

So what follows from the availability of the internal sources of the Eastern side, which have in principle surfaced as a result of the collapse of the Soviet Empire? How did it expand our notion of the Cold War, the knowledge of its context and developments? So far the Eastern archives have only been analyzed selectively; they are only partially accessible – and some, such as party and government documents of the Soviet Union, have already been closed again. Accordingly, many specific questions still have not been answered.[7] In principle, an image emerges that does not fundamentally alter the knowledge we had of the period prior to the opening up of Eastern archives; it does, however, present the Eastern side in a more colourful and more vivid light, and has, in some regards, brought out new features.[8]

First of all, a basic openness of the situation can be observed. Cooperation and confrontation were closely interlinked – the one could always turn into the other, "hawks" (hardliners) could always turn into "doves" and vice versa. This already applies to Stalin and the beginnings of the Cold War. The sources impressively confirm Stalin's paranoia and total restlessness; at the same time, however, it has become clear that his interest in the continuation of cooperation with the Western powers was even stronger and much more incessant than could be gathered before the opening of the Eastern archives.

In this manner, the first and most comprehensive war objectives programme of the Moscow leadership – edited by the chairman of the Commission for the Planning for Reparations to be Extracted from the Defeated Enemy States, Ivan Maiskii, and handed to Foreign Minister Vyacheslav Molotov on 11 January 1944 – considered the "strengthening of friendly relations with the USA and Britain" to be the first element of post-war politics. Here, Maiskii primarily focused on Great Britain, which he saw in a conflict of interests with the USA and which he intended to "utilize as counterbalance to the imperialist expansion of the USA." Regarding the internal order of the countries of freed Europe, he stated that it was to "be based on the principles of a broad democracy, in the spirit of the notions of the popular front." The allies were to cooperate in the realization of this objective: "There are reasons to assume that regarding the democratization of the regimes in post-war Europe it will be possible for the USSR, the USA and Britain to cooperate, even if it is not always going to be easy."[9]

The installation of Communist hegemony in Eastern Europe thus either appears to be the result of a power political confrontation with Anti-Soviet forces – such as in Poland, Bulgaria and Romania – or the product of the interaction of national revolutionaries and Soviet controllers, who were not up to the task of democratization and, therefore, adopted the Soviet model – such as in the Soviet zone of occupation in Germany and in Hungary.[10] Yet, even the national party leaderships included politicians who did not interpret the "democratic way to Socialism" merely as a temporarily necessitated tactical approach – such as Wladislaw Gomulka, who imposed a democratic programme on the Polish Workers' Party in December of 1945, or Imre Nagy in Hungary. It was only in 1947/48 that the old style party dogmatists were able to finally push through, when Stalin developed a pathological fear of "counterrevolutionary" actions of the "Imperialists" and their allies in the "people's democratic" countries.[11]

The dogmatic toughening of 1947/48, however, should not be equated with a complete rejection of cooperation with the Western powers. As the correspondence between Andreii Shdanov and Stalin in the autumn of

1947 shows, they really interpreted the conditions in Moscow the way they argued publicly: not only did Stalin really believe in the "subjugation" of the European countries to American imperialism; he also seriously hoped that the Communists would be able to mobilize the majority of the democratic and national forces against the Marshall Plan and Western bloc building. The thesis that "two camps" had formed in international politics did not mean – as has been gathered in view of later events – that the Soviet leadership now turned to the confrontation of the Eastern and the Western bloc. Rather, Stalin saw "two opposing lines in international politics." The victory of the "anti-imperialist and democratic" line in the West was to make it possible to continue with cooperation in the interest of securing the peace and of preventing the permanent division of Europe.[12]

However, the means Stalin applied indeed had the opposite effect: a "general strike" and "militant workers' demonstrations" were by no means likely to win the "struggle for the return of the Communists to the government" (as Shdanov told the Italian CP-secretary Luigi Longo[13]) in Western Europe, and by closing his own ranks the division between the East and the West grew. Both at the same time further increased the ever latent Western fear of aggressive Soviet Communism. This also increased the gap between intention and effect of Stalinist policies. The Soviet dictator acted more and more within an imaginary world of imagined dangers and chances; the ideologically blurred perception of reality made it impossible to influence the actual course of events outside of his sphere of power.[14] Regarding the Soviet side, therefore, ideologically based misperceptions of Western policies were one reason for the failure of East-West cooperation. The others were controlling weaknesses of a system in which the Soviet ruler wanted to decide everything himself, but presumably was told by his informants only what he wanted to hear.

It therefore shows that the Soviet interest in cooperation with the Western powers was even stronger than has previously been gathered. In the pursuit of his security and great power interests, Stalin deferred the export of the Bolshevist revolution even further; he had an even more pragmatic approach to the development of scenarios in Eastern Europe; he was obviously more constructive in his thoughts on Germany; and he even clung more tenaciously to the perspective of cooperation than should be assumed in light of the aggressive propaganda terminology in the Cominform style. On the other hand, the ideological limits of his ability to cooperate as well as those that were necessitated by the system have become clearer: the exaggerated fears and the illusions concerning political decision-making processes in the

West, the the insufficient provision of appropriate information input, or the inability to ensure trust-building diplomacy and the realization of democratization programmes – for which the Soviet Union was responsible as an occupation power. In view of these weaknesses of the Stalinist system, Communist movements and class struggle ideology were able to develop their own momentum within the sphere of power of the Red Army, which objectively were not in line with the strategic objectives of the Soviet dictator.[15]

Stalin's successors were more realistic in their perception of Soviet interests and Western politics, yet they were subjected to the pressure of the Communist bureaucracies, the interests of which amounted to little more than the extension of their own power and the basic conservation of the existing system of rule. It was this pressure and the perception of the aggressiveness of Western policies which were responsible for the decision to intervene in Hungary in 1956. It took Nikita Khrushchev one week to decide if a solution with the government of the reform communist Imre Nagy could be found. He only decided in favour of the "military path" after Mao Zedong and Palmiro Togliatti had voted accordingly. Next to his concern for his position as leader of the CPSU and World Communism, apparently, the continuous fear of Western imperialists played a role. "If we leave Hungary," he reasoned in the party executive committee, "it will give great impetus to the Americans, the British and the French – to the imperialists. They will consider it a weakness of our side and move into the offensive. [...] They will then add Hungary to Egypt."[16]

The pressure that motivated Khrushchev's risky Berlin Ultimatum had similar origins: the continuous wave of refugees from the GDR and the preparations for the atomic armament of the Federal Republic made him look like a loser in the eyes of his potential competitors. The threat to transfer the control of the transition routes to West Berlin to the GDR at least promised to force the acceptance of the GDR. It might also prevent the stationing of atomic weapons in the Federal Republic and remove the threat imposed by West Berlin. "It is our primary objective", he explained his endeavour to Foreign Minister Andrei Gromyko and his staff, "to squeeze them [i.e. the Western powers] out of Berlin like a disgusting pimple from the nose. This is our maximum programme, so to speak; but it should not be that easy to be realized. But we can wring out the recognition of the GDR from them and solve the German question on this basis. Then there will be two German states [...] and, of course, without nuclear or other modern weapons. This is our minimum programme."[17]

With the stationing of the Soviet atomic weapons in Cuba, Khrushchev on the one hand intended to compensate for the drastic superiority of the US in nuclear armament, which Deputy Defence Minister Roswell Gilpatric had now even made public in a speech delivered in October 1961. On the other hand, he wanted to prevent another American invasion on the sugar island, which threatened to damage his prestige as leader of the Communist world. The Americans, he later complained in his memoirs, "had surrounded our country with military bases and threatened us with nuclear weapons. Now they were to learn what it feels like to have enemy missiles pointed at oneself. We did not want anything more or less than have them have a taste of their own medicine."[18]

At the same time, Khrushchev was also very much interested in arms restriction and disarmament. In his eyes they were urgent "in order to reduce the pressure of military expenditures on our economy and they finally help the Soviet people to a better life."[19] He was sure that his own performance would be judged by whether and how well he succeeded. Ever since the detonation of the first Soviet hydrogen bomb in September 1953, he was worried about a nuclear catastrophe, and he concluded that an arrangement with the West had to be found by all means: "Either peaceful co-existence or the most destructive war in history – there is no third way."[20] He based his offensives on the conviction that a durable arrangement was possible after the confrontation with the Western powers. After the confrontation had been managed, he was indeed able to find a common terminology with Eisenhower in Camp David and later with Kennedy after the settlement of the missile crisis.[21]

Under Leonid Brezhnev the Soviet interest in arms restriction did not any longer show as evenly. The arms complex developed its own momentum, which was neither slowed down nor directed by any political leadership. In comparison, the interest in economic cooperation with the West showed all the more firmly. Progress in détente became a gauge for the power granted to the general secretary. Urged by KGB-boss Juri Andropov, Brezhnev in the spring of 1969 turned to a form of détente which consciously included Western Europeans and the Germans. "We have to build our house in Europe," Andropov argued as early as February 1968, "and that is impossible without Germany." The European interests were not to be put against those of the Americans, as Soviet diplomacy so often had attempted without success, and the victorious powers were not to impose a diktat on the West Germans. Rather, "thoroughly honest, trusting and dynamic relations" were to be developed, which would also help the Soviet leadership in the "civilization" of its country.[22]

When the intervention in Afghanistan was up for decision in 1979, the issue was not only the appropriate recognition of the endeavour's hopelessness, on which some in the Soviet leadership agreed, but also the concern about the breakdown of détente. In March 1979, Gromyko explained to the Politburo of the CPSU that the military intervention in Afghanistan "would throw everything over board that we have done in the past years in terms of efforts regarding détente, arms reduction and the like."[23] It was primarily because of the rivalries in the struggle for Brezhnev's succession that it took place after all. At the end of October, Minister of Defence Dimitri Ustinov began to argue in favour of a forceful intervention in the Afghan civil war, which to him promised to be a quick success and at the same time was to pave his way to the top of the Soviet regime. Andropov did not want to stand by quietly, so he, too, began to argue in favour of the intervention. On 8 December, the rivals were able to convince Brezhnev of the necessity of this operation.[24]

In 1981 it was the fear of the breakdown of détente that played in favour of the perfidiously skilful decision to leave the suppression of Solidarnosc up to the Polish government and party leader General Woyciech Jaruzelski. As late as 10 December, Suslov, Andropov and Gromyko stated in the Politburo that "the sending of troops [could] not at all be considered." Andropov added: "We have to adhere to our position until the end. I do not know how things will turn out in Poland, but even if Poland falls to the control of Solidarnosc, that is the way it is going to be. [...] Primarily we have to care for our own country and the strengthening of the Soviet Union. That is our main line."[25] The solidarity of the rulers and troops of the Warsaw Pact, which had allowed for the intervention in the "Prague Spring" of 1968, did not any longer work in view of the temptations of Western détente. It was Jaruzelski's own decision to suppress the democratization movement with the help of Polish troops – otherwise he obviously feared to be held accountable for the failure of "Socialism" in Poland.[26]

This already implies that despite their heaviness and the careless opportunist exploitation of liberation movements, the Brezhnev years did indeed show certain learning processes. Gorbachev came to power as a protégé of Andropov – that is, as the protégé of a politician, who, as we know now, had played an important role in Brezhnev's background for years. His actions can only be understood as the acceleration of these learning processes, which then led to a qualitative leap. "Perestroika" followed "Uskorenie", albeit not in the economic and social development Gorbachev proposed, but in the trains of thought.[27]

The West and the Overcoming the Cold War

Ambivalences and possibilities for development, of course, indicate that the West had a great influence on the actual development of East-West relations. And they generally underline the meaning of personal decisions, not only at the top of both sides, but also of the Allies and the respective opposition forces, that each played independent roles.[28] For example, the reconstruction of the negotiations on the creation of a Western alliance, of the reactions to the Stalin Note and of Churchill's peace initiative of the spring of 1953 brings out a much greater degree of openness of Western politicians for alternatives than has previously shown. The importance of Konrad Adenauer and the West Germans for the pushing through of the East-West bloc-building has become visible more clearly. By the same token it has become clear that the building of the blocs also served the containment of the Germans, while a lack of trust in the suitability of this path as a means for solving the German Question has played in favour of the search for constructive alternatives to the Cold War.[29]

The Cold War, this can also be gathered from the more intensive dealings with internal sources, is full of examples of statesmanlike ability, leadership, responsible acting – and for each of its respective opposites. Examining the different mixtures of these traits with numerous of the actors, both in the East and the West, is extremely worthwhile. Ronald Reagan, for example, was able to cooperate with Mikhail Gorbachev – after he managed to deal with his fears and restored the self-confidence of a society that had been traumatized by the defeat in Vietnam and the hostage crisis in Tehran. This was the essential effect of his arms policies, not the restoration of sufficient defence about which there had never been a question.[30] Reagan's development, therefore, shows an extreme example of the function of military armament in the East-West conflict: it was necessary for the reassurance of a basically uncertain situation and for not giving the opponent occasion to preventively obtain security advantages or to make use of military pressure in order to push their notions of order. However, this never required that degree of armament efforts which exaggerated threat perceptions, a mechanic notion of balance and the logic of the arms race suggested. Fear was a poor advisor that often prevented the actors from recognizing possibilities to communicate. Misperception played a major role in the conflict's escalations.

Insight into the decision-making processes of the Soviet sphere of power also reinforces the opinion that détente was in the interest of the West.

Military deterrence was necessary; it was, so to speak, the second best solution to the security problem after the design of a common peace order after World War II had failed in its early stages. But it had to be supplemented by arms control and trust building measures, if miscalculation or mistake were not to result in a self-destructive conflict. The decrease of the arms level was only to the advantage of both sides, and with the unfolding of economic productivity, which was connected to it, the need for reform in the Soviet bloc grew. Finally, détente helped in overcoming exaggerated threat perceptions and ideological blinkers. It was unable to force changes within the Soviet system; it was, however, able to encourage them.

Gorbachev indeed approached his reform with constant learning from Western think tanks. When Egon Bahr for the first time met the recently appointed general secretary in April 1985, he discovered that Gorbachev had already adopted Bahr's concept of "Common Security" which he had learned from Georgi Arbatov: "What he stated was astounding. A new way of thinking was necessary: superiority, atomic as well as conventional, had become senseless, deterrence dangerous; the East and the West would only be able to find security together and then also to disarm. In short: Much to my surprise Gorbachev developed the concept of Common Security. It was his foreign policy concept, ready to be carried through".[31] Indeed, due to Gorbachev's efforts, far reaching détente in the international situation preceded the disintegration of the Soviet Empire. By the same token, the reform forces which pushed the liberation from Communist rule through had been favoured by the CSCE process. Gorbachev was unable to use force against them, as this would have endangered the domestic reform process and the necessary support of the West. "Should we be required to apply force", Foreign Minister Eduard Shevardnaze told his American colleague James Baker in July 1989, "this would be the end of perestroika. We would have failed. It would be the end of all our hopes for the future, the end of all we aim to achieve – that is to design a new system based on humanity. The application of force would mean that the enemies of perestroika had been victorious. Because we would not be much different from our predecessors. But there is no way back".[32]

Regarding the end of the Cold War, it therefore has to be concluded that the West had undermined the Soviet system from above as well as from its Western periphery – albeit not in the sense of clumsy conspiracy theories or covered operations, but idealistically. Insofar as a victory of the West in the competition of models of order can be registered, for the other side it was self-liberation, which has many fathers: Western think tanks and pioneers, Soviet reformers and activists of the democratization movement in the countries of the Soviet sphere of power as well as Western partners, who supported the peaceful discharge of the Soviet system. It is both misleading and foolish to generally disqualify the self-liberation of the people of the Eastern bloc as the defeat of the Eastern side in the sense of the "Cold War" metaphor.

Finally, the perspective for the long term also shows the importance of the institutional and judicial frame which accompanied the East-West conflict and influenced it in the sense of containment. The agreements of Yalta and Potsdam were only partially realized; however, they were a frame of reference that gave an orientation to the communication between the East and the West. The United Nations served as a forum for de-escalation, and none of the four powers gave up its responsibility for Germany. The East-West tensions, therefore, could always serve as a factor of order in international relations, and steps for overcoming the conflict could take up these institutional basics – such as the agreements on disarmament and arms control and the final document of the CSCE, and finally the agreements to the peace settlement in 1990. In this sense, it is not totally unfounded to characterize East-West relations as the "long peace", even if this inadmissibly denies the precarious character of this peace and the underlying tensions.[33]

The big span and the ability to undergo changes in the conditions make it seem appropriate to choose the term "East-West conflict" as a generic term and to merely consider the "Cold War" as one state of this conflict, which reoccurred at different times and to different degrees.[34] This state was marked by the notion that the East-West conflict was not only a confrontation about different ways of life, social systems and spheres of power, but also a struggle of life and death, which existentially threatened the one side as much as the other. For fear that the opponent might attack one's own way of life contacts were cancelled, walls were built, the armament and militarization of the respective societies was spurred.

However, this was not the whole reality of the East-West conflict. Over and over again there were doubts if the opponent really was as aggressive and as powerful as the worriers and dogmatics claimed. Over and over again voices were to be heard that talked about the costs of the confrontation: the necessity to use extensive resources for armament without ever being quite sure if deterrence really worked; the militarization of societies; the risk of a nuclear catastrophe. Over and over again those who had suffered most from the building of the blocs tried to protect themselves. This was why the Cold War was permanently seen in relative terms. This is why it makes sense to talk about tendencies and climaxes of the Cold War; however, it is not possible to point to distinctly defined periods of the Cold War within the era of the East-West conflict or to an exact date of its end.

The term "Cold War", of course, is much more succinct than "East-West conflict". The English-speaking area does not know a catchy generic term. After the end of the conflict its peculiarities also emerge much more distinctively: force and despotism in the regimes of the Eastern bloc, the aggressiveness of the Communist notion of politics, deterrence's latent risk of annihilation. All this has contributed to the pushing through of the term "Cold War" as the generic term for the whole epoch. Certainly, this is reasonable. However, one has to be aware that this term is merely a metaphor that expresses essential points – but not all of them. The Cold War was not a war but a competition of the notions of order in coincidence with bipolar tensions.

Notes

1. For a broader foundation of the argument developed in this article, see my epilogue in the new edition of Wilfried Loth, *Die Teilung der Welt. Geschichte des Kalten Krieges 1941-1955* (Munich 2000), 352-389, as well as Wilfried Loth, *Overcoming the Cold War. A History of Détente, 1950-1991* (Houndsmills and New York 2002). For an excellent research overview in German, see Jost Dülffer, *Europa im Ost-West-Konflikt 1945-1990* (Munich 2004). Stimulating interpretations from slightly different points of view can be found in John Lewis Gaddis, *The Cold War. A New History* (New York and London 2005); and Bernd Stöver, *Der Kalte Krieg. Geschichte eines radikalen Zeitalters 1947-1991* (Munich 2007).
2. Cf. Walter Lippmann, *The Cold War. A Study of United States Foreign Policy* (New York 1947).
3. John Lewis Gaddis, *The Long Peace: Inquiries into the History of the Cold War* (Oxford and New York 1987).
4. Georges-Henri Soutou, *La guerre de Cinquante Ans. Les relations Est-Ouest 1943-1990* (Paris 2001).
5. Ibid., 11.
6. Cf. my analyzes in Wilfried Loth, "Der Ost-West-Konflikt", in Jörg Calließ and Reinhold E. Lob (eds), *Handbuch Praxis der Umwelt- und Friedenserziehung*, Vol. 1: *Grundlagen* (Düsseldorf 1987), 384-391; Wilfried Loth, "Der Krieg, der nicht stattfand. Ursprünge und Überwindung des Kalten Krieges", in Bernd Wegner (ed.), *Wie Kriege entstehen. Zum historischen Hintergrund von Staatenkonflikten* (Paderborn 2000), 285-298.
7. On the oftentimes laborious progress in the study of the sources see in particular

the information published in *Cold War International History Project Bulletin* (Washington, D.C. 1992), also available at <http://cwihp.si.edu>. A wealth of information can also be found in Vojtech Mastny, *The Cold War and Soviet Insecurity. The Stalin Years* (New York and Oxford 1996); Vladislav Zubok and Constantin Pleshakov, *Inside the Kremlin's Cold War: From Stalin to Khrushchev* (Cambridge, Mass. 1996); and Vladislav M. Zubok, *A Failed Empire. The Soviet Union in the Cold War from Stalin to Gorbatchev* (Chapel Hill 2007).

8   An overview of new research can be found in John Lewis Gaddis, *We Now Know. Rethinking Cold War History* (Oxford and New York 1997); Soutou, *La guerre*; Loth, *Teilung*, 352-389; Loth, *Overcoming*.

9   Investigated by Aleksei M. Filitov, "Problems of Post-War Construction in Soviet Foreign Policy Conceptions during World War II", in Francesca Gori and Silvio Pons (eds), *The Soviet Union and Europe in the Cold War, 1943-53* (London and New York 1996), 3-22; the whole text is published in *Istocnik* 4 (1995), 124-144.

10 Compare the articles in Norman M. Naimark and Leonid Gibianskii (eds), *The Establishment of Communist Regimes in Eastern Europe, 1944-1959* (Boulder, CO 1997); on the Soviet zone of occupation in Germany, see Wilfried Loth, *Stalin's Unwanted Child. The Soviet Union, the German Question and the Founding of the GDR* (London and New York 1998); as well as Norman M. Naimark, *The Russians in Germany. A History of the Soviet Zone Occupation, 1945-1949* (Cambridge, Mass. and London 1995).

11 Compare Galina P. Muraschko, Albina F. Noskowa and Tatjana W. Wolokitina, "Das Zentralkomitee der WKP (B) und das Ende der 'nationalen Wege zum Sozialismus'", *Jahrbuch für Historische Kommunismusforschung* (Berlin 1994), 9-37.

12 Compare Loth, *Stalin's Unwanted Child*, 79-84; the citation from the presentation of Georgi Malenkov at the founding conference of Cominform, in Boris Meissner (ed.), *Das Ostpakt-System* (Frankfurt/Main and Berlin 1955), 87-89.

13 Cited in Zubok and Pleshakov, *Inside*, 193.

14 For examples, see Loth, *Stalin's Unwanted Child*, passim, as well in the context of the coming about of the so-called "Stalin Note"; Wilfried Loth, "The Origins of Stalin's Note of 10 March 1952", *Cold War History*, vol. 4, no. 2 (January 2004), 66-88. On the continuing controversy on this crucial point of Stalinist policies on Germany, see Wilfried Loth, "Da Ende der Legende. Hermann Graml und die Stalin-Note. Eine Entgegnung", *Vierteljahrshefte für Zeitgeschichte* 50 (2002), 653-664; and Wilfried Loth, *Die Sowjetunion und die deutsche Frage. Studien zur sowjetischen Deutschlandpolitik von Stalin bis Chruschtschow* (Göttingen 2007). Peter Ruggenthaler, *Stalins großer Bluff. Die Geschichte der Stalin-Note in Dokumenten der sowjetischen Führung* (Munich 2007), claims without the slightest evidence that Stalin never aimed at negotiations on Germany.

15 John Lewis Gaddis only considers the second part and infers unlimited ambitions and the inevitability of the Cold War from Stalin's profound distrust, *We Now Know*, 25, 31 and 292. On Gaddis' return to a very "traditional" point of view, see also the criticism of Michael S. Sherry, "The Triumph of Democratic Capitalism without

the Democracy and the Capitalism", *Reviews in American History* 25 (1997 and Anders Stephanson, "Rethinking Cold War history", *Review of Inte Studies* 24 (1998), 119-124.

16 Minutes of the CK-official Vladimir N. Malin, presented by Mark Kramer occasion of the conference "Hungary and the World 1956. The New Archi dence", October 1996, Budapest.

17 Cited in Oleg Grinevskii, *Tauwetter. Entspannung, Krisen und neue Eiszeit* (Berlin 1996), 23f. On the pressure Walter Ulbricht imposed on Khrushchev, see also Hope M. Harrison, *Driving the Soviets up the Wall. Soviet-East German Relations, 1953-1961* (Princeton, NJ 2003).

18 *Khrushchev Remembers* (Boston 1970), 494. Compare Aleksandr Fursenko and Timothy Naftali, *"One Hell of a Gamble". Khrushchev, Castro, and Kennedy, 1958-1964* (London and New York 1997); Loth, *Overcoming*, 67-76.

19 Khrushchev in a conversation with his staff in the spring of 1959, cited in Grinevskii, *Tauwetter*, 153.

20 Khrushchev at the 20th Party Convention in February 1956, XX s"ezd KPSS, vol. 1 (Moscow 1956), 36.

21 See also William Taubman, *Khrushchev: The Man and His Era* (New York 2003).

22 Andropov in a conversation with the Germany-specialist Vyatcheslav Kevorkov on 13 February 1968, whom he assigned the creation a "direct line" to the Bonn government. Cited in Vyatcheslav Kevorkov, *Der geheime Kanal. Moskau, der KGB und die Bonner Ostpolitik* (Berlin 1995), 29f.

23 Minutes of the Politburo session of March 17-19, 1979, *CWIHP-Bulletin*, no. 8/9 (Winter 1996/97), 136-145.

24 See Loth, *Overcoming*, 157-160.

25 Excerpts from the minutes, *CWIHP-Bulletin*, no. 5 (Spring 1995), 121, 134-137.

26 See also Loth, "Moscow, Prague and Warsaw: Overcoming the Brezhnev Doctrine", *Cold War History*, vol. 1, no. 2 (January 2001), 103-118.

27 Important for the development of Gorbachev's thinking are Archie Brown, *The Gorbachev Factor* (Oxford and New York 1997); Archie Brown, *Seven Years that Changed the World: Perestroika in Perspective* (Oxford and New York 2007); Vladislav M. Zubok, "The Collapse of the Soviet Union. Leadership, Elites, and Legitimacy", in Geir Lundestad (ed.), *The Fall of Great Powers. Peace: Stability and Legitimacy* (Oslo and New York 1994), 156-174, Vladislav M. Zubok, "Gorbachev and the End of the Cold War. Perspectives on History and Personality", *Cold War History*, vol. 2, no. 2 (January 2002), 61-100.

28 The specific meaning of European actors is emphasized in a conference project, which has already produced four conference volumes: *The Failure of Peace in Europe, 1943-49*, edited by Antonio Varsori and Elena Clandri (Houndsmills and New York 2002); *L'Europe de l'Est et de L'Ouest dans la Guerre froide 1948-1953*, edited by Saki Dockrill, Robert Frank, Georges-Henri Soutou, Antonio Varsori (Paris 2002); *Europe, the Cold War and Coexistence, 1953-1965*, edited by Wilfried Loth (London and Portland 2004); *The Making of Détente. Eastern and Western Europe in the Cold*

    War, 1965-75, edited by Wilfried Loth and Georges-Henri Soutou (London and New York 2008).
29 See also Wilfried Loth, "Germany in the Cold War: Strategies and Decisions", in Odd Arne Westad (ed.), *Reviewing the Cold War: Approaches, Interpretations, Theory* (London and Portland 2000), 242-257.
30 See Loth, *Overcoming*, 165-172, 179-197.
31 Egon Bahr, *Zu meiner Zeit* (Munich 1996); see also Wilfried Loth, "Mikhail Gorbachev, Willy Brandt, and European Security", *Journal of European Integration History* 11.1 (2005), 45-59.
32 Conversation of 28 July, 1989, cited in Michael R. Beschloss and Strobe Talbott, *Auf höchster Ebene. Das Ende des Kalten Krieges und die Geheimdiplomatie der Supermächte 1989-1991* (Düsseldorf 1993), 128.
33 See also Soutou, *La guerre*, 729-732.
34 See also my proposal in Wilfried Loth, "Was war der Kalte Krieg? Annäherungen an ein unbewältigtes Erbe", in *Deutschland im Kalten Krieg 1945-1963. Eine Ausstellung des Deutschen Historischen Museums 28. August – 24. November 1992* (Berlin 1992), 11-28.

Polish Reactions to the West German Ostpolitik and East-West Détente, 1966-1978

Wanda Jarzabek

The time of détente and Ostpolitik was one of very intensive activity of the Polish authorities. This activity was to be observed first of all in Polish foreign policy, but détente also brought about changes in domestic policy, mostly information policy. The attitude of the Polish authorities to détente and Ostpolitik fluctuated – with fear continuously merging with hope. I will concentrate on the years 1966-1975, that is, from the so-called "peace note" to the East bloc countries issued by the Federal German Government to the agreement between German and Polish leaders on resolving the most urgent problems in bilateral relations reached in Helsinki during the last stage of the CSCE. As it is impossible to explore all aspects of the Polish attitude to détente and Ostpolitik in this article, I will limit myself to the official position of the authorities. Social attitudes and opposition perspectives will not be considered here.

The article is based mostly on Polish sources as they reflect the point of view of the then ruling group and in many cases provide historians with explanations of the diplomatic or political actions undertaken at the time. I have used documents stored in the Archive of Modern Records, primarily those in the collection of the Polish Communist Party – the Polish United Workers' Party – and in the Archives of the Ministry of Foreign Affairs.[1]

After 1945 Poland was a dependent country and we cannot therefore speak about an independent Polish foreign policy. The Polish room of manoeuvre was limited mostly by Soviet hegemony power – with the Warsaw Pact becoming one of the tools used to enforce it.[2] A human factor should also be considered as an element influencing Polish reactions to détente and Ostpolitik. The characters of individual politicians and their ideas of state interests had a big influence on Polish activity at the time. In the case of bilateral Polish-German relations one should add also very strong resentments shared by many Polish politicians and Polish society as such, caused mostly by the experiences of the Second World War.

After Wladyslaw Gomulka came back to power in October 1956, a new attitude towards the Polish role in the bloc can be observed. The authorities tried to rebuild relations with the Soviet Union and attempted to realize some political goals. Many of them were concerned with looking for confirmation of the post-war status quo in Europe. After the war, Poland lost almost half of its pre-war territory in the East, and following the Big Powers' decisions made in Yalta and Potsdam, the country gained new territories in the West. All the same, the territory was about twenty per cent smaller than in 1939. The final borderline was to be confirmed in a peace settlement – the so-called Potsdam agreement – which was in general understood as a peace treaty with Germany. The new territories have been settled mostly with Poles who had to leave homes in the East, but also with people from totally destroyed cities and towns, including Warsaw, and with peasants from the overpopulated territories of central and south Poland. For the Polish state and the majority of its citizens, including Polish émigrés, the new borderline in the West began to be a question of the Polish reason of state. A lack of *de jure* recognition of the Oder-Neisse line was the main source of Polish foreign activities in the West, especially as the Soviet Union sometimes treated this unstable character of Polish frontiers as a tool in bilateral relations with Poland.[3] However, the Polish Communist government was not interested in changing the political system in Poland, and after some years of close relations with the Soviet Union and the Soviet bloc it also realized that this alliance was in many ways neither sufficient for Polish security nor for economic development. This resulted in a growing Polish interest in opening to the West.

First Reactions to Détente and Ostpolitik

Even if in a limited form, the Polish authorities were interested in political and economic contacts with the Western countries, so the first signs of détente were in general welcomed. It was hoped that a new character of the East-West relations could create for Poland better opportunities to participate in economic exchange and also some political discussions. The first signals of greater interest in contacts with Poland came from the United States, France, Great Britain and smaller European countries such as Belgium and Denmark.[4] They resulted in an exchange of visits, concluding agreements on cultural and economic cooperation and also some political discussions, i.e. on the question of nonproliferation or the establishment of nuclear free zones in Europe.

Much more complex, however, was the Polish attitude to the German new Eastern policy. In March 1966 the Federal Republic of Germany proposed the Soviet bloc countries (East Germany was excluded) concluding treaties on the renunciation of force. The Soviet Union and some other bloc countries treated this proposal mostly as a chance to make bilateral relations better and to start closer economic collaboration. For Poland this proposal was not satisfactory as it did not include recognition of the Oder-Neisse border.[5] When the chief of the German Trade Mission in Warsaw, Ambassador Egon Emmel, was passing the German note to Mieczyslaw Lobodycz, the chief of the Department IV of the Foreign Ministry (dealing with the FRG and other Western countries also), Lobodycz stated that the Polish government would be ready to start bilateral talks if West Germany recognized the final character of the Oder-Neisse line and ceased to claim to be the only representative of the German nation.[6]

Poland feared that a possible mitigation of the conflict between the Soviet Union and the Federal Republic of Germany as well as the two German states could lead to German reunification in the future, and that this process would take place before Poland could obtain guarantees that its Western frontier had a final character.[7] Warsaw also thought that due to the Ostpolitik, Bonn's political position would be strengthened, which would in turn weaken the Polish situation.[8]

Ultimately the Polish answer to the German "peace note" was not encouraging.[9] The Federal Republic was accused of continuing its policy towards Poland and of being responsible for the strained bilateral relations with Poland. Warsaw's conditions for "security and peace", i.e. *de facto* for the establishment of bilateral relations, were the following: the renunciation of territorial claims towards Poland, which meant recognition of the Oder-Neisse borderline, recognition of the Munich convention of 1938 as null and void *ex tunc* (not valid from the beginning), acknowledgement of the German Democratic Republic German state on equal terms and official renunciation of nuclear weapons.

The Polish leaders thought that those bloc countries which had a less charged history would normalize their bilateral relations with the Federal Republic, and that Poland would be left alone with its problems. Also, the Soviet position was not so clear, and Polish fears were confirmed when Moscow sent its draft answer to the German note to Warsaw. Initially, the wording of the Soviet answer was very general and did not include controversial questions such as the borderline issues.

The initial Soviet (draft) note declared: "The line of the rivers Oder and

Neisse which comprises the state frontier between the Polish People's Republic and the German Democratic Republic, delineated in the Potsdam agreements and located hundreds of kilometers away from the eastern frontiers of West Germany, has nothing in common with the Federal Republic of Germany". Warsaw decided to intervene. In a handwritten note to Gomulka, Adam Rapacki listed numerous reservations concerning the draft of the Soviet response, but of greatest importance were those pertaining to the Oder-Neisse border. "For the sake of principles", Rapacki wrote, "I insisted on urgency in presenting our formula pertaining to the question of the Polish-German boundary (in accordance with our note), and even suggested to delay the presentation of the note in Bonn or Moscow, if it had not already been forwarded."[10] But apparently the Poles in general perceived talks with the Federal Republic as premature. In an analysis of the document received from Moscow, a Polish expert on German affairs wrote: "The interpretation of the Soviet note differs from our response and the one given by Czechoslovakia primarily due to the fact that it expresses readiness to conduct a dialogue with West Germany about certain issues."[11]

In a sense, the Poles were successful in influencing the wording of the Soviet answer to West Germany's note. The Soviet note handed on 17 May 1966 to the German Secretary of State Karl Carstens presented the question of the frontier in a manner acceptable to Warsaw and made references to the Potsdam agreements and the Polish-East German border treaty of Görlitz from 1950.[12] This Soviet readiness for compromise – with the note addressing the Oder-Neisse border – was probably caused by the fact that including such a formulation did not mean too much and was not against current Soviet interest. And any position could be changed or softened during negotiations, as the talks on the CSCE shows.

In the spring and summer of 1966, the other countries of the bloc engaged themselves in discreet talks with the FRG, but not Warsaw. To some diplomats such as Hans Ruete, the chief of subdivision A in the Political Department of the West German Foreign Ministry, dealing with Eastern Europe, Gomulka was perceived as the motor of the bloc's hard line towards the West German Ostpolitik.[13]

Helmut Schmidt, who visited some Eastern countries in the summer of 1966, reported that only in Warsaw was he not met by high-level politicians, and he pointed out that this was a result of Ulbricht's actions.[14] Undoubtedly, however, Schmidt was not right in perceiving Ulbricht's role as negative. The unpleasant atmosphere in Warsaw was caused first of all by Gomulka's perception of the German problem and Warsaw's evaluation of the West

German "peace note". Taking into account the policy implemented since 1956, this position should not be treated as extraordinary or difficult to understand.

Gomulka tried to influence the Soviet Union and the other bloc countries and to encourage them to engage in closer collaboration on the German question, or even coordination of the Soviet bloc's German policy. In realization of this plan, Poland cooperated with the GDR leaders, for whom the Soviet attitude to Ostpolitik was also in fact difficult to accept. As early as in March 1956, Gomulka and Ulbricht agreed that the other bloc countries should accept preconditions for their talks with the FRG, which would match Polish and East German interests.

The Polish side intensified its attempts in the beginning of 1967, especially during a bilateral meeting in January 1967 (in Lansk, Poland), when Leonid Brezhnev informed the Polish leadership about his plan to give the bloc countries green light for talks with West Germany.[15] Finally, Moscow agreed to the ministers' talks which took place in Warsaw in February 1967.[16] As preconditions for establishing relations with the FRG were included: borderlines recognition (Oder-Neisse and the FRG-GDR frontier), recognition of the GDR (although Gomulka explained that for Poland it did not mean *de jure* recognition), renunciation of nuclear arms by Bonn, and recognition that the Munich agreement was not valid *ex tunc*.[17]

After the Warsaw Pact meeting, the Poles started to think about forcing through their position, including into bilateral treaties, which were to be renewed during 1967 and 1968. Already in the fall of 1966, East Berlin proposed signing bilateral treaties with the other bloc countries, thinking also about a trilateral treaty with Poland and Czechoslovakia, but this idea failed. In the case of the Polish-East German bilateral treaty, Poland refused to accept the East German draft as a basis for negotiations, presenting its own project, which aimed mostly at securing Warsaw interests. Finally, Warsaw was successful in rejecting wording and obligations which could complicate its conduct of an individual German policy.[18] During negotiations with the other bloc members, i.e. Czechoslovakia, Hungary and Bulgaria, which took place in 1967 and 1968, Warsaw wanted to introduce to the renewed bilateral treaties formulations with an anti-West German timbre and a kind of commitment to consultations on German policy. In this way, Warsaw wanted to strengthen its position within the bloc. Although Hungary and Bulgaria in particular were trying to avoid it, they nevertheless finally accepted some Polish proposals. In the case of Bulgaria, the Polish side stated that if Bulgaria refused to accept, it would be better not to sign the bilateral treaty at all at this time.[19] It seems that by laying down the preliminary conditions and signing the bilateral treaties, including obligations on policies towards Germany, Gomulka wished to delay the establishment of relations between the FRG and the Eastern bloc countries for as long as possible. The Polish first secretary's actions should not be treated as extraordinary; rather, they were an application of "the Gomulka doctrine."[20]

The CSCE

In the second half of the 1960s, Polish reactions to détente and Ostpolitik can also be observed and evaluated through Polish reactions to the idea of the CSCE. Activation of the Polish preparatory work for the "European conference" or the Conference on Security and Cooperation in Europe was a part of the Polish German policy. Authors of the government studies looked for different options of minimizing dangers which, according to them, stemmed from Bonn's policy. As the documents indicate, initially the conference was treated in Warsaw mostly as a method to solve, on a multilateral basis, the question of the Oder-Neisse line and some other issues connected with the so-called German problem and an attempt to avoid a situation in which the Soviet Union could subordinate the borderline problem to its state and national interests. We can assume that the Polish side was inclined to regard the conference partly as a substitute for the peace conference with Germany.

But this was not the only reason behind Polish interest in the CSCE. From the late 1960s, the Polish authorities expected the conference to promote a change in international relations. The conference was perceived as a tool which would enable the smaller countries – including dependent countries such as Poland – to participate in international relations.[21] In the second half of the 1960s, Poland was engaged in bilateral talks with Belgium and Denmark concerning the agenda of the conference. During the talks with Belgium, disarmament questions were frequently raised. An important part of the preparatory works concerned economic issues; this idea was suggested by Poland as part of a conference agenda in the United Nations in 1965, and was an extension of the general idea presented by Adam Rapacki in 1964.[22] Polish political and diplomatic activities were interrupted in 1968 due to the Soviet bloc intervention against the Prague Spring and in terms of an attempt to remove Gomulka from the position as first secretary of the PUWP.

In March 1969 the Warsaw Pact countries announced in Budapest the "Appeal for a European Security Conference." This document mentioned the question of inviolability (not recognition, as the Poles wanted) of the Oder-Neisse line and the GDR-FRG borderline as a "fundamental prerequisite for Europe's security", but not for the convening of a European conference.[23] This wording did not meet Polish expectations and made it clear for the Poles that they should intensify their pressure on the Soviet Union, the bloc countries, and diplomatic action in the West. In the beginning of April 1969, the Minister of Foreign Affairs Stefan Jedrychowski prepared a note on further Polish activities addressed to the party leaders, who subsequently accepted them as guidelines.[24] Concerning the need to intensify Polish diplomatic activities, the minister underlined that the Soviet Union gave priority to its global interests and was not interested in stressing the question of the territorial status quo. He pointed out the need of "better coordination of the activities of the socialist countries." However, he was of the opinion that the other bloc countries did not consider the territorial questions to be as important to them as they were to Poland. At this time, Warsaw became concerned that détente would be realized mostly as a process between the superpowers, and Polish leaders tried to change it at least by being active in the inner bloc planning, although Polish possibilities to influence the Soviet position were limited.[25]

There were many reasons for Polish anxiety. In the spring of 1969 the FRD and the GDR concluded an agreement on economic collaboration, and the GDR was successful in blocking a decision on closer collaboration within COMECON.[26] The Polish leadership was not informed about the details of the Soviet-West German talks, but they knew that since the Soviet Union was interested in progress of its talks with the FRG, it was interested in setting preconditions. Probably the feeling of concern was the main reason for the change in the Polish German policy as announced by Gomulka in his electoral speech on 17 May 1969.[27] Gomulka stated that Warsaw was ready to begin talks on a bilateral treaty, and as a precondition he only mentioned the recognition of the Oder-Neisse line and not the whole bundle of problems mentioned in the Warsaw Declaration from February 1967. Gomulka also expressed his expectations of the future European conference, namely that among the many problems of European security also those concerning the Oder-Neisse line and GDR recognition should be solved. Presumably, the first secretary calculated that such a public proposal would create a stir in international relations since it would be difficult for Bonn not to respond. Gomulka did not inform Moscow about his plans.[28]

It seems as if the Polish authorities hoped that their proposal would make it possible to dissolve the borderline question on a bilateral level, but soon it appeared not to be the case. It was not a favourable moment for such a proposal since the FRG was preparing itself for parliamentary elections, and the Oder-Neisse line played an important role in West German domestic politics. In effect, the first reactions were moderate and did not sound encouraging to Warsaw.[29] Also, the new Bonn government formed after the elections in October 1969 was not capable of meeting the expectations of Warsaw. Polish-German relations were a function of the Federal Republic's Eastern Policy and German policy, in which the USSR played a crucial role, even if some German politicians thought that it might be a good idea to give priority to relations with Poland.[30] On the other hand, the legal doctrine of the FRG postponed any final borderline decisions until a peace conference and reunification.[31] In this situation, the conference on security and cooperation still seemed to be the only chance for Warsaw to gain borderline recognition.

In the late spring of 1969 the Poles intensified their work on the CSCE by preparing a draft entitled "Treaty on Security and Cooperation in Europe".[32] This draft included several premises. According to the perception of states interests of the Polish authorities, the problem of territorial status quo was the main issue. But Poland also suggested some other very important elements. First of all, the Poles wanted the European conference to be a starting point for further cooperation in Europe. This cooperation should include questions of disarmament and economic cooperation. The latter issue was an element of the multilevel studies at the Polish Ministry of Foreign Affairs and other ministries, which were included in the planning process. Poland was interested in broadening the East-West exchange because its economic problems were difficult to solve solely from within the bloc.

Polish work on the rules of economic collaboration within the CSCE concentrated on facilitating inter-bloc trade and was a consequence of Poland's experience with a deteriorated international economic environment in the mid-1960s. Poland needed hard currency to buy Western products and was very interested in the possibility of selling its products to the West to fulfil its international commitments. At this time, more gates to the West were closing just as Warsaw was looking for new markets. This need was partly spurred by Poland's accession to the GATT in 1967. Imports from the West were especially dependent on détente; according to regulations set by COCOM (the Coordinating Committee for Multilateral Export Controls), many products with potential or actual military application were banned from export to the bloc countries, and in many cases this included the most recent in civilian technologies. The Poles considered building a common system of roads, including two special projects: 1) highways from North-South and East-West, a common train-cars system, connecting energetic systems in Europe, and 2) deepening financial cooperation and liberalization of taxes. Of course this programme was also, but not exclusively, an effect of observing changes in European Common Market (EEC) and the ongoing Western integration. Stressing the need for cooperation can and should also be placed among Poland's desires to overcome the European inner border between East and West – or at least to make this division less painful for Poland. The opening of economic relations with the West would change Polish relations with Moscow and give the Polish authorities more room to manoeuvre; but this did not mean that, at least in the short term, there would be any change in Poland's political system. The authorities were not interested in change. Moreover, carefully designed economic collaboration with the West could serve the regime, which faced serious economic problems which might lead, and in fact led, to social unrest. Successful economic cooperation would give the ruling class greater legitimacy in the eyes of the people. But also Polish society at large would be served due to the rise in the standard of living. However, the possibility of an entirely different effect cannot be excluded. In the long run, contacts with the West would change not only the character of Poland's ties with the Soviet Union but also its domestic system.

In the years 1969-1972 the Poles tried in vain to convince Moscow to accept at least some of their ideas on economic cooperation. It seems that Soviet interest in broadening economic and trade cooperation with the West was very limited, and that Moscow did not want the opportunities which arose from détente to be extended to its satellites, at least not until Moscow would be able to construct new instruments of social and political control over the bloc. However, it was not the question of economic cooperation but the borderline question which still caused most of the bilateral Polish-Soviet controversies in 1969. Warsaw wanted to influence the shape of common bloc documents and to gain certainty that during the forthcoming meeting of the foreign ministers and at the following European conference "the question of recognizing and respecting territorial integrity would be regarded as crucial for security."[33] Also, during a meeting of the deputy ministers of the bloc in Moscow on 26 October, the Poles wanted to convince Moscow and the bloc countries to support their postulates on two counts – territorial status quo and economic cooperation.[34] Finally, at least the question of the recognition of status quo as one of the main topics to be solved during the conference was accepted. The Warsaw Pact Prague

Declaration from October 1969, however, was regarded by the West as too limited. After the NATO meeting in December 1969 it also became clear that some other questions should be settled frst, such as the question of West Berlin. The West also expected the conference to deal with more complex issues, and therefore the Soviet vision of the conference had no chance of being realized. Apparently, the Western position was perceived by Warsaw as a chance for a revision of the narrow bloc proposal and for the inclusion of some of the Polish ideas.

Normalization of Bilateral Relations with the FRG

When the Polish-German bilateral talks started in February 1970, the Polish leadership did not expect them to continue for a long time. The duration of the negotiations was dependent on the scope of issues which were to be discussed, but also on the Polish position in international relations. The Moscow Treaty was to be concluded first, and Poland had to wait. The Warsaw Treaty between Poland and the FRG was signed in December 1970, and as its title indicated – "Treaty on the principles (basis) of bilateral relations normalization between the PPR and the FRG"[35] – it was conceived as an introduction to further talks. The Polish government expected that diplomatic relations would soon be established and that bilateral talks would lead to agreements on economic cooperation, scientific and cultural collaboration including the question of text books revision, solving the question of compensation for the victims of Nazi Germany's occupation policy in Poland, and the problem of health insurance and pension premiums paid by present-day Polish citizens (having Polish citizenship after 1945) to German institutions before and during the Second World War. The Poles counted upon the liquidation of Radio Free Europe; they did not want the Federal Republic to prolong the validity of the German-American agreement which made it possible to broadcast from Germany territory. West Germany expected first of all that it would be possible to solve the problem of Germans living in Poland, including consular custody of them and recognition of their right to leave Poland. All the questions started to be treated as part of a "package deal" during the following years, and the road to an agreement turned out to be a long one.

The first disappointment for the Polish authorities came when the FRG did not ratify the Warsaw Treaty (as well as the Moscow Treaty) shortly after signing it. The ratification process lasted until May 1972. Divergences also occurred in the interpretation of the character of the Oder-Neisse borderline. In a memorandum issued in December 1971, the Federal Government presented its interpretation, according to which the Warsaw Treaty was signed in its name only – without obligating the future government of a united Germany to respect the stipulation. The formulations used in the Warsaw Treaty, perceived by the Poles as more favourable, were not quoted. In an answer to this document the Polish government decided that it should prepare its own interpretation and announce that the treaty would be ratified by Poland after being ratified by the Bundestag.[36] Thus, the establishment of bilateral relations also had to wait until ratification, including and question of emigration from Poland, which was important to the Federal Republic for domestic reasons.

After the ratification of the bilateral treaty in May 1972, Poland was interested in the early establishment of regular diplomatic relations. However, certain external obstacles now appeared. The Soviet Union and the bloc countries, such as the GDR and Czechoslovakia, which had not completed their talks with the FRG, were against Poland's establishment of diplomatic relations at this time.[37] Without a clear "yes" from Moscow, Prague and Berlin (fortunately for Poland, a "no" was not clear either, although Poland prepared the way by explaining to Bonn why it was not possible to exchange ambassadors in case Moscow would say no), Poland decided to establish bilateral relations in September 1972. Shortly before the first visit of the Polish foreign minister in West Germany, a note describing the Polish attitude to further negotiations was prepared. The Polish side was aware of the importance of the family reuniting problem to the West German government and society.[38] But Warsaw wanted to achieve its goals, too, primarily the question of individual compensation for Polish citizens paid on a similar basis as for citizens of the Western states. The Poles did not demand war reparations, as it is often presented in literature and press comments. As a negotiating strategy, it was decided to make allowance for citizens to leave Poland dependent on the West German attitude to the question of individual compensations. What is worth stressing here is that much has been written about the coupling between the negotiations between family reuniting and the German credits for the Polish communist government. However, it has not been noticed that there was a second coupling between compensation and emigration. The problem of individual compensations was treated as having a moral meaning as well as an economic one.[39]

The question of individual compensations was also treated by the Polish government in categories of power legitimization. There existed a pressure from the veterans organizations: the compensation problem was treated by many Poles as a question of historical justice. In the case of Poles with Polish citizenship, only the victims of paramedical experiments received compensations.[40] Some Poles, who accepted foreign citizenship after the war, including British or French, were given individual compensations. German Foreign Minister Walter Scheel declared that, "The German Federal Republic does not feel authorized to raise the compensation issue before the peace conference, and until such a conference is convened, these matters should be put off, as it cannot be excluded that other states of Eastern Europe may lay similar claims."[41] This point of view was difficult to accept in Warsaw, and as the Federal Republic refused to raise the issue of compensations for individuals, the Polish government stopped giving allowances for Germans to leave Poland.

Bilateral relations rapidly deteriorated in late 1972, and the first half of the next year did not bring about any change. The impasse was overcome after talks between the German and Polish Foreign Ministers Walter Scheel and Stefan Olszowski in July 1973 in Helsinki, during the first stage of the CSCE.[42] During the talks the Poles told the German side that the citizens leaving Poland, especially young people, also caused losses for the Polish economy. The Poles pointed out that without serious talks on economic collaboration – which meant concluding a long-term agreement – and without an attempt to solve the compensation problem, the government would not facilitate further emigration. According to the Polish documents, it was the German side which suggested during these talks that a "profitable credit would be a compensation for Poland, as any payment of individual damages is not possible."[43]

In April 1974 the so called "non-paper" was presented to the German government. The Poles presented this document as an attempt to break the impasse in the talks; however, the posture contained in it was not in fact a serious mitigation of the former hard negotiation positions taken by Warsaw.[44] Warsaw still demanded an amount no lower than 600 million DM for individual compensation and one billion DM for payment of pensions and other social benefits, especially to the former prisoners of concentration camps. Some German politicians were of the opinion that the Poles tried to avoid a coupling between compensations and credits because they did not want to weaken the moral character of the compensation problem.[45] The Polish side declared that it would be eager to allow 80,000 individuals to leave Poland, claiming that this was the real number of Germans in Poland. Emigration was to be accomplished in three to five years. Still, economic cooperation between Poland and Germany was still perceived by the Polish government as a kind of gesture of "good will". Warsaw expected 3 billion DM of financial credit, 7 billion as investment loans, and the signing of a long-term agreement on economic cooperation. In fact, the huge amount of 10 billion was re-emerged in many different "combinations" since December 1970, and this demand was not to be met by West Germany. After the change of government in Germany in May 1974, Warsaw decided to change its position: to lower the amount of expected credits, to agree on a lower sum of pension payments, and to raise the number of Germans who would be allowed to leave Poland. Some people perceived the emigration as positive in terms of Polish interests. Henryk Sokolak, an earlier employee in the Ministry of Interior and chief of the civil intelligence, who later became director of the Ministry of Foreign Affairs German department, was working on the new negotiation position and stated that "allowing some 90,000 people to leave Poland gives us a guarantee that we would never be confronted with the problem of German national minority in our future history."[46] The Politburo of the Central Committee of PUWP also agreed to limit the compensation claims to compensations for the former prisoners of concentration camps.

An agreement was reached in Helsinki during long-lasting talks between Edward Gierek and Helmut Schmidt on the night of 1 August 1975. Both top politicians participated in the last stage of the CSCE. A complex of agreements was discussed and initiated, among them the pension questions and related claims (1.3 billion), financial credit (1 billion), and an emigration protocol (120,000-125,000 Germans within four years). Poland and Germany also defined a long-term programme of industrial, technical, and economic cooperation. Agreements were signed in Warsaw during Minister Hans-Dietrich Genscher's visit in October 1975. Their ratification completed this stage of normalizing bilateral relations.

After the Helsinki Final Act

The first phase of the CSCE began in 1973, when the bilateral treaty between the Federal Republic of Germany and Poland signed in December 1970 was ratified by the Bundestag. At this point, it appeared that at least some of Poland's political aims were achieved. The Polish authorities wanted to strengthen the border guarantees by ensconcing them in the CSCE principles of international relations. Although Poland still had its own ideas concerning the conference agenda, it decided to adjust itself to the bloc position. During the Multilateral Preparatory Talks and the first stage of the conference, the Poles presented documents written in Moscow and passed to them, exactly as did the other bloc countries. The internal Polish documents demonstrate, however, that the Poles were critical towards them and concerned that they would have a negative impact on Polish bilateral relations with some countries.

What was still left to the Poles during the second phase of the CSCE in Geneva was an attempt to add some ideas to the agenda and also to influence the Soviet position. According to members of the Polish delegation as well as diplomats from the other bloc countries, this was indeed possible, and the Poles were relatively active.[47] The Communist Polish government wanted to secure its own interests in the CSCE talks mostly by gaining acceptance of the political status quo. The Helsinki Final Act was perceived as an acceptance of the political system in the East European countries and the ideology which dominated there. The Polish authorities expected that as a consequence of this, it would be possible to limit the activity of Radio Free Europe because it was contradictory to détente and the principle of non-interference.

After reaching the final agreement in Helsinki, a formal interpretation of the documents was prepared in Poland in the summer of 1975.[48] It was concluded that most crucial from the Polish point of view was describing the ten principles of international relations, especially the wording of the principle of sovereign equality, renunciation of the use of force, the inviolability of frontiers, territorial integrity and non-intervention in internal affairs (understood in Poland and in the rest of the Eastern bloc as non-interference). Subordinating the formula concerning peaceful change of boundaries to the principal of sovereign equality, and not to the principle of inviolability of frontiers, was presented as the success of Polish diplomacy, and in general for the diplomacy of the "socialist countries." The results of the Basket II negotiations were presented as partly satisfactory. Much attention was paid to Principle VII and Basket III. As the Basket III recommendations, among them the principle of non-intervention, were subordinated the ten principles of international relations; they were shown as dependent upon them and also upon the "stage of détente."

Despite the fact that many of the early Polish ideas concerning the agenda and the effects of the European conference were never realized, the CSCE was seen as a success. It is hard to find documents demonstrating Polish disappointments or regrets. The potential dangers were not emphasized, but this does not mean that they were not envisaged. Most likely some of them were understood, but not necessarily voiced. There were opinions that aspects of the CSCE could be dangerous for communist Poland, but there was also a belief that it would be possible to limit this peril.[49]

After 1975, relations with the FRG began to be smoother, which also resulted in better economic relations. The family reuniting action stopped to be an important issue in the bilateral talks, because Poland kept her promises and even agreed to a higher number of individuals to be allowed to emigrate. However, the CSCE was not able to create a visible change in the legal regulations concerning economic cooperation between Poland and Western countries. New opportunities for better economic collaboration were created by the détente process itself, and some of the hopes engendered by the détente process came to fruition. Another problem is how the new opportunities were exploited by the authorities. Poland soon became indebted, and serious economic problems emerged.

Due to the new character of the political contacts between Poland and the Western countries, the amount of social contacts increased, and the government tried to stop the possibilities of uncontrolled meetings. The number of social contacts grew visibly due to tourism, contacts between families and the exchange of scientists and students. In fact, uncontrolled contacts were against the founding principles of the communist power. Nevertheless, especially at the beginning of 1970s, the danger was perceived as not so strong, or at least possible to control. Moreover, the passport policy of the communist government remained unchanged. Most of the exchange programmes were centralized, and only persons approved by the authorities could take part in them. The government wanted also to limit the contacts to contacts between certain specialists.[50]

The real dangers appeared after 1975. In the 1970s, the state of human rights protection in Poland was relatively good compared to the other Soviet bloc countries.[51] But it began to deteriorate. What was important for the Polish case was that the growing importance of humanitarian questions manifested itself at the moment of growing criticism of the Communist Party activity in Poland, ending up in anti-government demonstrations. The number of opposition organizations increased and at least some of them began to call upon the CSCE stipulations.[52]

Human rights issues now occupied a much more important place in the planning of Western policy towards Eastern Europe.[53] In the late 1970s the atmosphere of cooperation in East-West relations began to deteriorate. During the Belgrade conference in 1977-1978, when human rights issues began to be treated as a tool in international relations, East bloc countries and Poland noticed how Basket III issues could be used in praxis. As the chief of the Polish delegation noted, the expected "deeply going exchange of views appeared to be rather a confrontation."54 Nevertheless, results of the first follow-up CSCE conference did not mean that Poland lost interest in the conference or détente.55

Conclusions

Polish reactions to détente and Ostpolitik emerged from the Polish government's and party leaders' perception of the European order. After the initiation of the so-called new Eastern policy by the Federal Republic of Germany, Warsaw remained anxious about the possibility of being left isolated within the bloc. This could happen if the member states of the bloc, unfettered in terms of the border controversies with West Germany, decided to establish relations with Bonn. In addition, for the Polish side, the Soviet intentions did not appear to be quite transparent, and fears arose of the so-called Rapallo policy (in Poland understood as an anti-Polish alliance between Russia/Soviet Union and Germany). These fears resulted in an attempt to convince the USSR to coordinate the bloc's German policy, in effect by forcing the other bloc countries to partly subordinate their state interests to Polish interests. The attitude to Ostpolitik changed in the late 1960s. Still, it was seen as including some dangers from the Polish point of view; nevertheless the Polish leadership wanted to use it to realize some state interests, among them to establish diplomatic relations with Germany and to find a solution to bilateral problems. The process of normalization of bilateral relations between Poland and Germany was realized by the new ruling group led by Edward Gierek as the first secretary of the PUWP. The new authorities expected that Ostpolitik would have a positive effect on bilateral relations mostly due to solving problems related with the past and creating better chances for economic cooperation. It was expected that the Polish need of hard currency and access to modern technologies would be satisfied.

Some similar expectations were set on détente, especially as to economic cooperation. But Polish hopes went beyond this. It was especially visible when Polish plans for the European conference were prepared in the second half of the 1960s. Especially at that time these plans could be placed within the framework of broad discussion on the nature of détente in the West. For the Poles, détente was to be a tool for changing the character of international relations. The Poles expected that détente would open new channels of communication and enable the smaller and dependent countries to be more present in internal politics. They hoped for more substantive dialogue with the West on certain topics, including disarmament questions and economic problems. However, it was never mentioned in a direct way, and apparently the Poles also hoped that internal relations in the Soviet bloc would change, and that Poland would gain larger room of manoeuvre. But it does not appear that they thought about changing the political system. Rather, they expected that due to détente, Ostpolitik and the CSCE, the Polish power system would be stabilized.

In the first half of the 1970s, the level of optimism was high, although many of the Polish ideas were not included in the documents presented by the bloc or by the Western countries. It seems as if potential dangers to the system which could occur due to détente were not treated as being serious. This position changed in the second half of the 1970s. However, according to the Polish ruling group, potential gains of détente still prevailed over potential drawbacks.

Notes

1 These documents include minutes of conversations, background reports, dispatches from the Polish embassies, and evaluating notes.
2 On the meanders of Polish membership in the Warsaw Pact, see Wanda Jarzabek, *Polska w politycznych stukturach Układu Warszawskiego w latach 1955–1980* (Warsaw 2008), 9f.
3 Wanda Jarzabek, "'Ulbricht-Doktrin' oder 'Gomulka-Doktrin'? Das Bemühen der Volksrepublik Polen um eine geschlossene Politik des kommunistischen Blocks gegenüber der westdeutschen Ostpolitik 1966/1967", *Zeitschrift für Ostmitteleuropa – Forschung*, no. 1, 55 (2006), 79ff.
4 In the case of the United States, economic cooperation with Poland (and the Eastern countries) was a part of the strategy aimed at loosening ties within the bloc. See, for instance, Bennett Kovring, *Of Walls and Bridges. The United States and Eastern Europe* (New York and London 1991), 75f., 105f. Also Great Britain was interested in cooperation, at least until 1968. See Jacek Tebinka, *Nadzieje i rozczarowania. Polityka Wielkiej Brytanii wobec Polski 1956–1970* (Warsaw 2005), 240f. On the Polish relations with Belgium and Denmark, see Wanda Jarzabek, *Polska wobec Konferencji Bezpieczeństwa i Współpracy w Europie. Plany i rzeczywistość 1964–1975* (Warsaw 2008), 23f.
5 Jarzabek, "Ulbricht-Doktrin", 83f.; Christian Hacke, *Die Außenpolitik der Bundesrepublik Deutschland* (Frankfurt/Main 2003), 165.

6   Akten zur Auswärtigen Politik der Bundesrepublik Deutschland 1967 (hereafter AAPD), Bd. 1, Botschafter Emmel an das Auswärtige Amt, March 26, 1966 (Munich 1997), 374.

7   Gomulka spoke about his fears in a direct way, for instance in a conversation with the Hungarian Communist party First Secretary Janos Kadar, Archiwum Akt Nowych (Archive of the Modern Records, hereafter AAN), Komitet Centralny Polskiej Zjednoczonej Partii Robotniczej (Central Committee of the Polish United Workers' Party, hereafter KC PZPR), XIA/64, Protocol from the First Secretary Cde. Wladyslaw Gomulka and the Prime Minister Cde. Józef Cyrankiewicz unofficial visit in Hungary, Budapest, 8-9 March, 1967.

8   The Polish fears were in a sense unique due to the difficult borderline problem, which included the problem of citizenship, but the FRG's growing participation in international relations gave rise to some apprehensions also in the West. See, for instance, Wilfried Loth, *Overcoming the Cold War. A History of Détente 1950-1991* (New York 2002), 103f.; Andreas Wilkens, *Der unstete Nachbar. Frankreich, die deutsche Ostpolitik und die Berliner Vier-Mächte Verhandlungen 1969-1974* (Oldenburg 1990), 78ff., William R. Smyser, *From Yalta to Berlin. The Cold War Struggle over Germany* (London 1999), 258f.

9   The Polish answer: Odpowiedź rządu Polskiej Rzeczpospolitej Ludowej na notę rządu RFN z 24 III 1966 w sprawie pokojowej polityki Niemieckiej Republiki Federalnej, 28 April 1966, in *Zbiór Dokumentów*, no. 4 (1966), 363.

10 AAN, KC PZPR, 237/V – 668, Note from Rapacki to Gomulka, undated.

11 AAN, KC PZPR, 237/V – 668 (original emphasis in text), Comments on the project of a reply of the U.S.S.R. to the note from the government of the FRG of 24 March, by M. Lobodycz, 14 May 1966.

12 Dokumente zur Deutschlandpolitik (hereafter DzD), IV Reihe Bd. 12, Antwortnote der Regierung der UdSSR an die Note der Regierung Bundesrepublik Deutschland zur deutschen Friedenspolitik, 726. In the Görlitz (Zgorzelec) Treaty, the GDR, answering the wish of Moscow, recognized the Oder-Neisse line as a permanent Polish-German borderline. Next, during the talks on the PPR-DDR bilateral treaty, East Berlin tried to play down the importance of the Zgorzelec (Görlitz) Treaty.

13 AAPD, 1967, Bd. 2, Aufzeichnung des Ministerialdirectors Ruete. Betr. Stand und Fortentwicklung unseres Verhältnisses zu den östlischen Nachbarn, 26 May 1967, 789.

14 Hans Georg Lehmann, *Öffnung nach Osten. Die Ostreisen Helmut Schmidts und die Entstehung der Ost- und Entspannungspolitik* (Bonn 1984), 43.

15 Protocol from the Polish-Soviet talks in Andrzej Paczkowski (ed.), *Tajne dokumenty Biura Politycznego. PRL-ZSRR, 1956-1970* (Londyn 1998), 242.

16 Douglas Selvage, "The Treaty of Warsaw: The Warsaw Pact Context", in David Geyer and Bernd Schaefer (eds), *American Détente and German Ostpolitik, 1969-1972* (Washington, D.C. 2004), 70.

17 Protocol from the First Secretary Wladyslaw Gomulka meeting with the participants of the Council of the Foreign Ministers of the Warsaw Pact, Warsaw, 9 February

1967, published in Jarzabek, *PRL w politycznych strukturach* (Listopad 2008), 206f.; AAN, KC PZPR, XIA/104, the Protocol of agreement.

18 AAN, KC PZPR, XIA/46, Note on Gomulka-Ulbricht talks in Warsaw, 14 March 1967, ibid., Draft of Polish-East Germany Treaty on bilateral relations.

19 On the policy towards the bloc countries and bilateral talks, see Jarzabek, "Ulbricht-Doktrin", 98f.

20 Ibid. In my article, I use the term "Gomulka doctrine" to describe a clear line in Polish foreign policy in the years 1956-1970, according to which Poland was trying to exert influence on bloc policies towards Germany, in order to achieve recognition of the Oder-Neisse line and to avoid a situation in which this recognition would be a playing card in international relations. Gomulka was a figurehead of this policy. To reach these aims, the first secretary was ready to dispute with the Soviet Union and also attempted to limit the other bloc countries' room of manoeuvre. I do not use the term with the intention to replace Ulbricht's name with Gomulka in the term "Ulbricht doctrine" used by many historians. However, I believe that Ulbricht's role in coordinating East bloc policies towards Ostpolitik has often been overestimated.

21 For more on Polish planning and diplomatic actions for the European conference, see Jarzabek, *Polska wobec Konferencji*. 23f.; see also Wanda Jarzabek, "Hope and Reality: Poland and the Conference on Security and Cooperation in Europe, 1964-1989", *Cold War International History Project Working Paper*, no. 56 (Washington, D.C. 2008), 4-11.

22 The Polish eyewitnesses – among them Bogumil Rychlowski (Gomulka's interpreter and later chief of the Planning Department at the Polish MFA) – stated that the Rapacki pronouncement was not consulted with the Soviet Union. Interviewed by the author in December 2004. Another document that can serve as proof of this position is Gomulka's pronouncement during the Warsaw Pact Advisory Committee meeting in Warsaw in January 1965, published in Jarzabek, *PRL w politycznych strukturach*, 165.

23 Appeal for a European Security Conference, 17 March 1969 in Vojtech Mastny and Malcolm Byrne (eds), *A Cardboard Castle? An Inside History of the Warsaw Pact 1955-1991* (Budapest 2005), 330; Timothy Garton Ash, *W imieniu Europy Niemcy i podzielony kontynent* (Londyn 1996), 76.

24 AAN, KC PZPR, XIA/ 87, Note by S. Jedrychowski, 4 April 1969.

25 In fact, at this time both superpowers perceived the process as primarily important for their bilateral relations. See, for instance, Raymond L. Garthoff, *Détente and Confrontation: American-Soviet Relations from Nixon to Reagan* (Washington, D.C. 1994), 5.

26 Mieczyslaw Tomala, *Patrząc na Niemcy. Od wrogości do porozumienia 1945-1991* (Warsaw 1997), 157.

27 Wladyslaw Gomulka, "Zgodnie z najbardziej żywotnymi interesami narodu polskiego", Z przemówienia na spotkaniu z wyborcami w Warszawie, wygłoszonego 17 maja 1959 (Gomulka's speech from 17 May 1969), in *O problemie niemieckim. Artykuły i przemówienia* (Warsaw 1984), 76.

28 Jarzabek, "Ulbricht-Doktrin", 113. The Polish Ambassador to Moscow Jan Ptasiński explained to V. Semenov in late May the reason for the lack of earlier consultations.
29 Dieter Bingen, *Polityka Republiki Bońskiej wobec Polski. Od Adenauera do Kohla 1949-1991* (Kraków 1997), 108f.
30 Ibid., 119f.
31 Garton Ash, *W imieniu Europy*, 86ff. On Ostpolitik's place in Bonn's foreign policy, see p. 41, ibid. See also Gottfried Niedhart, "Ostpolitik, Short-Term Objectives, and Grand Design", *Bulletin of the German Historical Institute. American Détente*, 118.
32 Several drafts of a "Treaty on Security and Cooperation" can be located in AAN KC PZPR, XIA/246, Project of the Treaty, September 1969. A draft from 24 October, partly translated into English, can be found in Vojtech Mastny and Malcolm Byrne (eds), *A Cardboard Castle?*, 350ff.
33 AAN, KC PZPR, XIA/87, Short note on consultations with Deputy Minister Vladimir Semenov on 30 September 1969, by Deputy Minister Zygfryd Wolniak. The full version is in Jarzabek, *Polska wobec Konferencji*, 200f.
34 Archiwum Ministerstwa Spraw Zagranicznych Rzeczpospolitej Polskiej (hereafter AMSZ), DSiP 66/77, v. 1, Note from the meeting of the Deputy Foreign Ministers in Prague, J. Winiewicz, 26 October 1969.
35 Układ o podstawach normalizacji stosunków między Polską Rzeczpospolitą Ludową i Republiką Federalną Niemiec.
36 AMSZ, Dep. IV 28/77, v. 4, Note on German Memorandum, December 1971.
37 AAN, KC PZPR, XI/127, A note on consultations with A. Gromyko, 24 July 1972. See also Jarzabek, "Die Haltung der Volksrepublik Polen zur Normalisierung der Beziehungen mit der Bundesrepublik Deutschland 1970-1975", *Deutsch-Polnisches Jahrbuch*, no. 13 (2006), 44f.
38 Ibid.
39 Jerzy Sulek, "Niemiecka pomoc humanitarna i finansowa w latach 1991-2004 dla poszkodowanych przez III Rzeszę w Polsce. Problemy polityczne i prawne", in Witold Góralski (ed.), *Problem reparacji, odszkodowań i świadczeń w stosunkach polsko – niemieckich 1944-2004* (Warsaw 2004), 337ff.
40 It is worth mentioning that part of the amount passed by the West German government through the German Red Cross to the Polish counterpart as compensation for the victims of medical experiments was misused by the Polish government, and a special commission in the 1980s tried to follow the way the compensations had been paid to the victims. The problem was also caused by the fact that the government disposed over a general amount to be distributed, and it was not detailed how much should be transferred to individual persons.
41 Note of conversation, published by Wanda Jarzabek in "Rozmowy ministra Stefana Olszowskiego w czasie wizyty w Bonn w dniach 13-14 września 1972", *Rocznik Polsko-Niemiecki*, no. 11 (2003), 179f.
42 AMSZ, Dep. IV 44/77, v. 1, Minute of conversation between W. Scheel and S. Olszowski, 3 July 1973.

43 AMSZ, Dep. IV 20/79, v. 6, Note: Some remarks on the Polish-German relations, 27 July 1974.
44 Politisches Archive des Auswärtigen Amts, Zwischenarchive, Bd. 116627, Thesen zum Gespräch, April, 1974, Jarzabek, "Die Haltung der Volksrepublik Polen", 121f.
45 AAPD, Bd. 1/1974, München 2004, Aufzeichnung des Ministerialdirektors van Well, 26 April 1974, 581. van Well wrote: "Die polnische Seite wolle diese Frage [of individual compensation, W.J.] nicht in indirekter Form mit Hilfe eines Kredites regeln. Dadurch würde die politisch-moralische Qualität zu sehr geschwächt."
46 AMSZ, Dep. IV 20/77, v. 6, Note: Some remarks on Polish-German relations, 25 July 1974. The Poles wanted to treat as Germans only "ethnic Germans" and not people having German citizenship before 1937, arguing that there were also so-called autochthons in the territories of Silesia and East Prussia. This term autochtons was often used in Poland to describe the original/native/autochthonous population in Silesia, basically of Slavic origin and Catholic, speaking a language resembling medieval Polish with Czech and German influence. Silesia ceased being a part of the Polish state in the fourteenth century and became part of the Czech state. In the eighteenth century it was captured by Prussia. The Polish, Czech and German interests crossed there. In a referendum organized according to the Versailles Treaty after the Great War, the majority of this population voted for Poland.
47 Jarzabek interviews with Adam Daniel Rotfeld, Marian Dobrosielski in March 2007. Talks with Jacques Andréani, Eduard Brunner, Luigi Vittorio Ferraris in September 2005.
48 AMSZ, DSiP 3/82, v. 5, Interpretation of the CSCE decision, 2 August 1975.
49 Jarzabek, *Polska wobec*, 149ff.
50 It was especially visible in the case of the Polish-German exchange, but this can be treated as a good example of the official attitude to the contacts with Germany, AAN, KC PZPR, X A/636, Note on our problems and plans in relations with the RFG, probably 1977.
51 Vojtech Mastny, *Helisnki, Human Rights and European Security. Analysis and Documentation* (Durham, NC 1986), 14.
52 On dissent movements in Poland, see R. Zuzowski, *Political Dissent and Opposition in Poland. The Workers' Defense Committee "KOR"* (New York 1992), 6f.
53 On human rights, see Daniel C. Thomas, *The Helsinki Effect. International Norms, Human Rights, and the Demise of Communism* (New Haven 2001).
54 AMSZ, DSiP 5/82, v. 7, Belgrade 1977. Estimation of results, 28 March 1978.
55 Jarzabek, "Hope and Reality", 48f.

The GDR in the Era of Détente

Conflicting Perceptions and Strategies, 1965-1975[1]

Oliver Bange[2]

If one assumes that the intensifying contacts between East and West both initiated and allowed for pressures for reform – that this eventually led to the end of the Soviet empire and the end of communist rule in Central and Eastern Europe – then the GDR has to be seen as the main victim of détente. If, on the other hand, the codification and multilateralization of East-West contacts, of behavioural standards and of individual liberties in the CSCE's Final Act really constituted the climax of détente, as is often claimed, then the GDR actually negotiated her own demise at Helsinki.

If so, a whole number of questions remain to be answered: when and why did the GDR give up her plans for a German-German confederation and start pursuing a rather defensive posture in facing the FRG? When and how did Moscow communicate its guidelines for a new, more constructive GDR course in the détente era to the East Germans? Why did the new SED leadership under Erich Honecker eventually fail to pursue its security interests more forcefully in the CSCE negotiations, specifically after the warnings by its own diplomats and secret service over the consequences of a CSCE agreement to the GDR's internal stability? The following analysis, while providing some answers, raises even more questions. It does, however, draw attention to a whole set of crucial changes in the GDR's foreign and German policy posture – from Ulbricht to Honecker, from an offensive to a defensive strategy, from an aggressive rhetoric to détente-compatible official language, from "delimitation" to more and more communication, contacts and cooperation. And this was essentially what transformation strategies in the West had been aiming at.

Walter Ulbricht's "Counter Offensive" versus Soviet Status Quo-Policies

Walter Ulbricht's reaction to the Neue Ostpolitik – as devised by Willy Brandt and Egon Bahr – was a mixture of antagonism, hardly surprising, and yet remarkable parallelism. At the same time, Ulbricht's counter-strategy was neither necessarily nor continuously the kind of policy advocated by the majority of the SED's Politburo, particularly by the group formed around Erich Honecker. The same was true of the perceptions and reactions in the Politburos of the CPSU and of other communist parties within the Warsaw Pact. In the following analysis, Walter Ulbricht appears as an unwavering, even obstinate, man of strong convictions. This understanding of the motivations and goals behind Ulbricht's actions offers an explanation for what has often caused confusion in the historiography of the GDR's foreign policy, leading to the established image of a "jumpy", unpredictable Walter Ulbricht. This study points to the exact opposite: namely that Ulbricht persistently worked towards his ultimate goal – a united Germany under communist rule. It also describes how Ulbricht, one of the last leaders of the Warsaw Pact still focused on class struggle, became increasingly isolated through his strategy of a permanent ideological struggle (a key concept for the survival of the early GDR).

In the late 1960s Ulbricht and his offensive approach were instrumentalized by his Soviet "friends" to push the Federal Government in Bonn towards détente and East-West cooperation. This in itself was a trick to force the new Nixon administration in the United States back to the negotiating table. Thereafter – and practically already during this early détente process – Ulbricht was increasingly seen as an obstacle to the status quo-policy the other Communist leaders (Soviet, Polish, Bulgarian, etc.) preferred in Europe. Ulbricht's revolutionary zest when it came to the future of communism in Germany led to both parallels and friction with the Western policies of the other Warsaw Pact member states in the détente era. The permanent attempt at changing political realities in Europe – an attitude shared by Willy Brandt and Walter Ulbricht for conflicting ends – appeared outmoded in the new Nixon-Brezhnev era. Brandt was able to hide the transformation-rationale of his policy behind both ingenious rhetoric and the day-to-day politics of his Eastern treaties – thereby satisfying both the proponents of a status-quo policy and the economic interests of East and West alike. On the other side, Walter Ulbricht's room for manoeuvre in pursuit of a similar tactic was decisively narrowed by Eastern bloc policies, the GDR's position at the frontline of the East-West conflict, and by the necessity to maintain his state's territorial existence. The resulting geopolitical pressures (emigration, economic dependencies, border regime, etc.) persistently hindered the organization of revolutionary change in the other part of Germany, something which Ulbricht following his personal experiences in the 1930s obviously would have preferred. Accordingly, Ulbricht saw the new elites which replaced the wartime or pre-war communist guards throughout the Warsaw Pact in the mid- and late-1960s as un-inspired, un-revolutionary and overly bureaucratic. This attitude was not so much caused by his personal stubbornness (as is often cited in historiography) but by his own convictions and values. However, his connection with Stalinism, his age, and his obstinacy and self-righteousness in dealing with the new communist leaders were increasingly perceived in Moscow and also by certain groups in East Berlin as a threat to the new and more cooperative approach to East-West relations, which the CPSU's Politburo had set out after tense discussions in early 1969. Walter Ulbricht had to be removed, or – and this appears to have been the solution preferred by Leonid Brezhnev – to be manoeuvred towards a siding where he could be isolated from foreign policy decision-making.

Ulbricht's basic rationale did not alter during the 1960s – a decade otherwise marked by important domestic and international shifts. What changed were his politics and tactics, which he – sometimes abruptly – had to adapt to new situations, threats and opportunities. Walter Ulbricht remained true to himself and his ideals – and was therefore much more predictable than most of his contemporaries, and some historians today, have claimed.[2]

Early Strategies for Dealing with the Dangers of "Socialdemocratism" and Ostpolitik

Ulbricht's life-long dream was a communist Germany. His experiences from Weimar taught him that the precondition for this was a united front of workers and employees. Before the war this was called *Volksfront* (peoples' front), in the 1960s the somewhat more modern and less pathetic *Aktionsgemeinschaft* (community for action). Both terms meant the same, and, in the 1920s/1930s as well as in the 1960s, German communists saw the SPD – the German social democrats – as the main obstacle on their path to revolution. Be that as it may, only the classic clientele of both social democrats and trade unions could possibly bring the broad support necessary for revolutionary change. In 1965, when Ulbricht talked to his comrades in Moscow, he defined the basic rationale of his all-German policy: "Besides a broad movement of the intelligentsia and all bourgeois classes, what is really needed is a planned orientation towards the working classes and towards the trade unions and also towards the social democratic parties".[3] In Ulbricht's view, the SPD with its "bourgeois" idea of individual liberties stood like a block between the socialist revolution and its "masses". It is therefore not surprising that old-style revolutionaries like Ulbricht and Mielke maintained a "life-long obsession"[4] with regard to Germany's social democracy. *Sozialdemokratismus* (socialdemocratism) was a derogative term introduced by the KPD (the German Communist Party) in the 1930s, describing the apparent rescue of the hated bourgeoisie by the "social traitors" of the workers' own social class. During the Third Reich and the post-war years the CP's strategy for the construction of a "new Germany" centred on the idea of a *Volksfront* between communists and social democrats. However, as soon as the respective organizations were merged into one party and one trade union (the SED and the FDGB) in the Soviet Occupation Zone, the crusade against "socialdemocratism" was revitalized. *Sozialdemokratismus* soon took on a double function both as a label for life-threatening aberrations within one's own party and as a dirt-campaign against German social democracy. During the Cold War years the latter appeared to be on the wrong side, the other side of the conflict, and was therefore – in communist eyes – responsible for the "preservation of the bourgeois system".[5]

Thus, Germany's communists possessed – at least in their self-perception – an unparalleled, decades-long experience and detailed expert knowledge in dealing with their social democratic adversaries. Combined with the analytical and information-gathering apparatus of state and party, this seemed to predestine East Berlin to realize earlier than anyone else in East and West (and even within the SPD) the true strategy and goals behind the new Ostpolitik and its "thrust" – as Ulbricht liked to call it – against the GDR. Winzer's much cited (though never proven) immediate characterization of Bahr's famous 1963 speech at Tutzing ("Wandel durch Annäherung" – change through rapprochement) as a blueprint for "aggression on felt slippers" provides an indication of the early and correct interpretation of Brandt's *Neue Ostpolitik* in East Berlin. As long as the SPD remained on the opposition benches in the West German Bundestag, Ulbricht and other leading members of the SED still maintained some hope for eventual cooperation with West Germany's social democracy. Of course, there could never be a pact with the SPD's leadership. Walter Ulbricht left no doubt about this.

Instead, the GDR's Westpolitik focused on presenting German communism as a natural ally to SPD voters, to "workers and intellectuals" in the FRG in their fight against the social conservatism of the CDU government and its rearmament policy.[6] On Ulbricht's personal order, experts in the SED's Central Committee and Politburo, as well as the GDR's ministries for foreign affairs and state security, drafted a comprehensive strategy paper for the fight against "socialdemocratism" – which amounted to nothing less than an Eastern variant of Western transformation strategies. This was the same fight for people's minds, which Willy Brandt, Dean Rusk, Charles de Gaulle and many others had been devising in and for the West, in reverse.

These ideas formed the very contemporary background against which East Berlin's initiative for an exchange of speakers between the SED and the SPD has to be interpreted and judged.[7] The logic of this undertaking would have necessitated at least a partial opening up towards the West – and was therefore not without risks. But Walter Ulbricht – partially blinded by multiple distorted and falsified economic data – remained convinced that the GDR could catch up economically with the FRG within four or five years (i.e. by the early 1970s) with the help of its allies, particularly the USSR. This would curb the FRG's economic magnetism, the source of the West Germans' self-esteem and perceived superiority, and the GDR would become a "model" of the social progress made in the East, a "show room" aimed at the West. The logic of this offensive approach demanded at least a partial opening towards the West – a truly risky affair for a state which only recently had to be stabilized by building a wall around it. Consequently, Ulbricht's repeated attempts at launching a political offensive against the West were vetoed by Moscow until his removal in 1971. Thus, in September 1966 Ulbricht pressed Brezhnev for economic and political support for his Westpolitik. Brezhnev retorted by demanding a more confrontational approach by East Berlin in its dealings with the FRG and its parties. Ulbricht understood immediately: "The opponent will surely declare that we intend to deepen Germany's division." To which Brezhnev dryly replied: "The West German government itself is not pursuing measures for reunification."[8]

Strategies for Coping with the Ostpolitik of the Grand Coalition: The Letter Exchange with Kiesinger and Moscow's Delaying Tactics

The situation was further complicated in December 1966 when the SPD joined the conservative parties as the junior partner in a Grand Coalition headed by a CDU chancellor. From now on, a direct appeal to SPD members to topple the FRG's conservative rulers was tantamount to a call to fight their own party leadership – and was therefore likely to backfire. Ulbricht seemed to have lost a crucial tactical lever for his long-term strategy. Together with the increasing recognition of the risks inherent in a strategy of influence-through-contact, this led in 1966/67 to the acknowledgement in East Berlin that the time (or the GDR) was not yet ripe for the realization of a more forceful *Westpolitik*. Even the discussion about the exchange of speakers was soon to be dropped.[9]

At the same time, Brandt and Wehner took charge of West Germany's foreign office and its ministry for all-German affairs – the key departments for a new Ostpolitik to be initiated by the Grand Coalition – and immediately set out to make the best possible use of these new instruments. Ulbricht conceded: "The opponent [Bonn] is leading the fight scientifically" – which was highest praise from a science fanatic like the SED's first secretary. The first signs of panic showed in East Berlin. In late January 1967, the Romanians appeared to confirm the worst fears of a "breach of the dam" within the Warsaw Pact's member states. Once again, East German anxieties mirrored those in Bonn, where the "breach of the dam" remained a public allegory for the possibility of the GDR's world-wide diplomatic recognition and the end of the Hallstein doctrine.[10] For Ulbricht, 1967 became a frustrating year of defensive actions. To Semjonov he promised to "correct all language based on the previous situation, for example concerning reunification, national unity, a united peaceful Germany […] We had suggested the agreement on border passes in the interest of détente and with the intention to move the SPD further to the left. This did not succeed. This is why we now have to engage in a conflict of principles."[11] The year at least showed that the GDR was still able to effectively block Bonn's new Eastern initiatives by cooperating with the Polish leadership and by using its relative economic strength within the COMECON.

Ulbricht then set out to pursue this new strategy for a "conflict of principles" through initiating an exchange of letters between the heads of governments in Bonn and East Berlin, Kiesinger and Stoph. This he thought might help to deflect or even repel the "psychological attack" from Bonn. But, once again, this operational approach was stopped by the USSR's leadership at the very moment when Ulbricht and Stoph were ready to regain the offensive by presenting the draft for a comprehensive inner-German treaty to the German public. In late August 1967 Brezhnev and Kosygin advised a "tactical limitation" on only a few topics, and in mid-September – only the Democracy and the Capitalism", *Reviews in American History* 25 (1997), 531-536; and Anders Stephanson, "Rethinking Cold War history", *Review of International Studies* 24 (1998), 119-124.

16   Minutes of the CK-official Vladimir N. Malin, presented by Mark Kramer on the occasion of the conference "Hungary and the World 1956. The New Archival Evidence", October 1996, Budapest.

17   Cited in Oleg Grinevskii, *Tauwetter. Entspannung, Krisen und neue Eiszeit* (Berlin 1996), 23f. On the pressure Walter Ulbricht imposed on Khrushchev, see also Hope M. Harrison, *Driving the Soviets up the Wall. Soviet-East German Relations, 1953-1961* (Princeton, NJ 2003).

18   *Khrushchev Remembers* (Boston 1970), 494. Compare Aleksandr Fursenko and Timothy Naftali, *"One Hell of a Gamble". Khrushchev, Castro, and Kennedy, 1958-1964* (London and New York 1997); Loth, *Overcoming*, 67-76.

19   Khrushchev in a conversation with his staff in the spring of 1959, cited in Grinevskii, *Tauwetter*, 153.

20   Khrushchev at the 20th Party Convention in February 1956, XX s"ezd KPSS, vol. 1 (Moscow 1956), 36.

21   See also William Taubman, *Khrushchev: The Man and His Era* (New York 2003).

22   Andropov in a conversation with the Germany-specialist Vyatcheslav Kevorkov on 13 February 1968, whom he assigned the creation a "direct line" to the Bonn government. Cited in Vyatcheslav Kevorkov, *Der geheime Kanal. Moskau, der KGB und die Bonner Ostpolitik* (Berlin 1995), 29f.

23   Minutes of the Politburo session of March 17-19, 1979, *CWIHP-Bulletin*, no. 8/9 (Winter 1996/97), 136-145.

24   See Loth, *Overcoming*, 157-160.

25   Excerpts from the minutes, *CWIHP-Bulletin*, no. 5 (Spring 1995), 121, 134-137.

26   See also Loth, "Moscow, Prague and Warsaw: Overcoming the Brezhnev Doctrine", *Cold War History*, vol. 1, no. 2 (January 2001), 103-118.

27   Important for the development of Gorbachev's thinking are Archie Brown, *The Gorbachev Factor* (Oxford and New York 1997); Archie Brown, *Seven Years that Changed the World: Perestroika in Perspective* (Oxford and New York 2007); Vladislav M. Zubok, "The Collapse of the Soviet Union. Leadership, Elites, and Legitimacy", in Geir Lundestad (ed.), *The Fall of Great Powers. Peace: Stability and Legitimacy* (Oslo and New York 1994), 156-174, Vladislav M. Zubok, "Gorbachev and the End of the Cold War. Perspectives on History and Personality", *Cold War History*, vol. 2, no. 2 (January 2002), 61-100.

28   The specific meaning of European actors is emphasized in a conference project, which has already produced four conference volumes: *The Failure of Peace in Europe, 1943-49*, edited by Antonio Varsori and Elena Clandri (Houndsmills and New York 2002); *L'Europe de l'Est et de L'Ouest dans la Guerre froide 1948-1953*, edited by Saki Dockrill, Robert Frank, Georges-Henri Soutou, Antonio Varsori (Paris 2002); *Europe, the Cold War and Coexistence, 1953-1965*, edited by Wilfried Loth (London and Portland 2004); *The Making of Détente. Eastern and Western Europe in the Cold*

War, 1965-75, edited by Wilfried Loth and Georges-Henri Soutou (London and New York 2008).

29 See also Wilfried Loth, "Germany in the Cold War: Strategies and Decisions", in Odd Arne Westad (ed.), *Reviewing the Cold War: Approaches, Interpretations, Theory* (London and Portland 2000), 242-257.

30 See Loth, *Overcoming*, 165-172, 179-197.

31 Egon Bahr, *Zu meiner Zeit* (Munich 1996); see also Wilfried Loth, "Mikhail Gorbachev, Willy Brandt, and European Security", *Journal of European Integration History* 11.1 (2005), 45-59.

32 Conversation of 28 July, 1989, cited in Michael R. Beschloss and Strobe Talbott, *Auf höchster Ebene. Das Ende des Kalten Krieges und die Geheimdiplomatie der Supermächte 1989-1991* (Düsseldorf 1993), 128.

33 See also Soutou, *La guerre*, 729-732.

34 See also my proposal in Wilfried Loth, "Was war der Kalte Krieg? Annäherungen an ein unbewältigtes Erbe", in *Deutschland im Kalten Krieg 1945-1963. Eine Ausstellung des Deutschen Historischen Museums 28. August – 24. November 1992* (Berlin 1992), 11-28.

from "democratic initiatives" and possible tactical coalitions for the new DKP in West German election campaigns to support for the reform programmes of Western trade unions and public campaigns against the nuclear war scare in the FRG.[21] Moscow also now realized the potential threat posed by West Germany's social democracy and its new Eastern policies. Soviet experts and leadership alike assumed that the SPD after the early successes in Czechoslovakia was set to continue with this new approach, particularly as "there was no alternative which could lead to a reunification of Germany according to Bonn's conditions."[22]

But there were also some endogenous reasons hindering an effective counter-strategy against the transformative intentions hidden behind Brandt's and Bahr's rhetoric of détente and rapprochement. One reason was the difficulties East German officials encountered in squaring the dichotomy of the new and the established images of the FRG. While the old stereotypes of the FRG were based on an alleged revanchism and militarism, the Eastern bloc's increasingly cooperative dealings with West Germany suggested a rather different interpretation, namely that of a country interested in security and stability combined with intellectual exchange across the blocs and an opening up of Eastern societies. This resulted in an indifferent equation of the détente concepts favoured by Kiesinger, Strauss, Brandt, Bahr, Wehner and Brzezinski (who East Berlin wrongly suspected to be the master-brain behind Lyndon B. Johnson's "bridge building" strategy, which was known to have been a strong influence on the conceptualization of Ostpolitik). All of these approaches were perceived as being interconnected – and therefore essentially the same. The resulting analytical framework made for a gross underestimation of the dynamic aspects in Brandt's and Bahr's Ostpolitik – as well as in the "bridge building" concept of Dean Rusk and Francis Bator – when compared to Zbigniew Brzezinski's zero-sum game.[23]

Between Dölln and Moscow: Ulbricht's "Westpolitik" Plans and Brezhnev's "Peaceful Coexistence"

By late 1969 it seems that Ulbricht had lost both his luck and perhaps also his sense of what could be done. The louder and more impertinent his demands became, the more concern they raised in Moscow over their eventual repercussions for the USSR's own policy of "peaceful coexistence" with the West. At the same time, Willy Brandt won the federal German elections in September 1969 (thereafter forming a new coalition with the FDP, the small liberal party in West Germany). Without the former restrictions of an anti-Ostpolitik majority amongst the conservative members of parliament, Bonn's negotiations with other Warsaw Pact capitals advanced rapidly – adding credibility, weight and a wealth of new tactical possibilities to the chancellor's approach towards Central and Eastern Europe. The conflict between East Berlin and Moscow came to a head when in the summer months of 1969 Ulbricht repeatedly pushed for the "political and economic strengthening of the GDR by making up for the *GDR's backwardness* in comparison with West Germany until 1975".[24]

When Ulbricht's ideas were pressed once again by a high-ranking East German delegation in Moscow in July, the Soviet leadership finally reacted. Instead of agreeing to the inner-German initiative, the Soviet comrades replied with a forthright demand for "one million tons of tubes". This was a blatant provocation, because the East Germans of course knew about the parallel negotiations between Bonn and Moscow over such a deal – but, unlike the Federal Republic, the GDR lacked the necessary raw materials, production capacities and probably even the know-how needed to make the seamless tubes developed by Thyssen. This provocation encapsulated a demonstration of the necessity for peaceful coexistence and cooperation. Ulbricht's demands for the continuation of the revolutionary fight against and within West Germany by all means following from international solidarity (particularly within the Warsaw Pact) correctly followed and cited communist ideology and dogma. But the politics pursued by Breshnev, Ceausescu, Kadar, Gomulka and others had long set out on a path which Western terminology characterized as "national communism" – a prescription for status-quo policies combined with the prioritization of national interests.

Still Ulbricht was unwilling to take no for an answer to his essential ambition. On 30 October 1969, he called the SED's Politburo for an extraordinary meeting to his country house at Dölln. While in Bonn the Bundestag was in the midst of a heated debate over Brandt's recognition of the GDR's statehood in his inaugural address,[25] in Dölln, Ulbricht staged the final curtain of his regency. He declared that Brandt's apparent change in tactics was solely intended "to penetrate us". And he was realistic enough to recognize: "This could have an effect on us." In the best agitprop-style of the election hall battles of the 1930s, he then called upon his troops for a counterattack: "If Brandt makes a new Ostpolitik, then will we make a new Westpolitik, and one that truly deserves its name. We will make him sweat."[26] Although the Politburo eventually agreed that Moscow should be informed about the

SED's new initiative, Ulbricht's forceful appearance had led to a number of clashes in Dölln, particularly with Norden, Hager, and Honecker, whose statements he had simply discarded as "not correct". Honecker, with silent support from Soviet ambassador Abrassimov, almost immediately set out to block the initiative. While Ulbricht was still recovering at Dölln, the next Politburo meeting under Honecker blocked further contacts between the East and West German trade union organizations, agreed on a slander campaign against the figureheads of Bonn's new Ostpolitik, and ordered Foreign Minister Winzer to draft a "principal commentary" on the GDR's recognition under international law.[27]

From Ulbricht to Honecker – from Offensive Dreams to Defensive Pragmatism

Ulbricht's ideas for a communist offensive in inner-German politics were diverted to a siding in European history – in fact much earlier than his official dismissal in May 1971 might indicate. Already in December 1969, the head of government Stoph, the Minister of Defence Hoffmann, and the almighty Minister of the State Security Mielke, staged a common front against Ulbricht's rapprochement strategy. Mielke's explanations were less stringent than robust: the SPD leaders would perceive themselves as "better experts in subversion" than the Americans. Their Ostpolitik was "an intensified strategy for political-ideological softening-up", their weapon was to be the infamous "socialdemocratism" – everything would be done according to a tactical blueprint. What was needed now was true "revolutionary attention".[28]

Over the following months, Ulbricht lost much of his former influence. His almost unchallenged ability to forge both domestic and foreign policy decisions within the GDR according to his own ideas, still apparent in spring 1969, quickly vanished. From February 1970 onwards, the tone in official analyzes by the GDR's foreign minister and his diplomats, when dealing, for example, with Brandt's letters to Stoph, or the situation in Berlin, sharpened considerably. In addition, before these memoranda were sent on to Ulbricht and Moscow they were first checked by Erich Honecker.[29] And when it came to the issue of an inner-German summit, initiated in a letter from Ulbricht to the ceremonial/formal head of West Germany, Federal President Gustav Heinemann in December 1969,[30] the course of the new SED leadership was so restrictive that Moscow already feared a public loss of face for Brandt and accordingly warned East Berlin to start preparations in earnest for what would become the Erfurt and Kassel meetings.³¹

During the negotiations between Bahr, Gromyko and Falin in the first half of 1970 leading up to the Treaty of Moscow, Ulbricht was denied any contacts with the CPSU leaders. When the treaty was signed he was merely informed of it and a letter by Brezhnev told him that the "principal SED course ought to be one of consistent delimitation".³² Essentially this was a double warning: against the evil brother in the West and the big friend in the East. Two weeks later, Soviet Foreign Minister Gromyko spelt out to Ulbricht what this meant and what was expected from the GDR: "You are informed about the line taken by the Brandt government. This line will be supported."³³ Walter Ulbricht was voluntarily dismissed on 3 May 1971. Only a fortnight later, the SED's new first secretary, Erich Honecker, visited Moscow and explained the dangers of "socialdemocratism", apparently in the same language as his predecessor. He talked about penetration and "diversion" by "refined methods". He went on to describe Brandt as a demagogue "pretending to represent the left wing of the SPD", and declared that counter-measures had to focus on contacts with ordinary social democrats, on ideological work within the GDR, and on the reduction of debts in the FRG (something he was soon to forget). The most important sentence came at the end: "Time works for us!"³⁴ What was once thought up by Walter Ulbricht as an initiative towards a communist future in Germany declined under Erich Honecker to a rhetorical disguise for international status-quo politics and domestic standstill.

The effect of the change from Ulbricht to Honecker was also a change of paradigms: from ideology to power pragmatism, from offensive to defensive. Brezhnev's part also changed, perhaps not even unintentionally. Now it seemed to be his role to protect Brandt from the obstructionists in East Berlin. Yet no one in Moscow was under any illusions about Bonn's political concepts and goals – which was why Brezhnev argued for a strict separation between contacts and even cooperation at state level and ideological struggle. This meant that the USSR had a free hand to continue its policy of negotiations and treaties (over Berlin, SALT, etc.) while all others and particularly the East Germans were asked to provide a "broad frontline" for the "ongoing observation" of Western socialdemocratism – all of course the subject of continuous consultation with Moscow.³⁵ The SED's Politburo understood and immediately set out to redefine its concept for the fight against Western transformation strategies. Within a few months the Politburo's agreed policy posture shifted from Ulbricht's concept of intensified class struggle to Honecker's posture of drawing a dividing line and digging in. Even the

Central Committee's foreign policy task force (AG Außenpolitik), once founded by Ulbricht, now delivered appropriate reasoning for Brezhnev's "consistent policy of delimitation", meant to preclude any so-called "inner-German relations".36 In early 1971 the outlook was as grey as the so-called real-existent socialism: "The socialist countries will have to face the task to foil this imperialist strategy and tactic for many years ahead."

Throughout the détente era, the GDR's position did not improve through the politics of linkage created by Washington, Moscow and Bonn. The ratification procedures for Bonn's Eastern treaties, the Quadripartite Agreement, SALT, and the inner-German Basic Treaty were all linked to each other and to the convocation of negotiations on a pan-European peace conference and the reduction of military forces in Europe.

Between the Devil and the Deep Blue Sea: East Berlin's Diplomacy during the CSCE Negotiations

The shift in personnel and policies almost immediately translated not only into a new official foreign policy posture but also into a change towards a détente-compatible language. This was nowhere more apparent then in East Berlin's approach towards Brezhnev's pet project of an all-European security conference.37 Back in October 1969 a position paper prepared by the *Grundsatzabteilung* of the GDR's Foreign Ministry (the MfAA) clearly perceived what would later become the Conference on Security and Cooperation in Europe (CSCE), as an ideal platform for Walter Ulbricht's offensive goals. The paper digressed for over fifty pages about "containment of the effects of the aggressive special pact between West German and American imperialism", "rollback of US influence in Europe", "preventing the further development of Western European integration towards a political unit", "rollback of NATO's influence and the eventual overcoming of this aggressive pact system", and "support for the struggle for socialism and democracy in Western European countries".38

In October 1970 the same department, under Siegfried Bock, focused another memorandum almost exclusively on the CSCE's limitations for guaranteeing the status quo. Instead, the paper lamented the fact that the Warsaw Pact's proposal for intensified East-West cooperation in the fields of commercial, economic and scientific/technological relations paved the way for Western efforts "to use the comprehensive application of relations of peaceful coexistence to increase the antisocialist subversion and diversion of the Warsaw Treaty states",[39] thus putting the GDR on the spot. By autumn 1971, due to pressure from Moscow to accelerate the inner-German negotiations, the GDR had completed its 180-degree turn in its policies both towards Moscow as well as towards Bonn. Now the GDR goals were reduced to "keeping peace in Europe", guaranteeing state borders, and economic and other cooperation.[40] East Berlin's essentially defensive posture was from now on to focus on developing socialism within the GDR.

From the very beginning of the negotiations, the MfAA succinctly identified Western interests in the CSCE. As the very first conversation between the foreign ministers of the two German states, Walter Scheel and Otto Winzer, indicated,[41] in the long term nothing less than the existence of the GDR as a socialist state was at stake in the CSCE process. The head of the GDR's CSCE delegation also realized that "with their demagogic performance, the Western states are trying to pretend to the public that they represent the true interests of the people. According to the West's assumption the socialist states have to pay the 'price' of so called 'human reliefs' in return for a multilateral recognition of frontiers."[42] Bock accurately predicted the Helsinki Final Act's character as a tit-for-tat deal already in July 1973, two years before its signature. In his report to Foreign Minister Winzer, he left no doubt that the NATO and EEC states' proposals concerning the second and third item of the agenda[43] "are aimed at eroding sovereignty by means of multilateral agreements and broad 'freedom of movement of persons and ideas.'"[44]

Another, perhaps even *the* crux of the conference – which was after all meant as an "Ersatz-peace"[45] agreement over Germany to legalize the territorial gains and losses after the Second World War – was Bonn's demand for the insertion of a clause on "peaceful change of frontiers". The West German delegation tabled this demand already at the very start of CSCE's stage II, in Geneva in September 1973 – and East Germany's diplomats instantly knew what this could mean for the future of their state. Siegfried Bock strongly advised both his minister and Erich Honecker not to sign any final document containing this clause – and instead to gamble on the increasing international pressures on Bonn to give in during the final stages of the conference.[46] Eventually, in February 1975, Bonn, Washington and Moscow reached an agreement over the positioning of the disputed clause in the list of principles. The USSR's leadership thereby acknowledged that in order to bring the conference – on which Brezhnev had staked his reputation at home and abroad – to a successful end it had to accept Bonn's request for prospective "peaceful changes".[47] As had been the case with the shift from

Ulbricht to Honecker in the run-up to the Moscow treaty in 1969/1970, the Helsinki Final Act of 1975 again proved that Moscow's national interest by far outweighed the GDR's national security concerns. The GDR indeed had to pay the price. Heading the Warsaw Pact's most Western outpost, Honecker's team remained rightfully concerned that the West used inter-systemic cooperation for "systematically and permanently exercising influence on the economic, political and ideological processes in the countries of the socialist community of states in order to induce the erosion of their social orders".[48]

"And there will always be the Staatssicherheit": The SED Leadership between Realism and Self-deception

In October 1975 Klaus Blech – head of the planning staff in Bonn's *Auswärtiges Amt* and for obvious reasons its chief negotiator in the CSCE talks – allowed his British colleagues a glimpse of Bonn's long-term expectations when he drew an optimistic outlook on the CSCE process, "if one sees over a longer period – 50 years – and assumes a waning of ideological confrontation over this period."[49] Seen from East Berlin, this was of course exactly what the GDR had to avoid.

Like the GDR's diplomats, the ministry of state security from very early on sensed and predicted the dangers inherent in a CSCE process. Already a year before the conclusion of the CSCE summit in Helsinki, the East German security services – the *Staatssicherheit*, MfS or Stasi – had a clear picture of the eventual outcome and its momentous consequences for the GDR's internal situation.[50] Numerous departments were involved in an exercise listing various forms of ideological subversion expected to flood the country from the West and thinking up a "catalogue" of ways and means to counteract this.[51] It was clearly realized that an increase both in the volume of East-West traffic and in economic and technical cooperation was to form an integral part of the FRG's "policy of contacts" aiming at the "diversion" (subversion) of socialism in the GDR.

Why then did the SED leadership go along with the Helsinki Final Act? On a general level, Honecker's team had to balance out their justified fears over what they saw as "illegal" outside interference in the GDR's socialist society against its own economic, financial and technological needs (which could only be satisfied in cooperation with the West) and Soviet pressure for a "peace offensive" on the part of the Warsaw Pact states, coupled with demands for strict sealing (*Abgrenzung* or "delimitation") of the GDR from the corrupting influences of West German society and politics. The result was a delicate balancing act, much helped by two assumptions obviously shared by the entire SED leadership: on the international level, the long-term effect of the status quo; and on the domestic level, the ability of the state security to cope. Internationally, both Moscow and East Berlin banked on the impact of post-war realities and their recognition in Helsinki. The mere fact of the "German peace border" – plus the sheer numbers of East German and Soviet troops on GDR territory to uphold it, and a new generation growing up within this reality – would cement the status quo and guarantee a socialist future for East Germany.[52] Internally, as Honecker put it with a smile to Brezhnev at their last consultative meeting before Helsinki, "there had always been the *Staatssicherheit*, and it is still in existence."[53]

This misleading notion of a safety net simultaneously formed an important psychological background for the GDR leadership's final decision to bow to Moscow's pressure not to stand in the way of a successful conclusion of the conference. The irony of this was that the intensification of domestic surveillance and oppression by the state security during the détente years[54] decisively contributed to its negative image with the East Germans. The State Security and its ever threatening presence dominated the internal perception of the GDR's society; and it proved to be an important reason for why, in 1989, the reform of the communist system – intended by a majority of the GDR's leftist opposition groups – was unacceptable to the majority of the East Germans.

Notes

1. This chapter draws on some of the preliminary findings of the VW project on "CSCE and the Transformation of Europe" at Mannheim University, coordinated by Gottfried Niedhart and Oliver Bange (see <http://www.CSCE-1975.net>).
   Archival abbreviations: BStU – Beauftragte für Stasi-Unterlagen, archives of the GDR's Ministry for State Security (Berlin); PA AA/MfAA – Records of the GDR's Foreign Ministry (Ministerium für Auswärtige Angelegenheiten, MfAA) in the Political Archives of the Auswärtiges Amt (Berlin); BNA – British National Archives (London); SAPMO – Stiftung Archiv der Parteien und Massenorganisationen der DDR (Berlin).
2. Repeated evaluations of Ulbricht in Monika Kaiser, *Machtwechsel von Ulbricht zu Honecker – Funktionsmechanismen der SED-Diktatur in Konfliktsituationen 1962 bis 1972* (Berlin 1997), who on page 233 even talks about Ulbricht's zig-zag course), and Norbert Podewin, *Walter Ulbricht – eine neue Biographie* (Berlin 1995).

3   Ulbricht to Brezhnev, Moscow, 18.9.1965. SAPMO: DY30/J IV 2/201/725. What looks like a bad translation is indeed odd language in the original, typical of Ulbricht.
4   Markus Wolf, *Man Without a Face: The Autobiography of Communism's Greatest Spymaster* (New York 1999), 236.
5   On this – although exclusively based on official GDR publications – see Hans-Joachim Spanger, *Die SED und der Sozialdemokratismus – ideologische Abgrenzung in der DDR* (Diss. Frankfurt/M. and Cologne 1981). More differentiation may be found in the article by Michael Lemke, "Eine neue Konzeption? – Die SED im Umgang mit der SPD 1956 bis 1960", in Jürgen Kocka (ed.), *Historische DDR-Forschung – Aufsätze und Studien* (Berlin 1993), 361-377. Lemke proves already at this early phase that socialdemocratism was anything but a consistent ideological concept. Instead, it provided a container which could be filled with various strategies in the fight against the West German SPD. Accordingly, the change from a frontal assault on socialdemocratism towards partial and informal cooperation at and with the lower levels of West German social democracy and trade unions – a tactic preferred by Ulbricht – would have taken place already in the late 1950s.
6   For Ulbricht's rationale, see the cited conversation with Brezhnev, Moscow, 18.9 1965; and, for a more detailed description and analysis of this, Jochen Staadt, Die *geheime Westpolitik der SED 1960-1970 – Von der gesamtdeutschen Orientierung zur sozialistischen Nation* (Berlin 1993), particularly 107ff.; and Monika Kaiser, *Machtwechsel von Ulbricht zu Honecker*, 233ff.
7   For the letters between the Central Committee of the SED of 1.2 and 25.3.1966, and those by the SPD's party directorate of 18.3.1966, see SBZ-Archiv 1966, no. 7, 105-112; for the SPD's public answer in early June see *Deutsche Aussenpolitik* (East Berlin 1966), 139; for Ulbricht's letter to Brandt of 22.6.1966 and Brandt's reply, see SBZ-Archiv 1966, no. 13, 204-206. The end to these discussions is provided by a press declaration of Albert Norden in *Neues Deutschland*, 30.6.1966.
8   Conversation between Ulbricht and Brezhnev in Moscow on 10.9.1966. SAPMO: (Ulbricht's office) DY 30/3518 and -/3294.
9   The discussion between Ulbricht and Norden during the Central Committee meeting on 27/28.4.1966 showed up the different positions within the SED. See also Ulbricht's handwritten notes from 8.5.1966 on the necessity for a strong public stance over the question. SAPMO: DY 30/J IV 2/202/343; DY 30/IV 2/1/342; DY 30/3294.
10 For the importance of the January/February 1967 Warsaw Pact crisis for the future course of the détente era, see Oliver Bange, "Ostpolitik as a Source of Intra-Bloc Tensions", in Mary Ann Heiss and S. Victor Papacosma (eds), *NATO and the Warsaw Pact – Intra-Bloc Conflicts* (Kent, OH 2008), 106-121.
11 Conversation Ulbricht – Semjonov, 17.1.1967. SAPMO: DY 30/3520.
12 Therefore the historiographical assumption that the GDR "did not want" to engage in a serious inner-German discussion (the latest uncritical repetition can be found in Christoph Meyer, *Herbert Wehner – eine Biographie* [Munich 2006], 310) is based on a forty-year old misperception in Bonn.

13 Conversation Ulbricht, Semjonov, Rapacki, 15.9.1967 in East Berlin. SAPMO: DY 30/3519.
14 Conversation Ulbricht – Zarapkin, 18.9.1967. SAPMO: DY 30/3495.
15 Personal and strictly confidential "Disposition für die Skizze einer langfristigen Politik gegenüber Westdeutschland", 8.2.1968, by the AG Außen- und Deutschlandpolitik. SAPMO (Ulbricht's office files) DY 30/3311.
16 Author's conversation with Norbert Podewin, Odense, 17.11.2007. In 1968 Podewin was working for Albert Norden and frequently discussed the situation in Prague with Ulbricht. See also Oliver Bange, "Die CSSR-Krise 1968 – Die 'Special Role' der Neuen Ostpolitik vor dem Hintergrund westlicher Transformationsstrategien", in Bernd Greiner, Christian Th. Müller and Dierk Walter (eds), *Krisen im Kalten Krieg*, vol. 2 (Hamburg 2008), 411-445.
17 While Mark Kramer and Manfred Wilke (in their contributions in Jaromir Navratil et al. (eds), *The Prague Spring 1968 – A NSA Documents Reader* [Prague 1998]) and Vaclav Kural and Lutz Priess, *Die SED und der 'Prager Frühling' – Politik gegen einen 'Sozialismus mit menschlichem Antlitz'* (Berlin 1996) describe Ulbricht as a proponent of a harsh military reaction by the Warsaw Pact, Kaiser in *Machtwechsel*, op. cit., argues that Ulbricht continued to prefer a peaceful solution, but was forced by Honecker and Norden to support the course of the hardliners. A similar argument is put forward by the former East German ambassador to Prague, Karl Seidel, in Siegfried Bock et al. (eds), *DDR-Außenpolitik im Rückspiegel – Diplomaten im Gespräch* (Münster 2004), 60. I argue for a different, third interpretation of Ulbricht's and the GDR leadership's reaction to the CSSR crisis in several stages, in close interdependence with the GDR's inner-German policies.
18 Memorandum by Norden for Ulbricht, 12.7.1968; telegram from Florin to Winzer, 18.7.1968; draft speech by Ulbricht for the meeting in Warsaw on 14/15.7.1968. SAPMO: DY 30/3556 and -/3618.
19 The irony of this statement was that Benno Ohnesorg – whose death Ulbricht was obviously referring to – had been shot under dubious circumstances by a West Berlin police officer, secretly enlisted by East Germany's State Security, as has been revealed by BStU research staff in May 2009. Conversation Ulbricht-Kolar (Prague's ambassador to East Berlin), 17.4.1968. SAPMO: DY 30/3616. Author's conversation with Siegfried Bock in September 2005. Bock headed the analytical unit of the GDR's Foreign Ministry at the time.
20 Note by Winzer for Ulbricht, 9.10.1968; note from Belezki, 22.10.1968; draft peace treaty, 21.10.1968. SAPMO: DY 30/3522.
21 Letter by Max Spangenberg to Ulbricht, 30.9.1968; memorandum by Spangenberg, 14.1.1969. SAPMO: DY 30/3558. Similar, though more general, conclusions due to the lack of archival material can be found in Michael Roik, *Die DKP und die demokratischen Parteien 1968-1984* (Paderborn 2006), 73ff.
22 Soviet memorandum (in Russian and German) on "The reactions of the FRG to the events in Czechoslovakia", 11.11.1968. SAPMO: DY 30/3496 and -/3624.
23 For a comparison and analysis of the various and often antagonistic concepts for

East-West détente in the USA see Oliver Bange, "Die USA und die oppositionellen Bewegungen in Osteuropa 1961-1990", in Hans-Joachim Veen, Ulrich Mählert and Peter März (eds), *Wechselwirkungen Ost-West – Dissidenz, Opposition und Zivilgesellschaft 1975 bis 1989* (Weimar 2007), 79-95.

24 Author's added emphasis. Letter from Ulbricht to Brezhnev, 21.4.1969. Attached to this letter was a comprehensive analysis of the Grand Coalition's new Ostpolitik. Ulbricht's letter to Brezhnev of 3.6.1969 and the statements by the East German delegation in Moscow in July 1969 (without Ulbricht who had fallen ill at the time) were written in a similar vein. The Soviet demand for "one million tons of tubes" was tabled at the final meeting of the delegation in Moscow on 14.7.1969. SAPMO: DY 30/3525; DY 30/J IV 2/202/346; DY 30/J IV 2/2/1235.

25 Brandt had provided the SED leadership with a copy of his speech in advance through a secret back-channel between Bahr and von Berg. Note by von Berg, 26.10.1969 BStU: GH 25/87.

26 Stenograph protocol of the Politburo meeting in Dölln on 30.10.1969 by Ulbricht's personal assistant, Wolfgang Berger. SAPMO: DY 30/3294. This appears to be much more reliable than Honecker's handwritten notes, cited by Kaiser, *Machtwechsel*, 326-331.

27 Decisions taken at the meeting of SED Politburo on 4.11.1969. SAPMO: DY 30/J IV 2/2A/1400.

28 12th meeting of the CC of the SED, 12/13.12.1969. SAPMO: DY 30/IV 2/1/404. The state security's analysis of Brandt's and Bahr's self-perception is indeed mirrored in Bahr's memoirs (Egon Bahr, *Zu meiner Zeit* [Munich 1996], 552). For an interpretation of Mielke's statement in the context of East German State Security reactions triggered by the beginnings of East-West détente, see Oliver Bange, "Zwischen Bedrohungsperzeption und sozialistischem Selbstverständnis – Das Wissen der Staatssicherheit über westliche Transformationsstrategien, ihre Politikberatung und Gegenstrategien 1966-1975", in Torsten Diedrich and Walter Süß (eds), *Die Rolle von Militär und Staatssicherheit im inneren und äußeren Sicherheitskonzept der WVO-Staaten* (Berlin 2009) (forthcoming).

29 See, for example, the memorandum on Bonn's Berlin policy, which was forwarded on 27.1.1970 to Moscow, but only submitted by Winzer to Ulbricht on 10.2.1970. SAPMO: DY 30/3526.

30 The text is published in "Bundesministerium für innerdeutsche Beziehungen" (ed.), *Texte zur Deutschlandpolitik 1969 (TzDP)*, vol. IV (Bonn 1970), 143-147. For Ulbricht's considerations, see SAPMO: DY 30/J IV 2/202/103.

31 Letter from Winzer to Ulbricht on a meeting with Abrassimov, 11.3.1970. SAPMO: DY 30/3526.

32 Letters from Ulbricht to Brezhnev of 2.6 and 17.8.1970; conversations Ulbricht – Brezhnev on 19 and 21.8.1970; letter from Brezhnev from 16.10.1970. SAPMO: DY 30/3530.

33 Conversation Ulbricht – Gromyko, 29.10.1970. SAPMO: DY 30/3654.

34 Honecker's memory cards for his talks with the CPSU leadership on 18.5.1971 in Moscow. SAPMO: (Honecker's office) DY 30/2375.

35 Brezhnev's explanations at the meeting of the Warsaw Pact's Permanent Consultative Committee in East Berlin, 2.12.1970. SAPMO: DY 30/3391.

36 Memorandum "The FRG in the class struggle of our time – analysis and prognosis", 121 pp., November 1970/January 1971, by AG Außenpolitik. SAPMO: DY 30/3317. The study began with a "scientific" definition of "socialdemoratism" as a pretended change of capitalism and an attempt at liquidating socialism step by step. Its goal was, according to the paper, "to remove the GDR from the socialist camp and to use the pretended claim of a continuing 'unity of the nation' finally to attach her to the FRG."

37 For a more detailed analysis of the GDR's role in the CSCE negotiations, an English edition of key MfAA documents, and a comment by Siegfried Bock, see Oliver Bange and Stephan Kieninger (eds), *Negotiating one's own demise? The GDR's Foreign Ministry and the CSCE negotiations – plans, preparations, tactics and presumptions* (Mannheim 2008), e-dossier at <http:www.wilsoncenter.org/index> and <http://www.CSCE-1975.net>.

38 Memorandum "Working Material for the Preparation of a European Security Conference", 10.10.1969, by the Department for Analysis, Planning and Prognosis. PA AA: MfAA C 367/78.

39 Memorandum "Some questions regarding the preparation and realisation of a European Security Conference in the struggle for establishing a European Security System", 20.10.1970, by HA GP Sector ESC. PA AA: MfAA C 366/78.

40 "Factor Analysis concerning the state of preparation for a European Security Conference", Berlin, 25.9.1971, by the Grundsatzabteilung. PA AA: MfAA C 368/78.

41 Scheel and Winzer met on 3 and 7.7.1973 in Helsinki. The East German records of these conversations can be found in PA AA: MfAA C 376/78. The West German records are edited in Auswärtiges Amt (ed.), Akten zur Auswärtigen Politik der Bundesrepublik Deutschland 1973 (Munich 2004), docs 215 and 220. In their first conversation, Scheel explained his 'Verklammerungsstrategie' (though he did not mention the term – meaning: strategy for clipping together) with regard to all kinds of contacts between the FRG and the GDR, including Berlin, of course.

42 Undated memorandum "Possible ideas for the introduction of a submission in the Politburo", by Bock, July 1973. PA AA: MfAA C 388/78. For a comprehensive analysis of the history and effect of the memorandum see Bange and Kieninger, e-dossier, doc. 10.

43 The proposals from NATO and EEC states concerning cooperation in the field of trade, economy, science/technology, and freer movement of people, information and ideas can be found in PA AA: MfAA C 374/78.

44 Report "The course and the results of the first phase of the European Security Conference", 23.7.1973, for Winzer. PA AA: MfAA C 851/75.

45 John J. Maresca, *To Helsinki – The Conference on Security and Cooperation in Europe, 1973-1975* (Durham 1987), 80. Maresca was a member of the American delegation to the conference.

46 Conversations and letter exchange between the author and Siegfried Bock, 2005-2007. See also Siegfried Bock, "The CSCE – an Era of Dissent *and* Consensus", in Oliver Bange and Stephan Kieninger (eds), *Negotiating one's own demise? The GDR's Foreign Ministry and the CSCE negotiations – plans, preparations, tactics and presumptions* (Mannheim 2007), e-dossier at <http:www.wilsoncenter.org/index> and <http://www.CSCE-1975.net>.

47 For a detailed study, see Gottfried Niedhart, "Peaceful Change of Frontiers as a Crucial Element in the West German Strategy of Transformation", in Oliver Bange and Gottfried Niedhart (eds), *Helsinki 1975 and the Transformation of Europe* (Oxford and New York 2007), 65-84.

48 Information about the plenary session of the socialist countries' permanent commission of scientific institutions about issues of European security and cooperation, Sofia, 9-13.11.1976. PA AA: MfAA C 385/78.

49 Summary of planning staff talks, 31.10.1975. BNA: FCO 49/589. While Hibbert for the British side wondered in a commentary of 10.11.1975 if one should not admit that Basket III was "a form of ideological confrontation on our side", Blech advised against further confrontation over the implementation of results during the follow-up conference at Belgrade, obviously banking on the long-term effects of the CSCE process while not willing to put this in jeopardy.

50 Memorandum from ZAIG (the analytical unit of the MfS), 15.7.1974, on Western aims in connection with CSCE, filed in HA IX (the prosecution department). BStU: HA IX 1943; ZAIG 4645.

51 MfS planning on CSCE came to a head in the summer of 1975. Many memoranda from the numerous departments involved in this exercise were sent to the legal department for comment and – now filed – form a comprehensive overview of the various considerations and methods put forward. BStU: RS 289, 290, 347.

52 For this rationale, see, for example, expert legal comment on the "State border between the GDR and the FRG", February 1975, by Emmerich of the legal department of the MfS. BStU: HA II/13-2060. Letter by Erich Mielke to his officers from 6.8.1975 on the results of CSCE, drawing attention to the recognition of the existing post-war order and demanding close study of the Brezhnev and Honecker speeches at Helsinki. BStU: HA VI 6298. During his conversation with Honecker in Moscow on 18.6.1974, Brezhnev presented his own interpretation of the power of the factual: step by step, the old generation would be replaced by Young Pioneers with a socialist education, leading to a "natural form of delimitation between the GDR and the FRG". SAPMO: DY 30/11467.

53 Honecker-Brezhnev, Berlin, 18.6.1975. SAPMO: DY 30/ J IV 2/2/1567.

54 Between 1969 and 1975, the number of MfS officials (not counting its informers) increased tremendously from about 40,000 to about 60,000. See Jens Gieseke with Doris Hubert, *Die DDR-Staatssicherheit – Schild und Schwert der Partei* (Bonn 2000), 86; Helmut Müller-Enbergs, *Inoffizielle Mitarbeiter des Ministeriums für Staatssicherheit*, 2 vols (Berlin 1996/1998).

Forced to Cooperate

The Brandt Government and the Nixon Administration on the Road to Helsinki

Giovanni Bernardini

Introduction

The subject of this chapter is the analysis of the different, and substantially diverging, strategies that the Nixon administration of the United States and the Brandt Government of the Federal Republic of Germany deployed in their first approach to a proposal for a conference on security in Europe during the early 1970s, especially concerning the problem of multilateral negotiations on military forces reductions in Europe.[1] The sources available today at the German and American archives confirm that this topic was among the most debated inside the two respective governments, as in the course of the bilateral debates and in the wide range of multilateral (transatlantic) fora.[2] If détente "easily [came] to represent a challenge to the stability of American-European relations",[3] the problem of a redefinition of a new "security" for Europe involving a broader, continuous dialogue between the countries of the two blocs proved to be the most potentially divisive between the United States and its (until then) most loyal ally in Europe, the FRG.

Moreover, the issue of a conference on European security represents a useful *fil rouge* in the analysis of the relations between the two countries during the early 1970s for these main reasons:

1) initially, the proposal of a conference came neither from the two countries examined, nor from other partners of the Alliance: it was actually a long-standing Soviet aspiration, raised with greater emphasis by the "Budapest Appeal" of the Warsaw Pact at the beginning of 1969. Thanks to the sources available today, this "external" genesis allows us to understand the impact that the proposal had on the two administrations since its new launch;

2) however, during the age of the détente, the issue of European security did not represent a completely unexplored field, neither for the new Ameri-

can administration nor for the Social-Liberal coalition in Bonn. The "Budapest Appeal" arrived a few months after the invasion of Czechoslovakia by the troops of the Warsaw Pact, but also after the transatlantic tensions of the 1960s, signified by the exit of France from the NATO integrated command, the failure of the Multilateral Force project and the fear of a "condominium" between the United States and the Soviet Union over Europe, especially after the two superpowers signed the Non Proliferation Treaty. Thus, the debate following the Budapest Appeal did not erase but, on the contrary, quickened and emphasized the projects, the aspirations and the fears of the two governments;

3) projects and aspirations that, in their turn, were born out of a realistic evaluation of the material conditions in which the two countries found themselves at the beginning of the 1970s: the real or supposed decline of the United States as well as the consolidation of western German economic power represented important elements in the approach to the issue of European security, especially when the problem of a fairer share of the burden for the common defence was another source of tensions in transatlantic relations. The reduction of these expenses was a major thrust towards détente;

4) finally, the interest of the debate over a conference on European security mainly comes from the broad space-time coordinates involved by the issue, including a wide spectrum of further subjects concerning the relations between the United States and Western Europe, and of these within the communist bloc. The spatial dimension, attempting to cover the whole continent in a sole assembly, represented a substantial innovation with regard to the situation generated by the Cold War, full of new and stimulating opportunities (political, cultural and economic), but also of risks and doubts on the survival of the western Alliance and concerning a possible common direction towards détente.

The USA and European Détente

As the most recent historiography has underscored, the main task that confronted the Nixon administration since its coming to power was the reassessment of the international role of the United States, taking into account on the one hand the interests and resources of the nation, on the other hand the dramatic changes that were intervening on a global scale. Nixon became president during an extremely critical stage in the history of his country, full of vigorous isolationist tendencies[4] and characterized by a refusal of the military commitment abroad, which was emblematically symbolized by the tragic Vietnamese adventure.[5] The needs, interests and goals of the United States were no longer those of the winning power of the Second World War that presided over the reconstruction of the "free world" and its direct protection, the ideological being the basis of its own foreign political action.[6] The world economic conditions were not the same that had seen the United States taking the lead of the western reorganization from the ruins of the world conflict in order to guide it towards a capitalist economic system based on the free market and guaranteed by US military protection. The western Europe that, immediately after the post-war period, Washington had helped to return to life was becoming more and more a serious economic and commercial rival. The economic statistics appeared worrying due to the deterioration of the balances of payments and trade, besides the enormous costs of the armaments race and the military support to countries threatened by communism all over the world. Nixon and his national security adviser, Henry Kissinger, did not conceive the necessary "partial dissolution of the American Empire" (to quote a member of the administration[7]) as a withdrawal of the United States from world affairs, but more as an adaptation of their international commitments to the world and the country's changed conditions: the aim was a "cheap price containment", which first of all needed to bring back the Soviet Union to the negotiation table for the common resolution of issues like the Vietnamese withdrawal and the limitation of strategic armaments.[8] As the same president pre-announced, it was time to pass "from an era of confrontation to an era of negotiation": negotiations that were intended to remain a prerogative of the two superpowers.

Europe continued to be a priority for the administration, as shown by Nixon's early journey to the main capitals of the Old World. Started just a month after his entry to the White House, the visit had been conceived as the assertion of a willingness to repair the strains that the Atlantic Alliance had suffered during the 1960s. It was necessary to recover the confidence of some of the allies that during a period of time had been disregarded due to the shift of American attention towards new areas of the world and for the beginning of a dialogue among the superpowers that, due to a certain lack of tact, had raised the suspicion of a "condominium" confining the same Europeans to the role of objects of someone else's decisions.[9] Within NATO, Nixon became the promoter of projects that should have given a new life to the Alliance, which risked becoming obsolescent compared to a world that had changed so much in the last twenty-five years. He also became guarantor of a continuous and opportune consultation that should have avoided the past tensions. The European Community was now a commercial power to deal with in order to find a solution to the crisis of American exports, and to ease some forms of protectionism hindering the free market. Furthermore, Europe was absorbing a growing part of US capital as foreign direct investments, to the detriment of the US balance of payments. The European partners appeared to be also essential interlocutors even in the issue of the international monetary system reform.[10] Therefore, the relation that the Nixon administration tried to establish with Europe from the very first months was one of collaboration in order to solve the problems in Atlantic relations and to plan future relations, in the light of the reassessment of the American potentiality and the growth of the European ones.[11]

However, during talks with the partners, there had been no hint as to a possible European initiative concerning détente with the communist bloc. The projects of the administration did not include any initiative aimed at modifying the balance of forces determined by the end of the Second World War in Europe. Nixon's White House disliked the potentially disturbing agenda of west European promoters of détente; his administration, mainly committed to obtain Soviet help for the solution of the Vietnamese conflict and draft a negotiation on strategic armaments, did not have any real intention to challenge the Kremlin about its "sphere of influence" in Eastern Europe.[12] Nixon and Kissinger did not go beyond the verbal denunciation of the "Brezhnev Doctrine" and the refusal to give it any validity;[13] furthermore, the persistence they placed in trying to dissuade the allies from easy enthusiasms towards détente in Europe showed that there was not a real willingness to discuss the European order, as much as there was no intention to ratify it.[14]

A similar treatment was given to the unsolved issue in the centre of Europe, that of Germany. On the eve of the halting of the presidential journey to Bonn, Kissinger suggested to Nixon that it would not have been "really wise to express opinions voluntarily" on the delicate subject of East German politics; in case the counterpart had mentioned it, the president should have expressed support for the goals but also awareness of their limits and insist on the "need of a coordinated action of the western approach in dealing with Soviets and (...) the importance of opportune consultations". The problem of reunification too did not have to be raised, and to a specific question on the German behalf, the president would have confirmed the American idea of a "fair solution for the division of Germany within the context of European security". However, this primary aim would have been "the result of a long term process (involving) changes in the Soviet politics, in eastern Europe and in eastern Germany".[15] At the same time, the Germans, the first among all the allies, had to be warned against the uselessness of multilateral initiatives between East and West, and against the pressure coming from public opinion for some short-term results of détente. The evident contradiction in the repeated statements of the White House about the fact that a major multilateral initiative on security in Europe would have been useful only to Soviet propaganda and that it would have been better to start solving "concrete problems", possibly among superpowers,[16] showed that the administration was all but "ready for the vigorous and innovative approach that Brandt's government would have adopted at the end of the year".[17] The problem of Berlin represents the exception confirming the rule: President Nixon had declared in the divided city that rejecting any unilateral modification of the situation did not mean having to consider satisfying the status quo. However, facing the Soviet willingness to discuss the solution of some real problems of the former German capital, the White House would have relied for a long time on a hesitating and not very incisive conduction of the quadripartite discussions at the State Department (as it has been noticed, submitting the problem to traditional diplomacy had always meant a degradation for Nixon and Kissinger of the very same theme from the list of the urgent and vital issues).[18]

From Plan to Reality: Beyond the "Budapest Appeal"

The close link between Washington and Bonn, established since the rebirth of a German state at the beginning of the Cold War, had experienced growing strains during the 1960s. The apex was reached in the autumn of 1966, when Chancellor Erhard resigned after an unsuccessful visit to the other side of the Atlantic: the main topic was the German contribution to the common defence, which President Johnson considered unsatisfactory.[19] Subsequently, the two major German parties (CDU and SPD) gave birth to the experiment of a "Great Coalition" under the leadership of Chancellor Kiesinger. Willy Brandt, former mayor of West Berlin and secretary of the SPD, led the party to government for the first time since the Weimar Republic and became himself foreign minister. The Johnson administration greeted the change in Bonn, for the positive effects that it could produce on FRG foreign politics, after twenty years of total hostility towards any process of détente that would not begin with the reunification of Germany.[20] However, when Nixon became president, the precarious formula of the Great Coalition had entered into an irreversible crisis that the proximity to the natural terms of the legislation contributed to aggravate. The last year of Kiesinger's government was characterized by a growing sense of frustration in Washington, which tried in vain to involve its most important European ally in its projects in the field of foreign policy.[21]

During 1969 it was up to the SPD-led Foreign Ministry to conceive a renewal of the German foreign policy that the next Government in Bonn was obliged to attempt by necessity in order to secure a special role for the FRG during any East-West détente.[22] According to Egon Bahr, Director of the *Plannungstab* (the core of the Foreign Ministry), the aim was to "think the unthinkable", that is, to find a path to some forms of German reunification that would avoid raising the old Eastern (and Western) fears of a renewed "German danger".[23] The result was more than a programme for a coalition which would include the SPD again: it represented an explicit, though still confidential, long-term plan towards a "new European peace order".[24]

The projects of the *Plannungstab* were propelled by the constant concern that the powerful pressure of the Congress and of public opinion could lead to a withdrawal of American troops from Europe in the near future.[25] Moreover, a success in the US-USSR negotiations for a reduction of strategic armaments could lead to a substantial decrease of the American nuclear warranty for Western Europe.[26] However, the members of the *Plannungstab* were especially motivated by the "Budapest Appeal" for a conference on European security, issued by the Warsaw Pact on 17 March 1969, which clearly showed a renewed willingness in Moscow to discuss the European situation in a multilateral context. Compared with other similar invitations issued during the first decades of the Cold War, the letter sent to all the Western governments did not contain any explicit exclusion of the US from the conference, thus fulfilling one essential precondition posed by Bonn.[27] The main goal, which Moscow made explicit in the Appeal, was again a recognition of the status quo in Europe – and thereby of the Soviet sphere of influence; however, such a recognition was intended to be a premise for increased cooperation between East and West on economic and technological issues, but also a solution for the military opposition which divided the continent.

Immediately after the Budapest Appeal was issued, the *Plannungstab* started reflecting on the advantages that the conference proposed by Moscow could bring to the FRG.[28] Bahr esteemed the conference as highly advantageous, provided that the West would be able to advance its own priorities and would not limit itself to accept the aims of the Warsaw Pact. A conference on security would have had to be devoted to protect the European countries from any threat and the use of force, and from any interference in the internal affairs of other countries. Furthermore, a considerable amount of bilateral and multilateral contacts between East and West would have started since the first preparatory stage, fostering a better political climate in Europe, while the increase of economic and technological cooperation among European states was certainly desirable in terms of improving mutual understanding and of easing Soviet oppression of the people of the Eastern bloc; nevertheless, the two main working fields were political and military security. On the political front, all the participants to the conference should have subscribed a set of rules (respect of national sovereignty, non-interference in internal affairs) that, from the FRG point of view, would have represented a logical conclusion to the German efforts for normalizing its relations with the European communist countries.

On the military side, the conference would have to focus on the continental disarmament.[29] According to Bahr, the overcoming of the status quo towards a new European peace order could give Bonn the opportunity to keep a door open for a possible German reunification more than the situation at the time allowed.[30] A mutual, balanced withdrawal of troops from both sides of the Iron Curtain would not have reduced the security of the FRG: on the contrary, it could rather have produced a more dynamic dimension in the East-West relations. Moreover, this process appeared more urgent since (as aforementioned) a unilateral withdrawal of the US troops from Europe was more a concrete perspective than a working hypothesis. A negotiated withdrawal of Soviet troops from the German Democratic Republic could have shaken the regime of Pankow, forcing Secretary Ulbricht to a more conciliatory attitude towards a *modus vivendi* with Bonn.[31] In this context, it was clear to the *Planungstab* that the international recognition of the GDR was one major aim of the European conference convened by the Warsaw Pact. But Bahr and his collaborators had already considered for a long time that the FRG should have conceded the recognition of the other German state before the conference, as a last step of the normalization process with the communist countries.[32]

The middle-term goal to be achieved through the conference was to avoid the possibility that the two blocs could freeze permanently; in the long run, the reduction of military and political tensions could have led to a new European security system based on the code of conduct subscribed by all the governments, under the warranty of the two superpowers.[33] Therefore, even after a substantial withdrawal of the American troops, the German plans did not intend to expel the US from the "new order": they would have continued to play a major role as guarantor, but with a lighter economic burden. Even after the dissolution of the two military alliances, the same concept of a "neutral" Germany was meaningless to Bahr, if compared to the economic, demographic and territorial weight of Germany in Europe. Just after the German elections of autumn 1969, Bahr restated in a document for Brandt that the new government had to remove what remained of the "Hallstein Doctrine" and to become an active promoter inside the Western Alliance of a conference on European security and on the mutual reduction of troops, as a necessary step to establish a new peace order and to alter the terms of the German question for the benefit of the FRG.

Scepticism in Washington

The Nixon administration proved to be much more sceptical towards the "Budapest Appeal".[34] As recent historiography has underlined,

> the analytical and historical rigidity of the categories used by Kissinger to carry the United States out of the cold war (…) tended to lead local and national dynamics back to his own bipolar reading and, in Europe, to his own bipolarizing purposes.[35]

Kissinger confessed his concern over the enthusiasm displayed by some political entourages in Europe, since Moscow was only restating its traditional goal of an international recognition of its sphere of influence in Europe.[36] Helmut Sonnenfeldt, one of the most important members of the Kissinger staff, more explicitly suggested that the approach of the White House to the European security should stem from the observation that the current status quo was not unfavourable for the US national interests; on the other hand, a recognition *de jure* of Moscow's "free hand" in Eastern Europe was highly undesirable, because it would have jeopardized the "special relations" that Washington was trying to establish with the governments of Poland and Romania.[37] Furthermore, Moscow would have achieved its long-term aspiration without granting the West any concession in return.[38] Kissinger suggested to the president to maintain a tactical "non refusal" of the Soviet proposal. Washington should answer Moscow suggesting that the two superpowers would discuss more concrete topics that were preparatory to the "conference". Anyway, it did not mean that Kissinger had reconsidered his opinion about "the inutility and, indeed dangers of holding grandiose conferences at this stage".[39]

The NATO conference held in Washington in April 1969 to celebrate the twenty years of the Atlantic Alliance offered to Nixon a first opportunity to warn the European allies against an unjustified optimism towards a process of détente in Europe. The president took a further chance to appeal to the solidarity of the allied representatives, among them the German Minister of Foreign Affairs Brandt, against the attempts (and the temptations) of a "selective détente" periodically announced by the Kremlin towards the western European countries, chosen on the basis of the need of the moment.[40] The Alliance needed a more careful attitude in dealing with Moscow, since the last offers from the Soviet Union were only aimed at obtaining its long-term goals and did not offer any solutions to European problems.[41] Foreign Minister Brandt, on the other side, exposed a different perspective and did not refrain from urging the Alliance to seize the proposal on European collective security coming from Moscow.[42] Consequently, the German foreign minister proposed to test without delay the goodwill of the Kremlin in dealing with topics such as an improvement of the situation of Berlin.[43] The Netherlands, Italy and partially France and Great Britain approved the proposal, and the Washington meeting issued a communiqué which, though not explicitly quoting the "Budapest Appeal", confirmed the commitment of the Alliance to détente and urged the four powers responsible for the divided city to explore the chances to improve their conditions.[44] The coincidence with Nixon's proposals was only apparent, since Berlin was not one of the topics Washington intended to discuss with Moscow in the foreseeable future. For the first time, although not for the last, Brandt was skilful enough to impose to the administration a revision of its priority scale concerning its relations with Western Europe and détente with the East. Even if the CDU explicitly confirmed to Washington that Brandt had spoken only on behalf of his party and not of the whole government,[45] the White House could not ignore that Moscow answered positively to the proposal concerning an "exchange of opinions" about Berlin contained in the NATO communiqué.[46] Thus, the Nixon administration found itself involved in a long and difficult negotiation which finally led to the Berlin Agreement of 1971. Despite its own serious reserves, the Nixon administration started removing a major obstacle from the road to the conference on European security.

After the Washington meeting, the White House was repeatedly called to give an answer to the pressures coming from the German Foreign Ministry for a common reply to the Budapest Appeal. Brandt himself had repeatedly asked his Soviet interlocutors for their willingness to accept the US as a full participant to the conference, as an essential precondition for Bonn. On the contrary, Kissinger took every chance to warn his German interlocutors that Bonn could have "live[d] to regret" its enthusiasm, since "they would often be a minority of one". The German question would have become the main topic of the conference, offering much fewer guarantees to the legitimate interests of Bonn than other *fora*.[47] Surprised by the hyperactivism of the German foreign minister within and outside the Alliance, Kissinger advised the president to express clearly to the allies all his scepticism about the initiative, making it understood that the US would not have run "to save the Europeans from their madness" in case they followed Moscow.[48] For these reasons, Kissinger confirmed many times to the German representatives that the White House did not mean to "take any initiative in the European security field", and that "the whole subject was not a major point in the foreign policy of the United States".[49]

However, the White House did not take into consideration that a new German government could have imposed a real revolution in FRG foreign policy: as foreseen by Bahr, the "German question" would not have become the very object of the conference only if Bonn succeeded in changing its terms. While the administration was experiencing a two year period of intense frustration, due to its foreign policy goals – and in particular 1970 was defined "a lost year" as far as the relations with Moscow were concerned – the accession of the SPD-FDP coalition to the government of Bonn determined an impressive acceleration of the European process of détente. As a result of international circumstances, about which there is not the scope to elaborate in this chapter, in a few months Brandt's government signed the Moscow Treaty in the summer of 1970 and paved the way for a similar treaty with Poland. Moreover, new exchanges with the Pankow government were started in the light of its formal recognition, without reducing the pressure on the allies and Moscow in order to reach an agreement to improve the situation in Berlin.[50]

In its first stage the Ostpolitik surprised the White House, forcing it to answer periodically to the pressures coming from Bonn even where US interests were involved.[51] In particular, Kissinger would have confirmed to the president that, as a result of the signing of the Moscow Treaty, the European political relations had "turned the corner" not exactly in a favourable way to the interests of Washington. It was, then, necessary for the United

States to realize that their relations with Europe were entering a new and more dynamic phase than had been the case previously.[52] In this context, it soon became urgent for the US to support the project of a future East-West dialogue in Europe as a natural consequence of progress on the German question.[53]

The Multilateral Framework

In his inaugural speech to the Bundestag, a speech that was full of new elements compared to his predecessors' foreign policies, Brandt did not fail to underline that a European conference, carefully organized, would have been an important step towards a greater security for the continent.[54] And, quite soon, Washington was obliged to admit that Bonn was successfully exploiting the issue also from a tactical point of view: since, conceptually, the conference had to follow the phase of the normalization of bilateral relations between the RFT and its communist neighbours, Moscow should have had to ease this last process in order to have assured its own final goal.[55]

At this point, however, the issue would pass to the Atlantic Alliance, where it was necessary to express a collective willingness towards the Soviet Union. Immediately after its assumption of power, the Brandt government informed the US administration that it intended to relaunch in concrete terms the projects for détente in Europe during the Brussels NATO meeting to be held in December.[56] According to Bonn, it was necessary for the Alliance to introduce the topic of the mutual reduction of troops in Europe as an item of the agenda for the future East-West conference. As we have already seen, the SPD-FDP coalition considered the use of negotiations about troop reduction "as one of the instruments able to change the structure of the European security system".[57] Moreover, the chancellor deemed a diminishing of the American military commitment to Europe as unavoidable, since isolationism seemed to spread through Congress and public opinion.[58] Consequently, the promotion of a joint reduction of American *and* Soviet troops from Central Europe could have reduced the dangers coming from a unilateral US withdrawal.[59]

The Department of State seemed much more open to the suggestions coming from Bonn than the White House. In view of the NATO meeting, Secretary of State William Rogers repeatedly advised the president to take the lead on the multilateral reassessment of European security. According to his Department, the involvement of the European allies in détente, with a continuous and careful American contribution (and even respectful leadership), could help to fill a gap of participation deriving from the exclusiveness of the negotiations over strategic weapons between the two superpowers.[60] If Washington was trying to enhance the cohesion of the Alliance, to give the Western European "their SALT" in the form of Mutual and Balanced Force Reductions (MBFR), it could have fostered the sense of a common mission between the two shores of the Atlantic.[61] Kissinger's staff completely disagreed with that attitude and appeared to be rather alarmed by the "irresistible push forward" of the "bureaucratic steamroller" (as the Department of State was labelled).[62] While the White House had not yet issued a set of rules of conduct on the subject of European security, the "bureaucracy" was even suggesting that Washington should take the lead on the whole process inside the Alliance. Kissinger reminded the president that, particularly concerning the subject of MBFR, the military experts were still evaluating a platform coherent with the strong US interests at stake.[63] Furthermore, it seemed quite paradoxical to exhort the Alliance to issue a proposal about a withdrawal of troops from Europe while, at the very same time, the White House had denied the Soviets any agreement on arms control without a previous progress on political issues.[64] A last fundamental objection: though the Soviet diplomacy had been repeatedly challenged by the Germans about MBFR, it had displayed a total lack of interest in introducing that topic in the schedule of the conference. If the White House had accepted the advice of Rogers and his staff, it could have found itself struggling with Moscow over an issue which was still totally unclear and potentially dangerous for the whole of American foreign policy. All these considerations drove Nixon to issue a "National Security Study Memorandum" which required all the Departments concerned to produce further analysis of the European security issues: since the results were to be submitted in January 1970, the non-committal attitude towards the NATO meeting of December was more than evident.[65]

The line of conduct chosen by the presidency proved to be totally wrong. If Washington considered that the first positive results of the Ostpolitik could water down the common interest in a conference on European security,[66] it underestimated that the Bonn government was assuming the role of the main promoter of the conference among the European partners, since that commitment was not a secondary part of the very same negotiations held in Moscow.[67] At the Brussels meeting, the other European allies seemed to have accepted the summoning of the conference in the foreseeable future as "a fact of political life" (as stated by Foreign Minister Luns of the Netherlands without raising substantial objections among the other participants).[68] To the satisfaction of Bonn, almost all the allies seemed to share the same will to explore further the items under proposal for the agenda of the conference, while restating that Moscow was called to show concrete signs of goodwill in improving the situation of Berlin and in normalizing the relations between the FRG and the communist bloc. Secretary Rogers expressed the only dissenting opinion, suggesting that the conference could have produced a *de facto* recognition of the Soviet sphere of influence without any compensation for the West. However, US diplomacy was not able to prevent the North Atlantic Council from producing a "Declaration" in which the Alliance restated the goals of the Harmel Report[69] and raised the prospect of an MBFR negotiation with the East, while approving the quadripartite discussions over Berlin and the efforts undertaken by the FRG in normalizing its relations with the communist countries and the Democratic Republic.[70]

The results of the Brussels meeting forced the administration to reassess its stance towards the whole complex of European security. Washington was increasingly assuming the role as the only opponent of a process that seemed to be of some interest to all the allies, and even to the Eastern European countries which were seeking a more independent stance in relation to Moscow.[71] Kissinger's staff became persuaded that

> as long as the US takes simply a "hands off" posture toward intra-European relationships, those relationships will be posited on a kind of limited and sweetened American hegemony rather than on closer Western European collaboration – even in fact of the substantial US force reductions that our allies expect to take place before long. [...] Our continued failure to define our generalized approval of greater allied self-reliance in terms of structural concepts and specific policies tends to perpetuate allied separation and militate against any basic change in the US – European distribution of power.[72]

Since the latter was a major goal of the administration in view of a fairer share of the burden for the common defence, Washington could not oppose the trend that Brandt's Ostpolitik had set in motion and that the other allies seemed willing to adopt: as Kissinger confirmed to an interlocutor coming from the other side of the Iron Curtain after the NATO meeting, the White House did not intend to oppose "a meaningful eventual conference", and he and his staff would have watched developments in Europe with special care.[73]

Bonn judged the "Declaration" as a positive result of its efforts to promote a more active approach to a continental détente inside the Alliance.[74] The government of the FRG seemed even surprised by "the tremendous increase of interest" that the allied had displayed in a multilateral consultation in view of potential East-West contacts.[75] Moreover, the momentum engendered by the "Declaration" seemed the most favourable to make MBFR "the central subject of the international debate", including the preparations for the conference on European security.[76] According to the text issued by the NATO meeting, the Alliance had to elaborate the models of mutual forces reduction to be submitted to the Eastern bloc. After a long process of evaluation, the German government decided to adopt the approach which seemed more consistent with the prompt inclusion of MBFR in the schedule of the future conference on European security. Retracing the pattern adopted by the US administration in its approach to the Strategic Arms Limitation Talks, the Alliance had to avoid introducing technical questions in the first phase, while clearly underlining to Moscow the political principles and goals on which the negotiations had to be based.[77] According to Minister Scheel, the aim of the German government was that the following NATO meeting would have forced the Soviets to consider the MBFR issue as "an integral part" of the future debate over European security.[78] Although some allies had already showed signs of interest for the inclusion of MBFR in the conference, such as the British government,[79] Bonn deemed even more necessary to gain the approval of the US administration well before the NATO meeting to be held in Rome in May 1970.

The expectations of the German government were bound to be frustrated. Although the administration had accepted that it was impossible to avoid the whole Alliance becoming involved in a continental détente, the MBFR complex still raised strong objections in Washington. The White House seemed less eager than Bonn to downplay the objections raised by the military in Brussels, according to which the Alliance faced the paradox that all the negotiation models were either disadvantageous to the West or unacceptable to the Warsaw Pact.[80] Moreover, the reports submitted by the agencies to the president showed the need for a further evaluation of all the effects coming from MBFR over US foreign policy: a new "National Security Study Memorandum" was commissioned and the results were expected by the end of July, well after the NATO meeting.[81] According to Kissinger, not only Washington needed a further examination of MBFR: the whole Alliance had to find a common position before engaging itself into an issue that experience had shown to be too controversial on the Western side and too uninteresting to the Eastern side to be a manipulatable lever in the [European Security Conference] complex – despite the merits it may well have as a continuing American objective.[82]

Hence, Kissinger warned the German interlocutors that Washington was willing to accept that the meeting in Rome would have restated the interest of the Alliance in engaging the Warsaw Pact in negotiation on conventional weapons; but it deemed unlikely that the meeting could have issued a more concrete proposal in that field.[83]

The unmistakeable signal coming from the other shore of the Atlantic did not dissuade the German government from submitting to the North Atlantic Council its plan for early negotiations on MBFR. The document was aimed at speeding the internal debate in view of the following NATO ministerial meeting, and it contemplated details concerning the times and scope of future reductions. Furthermore, Bonn reaffirmed its persuasion that the MBFR complex could have merged into a European conference to avoid the traditional bloc-to-bloc approach between the Warsaw Pact and NATO. The plan received a quite cold reaction in Brussels and was strongly criticized by the US representative Robert Ellsworth. The German proposal seemed just too ambitious, and the US administration judged that a more careful planning was needed before releasing a common proposal. Furthermore, Ellsworth had stated that Washington had no interest in linking the MBFR complex to the conference on European security.[84] As confirmed a few weeks later to the Soviets, Washington had reached the conclusion that while the Alliance had already posed some preconditions for the conference on European security (such as a Berlin agreement and the success of German Ostpolitik) in order to assure that a continental meeting would not be held simply for propaganda effect, MBFR deserved negotiations on its own terms without reference to progress in other contexts.[85] After the setback suffered by Bonn in the North Atlantic Council, the NATO meeting held in Rome came with no surprise and signalled a victory for the US approach: the Alliance restated its interest in negotiating the MBFR complex, but no link was established with the project of the European conference. Confronted with the opposition of Washington, the government of Chancellor Willy Brandt was compelled towards a first major reassessment of its strategies: the military component of détente in Europe became more dependent on a bloc-to-bloc approach under the leadership of the two superpowers than on the activities deployed by the FRG and other European partners.[86]

Conclusions

The issue of a conference on European security, vigorously raised by the Soviet Union at the beginning of 1969, was a subject unrelated to the approach that the Nixon administration had assumed towards the problems of the divided continent. Kissinger and his staff were even hostile to the hypothesis of an involvement of the European partner in the process of détente with the East, which had to be an almost exclusive competence of the two superpowers. More than the signals of enthusiasm coming from other partners, it was the Ostpolitik of Chancellor Willy Brandt that set the debate in motion. Helped by favourable international conditions, between 1969 and 1971 the Brandt government was able to remove all the obstacles that had prevented a multilateral European conference on security from becoming a reality. Although the US administration repeatedly warned Bonn and the other European partners against the potential dangers deriving from a similar approach, Washington found itself involved in a process that it believed uncertain and potentially dangerous. Although Nixon and his administration were not persuaded about the approach chosen by the Allies, they were forced to cooperate for many reasons: the tensions of the previous ten years required an improvement in relations with western Europe, since it now represented a dangerous commercial rival and a vital contributor to the common defence and to the reorganization of the capitalist economy. After the elimination of the obstacles concerning the German issue, Washington had no excuses to refuse the project of the conference that, according to the State Department, the allies considered more and more to be the natural prosecution of the commitments taken in the "Harmel Report" and also an addition to the SALT negotiations between the superpowers.

On the other hand, Bonn supported the Warsaw Pact proposal with the intention of using it to complete its Ostpolitik and to recover, once and for all, the international status of the FRG. However, the approach to the conference was not only a continuous series of triumphs for the western German government. If from a bilateral point of view Brandt could act more freely being "a partner, not a client" of Washington, it was necessary for it to involve the entire Alliance in the project of the conference and, in particular, the United States, whose absence was simply inconceivable. Besides partial victories, Bonn suffered an important defeat concerning the negotiations on conventional armaments and troops in Europe. This was a fundamental point in the project of Brandt's staff aimed at reducing tensions within the continent. Faced with the poor interest shown by the Soviets, Bonn needed the support of the western allies to put pressure on Moscow and have the MBFR negotiations in the agenda of the conference (as was going to happen later on with the subject of human rights). The final denial of Washington, already clear on the occasion of the NATO meeting held in Rome in 1970, excluded the issue from the schedule of the conference on European security. The MBFR forum became exactly what Brandt's government wanted to avoid: the hostage of endless discussions on technical details, which diverted attention from the political principles and goals that were supposed to be their inspiration. Shortly a renewed atmosphere of Cold War came back to "remilitarize" the Iron Curtain between the two blocs in Europe, freezing again for a long time the hopes that the détente had raised for the divided continent.

Notes

1. This chapter is a part of a broader research project concerning the relations between the Federal Republic of Germany and the United States of America during the early 1970s G. Bernardini, "Le relazioni politiche europee hanno girato l'angolo" L'amministrazione Nixon e il governo Brandt: Europa, Occidente, rapporti con l'Est, 1969-1971 (*The Federal Republic of Germany and the United States of America 1969-1971: Ostpolitik, Détente, Europe and the West*), Ph.D. Dissertation presented at the University of Florence in 2005, under supervision of Prof. Antonio Varsori.
2. The chapter is based on sources from the Nixon Presidential Material Project (NPMP) at the National Archives in College Park (MD, USA), from the Bundesarchiv (BA) in Koblenz (Germany), from the Politische Archiv des Auswärtiges Amt (PA-AA, Berlin, Germany) and the Archiv der Sozialdemokratie (ADSD) of the Friedrich-Ebert-Stiftung in Bonn (Germany).
3. Geir Lundestad, *The United States and Western Europe* (Oxford 2005), 169.
4. In 1969 the Congress was debating three projects concerning the stationing of American troops in Europe: the Fullbright resolution, which tended to limit presidential powers in deploying the troops abroad; the Mansfield resolution, concerning a "substantial" reduction of American troops in Europe, and the Symington resolution, which intended to limit the expenses for defence abroad. The fate of these resolutions was a source of continued apprehension among the Western European governments. Politische Archiv – Auswärtiges Amt (PA-AA), B31 – USA, Box 353, Embassy in Washington to the Foreign Ministry, Unterausschuss des Senatsausschusses für Auswärtige Beziehungen zur Überprüfung der Amerikanischen militärischen Verpflichtungen.
5. Keith L. Nelson underlines how the Vietnam War brought to an end the general consensus which sustained the US policy pursued since the Second World War.

According to some polls, the share of American citizens willing to react militarily to a Soviet invasion of Western Europe had fallen dramatically between the 1960s and the 1970s. Keith L. Nelson, *The Making of Détente* (Baltimore 1995), 21. For a brilliant analysis of the end of the "Cold War consensus", see also Mario Del Pero, *Henry Kissinger e l'ascesa dei neoconservatori. Alle origini della politica estera americana* (Bari 2006), 3-35.

6 Anders Stephanson, "Liberty or Death: The Cold War as US ideology", in Odd Arne Westad (ed.), *Reviewing the Cold War: Approaches, Interpretations, Theory* (London 2000).

7 NARA (National Archives and Records Administration), RG 59, OFLF, entry 5339, HS, Box 2, Eagleburger to Kissinger, *The United States and Europe*, 15 October 1969.

8 Walter LaFeber, *America, Russia and the Cold War, 1945-1972* (New York 1997), 261.

9 Henry A. Kissinger, *The White House Years* (Boston 1979).

10 For a complete analysis of the strategies of the Nixon administration concerning a renewal of the international monetary system in accordance with the European allies, see Duccio Basosi, *Il governo del Dollaro: interdipendenza economica e potere statunitense negli anni di Richard Nixon (1969-1973)* (Firenze 2006).

11 Giovanni Bernardini, "'Getting the worst from both worlds': Washington e gli albori della Ostpolitik," in Antonio Varsori (ed.), *Alle origini del presente. L'Europa occidentale nella crisi degli anni Settanta* (Milan 2007).

12 Vojtech Mastny, "Superpower Détente: US-Soviet Relations, 1969-1972," in David C. Geyer and Bernd Schaefer (eds), *American Détente and German Ostpolitik, 1969-1972*, special issue of Bulletin of the German Historical Institute (Washington D.C. 2004), 21; Anatoly F. Dobrynin, *In Confidence: Moscow's Ambassador to Six Cold War Presidents* (Seattle 2001), 216.

13 Akten zur Auswärtigen Politik der Bundesrepublik Deutschland (AAP) 1969, Document 223, Ambassador Pauls to the Foreign Ministry, 6 July 1969.

14 In a conversation with Chancellor Kiesinger, Nixon warned against some "enthusiastic" European politicians who were "soft in their heads" concerning the concrete hope for disarmament and détente with the communist bloc. He would apply the same allusion to Chancellor Brandt and his Eastern policy. AAP-1969, Document 257, Memorandum of Conversation between Chancellor Kiesinger and President Nixon, 7 August 1969.

15 NARA, NPMP, NSC (National Security Council Files) Files, Trip Files – President's 1969 Trip to Europe, Box 442, Kissinger to Nixon, 20 February 1969.

16 NARA, NPMP, NSC Files, Country Files – Europe, USSR, Box 709, Kissinger to Nixon, *Soviet Initiative For A European Security Conference*, 4 April 1969.

17 Ruud van Dijk, *We will come to regret German 'Flexibility'*, 2; paper presented at the conference "NATO, the Warsaw Pact, and Détente, 1965-1973", Dobbiaco (Italy), 26-28 September 2002.

18 William Bundy, *A Tangled Web: The Making of Foreign Policy in the Nixon Presidency* (New York 1998), 58; Giovanni Bernardini, "Nessuna preferenza: l'amministrazione

Nixon, la 'Grande Coalizione' tedesca e le elezioni tedesche del 1969", in *Ventunesimo Secolo* (Soveria Mannelli 2006), n. 9.

19   David Wightman, "Money And Security. Financing American Troops in Germany and the Trilateral Negotiations of 1966-67, *Rivista di storia economica* 1 (Turin 1998).

20   Massimiliano Guderzo, *Interesse nazionale e responsabilità globale: gli Stati Uniti, l'Alleanza Atlantica e l'integrazione europea negli anni di Johnson 1963-1969* (Firenze 2000), 361ff.

21   William Bundy, *A Tangled Web*, 115; Giovanni Bernardini, "Nessuna preferenza", in *Ventunesimo Secolo* (Soveria Mannelli 2006), n. 9.

22   AAP-1969, Document 111, *Plannungstab* to Minister Brandt, *Konzeptionen der europäischen Sicherheit*, 24 March 1969.

23   Egon Bahr, *Zu meiner Zeit* (Berlin 1998), 226.

24   AAP-1969, Document 111, *Plannungstab* to Minister Brandt, Konzeptionen der europäischen Sicherheit, 24 March 1969.

25   NARA, RG56, General records of the Department of Treasury, Central Files of the Secretary of the Treasury, 1957-1965, Files of the Under Secretary for Monetary Affairs Pauls Volcker, 1969-1974, FRC 4 – Germany, Memorandum of Conversation between Secretary of Defence Laird and Minister of Defense Schröder, 4 February 1969.

26   AdSD, DEB (Depositum Egon Bahr), Box 334, Kielmansegg to Bahr, 23 February 1969.

27   NARA, NPMP, NSC Files, Country Files – Europe, Poland, Box 698, Intelligence and Research (INR – Department of State) to Secretary Rogers, Warsaw Pact Seemingly Resolves Impasse Over Military Coordination, 18 March 1969.

28   AAP-1969, Document 301, Memorandum of the Plannungsstab, 24 September 1969.

29   Cristian Bluth, "Détente and Conventional Arms Control: West German Policy Priorities and the Origins of MBFR", *German Politics*, vol. 8, no. 1 (London 1999), 181-206.

30   AAP-1969, Document 111, Memorandum of the Plannungsstab, Konzeptionen der europäischen Sicherheit, 24 March 1969.

31   AAP-1969, Document 116, Memorandum of conversation between Foreign Minister Brandt and Soviet Ambassador Zarapkin, 4 April 1969.

32   Bahr coined the expression "change through rapprochement" a long time before the SPD entered the government, and it soon became a codeword for the new Ostpolitik of Chancellor Brandt. Gottfried Niedhart, "Revisionistische Elemente und die Initiierung friedlichen Wandels in der neuen Ostpolitik, 1969-1974", *Geschichte und Gesellschaft*, 28.2 (2002).

33   Egon Bahr, *Zu meiner Zeit*, 226.

34   William Bundy, *A Tangled Web*, 77.

35   Mario del Pero, *L'Italia repubblicana negli anni Settanta – Kissinger e la politica estera americana nel Mediterraneo: il caso portoghese*, in "Studi Storici", 4 (2001), 973-988.

36   NARA, NPMP, NSC Files, Country Files – Europe, USSR, Box 709, Kissinger to Nixon, Soviet Initiative For A European Security Conference, 4 April 1969.

37 NARA, NPMP, NSC Files, Country Files – Europe, USSR, Box 711, Sonnenfeldt to Kissinger, US-Soviet Diplomacy On European Security, 8 January 1970.
38 According to Jussi M. Hanhimäki, Kissinger's reluctance to pursue European détente in a later phase "can be seen partly as a way of alleviating (…) Chinese concerns". Hanhimäki, *The Flawed Architect. Henry Kissinger and American Foreign Policy* (Oxford 2004), 271.
39 NARA, NPMP, NSC Files, Country Files – Europe, USSR, Box 709, Kissinger to Nixon, Soviet Initiative For A European Security Conference, 4 April 1969.
40 Willy Brandt, *La politica di un socialista* (Milan 1979), 217.
41 Public Papers of President Richard M. Nixon, Address at the Commemorative Session of the North Atlantic Council, Document 145, 10 April 1969 (from the website <www.nixonfoundation.org>).
42 NARA, NPMP, NSC Files, Country Files – Europe, Germany, Box 681, Memorandum of conversation between Secretary Rogers and Foreign Minister Brandt, 9 April 1969.
43 AAP-1969, Document 121, Ruete to Foreign Ministry, Ministerkonferenz der NATO in Washington, 11 April 1969.
44 Final Communiqué of the Conference of NATO Foreign Ministers, Washington, 10-11 April 1969 (from the website <www.nato.int>).
45 NARA, NPMP, NSC Files, VIP Visits – Kiesinger Visit, Box 917, Fessenden to Rogers, German Sounding On Berlin, 23 June 1969.
46 James S. Sutterlin and David Klein, *Berlin: From Symbol of Confrontation to Keystone of Stability* (New York 1989), 86.
47 NARA, NPMP, NSC Files, Country Files – Europe, Germany, Box 682, Memorandum of conversation between Kissinger and German Ambassador Pauls, 4 July 1969.
48 NARA, NPMP, WHSF – Confidential Files, Box 6 – Germany, Kissinger to President, Chancellor Kiesinger's Meetings with You, Undated.
49 NARA, NPMP, NSC Files, Country Files – Europe, Germany, Box 682, Sonnenfeldt, German Ambassador's Call on Mr. Kissinger, 28 October 1969.
50 See, for example, M.E. Sarotte, *Dealing with the Devil: East Germany, Détente, and Ostpolitik, 1969-1973* (Chapel Hill 2000).
51 NARA, NPMP, NSC Files, Country Files – Europe, Germany, Box 683, Hyland to Kissinger, Your Meeting with Ambassador Pauls, Monday, 29 December 1969.
52 NARA, NPMP, NSC Files, Country Files – Europe, Germany, Box 684, Kissinger to Nixon, *The German-Soviet Treaty*, 1 September 1970.
53 NARA, NPMP, NSC Files, Country Files – Europe, USSR, Box 711, Sonnenfeldt to Kissinger, US-Soviet Diplomacy On European Security, 8 January 1970.
54 NARA, NPMP, NSC Files, Country Files – Europe, Germany, Box 682, Ambassador Rush to Rogers, Willy Brandt's Policy Declaration-Preliminary Assessment, 28 October 1969.
55 NARA, NPMP, NSC Files, Country Files – Europe, USSR, Box 711, Memorandum

of the Intelligence and Research (INR) to Rogers, A good word for Bonn and a vision of Détente with the west, 5 December 1969.
56 NARA, NPMP, NSC Files, Country Files – Europe, Germany, Box 682, Sonnenfeldt to Kissinger, Your Meeting with German Ambassador Pauls, 27 October 1969.
57 Cristoph Bluth, "Détente and Conventional Arms Control: West German Policy Priorities and the Origins of MBFR", *German Politics*, vol. 8, no. 1 (April 1999), 181-206.
58 AAP-1970, Document 250, Report of Cabinet Meeting, 8 June 1970.
59 AAP-1970, Document 83, Document of the Foreign and Defence Ministries to the Council for National Security, 2 March 1970.
60 NARA, NPMP, NSC Files, Subject Files – HAK-Richardson Meetings, Box 337, Undersecretary Richardson to USNATO Mission, December Ministerial Meeting: European Security and East-West Relations, 30 September 1969.
61 NARA, NPMP, NSC Files, Country Files – Europe, Germany, Box 683, Rogers to Nixon, United States and Allied Approaches to the Current Issues of European Security, 31 October 1969.
62 NARA, NPMP, NSC Files, Subject Files – HAK-Richardson Meetings, Box 337, Sonnenfeldt to Kissinger, European Security and Forthcoming NATO Meetings – The Bureaucratic Steamroller Pushes Irresistibly Forward, 2 October 1969.
63 NARA, NPMP, NSC Files, Country Files – Europe, Germany, Box 683, Sonnenfeldt to Kissinger, Handling of Secretary Rogers' Memoranda on Berlin and European Security Conference, 5 November 1969.
64 NARA, NPMP, NSC Files, Subject Files – HAK-Richardson Meetings, Box 337, Sonnenfeldt to Kissinger, Your Meeting with Elliot Richardson – NATO Issues, 22 October 1969.
65 NARA, NPMP, NSC Files, Subject Files – NSSM, Box 365, Kissinger to Departments of State and Defence, National Security Study Memorandum 83 – U.S. Approach to Current Issues of European Security, 21 November 1969.
66 NARA, NPMP, NSC Files, Country Files – Europe, Germany, Box 682, Rogers to Nixon, United States and Allied Approaches to the Current Issues of European Security, 31 October 1969.
67 NARA, NPMP, NSC Files, Country Files – Europe, USSR, Box 711, Hyland to Kissinger, Recent Soviet Policy Developments: Germany, China, and SALT, 15 December 1969.
68 AAP-1969, Document 388, Ruete to the German Foreign Minister Scheel, 5 December 1969.
69 The "Harmel Report" was issued by the Atlantic Alliance in 1967, and it posed the dialogue and détente with the communist countries as a major goal of the same Alliance, together with collective defence (see <http://www.nato.int/archives/harmel/harmel.htm>).
70 Declaration of the North Atlantic Council, 5 December 1969 (<www.nato.int>).
71 NARA, NPMP, NSC Files, Country Files – Europe, USSR, Box 711, Sonnenfeldt to Kissinger, The Status of Ostpolitik and the Berlin Talks, 8 January 1970.

72   NARA, NPMP, NSC Files, Country Files – Europe, France, Box 676, Osgood and Hyland to Kissinger, The Role of France in U.S. European Policy, 3 February 1970.
73   NARA, NPMP, NSC Files, Country Files – Europe, Poland, Box 698, Polish Ambassador's Conversation With Mr. Kissinger, 9 February 1970.
74   AAP-1969, Document 388, Ruete to Scheel, 5 December 1969.
75   AAP-1969, Document 395, Ambassador Grewe to Scheel.
76   AAP-1970, Document 83, Document of the Foreign and Defence Ministries to the Council for National Security, 2 March 1970.
77   AAP-1970, Document 117, Undersecretary Roth to Scheel, 12 March 1970.
78   AAP-1970, Document 160, Scheel to the German representatives at the NATO Council, 16 April 1970.
79   AAP-1970, Document 132, Memorandum of conversation bewteen Minister Schmidt and Minister Healey, 24 March 1970.
80   AAP-1970, Document 117, Roth to Scheel, 12 March 1970.
81   NARA, NPMP, NSC Files, Subject Files – NSSM, Box 365, Kissinger to Departments of State and Defence, National Security Study Memorandum 92 – Mutual and Balanced Force Reductions Between NATO and the Warsaw Pact (MBFR), 13 April 1970.
82   NARA, RG 59, OFLF, entry 5339, HS, Box 2, Sutterlin to Hillenbrand and Sonnenfeldt, European Security Conference, 14 January 1970.
83   NARA, NPMP, NSC Files, Country Files – Europe, Germany, Box 683, Memorandum of Sonnenfeldt, Mr. Kissinger's Lunch with Helmut Schmidt, 9 April 1970.
84   AAP-1970, Document 166, Grewe to Scheel, 17 April 1970.
85   NARA, NPMP, NSC Files, Country Files – Europe, USSR, Box 712, Richardson, Meeting with Dobrynin – MBFR, 10 July 1970.
86   AAP-1970, Document 303, Ederer to Scheel, 10 July 1970.

Transformation versus Status Quo

The Survival of the Transformation Strategy during the Nixon Years

Stephan Kieninger

According to John Lewis Gaddis' interpretation of Cold War History – with Geir Lundestad one might call it "new traditionalism" – "détente sought to freeze the Cold War in place" whereas the Helsinki Final Act "did not freeze the Cold War in place".[1] Gaddis' dichotomic view lacks an understanding of the dialectal strategic rationale behind the Helsinki Final Act as well as behind several Western détente strategies like Lyndon B. Johnson's policy of "bridge building",[2] German Ostpolitik since Brandt,[3] as well as de Gaulle's,[4] Pompidou's[5] and Wilson's[6] policies towards the Soviet Union and Eastern Europe: The recognition of the territorial status quo in Europe was the first step in the process of overcoming it and inducing change in the Soviet orbit. Both the above mentioned détente strategies as well as the Helsinki Final Act were a synthesis of stability and change, of power and mission.[7]

The establishment of the transformative elements in the Helsinki Final Act – above all the regulations on freer movement of people, information and ideas in Basket III as well as the Peaceful Change clause – were the result of a joint Western effort throughout almost three years of CSCE negotiations preceded by another three years of intra-NATO preparations from 1969 to 1972.

Despite the hostile attitude displayed towards the CSCE by Richard Nixon and Henry Kissinger, the Department of State succeeded in playing a crucial role during the intra-alliance preparations and the Multilateral Preparatory Talks. Particularly its Bureau of European Affairs continued pursuing Johnson's and Rusk's euphemistically labelled "bridge building" policy intending a softening up from within of Communist rule via intensified ideological competition.[8] The Department of State essentially helped to bring about the eventual Western CSCE concept in 1972 which was directed at opening up the Soviet-reigned sphere and at transforming it in an open ended process via increased inter-bloc communication by means of trade, culture, and exchange of people, information and ideas.[9]

The gap between bridge building and the White House approach towards European Security could not have been wider. Presidents Nixon and Ford as well as Henry Kissinger in his capacity as national security adviser – and later secretary of state – viewed détente first and foremost as a tool of their stabilization policy aimed at slowing down the decline of US power on a global scale in the aftermath of the Vietnam War, the spirit of the youth revolts in 1968, and the uncoupling of the US dollar from the Bretton Woods System.[10] From this background, White House policy towards the Soviet Union was particularly focused on internationally integrating and thereby containing the second super power in order to stabilize the post war order in Europe.[11] Stability was an end in itself. The dualism[12] in concepts and policies between the White House and the State Department's policy towards Europe manifested itself particularly in the preparation for the ESC/CSCE.[13]

However, an explanation of the basic assumptions lying at the heart of both concepts necessitates a wider frame of examining the interdependences between ESC/CSCE, MBFR and Ostpolitik. At the core of all three issues was Europe's security system dealing with the German question as its nucleus. In this respect both Kissinger's National Security Council and the State Department's Bureau of European Affairs viewed ESC/CSCE and MBFR as Siamese twins. Ostpolitik, until the inner-German modus vivendi in late 1972, set the pace for conceptualizing both approaches and, at the same time, stimulated the State Department's strategy of transformation. So far historiographical analysis – recently by Hanhimäki, Suri, Morgan and Gaddis – has failed to take sufficient account of this interconnection and was therefore unable to explain the breadth of American diplomacy over the Ostpolitik-ESC/CSCE-MBFR package.[14] This essay will comparatively analyze the attitude in the White House towards ESC/CSCE, MBFR and Ostpolitik as well as the State Department's respective views, in order to give sufficient explanations for both the conceptual struggle and the eventual survival of the transformative elements within the CSCE frame.

Status Quo Détente versus Bridge Building: The Story of Conflicting Perceptions

The intra-American discussions about the implications of Willy Brandt's Neue Ostpolitik offer a good litmus test for the underlying perceptions behind the détente concepts pursued in the White House and the Department of State. In the aftermath of the Moscow Treaty, a highly revealing conversation between Henry Kissinger and Assistant Secretary of State for European Affairs Martin Hillenbrand took place, each being a key representative of the respective stratagem of US policy. During a meeting of the National Security Council's Senior Review Group on 31 August 1970, they had an intense encounter about the long-term objectives of Brandt's Ostpolitik. Hillenbrand perceptively pointed out that Brandt "hopes increasing Soviet permissiveness will accelerate the process of change in Eastern Europe. This could lead to a situation in which the Soviets do not see control over East Germany as essential to their security." Kissinger directly replied that "no rational Soviet leader would consider it preferable that there is a united Germany particularly if a united Germany could get there only by loosening Soviet influence in Eastern Europe". Hillenbrand admittedly mentioned that there was "some wishful thinking" on the FRG side, but he emphasized that "the Germans regard power as divisible". He pointed out that "they [the Germans] are thinking in terms of economic power and are impressed by the fact that the Eastern European economy is falling back behind that of Western Europe. They believe the Soviets are motivated by a desire for access to Western technology and Western credits". Equally important, "the Germans also see a waning of ideological fervor in the East" which in Hillenbrand's view had undoubtedly had some influence on SPD thinking. Kissinger did not deny that this was a rational construction, but insisted "that we should at least consider that this could have a very unhappy ending",[15] obviously referring to his leitmotif predictions of a revival of German nationalism.[16] Whereas Hillenbrand perceptively distilled the transformative rationale behind Ostpolitik, Kissinger selectively perceived possible dangers.[17] The reason for their conflicting judgments almost solely lay in conflicting perceptions.

In contrast to Nixon's and Kissinger's static, Realpolitik view of international relations and their neglect of the conceptual role of perceptions in international politics, the members of Bill Cargo's Policy Planning Staff in the State Department were fully conscious that "the internal evolution of the Warsaw Pact will be shaped by its members perceptions of the evolution of NATO" – and vice versa. The State Department Policy Planners succinctly pointed out that "mutual perceptions are not mirror images of each other." They claimed that NATO members had a "more realistic perception of the pact than Pact members have of NATO." The State Department's planners emphasized that reduced "paranoia about West German revanchism" in the wake of Ostpolitik would lead to a more realistic Warsaw Pact perception of NATO and would therefore encourage Eastern European efforts for more independence.[18] Hence, it is fair to say that their systematic thinking about the conceptual role of perceptions in international politics led the State Department planners to believe that changing the Soviet system was possible. Along these lines, Bill Cargo himself wanted to convince Henry Kissinger that "the Russians see a European security conference as a 'controlled reaction' vehicle to let the necessary and inevitable process of technological adaptation occur in Eastern Europe – with absolutely essential Western assistance but in such a manner that it will not assume a 'critical mass' as Czechoslovakia did". In Cargo's view "detente and greater freedom of action in Eastern Europe go hand in hand".[19]

As early as in late 1969, the State Department's Bureau of European Affairs realized that the Soviet Union's policy of trying to slow down the erosion of its power in Eastern Europe necessitated increased coordination within the Warsaw Pact on account of the start of Brandt's Neue Ostpolitik. The Bureau of European Affairs considered the two-item declaration of the Warsaw Pact's Prague Declaration[20] – renunciation of force and increased East-West trade – as being open to negotiation. The trade-item could even be reinterpreted as a means of "promoting greater freedom of movement for goods, people and ideas"[21] as Lewis Bowden of the Office of Soviet Union Affairs pointed out. Proposing freer movement of people, information and ideas as a separate item for a future ESC, and assuming that the Soviet Union might be prepared to accept this as a concession for the convocation of a conference, Bowden pleaded for a US strategy that would in effect be a "preemptive movement to take the initiative away from the Soviets and use any European meeting to force concessions from them in the sense of allowing greater independence of Eastern European states."[22] Along these lines, Secretary of State William Rogers stressed that in a European Security Conference the US would not just give in – recognizing the status quo to the benefit of the Soviet Union.[23] Naturally, the Department of State was prepared to accept the status quo, but at the same time it forcefully pleaded for fostering "national independence and liberalization in the East."[24] In essence, accepting the status quo should be the first step in the process of overcoming it.

In sharp contrast, Nixon and Kissinger viewed the recognition of the status as a means for international stability – and for them, stability was as an end in itself.[25] At this point, it is important to note that solely Richard Nixon in his capacity as president of the United States set out the overall objectives of US foreign policy. Kissinger's influence on defining the strategic framework of US policy was rather limited.[26]

Assuming that self-perceptions and perceptions of the other side – based on both a relatively rigid historical picture of the other side and simultaneously on long-term changes in attitude – decisively determine policies,[27] it is of utmost importance to examine Richard Nixon's mental map. Nixon's perception of the Soviet Union was particularly influenced by his experience as vice president during the Eisenhower administrations in the 1950s. His famous kitchen debate encounter with Nikita Khrushchev at the American National Exhibition in Moscow on 24 July 1959[28] contributed to his perception of the Soviet Union as a revolutionary power seeking competition with the West in every possible respect. Despite the new Soviet leadership's turn to tend to a purely status quo-oriented European policy in the aftermath of the double crisis of Berlin and Cuba,[29] Nixon continued perceiving the new Soviet leadership along the lines of the 1950s. "They are still Communists and they are committed to the goal of a Communist world. [...] They seek victory with peace [...]."[30] In an address to the Bohemian Club in San Francisco in July 1967 – one year before the Soviet clamp-down of the Prague Spring in August 1968 – Nixon falsely predicted that "the differences in Eastern Europe still cause less trouble to the Soviet Union than the differences in Western Europe cause to the United States".[31]

And worse, after the events of Czechoslovakia and the first successes of Brandt's Neue Ostpolitik, Nixon still thought in the categories of the 1950s. Although he set out the goal of an "era of negotiation",[32] Nixon for the most part failed to adapt his old Cold War perceptions to the new era of détente. Vis-à-vis Italian Prime Minister Colombo, he emphasized that he saw some validity in applying the "Domino-Theory"[33] to the situation in Europe in the 1970s. Nixon feared that Italy – governed by a four-party coalition including two Socialist parties[34] – could get lost to Communism and could become the first falling domino in Europe: "As Italy goes, so goes Europe."[35] The Vietnam War weighed so heavily on Nixon's self perception that he feared Germany and Japan as the "two key nations on the periphery of the Communist bloc" might be inclined to see the US as being "satisfied to become a second rate power" and not being able to provide the security of its allies.[36] After all, from this standpoint, a European status quo arrangement with the Soviet Union did not look all that bad.

As long as Nixon and Kissinger perceived Germany to be firmly anchored in NATO, they did not want to reject the Warsaw Pact's Budapest Appeal out of hand.[37] The White House would put the Western Europeans no obstacles in their way towards a European Security Conference, but the Europeans had to know what they wanted – that was of the essence of what Kissinger told Egon Bahr, Brandt's chief foreign policy advisor and the architect of Brandt's Neue Ostpolitik, during their first encounter in mid-October 1969.[38] However, in late 1969 Nixon's and Kissinger's rather relaxed attitude towards European Security issues as displayed in spring 1969 was replaced by severe misgivings that Brandt's Neue Ostpolitik gave the Soviet Union leverage for pursuing "selective détente",[39] reducing tensions vis-à-vis the FRG and Western Europe and at the same time being intransigent towards the US. In the White House view, the Soviet Union could lead the Brandt government astray to gradually reducing its Western ties in order to open a window for the reunification of one neutralized German state.[40] After the take-off of Brandt's Ostpolitik, the Warsaw Pact's initiative towards an ESC was suddenly perceived in the White House as increasing the Soviet Union's chances for slowly – and at first imperceptibly – taking the FRG out of NATO. In January 1970, Lawrence Eagleburger, one of Kissinger's closest confidants, noted that "we have already slipped into a relatively dangerous position on the Soviet proposal for a European Security Conference" because "by focussing on the Soviet proposal, talking about it, and trying to shape it into something we might be able to live with we have already agreed to play in the Russian ball park".[41] The causal nexus between the perception of Ostpolitik and the judgement of an ESC is evident. In the wake of Ostpolitik's growing success, Kissinger judged the implications of a future ESC as inherently including the danger of "disintegrating NATO".[42] In Eagleburger's outlook, Brandt's Neue Ostpolitik added a new and decisive dimension to Nixon's perception of "presiding over the partial dissolution of the American empire".[43]

The Conceptual Relevance of Perceptions for the Respective ESC/CSCE and MBFR Stratagems in Washington: Preserving the Status Quo or Gradually Overcoming It

Richard Nixon and Henry Kissinger did nothing to revise their perception that "the Conference could do harm".[44] In the spring of 1971, they saw their predictions concerning disintegrative effects on NATO's cohesion confirmed, as different tactical options with regards to freer movement emerged within intra-alliance preparations. Supported by the Bureau of European Affairs, the US mission to NATO pleaded forcefully for taking an intransigent position confronting the Soviet Union with open demands for freer movement.⁴⁵ Moscow's interest in an ESC should be used for extracting Soviet concessions with regards to extending East-West communication. Even though Bonn, like the State Department, pursued détente as a long-term means for challenging the status quo and inducing change in the Soviet Union and Eastern Europe, views differed about tactics in a future ESC.

With respect towards the process of gradually reducing the barriers between the two German states, Bonn intended to avoid immediate confrontations with the Soviet Union about the highly controversial freer movement issue within the ESC context.⁴⁶ Nevertheless, the State Department, in accordance with Paris and Bonn, shared the common pursuit of trying to transform Soviet-style communist rule. One may call it "peaceful rollback"⁴⁷ like French Foreign Minister Schumann did or "gradual bridging of the divisions of Europe" reasserting "the Western interest in constructive, liberalizing change"⁴⁸ as Ralph McGuire did in his capacity as Director of the Office of Regional Politico-Military Affairs (RPM) in the State Department's Bureau of European Affairs. Hence, NATO eventually proved to be a highly robust and efficient political consulting mechanism. In the autumn of 1972, NATO's permanent representatives found a compromise solution, taking a hard stance in the substance of freer movement, but labelling it "human contacts".⁴⁹ Kissinger considered this policy of transformation towards the Soviet Union as absolutely illusory. It was beyond his imagination that one could induce liberalizing change via freer movement. Thinking strictly in realist terms and viewing states as black boxes, in his dealings with the Soviets, Kissinger just hit the Soviet Union's rock-hard external mantle.⁵⁰ The State Department's policy of trying to penetrate the Soviet system and change its weak internal sphere provoked Kissinger's anger. He could not find an answer to his question of what it was "that suddenly possesses the West to believe that it can affect the domestic structure of the Soviet Union through a treaty signed in Geneva with peripheral significance".⁵¹

But at the same time, every Western decision-maker identified Mutual and Balanced Force Reductions (MBFR) as the true crunch European Security issue of the day. Brandt and Bahr as well as the White House realized that MBFRs – always viewed in connection with an ESC – were "the real one substantive subject"⁵² in terms of European Security. There was agreement that an ESC itself just meant carefully negotiating a multilateral modus vivendi in Europe and not immediately creating a new European security structure like the Vienna Congress had done. Compared to an ESC, troop reductions could have a more immediate political impact. Brandt and Bahr wanted to use MBFRs – via an ESC as institutional provisional – both as a lever and a core for eventually establishing a European security system, aimed at bringing about peaceful change in the Soviet sphere and finally allowing a unification of the two German states.[53]

In their approach towards MBFR, Nixon and Kissinger faced a real dilemma. Although they saw actual reductions of troops synonymous with strong Soviet influence in Europe, they were forced to use the mere idea of MBFR as a means for preventing unilateral US withdrawals as Senator Mike Mansfield had been demanding for years.[54] Nixon and Kissinger were in agreement about not being able "to foresee an outcome for MBFR that is both manifestly negotiable and clearly in our security interest". Hence, they were "not in a position to commit ourselves to reaching agreement in MBFR". They wanted to use "the process of MBFR to hold the line against unilateral reductions on the Western side and, if satisfactory reductions prove non-negotiable, to maintain public support for an adequate defense effort".[55] These objectives required that the president and his national security advisor permanently made visible efforts to get MBFR underway by demanding several MBFR studies from various departments and agencies, but at the same time they denied giving basic criteria, assumptions or commitments for judging MBFR scenarios.[56] This strategy necessitated Kissinger's tight control over decision-making with regards to the MBFR issue via the National Security Council.

Nixon's and Kissinger's rationale reflected itself particularly in Kissinger's actions in May 1971 when Mansfield's success in Congress seemed to be in reach. Both Kissinger and Secretary of Defense Melvin Laird agreed that offering Congress an MBFR proposal including US reductions of 50,000 soldiers would be too high a price for preventing a successful Mansfield resolution.[57] Brezhnev's immediate reaction towards an impending unilateral US withdrawal did not fit in with the White House's expectations for he signalled Soviet readiness towards MBFR negotiations.[58] Brezhnev obviously viewed the United States as the only Western power being able to preserve the status quo in the heart of Europe.[59] Therefore, in the immediate wake of the MBFR crisis in May 1971 the Soviet Union was even ready to start MBFR negotiations in advance of ESC negotiations.[60] Nevertheless, in the White House a completely different perception of Soviet motives with regards to MBFR prevailed – seen in context with an ESC. Sonnenfeldt assumed that, although from the Soviet perspective the overall purpose of an ESC obviously lay in the recognition of the political and territorial status quo in Europe, "MBFR would detract from this concept, suggesting as it does some blurring of the line between East and West, and some aura of disengagement in the East. A deferred MBFR, however, might be manageable from the Soviet viewpoint if the political foundation had already been laid in the CSCE. In this scenario, subsequent MBFR negotiations would be directed at making West Germany a grey area for special consideration (this is the basic French fear about MBFR and it is a justified one)."[61]

In the State Department, ESC and MBFR as the Siamese twins of European security policy were seen from a completely different perspective. However, faced with Kissinger's supreme stance in the National Security Council, the conceptual thinkers of bridge building were more and more averse to putting the cards on the table openly vis-à-vis the White House, in order to prevent sanctions either against their policy or their careers. Directly challenging Kissinger, like Hillenbrand had done in 1970, seemed to become counterproductive. Phil Farley, Deputy Director of the Arms Control and Disarmament Agency (ACDA), avoided confronting Kissinger's conceptual hegemony openly in the National Security Council's Senior Review Group. Instead Farley decided to write a letter to Kissinger questioning the latter's basic MBFR assessments. Contrary to Kissinger's leitmotif expectation that MBFRs would result in the FRG's Finlandization, Farley drew up a rationale using MBFR as a mechanism of gradually transforming Soviet rule in Eastern Europe and in the Soviet Union itself. He regarded MBFR as a lever for inducing change. Farley argued lucidly that Finlandization was out of the question "as the weight of Soviet pressures would diminish as their forces shifted eastward." He expected that in "Eastern Europe, the effect on declining Soviet force levels would also be positive and stabilizing." If the peoples in Eastern Europe "see a process under way through which the Soviet presence will gradually be eroded and Soviet freedom to intervene massively in their affairs will gradually be constrained, then they are more likely to be patient and to hope and scheme to follow the Romanian rather than the Czech or Hungarian pattern."[62] In the long run, Farley clearly did not intend spreading Ceausescu style despotism, but liberalizing change in the Soviet kraal. The key lay with Moscow. Farley saw MBFR as a means of strengthening the détente-minded parts in the Politburo by mutually recognizing the legitimacy of concerns about troop levels. In his view, MBFR negotiations could "contribute to a transformation of attitudes in Moscow"[63] as the essential precondition for change in the Soviet orbit.

Kissinger's answer to Farley's letter was most revealing: "It should be easy for us to agree, however, our analytical work to date gives us reasons for proceeding cautiously, and that it demonstrates that we have only begun to grapple what is a most difficult subject."⁶⁴ In essence, Kissinger's and Farley's contrary views with regards to MBFR were based on their contrary perceptions of the United States and their inherently dependent perceptions of the Soviet Union. Self-perception, self-image and self-confidence constituted the gap between bridge building and the White House status quo-détente.

No End to Conceptual Dualism: Implications for the Character of the Helsinki Final Act until the Start of the Multilateral Preparatory Talks (MPT)

After having analyzed the roots of conceptual dualism, the analysis will now address the question of how the struggle between bridge building and status quo-détente found its expression at the level of political action. Due to various linkages and reverse-linkages, the preparations for an ESC/CSCE could only take place after the ratification of the Eastern Treaties in the German Bundestag and the ratification of the Berlin Agreement by the Four Powers. The relevance of the Berlin Agreement on the road towards an ESC was reflected in the quickly changing label of the conference in late 1971. NATO's turning away from the initial Soviet label "ESC" was an obvious challenge to the Soviet view of the conference as a surrogate treaty for World War II. With the bridge building strategy in mind, State Department Counselor Richard F. Pederson proposed the title "Conference on European Cooperation".⁶⁵ In November 1971 the permanent NATO council opted for the name "Conference on European Security and Cooperation (CESC)".⁶⁶ However, in December 1971 the French finally succeeded in naming it "Conference on Security and Cooperation in Europe" (CSCE) because "CESC" from the Paris viewpoint implied an immediate decrease for the US role in Europe's affairs. In Foreign Minister Schumann's words France "could not conceive of a balanced situation in Europe without US participation".⁶⁷

Within NATO, there was consensus that in the wake of the Berlin Agreement there should be a focus on preparing an ESC instead of MBFR although the latter was not linked to preconditions.⁶⁸ After the intra-Western frictions on the tide of Brandt's Ostpolitik, in the interest of NATO's cohesion there was eagerness to prevent "a sharp revival of interest",⁶⁹ which would occur in MBFR negotiations. In the White House, in Paris and London extensive mutual force reductions were seen as being erosive with regards to the Four Power rights in Germany and Berlin.⁷⁰ However, the State Department and

Bonn were ready for beginning MBFR exploration talks even before – as well as after – the ratification of the Berlin Protocol – which meant after beginning ESC preparations.[71] The social-liberal Bonn government insisted that, in the second case, MBFR elements as the heart of an eventual European peace structure should be included within the wider ESC frame.[72] This approach raised the negative effect of involving countries not directly affected by reductions in decision-making about superpower force levels. George Vest, the acting chief of the US mission to NATO, proposed establishing a special MBFR group in the framework of preparatory talks for an ESC as a mechanism of resolving this critical point.[73] Although Haig and Sonnenfeldt both disliked negotiations per se, they did not turn down Vest's special group idea, since from the White House perspective, it could be used as a vehicle for containing Congressional pressure for unilateral US reductions.[74]

But that was about all the White House accomplished with respect to European security in autumn 1971, for the beginning of ESC preparatory talks depended on the fate of Ostpolitik being on the agenda in mid 1972. Nixon and Kissinger completely ignored the permanent work of the US mission to NATO during the intra-alliance preparations for a conference. They considered it sufficient starting with NATO preparations after the success of Ostpolitik.[75] Despite their common dislike of an ESC, both Nixon and Kissinger recognized that they couldn't prevent a conference from taking place. Both men also considered the potential of MBFR with respect to changing the status quo – in their view solely to the West's disadvantage – far superior to that of an ESC.[76]

Hence, in early October 1971, in the wake of the Berlin Protocol, Nixon decided not only to accept the conceptual dualism with regards to the ESC, but to institutionalize it by letting the State Department pursue its bridge building policy for the sake of the White House damage-limiting strategy. Nixon and Kissinger played a "double track game".[77] As the president put it, "Dobrynin has word to handle it [the ESC] through channels and also preparations for the summit". But on the other hand, Nixon wanted to "give State things to do". Nixon wanted "Dobrynin to understand that he can talk with Rogers but I will make the decisions".[78] Nixon planned to focus on bilateral dealings with Moscow and Beijing and he did not want to get involved in confrontations with the State Department's bridge building bureaucracy.[79] Finally, in late October 1971, Nixon told Rogers that from then on, the secretary was officially in charge of the conference issue. Nixon instructed Rogers how he wanted the ESC issue to be played. Towards the Soviet Union, Rogers should "just sort of indicate, well this is a gingerly thing and we've gotta consider it and we've talked about. Because the press would love to push us into this god damn thing."[80]

In keeping with their cautious rationale, Nixon and Kissinger were holding their efforts until just before the Moscow summit in the spring of 1972 in order to, on the one hand, pull the Soviets in MBFR negotiations as a counter to Congressional pressure. On the other hand, the White House's maximum goal was still "not to reduce or limit the size character and activities of military forces in the heart of Europe".[81] Having this rationale in mind – and keeping it secret from State and Pentagon – Kissinger approached the decisive National Security Council meeting on 29 March 1972, which solely dealt with European security. Under the assumption of Ostpolitik's success, the NSC Senior Review Group agreed to establish a special MBFR group through CSCE preparatory talks, permitting the commencement of MBFR talks and restricting them to states directly involved, as proposed by Vest in autumn 1971. NSDM 162 reflected this broad consensus,[82] which was clearly in the interest of the State Department.

However, Nixon's and Kissinger's verdict against substantial MBFR exploratory talks within a "special MBFR group" had been taken.[83] NSDM 162 was useless paper. Rogers was already worried that Kissinger wanted to deal with the decisive MBFR issue in bilateral talks between the superpowers.[84] In his talks with Brezhnev during a top secret trip to Moscow in April 1972, Kissinger tried to get definitive Soviet acceptance for starting MBFR preparatory talks, but he just accomplished vague agreement.[85] Only during the Moscow summit in late May 1972 could Nixon get Brezhnev's consent to MBFR negotiations, since the Eastern Treaties had been ratified in the German Bundestag a few days earlier. The road towards a CSCE was open. However, until the Moscow summit, the State Department as well as the Pentagon were convinced that the NSDM 162 "special group approach" still remained relevant.[86] During the Moscow summit, Rogers realized that both Nixon and Brezhnev were already determined to prevent MBFR exploratory talks from taking place under the roof of CSCE preparations, but wanted to deal with MBFR strictly on a bilateral basis. Rogers' open opposition against this MBFR superpower condominium forced Nixon to break off the summit talk to avoid a further escalation before the assembled Soviet leadership.[87] Finally, in September 1972 Kissinger got definitive Soviet assent to begin MBFR exploratory talks in late January 1973.[88]

In summary, Nixon and Kissinger succeeded in keeping complete control over the MBFR issue. They fully implemented their MBFR blueprint into operative politics. Therefore, Nixon and Kissinger could afford accepting the conceptual dualism with regards to an ESC in order to use the State Department's bridge building policy for their purpose of a damage-limiting approach. However, the State Department's Bureau of European Affairs did not accept restricting its studies to damage limiting, but consequently stayed with its bridge building concept.[89] Secretary Rogers even transformed the recently established Interdepartmental Group for Europe into a permanent Interagency Task Force in order to support the search for a common position on freer movement in NATO.[90] Even in an NSC meeting with Nixon and Kissinger, Rogers contradicted the White House view of the ESC as a "nightmare"[91] when he emphasized that "a conference might be turned to our advantage".[92]

Although Rogers violated Nixon's out of touch with reality guideline of postponing preparations in NATO until after the ratification of the Berlin Protocol,[93] Nixon and Kissinger let Rogers have his way on account of their double track game rationale. Therefore, the Interagency Task Force under Hillenbrand's auspices could draw up guidelines reflecting the State Department's bridge building approach until the start of the Multilateral Preparatory Talks (MPT) for the CSCE in November 1972.[94] The US mission to NATO under the aegis of George Vest could thus substantially contribute to NATO's success in finding a common stance in the freer movement issue, basically reflecting the bridge building blueprint.

Implications of the Conceptual Dualism for the Character of the Helsinki Final Act after the Start of the Multilateral Preparatory Talks (MPT)

Whereas in NATO's preparations for the conference Vest could take an intransigent position on the freer movement issue, as the head of the US delegation at the MPT he consciously decided to take a behind the scenes role in the negotiations between the thirty-five participants in order to avoid a superpower showdown.[95] Nevertheless, in intra-NATO consultations during the MPT, Vest forcefully supported NATO's stance continuing with State's bridge building policy.[96] Due to their united position during the MPT, the NATO states eventually succeeded in establishing a separate agenda item on freer movement in Stage I of the CSCE in July 1973. This was against Kissinger's conviction. With NATO's united front, Kissinger's damage-limiting approach was fully served. Kissinger planned to trade what he perceived as absolutely illusory – NATO's ambitions for transforming

Soviet rule – in exchange for Soviet concessions with respect to his common ceiling approach in MBFR, implying asymmetrical reductions to the advantage of the US.[97]

Just before Stage I of the CSCE in July 1973, Nixon and Kissinger even put overt pressure on their NATO allies – trying to force them to abandon their tough negotiation stance on the freer movement issue. To that end, a group consisting of Permanent Representatives to the North Atlantic Council and of Western European Chiefs of Missions in Washington was assembled in Nixon's resort in San Clemente – without any tangible success for the White House.[98] Additionally, from 1974 onwards, Harold Wilson's newly elected Labour government made it more difficult for Kissinger to sell his defensive détente approach in Great Britain. Wilson pursued a more dynamic British détente policy than the previous Heath cabinet.[99] As Kissinger, despite persistent efforts, was not able to persuade his NATO allies to give up their ambitious freer movement position, the Soviets refused accepting his common ceiling MBFR approach.[100] Additionally, due to the Jackson-Vanik Amendment's definitive success in Congress in late 1974,[101] the SALT II negotiations got stuck although Ford and Brezhnev had been able to create a framework for strategic arms control at their first meeting in Vladivostok in November 1974.[102] Hence, Kissinger's only option to save his détente policy lay in supporting the key elements of bridge building in the CSCE, namely freer movement and peaceful change – despite his still disparaging views.[103]

In sum, the importance of the State Department's bridge building policy in the Nixon years as a basis for the prevailing of the dynamic elements of liberalizing change over the status quo factors within the Helsinki process can hardly by overestimated. Since William Rogers until his dismissal consequently continued pursuing State's bridge building policy supporting the West German position on peaceful change[104] and confronting Gromyko with demands for freer movement of people, ideas and information,[105] he strengthened NATO's intransigence – vis-à-vis both the Soviets and Kissinger's linkage policy of trying to trade freer movement for common ceiling.[106]

Despite suggesting the contrary in his memoirs,[107] Kissinger did never share the joint NATO and EC policy of trying to transform Communist rule, but still viewed the Helsinki Final Act from the perspective of his status quo approach. Although he gave positive accounts before the US cabinet to justify the United States' signing the Final Act,[108] Kissinger was worried about "communist inroads"[109] in the future CSCE process. In Kissinger's outlook, that was particularly true for Germany: "In terms of Euro-communism, one third of Germany is Communist. If the GDR ever does manage to present an acceptable image of herself, we will have a Euro-communist problem in Central Europe."[110]

Notes

1. Geir Lundestad, "The Cold War according to John Lewis Gaddis", *Cold War History*, vol. 6, no. 4 (November 2006), 535-542, here 539. Lundestad refers to John Lewis Gaddis, *The Cold War* (New York and London 2005).
2. Thomas A. Schwartz, *Lyndon Johnson and Europe: In the Shadow of Vietnam* (Cambridge, Mass. 2003).
3. Gottfried Niedhart, "Revisionistische Elemente und die Initiierung friedlichen Wandels in der neuen Ostpolitik 1967-1974", *Geschichte und Gesellschaft* 28 (2002), 233-266; Oliver Bange and Gottfried Niedhart, "Die 'Relikte der Nachkriegszeit' beseitigen: Ostpolitik in der zweiten außenpolitischen Formationsphase der Bundesrepublik Deutschland im Übergang von den Sechziger- zu den Siebzigerjahren", *Archiv für Sozialgeschichte* 44 (2004), 415-448.
4. Maurice Vaïsse, *La grandeur: Politique étrangère du général de Gaulle 1958-1969* (Paris 1998).
5. Mary Pierre Rey, *La tentation du rapprochement: France et URSS à l'heure de la détente, 1964-1974* (Paris 1991).
6. Lucca Ratti, "Britain, The German Question and the Transformation of Europe: From Ostpolitik to the Helsinki Conference (1963-1975)", in Oliver Bange and Gottfried Niedhart (eds), *Helsinki 1975 and the Transformation of Europe* (New York and Oxford 2008).
7. For an analysis of power and mission as the driving forces of US Foreign Policy, see Detlef Junker, *Power and Mission – Was Amerika antreibt* (Freiburg 2003). One of Kissinger's most famous biographers, Walter Isaacson, comes to the conclusion that Nixon's and Kissinger's balance-of-power thinking was oriented far too much to power than towards ideas. See Walter Isaacson, *Kissinger* (New York 1992), 760, 767.
8. James Goodby, *Europe Undivided, The New Logic of Peace in US-Russian Relations* (Washington D.C. 1998), 37-64.
9. Stephan Kieninger, "Transformation or Status Quo: The Conflict of Stratagems in Washington over the Meaning and Purpose of CSCE and MBFR, 1969-1973", in Oliver Bange and Gottfried Niedhart (eds), *Helsinki 1975 and the Transformation of Europe* (New York and Oxford 2008).
10. For the contextualization of détente, see Jussi M. Hanhimäki, "Ironies and Turning Points: Détente in Perspective", in Odd Arne Westad (ed.), *Reviewing the Cold War. Approaches, Interpretations, Theory* (London 2000), 326-342.

11 Richard M. Nixon, *The Memoirs of Richard Nixon* (New York 1978); Henry A. Kissinger, *White House Years* (Boston 1979).

12 For the conceptual and political dualism between the White House and the Department of State in the Nixon years, see Stephan Kieninger, "Transformation or Status Quo", in Bange and Niedhart, *Helsinki 1975*, and cited above.

13 In labelling the conference I stick to the respective changing contemporary name. NATO's turning away from the initial Soviet label "ESC" was an obvious challenge to the Soviet view of the conference as a surrogate peace treaty for World War II. In December 1971 NATO named it "Conference on Security and Cooperation in Europe" (CSCE).

14 Hanhimäki in 2003 just gave a hint concerning the State Department's "own policy with regards to the CSCE". Jussi M. Hanhimäki, "'They can write it in Swahili': Kissinger, the Soviets and the Helsinki Accords, 1973-1975", *Journal of Transatlantic Studies* 1 (2003), 40.

15 National Archives and Record Administration, College Park (NARA), Nixon Presidential Material Project (Nixon), NSC, Institutional Files, Box H-111, memcon Kissinger-Hillenbrand, 31 August 1970.

16 See Holger Klitzing, *The Nemesis of Stability. Henry A. Kissinger's Ambivalent Relationship with Germany* (Trier 2007).

17 For the US reactions towards Ostpolitik see Gottfried Niedhart, "Zustimmung und Irritationen: Die Westmächte und die deutsche Ostpolitik, 1969-1970", in U. Lehmkuhl, C.A. Wurm and H. Zimmermann (eds), *Deutschland, Großbritannien, Amerika. Politik, Gesellschaft und Internationale Geschichte im 20. Jahrhundert, Festschrift für Gustav Schmidt* (Stuttgart 2003), 227-245. See also Gottfried Niedhart, "Ostpolitik: Phases, Short-Term objectives, and Grand Design", in David C. Geyer and Bernd Schaefer (eds), *American Détente and German Ostpolitik 1969-1972: Bulletin of the German Historical Institute, Supplement 1* (Washington D.C. 2004), 118-136; idem, "Frankreich und die USA im Dialog über Détente und Ostpolitik 1969-1970", *Francia. Forschungen zur westeuropäischen Geschichte Band* 31/3 (Deutsches Historisches Institut Paris 2004), 65-85.

18 NARA, Records of the Department of State, Record Group 59 (RG 59), Subject and Country Files of the Policy Planning Council, 1967-1973, Box 401, undated Policy Planning Staff Paper entitled "Relations among the Warsaw Pact Members in the 1970's" for the Meeting of the Atlantic Policy Advisory Group (APAG), 7-10 September 1971.

19 NARA, Nixon, NSC, Institutional Files, Box H-166, memorandum from Cargo to Kissinger, 17 August 1970.

20 For the Records of the Meetings of the Warsaw Pact Deputy Foreign Ministers in Prague on 30-31 October 1969, see the edited documents by Csaba Békés, Anna Locher and Christian Nuenlist on the webpage of the Parallel History Project <http://www.php.isn.ethz.ch/collections/cfm>.

21 NARA, RG 59, Lot Files, Entry A1-5574, Bureau of European Affairs, Office of Soviet Union Affairs, Multilateral Political Subject Files, 1958-1976, Box 4, memorandum

from Bowden to Swank, 1 December 1969. A few days later the freer movement item was for the first time implemented in the Declaration of the NATO Ministerial Meeting in Brussels taking place on 4-5 December 1969 <http://www.nato.int/docu/comm/49-95/c691204b.htm>.

22 Memorandum from Bowden to Swank, cited above.
23 AAPD 1969, 1384, memcon Rogers-Brandt, 6 December 1969.
24 NARA, RG 59, Lot Files, Entry A1-5574, Bureau of European Affairs, Office of Soviet Union Affairs, Multilateral Political Subject Files, 1958-1976, Box 2, Talking Points for President Nixon's first trip to Europe in February 1969, set out by the Office of Soviet Union Affairs on 11 February 1969.
25 For Nixon's and Kissinger's strong focus on a balance-of-power policy and their utter neglect of any kind of ideas in foreign policy, see numerous conversations between Kissinger and Dobrynin in FRUS 1969-1976, vol. XII (Soviet Union, January 1969-October 1970). Furthermore, the document collection "Soviet-American Relations – The Détente Years 1969-1972" provides ample evidence of the broad agreement in the scope and the objectives of détente between the White House and the Kremlin. The collection was jointly edited and published in 2007 by the US Office of the Historian in the State Department and the History and Records Department of the Russian Federation's Ministry of Foreign Affairs.
26 See William Bundy, *A Tangled Web, The Making of Foreign Policy in the Nixon Presidency* (London 1998). See Alexander M. Haig Jr., *Inner Circles: How America Changed the World* (New York 1992). With regards to the US opening to China, according to Haig, "the diplomatic point man in all these events was, of course, Henry Kissinger, but it was Nixon who, in successive flashes of inspiration, conceived the grand design", ibid., 257. For an overview on the literature on Kissinger, see Jussi M. Hanhimäki, "'Dr. Kissinger or Mr. Henry'. Kissingerology, Thirty Years and Counting", *Diplomatic History* 27.5 (2003), 637-676.
27 For the methodological background, see Robert L. Jervis, *The Logic of Images in International Relations* (Princeton 1970); idem, *Perception and Misperception in International Politics* (Princeton 1976); idem et al., *Psychology and Deterrence* (Baltimore, MD 1985); M.W. Richter, "The Perception Method for Analyzing Political Conflict", in Klaus Gottstein (ed.), *Tomorrow's Europe: The Views of Those Concerned* (Frankfurt and New York 1995), 731ff.; R. Frank, "Mentalitäten, Vorstellungen und internationale Beziehungen", in Wilfried Loth and Jürgen Osterhammel (eds), *Internationale Geschichte: Themen – Ergebnisse – Aussichten* (Munich 2000), 159ff.; Gottfried Niedhart, "Selektive Wahrnehmung und politisches Handeln: internationale Beziehungen im Perzeptionsparadigma", in ibid., 141ff.
28 There is extensive documentation on Nixon's trip to the Soviet Union in July/August 1959. But the respective FRUS volume – FRUS 1958-1960, Vol. X 1 – does not contain any record of the so-called "Kitchen Debate" between Nixon and Khrushchev on 24 July 1959. The debate was not broadcast on television but was observed by many reporters and reported in the press. A reconstruction of their informal exchanges

is printed in *The New York Times*, 25 July 1959. Nixon's account of theses exchanges can be found in Richard Nixon, *Six Crises* (Garden City 1962), 272-279.

29 The elder members of the Soviet leadership, particularly Gromyko, were in favour of starting a new dialogue with Washington after John F. Kennedy's death in 1963 and Khrushchev's ouster in 1964. See Gromyko's memoranda on the Soviet Union's foreign policy from 13 January 1967 and "An Estimate of Foreign Policy and Soviet-American Relations" from 16 September 1969. Both memoranda can be found in an English translation in the appendix to Anatoly Dobrynin, "In Confidence – Moscow's Ambassador to America's Six Cold War Presidents" (Seattle 2001), 640-643.

30 FRUS 1969-1976, Vol. I, 2ff., here 8, address by Richard Nixon to the Bohemian Club in San Francisco, 29 July 1967.

31 Ibid., 3.

32 FRUS 1969-1976, Vol. I, 53, President Nixon's inaugural address on 20 January 1969.

33 The origins of the so-called "Domino-Theory" go back to President Eisenhower's remarks on 7 April 1954 when he proclaimed that in case South Vietnam became Communist, the surrounding countries would follow that way. See David L. Anderson, "J. Lawton Collins, John Foster Dulles and the Eisenhower's Administration's 'Point of No Return' in Vietnam", *Diplomatic History* 12.2 (1988), 127-148.

34 For the rise of the Italian left from 1953 onwards, see Leopoldo Nuti, "The United States, Italy and the Opening to the Left, 1953-1963", *Journal of Cold War Studies*, vol. 4, no. 3 (2002), 36-55.

35 NARA, Nixon, White House Special Files, President's Office Files, Box 84, memcon Nixon-Colombo, 18 February 1971.

36 Ibid., memcon Nixon-Senate Republican Royalists, 20 April 1971.

37 NARA, Nixon, NSC Country Files, Box 709, memorandum from Kissinger to Nixon, 4 April 1969. The Budapest Appeal of the Warsaw Pact states for convoking a European Security Conference was submitted on 17 March 1969. An excerpt is edited in Vojtech Mastny and Malcolm Byrne, *A Cardboard Castle? An Inside History of the Warsaw Pact 1955-1991* (Budapest 2005), 330-331. For the complete text of the Budapest Appeal see Europa-Archiv 7 (1969): D 151-153.

38 Akten zur Auswärtigen Politik der Bundesrepublik Deutschland (AAPD) 1969, 1117, memcon Kissinger-Bahr, 13 October, 1969.

39 Kissinger, *White House Years*, 410.

40 NARA, Nixon, NSC, HAK Telcons, Box 3, telcon Nixon-Kissinger, 13 December 1969.

41 NARA, RG 59, Records of the Counselor 1955-1977, hereafter Sonnenfeldt Records, Box 2, memorandum from Eagleburger to Kissinger, 26 January 1970.

42 NARA, RG 59, Sonnenfeldt Records, Box 5, memcon Kissinger-Frank, 1 December 1971.

43 Memorandum from Eagleburger to Kissinger, cited above.

44 *Documents on British Policy Overseas, Series III, Volume II, The Conference on Security and Cooperation in Europe, 1972-75*, edited by Gill Bennett and Keith

A. Hamilton (London 1997), 56 (hereafter DBPO, Series III, Vol. II), memcon Brimelow-Kissinger, 10 August 1972.

45 George Vest and James Goodby in their interviews with Oliver Bange and the author, 25 April 2005 respectively 13 April 2005; Politisches Archiv des Auswärtigen Amtes (PA AA), B 150/238, report from German NATO envoy Boss, 29 September 1971.

46 AAPD 1972, 242, memcon Irwin/Hillenbrand-Staden, 13 March 1972.

47 DBPO III/2, 41, memcon Schumann-Douglas Home, 11 November 1971.

48 Memorandum from McGuire for CSCE Task Force Working Group on Freer Movement, 19 November 1972, cited in Goodby, *Europe Undivided*, 61-62. In November 1972, a State Department's public affairs guidance on freer movement was sent to all European posts. The guidance set out that "the freer movement proposal [...] reasserts the Western interest in constructive, peaceful and liberalizing change, in contradiction to Soviet emphasis on legitimizing the status quo at the level of state-to-state relations". NARA, RG 59, Subject Numeric Files, 1970-73, Box 1712, U.S. Airgram A-11268: CSCE Public Affairs Guidance – Freer Movement of People, Information and Ideas, 16 November 1972, drafted by Arva Floyd, approved by George Springsteen.

49 See the Communiqué of the NATO Ministerial Meeting in Brussels, 8 December 1972 (<http://www.nato.int/docu/comm/49-95/c721207a.htm>).

50 Gottfried Niedhart, "Deutsch-Amerikanische Beziehungen in der Anfangsphase der sozial-liberalen Ostpolitik und Differenzen in der Perzeption der Sowjetunion 1969/1970", in Manfred Berg and Philipp Gassert (eds), *Deutschland und die USA in der Internationalen Geschichte des 20. Jahrhunderts* (Stuttgart 2004), 519-520.

51 Hedwig Gusto, Mircea Munteanu and Christian Ostermann (eds), *The Road to Helsinki: The Early Steps to the CSCE, Selected Documents* (Collection of Documents, distributed for the participants of the International Conference on the CSCE, Florence 2003), doc. no. 56; NARA, RG 59, Transcripts of Secretary of State, Henry A. Kissinger Staff Meetings, 1973-1977, memcon Kissinger-Springsteen, 29 October 1973.

52 NARA, Nixon, NSC, President's Trip Files, Box 667, memorandum from Sonnenfeldt for Kissinger, 8 January 1970.

53 See Oliver Bange, "An Intricate Web – Ostpolitik, the European Security System and German Unification", in Oliver Bange and Gottfried Niedhart (eds), *Helsinki 1975 and the Transformation of Europe* (New York and Oxford 2008)

54 NARA, Nixon, NSC, Box 1027, memcon Kissinger-Meany/Lovestone, 14 September 1973.

55 NARA, Nixon, NSC, HAK Office Files, Box 21, undated memorandum from Kissinger to Nixon, April 1972.

56 NARA, Nixon, NSC, Institutional Files, Box H-64, memorandum from Sonnenfeldt and Odeen to Kissinger, 28 June 1972. Even Sonnenfeldt, Kissinger's most senior advisor, complained about the lack of criteria for developing MBFR studies.

57 NARA, Nixon, NSC, HAK Telcons, Box 10, telcon Kissinger-Laird, 1 June 1971.

58 L. Breschnew, *Auf dem Wege Lenins: Reden und Aufsätze*, vol. 3, *May 1970 to March 1972* (East Berlin 1973), 382.
59 AAPD 1972, 351, letter from Bahr to Kissinger, 1 April 1972.
60 NARA, Nixon, HAK Telcons, Box 10, telcon Kissinger-Rogers, 16 June 1971.
61 NARA, Nixon, NSC, Institutional Files, Box H-61, memorandum from Sonnenfeldt to Kissinger, 29 March 1972.
62 NARA, Nixon, NSC, Institutional Files, Box H-61, letter from Farley to Kissinger, 31 March 1972.
63 Ibid.
64 Kissinger undated answer to Farley's letter, ibid.
65 NARA, RG 59, Sonnenfeldt Records, Box 15, memorandum from Pederson to Irwin, 29 September 1971.
66 NARA, Nixon, NSC, Institutional Files, Box H-187, telegram from Vest to State Department (No. 4734), 12 November 1971.
67 NARA, RG 59, Executive Secretariat, Conference Files, 1966-1972, box 531, memcon Schumann-Irwin, 6 December 1971.
68 NARA, Nixon, NSC, Institutional Files, Box H-187, memorandum from Sonnenfeldt to Kissinger, 20 September 1971.
69 NARA, Nixon, NSC, Institutional Files, Box H-032, memorandum from Kissinger to Nixon, 1 December 1971.
70 NARA, Nixon, NSC, CF Europe, Box 678, memcon Kissinger-Debré 7 July 1972; NARA, RG 59, Executive Secretariat, Conference Files, 1966-1972, Box 532, memcon Douglas Home-Irwin, 20 July 1971.
71 NARA, RG 59, Subject Numeric Files, 1970-1973, Box 2317, memcon Hillenbrand-Roth, 30 June 1971; letter from Bahr to Kissinger, 24 May 1971, AAPD 1971, 851-852.
72 PA AA, B 150/228, memorandum from Ruth to Roth, 30 April 1971.
73 NARA, Nixon, NSC, Institutional Files, Box H-187, telegram from Vest to State Department (No. 3721), 10 September 1971.
74 Ibid, memorandum from Haig to Nixon, 21 October 1971; memorandum from Sonnenfeldt to Haig, 21 October 1971.
75 NARA, Nixon, NSC, Institutional Files, Box H-187, National Security Decision Memorandum 142, 2 December 1971.
76 In advance of Kissinger's top secret trip to Moscow in April 1972, the president and his national security adviser tried to sort out their policy with regard to CSCE and MBFR. Nixon thought that "[…] when you have European security, you can damn near forget NATO." He was even convinced that "NATO is done anyway". Kissinger responded that "[…] European security won't hurt it as much as […] MBFR will". Nixon concluded that "maybe then we'll just take European security and talk about peace and good will and exchange". Memcon Nixon-Kissinger, 19 April 1972, FRUS 1969-1976, Vol XIV, 427ff., here 445.
77 NARA, Nixon, NSC, HAK Telcons, Box 11, telcon Kissinger-Nixon, 2 October 1971.
78 Ibid.
79 Ibid.

80 White House Telephone Conversation 012-130, 26 October 1971, 8.49 am–8.55 am, White House Tape Records, cited in Werner Lippert, "Richard Nixon's Détente and Willy Brandt's Ostpolitik: The Politics and Economic Diplomacy of Engaging the East" (Ph.D. dissertation, Nashville 2005) (Ms.).
81 NARA, Nixon, NSC, Institutional Files, Box H-65, undated NSC comments on a memorandum from Laird to Nixon, 7 September 1972.
82 NARA, Nixon, NSC, Institutional Files, Box H-233, NSDM 162, 5 April 1972.
83 Memorandum from Kissinger to Nixon (undated), see n. 53.
84 NARA, Nixon, NSC, HAK Telcons, Box 13, telcon Kissinger-Rogers, 4 April 1972.
85 NARA, Nixon, NSC, HAK Office Files, Box 72, memcons Kissinger-Brezhnev, 21-22 April 1972.
86 NARA, Nixon, NSC, Institutional Files, Box H-233, memorandum from Laird to Nixon, 13 May 1972.
87 FRUS 1969-1976, Vol. XIV, 1023ff., here 1034f., Moscow Summit delegation memcon including Rogers and Hillenbrand, 24 May 1972.
88 NARA, Nixon, NSC, HAK Office Files, Box 74, memcon Kissinger-Brezhnev, 12 September 1972.
89 NARA, Nixon, NSC, Institutional Files, Box H-187, NSSM 138, 3 November 1971.
90 Memorandum from Rogers to Nixon, 22 December 1971, ibid.
91 Henry Kissinger characterized the CSCE as a "nightmare". NARA, Nixon, NSC, Institutional Files, Box H-110, NSC minutes, 1 December 1971.
92 NARA, Nixon, NSC, Institutional Files, Box H-110, NSC minutes, 1 December 1971. The following day, Rogers underpinned his point by writing a memorandum to Nixon telling the president that "on CSCE [...], I hope to generate a positive attitude about what the conference may be able to accomplish in opening up relations with Eastern Europe. To that end I will stress the importance of maintaining a separate agenda item covering freedom of movement of people, information and ideas." NARA, RG 59, Subject Numeric Files, 1970-1973, Box 3149, memorandum from Rogers to Nixon, 2 December 1971.
93 NSDM 142, cited above.
94 NARA, Nixon, NSC, Institutional Files, Box H-233, Interim Report of the Inter-Agency Task Force on CSCE, 20 March 1972.
95 George Vest in an interview with Oliver Bange and the author, 25 April 2005.
96 DBPO III/2, 103, memorandum from UK Embassy Helsinki, 12 March 1973.
97 NARA, Nixon, NSC, HAK Telcons, Box 19, telcons Kissinger-Rush 15 March, 10 April and 18 April 1973.
98 NARA, Nixon, White House Special Files, President's Office Files, Box 92, memcon between Nixon, Kissinger and NATO Ambassadors. The UK, Greece, Luxembourg and Denmark were represented by their Chiefs of Mission in Washington.
99 For the struggle between détente skeptics and proponents of the transformation strategy within the FCO, see *Documents on British Policy Overseas, Series III, Volume III, Détente in Europe 1972-76*, edited by Gill Bennett and Keith A. Hamilton

(London 2001). In 1975 at the latest, the British government was on the road of the Western transformation strategy.

100 NARA, RG 59, Sonnenfeldt Records, Box 8, memcon Kissinger-Gromyko, 20 September 1974.

101 Noam Kochavi, "Insights Abandoned, Flexibility Lost: Kissinger, Soviet Jewish Emigration, and the Demise of Détente", *Diplomatic History* 29.3 (2005), 503-530.

102 For a meticulous documentation on SALT II and the Vladivostok meeting in particular, see NARA, RG 59, Sonnenfeldt Records, Box 6.

103 Giusto et al., *The Road to Helsinki*, docs no. 105, 106; NARA, RG 59, Transcripts of Secretary of State, HAK Staff Meetings, 1973-1977, Kissinger staff memcons, 5 December 1974, 9 December 1974.

104 NARA, Nixon, NSC, CF Europe, Box 722, telegram from Rogers to Kissinger (No. 84507), 4 May 1973.

105 NARA, Nixon, NSC, HAK Office Files, Box 68, memcon Rogers-Gromyko, 7 July 1973.

106 However, at least from early 1973 onwards, Kissinger had two confidants at the top of the State Department hierarchy. Walter Stoessel, Hillenbrand's successor as director of the Bureau of European Affairs, and deputy secretary of state and former Ambassador to Germany Kenneth Rush were Kissinger's trusted top men in the Department of State. On Kissinger's and Rush's directive, Stoessel had regular exchanges with Vorontsov of the Soviet embassy in Washington to steer the White House linkage policy with regards to CSCE and MBFR. See NARA, Nixon, NSC, HAK Telcons, Boxes 19 and 20.

107 Kissinger, *Years of Renewal* (New York 1999), 635ff.

108 In a cabinet meeting immediately after President Ford's trip to Europe, he stated that "anyone observing from another planet would not have thought Communism was the wave of the future". Gerald Ford Library, Ann Arbor, Michigan, National Security Advisor, Memcons, Box 14, Cabinet Meeting on Ford's Trip to Europe, 8 August 1975.

109 NARA, RG 59, Sonnenfeldt Records, Box 3, memcon Kissinger-Tindemans, 1 August 1975.

110 NARA, RG 59, Secretary's Office Files, Records of Henry Kissinger 1973-77, Box 13, Kissinger's remarks before the General Advisory Committee on Arms Control and Disarmament, 6 January 1976.

The Main Task of the European Political Cooperation

Fostering Détente in Europe[1]

Angela Romano

The Genesis of the EPC and its First Task

On 1 and 2 December 1969 the heads of state and government of the six EC members gathered in The Hague for a summit that had to re-launch the process of Western European integration after the stalemate of the 1960s. De Gaulle's resignation and the more cooperative attitude of his successor to the French Presidency, George Pompidou, unlocked the EC doors to membership of Britain, Ireland, Denmark and Norway. The enlargement was coupled with – and somehow caused – farther integration: the consolidation of the Common Agricultural Policy (CAP) and its financing, which the French considered a sine qua non, and the widening of the cooperation to other fields.[2] This came to be known as The Hague ambitious triptych: enlargement/completion/deepening of the European Community.

The enlargement was also pivotal in EC efforts to face up more effectively to its international responsibilities. The Community à Neuf, with its 253 million citizens and being the biggest trade power in the world, had both the chance and the responsibility to play a more prominent role in the international arena. The Western European countries were facing challenges they could not manage effectively unless they united: East-West dialogue, commercial and monetary negotiations among industrialized countries, relations with developing countries. All these issues needed a careful study on Community interests and the political definition of values, strategic goals and tactical approaches. In addition, the new US President Richard Nixon had called the European allies to establish an actual transatlantic partnership that implied sharing of honours, duties and responsibilities. The US recognition of the existence of several centres of political power in the international scenario apart from the two superpowers – Western Europe, China, Japan – coupled with the process of détente in giving more room of manoeuvre to Western European states.

Hence, at The Hague the EC member states, not least as they all shared a feeling of anxiety about their marginality within the global scenario, decided to initiate the European Political Cooperation (EPC), in order "to prepare the way for a united Europe capable of assuming its responsibilities in the world of tomorrow and of making a contribution commensurate with its tradition and its mission".[3]

The foreign ministers were entrusted with studying practical measures to reach the aim. The resulting Luxembourg Report suggested that coordination of foreign policies would show the world that Europe had its own political mission. The Report proposed that the foreign ministers of the EC member states meet at least once every six months to discuss and try to agree on common attitudes to international problems. By endorsing the Luxembourg Report, the EC member states decided to harmonize their views, coordinate national positions and, where possible and desirable, take common actions. They committed themselves to consult each other, but not necessarily to reach agreement.[4]

Such statements and decisions were soon to be turned into action, and it is noteworthy that at the first EPC meeting in Munich, in November 1970, the EC foreign ministers agreed to devote the brand new political cooperation to the issue of East-West relations and détente. In particular, they agreed to a Belgian proposal of engaging the EPC with the Warsaw Pact proposal for a conference on security and cooperation in Europe, which was high on the agenda in the international debate at the time. Favoured by the flourishing of détente, on 17 March 1969 the Warsaw Pact Political Committee had re-launched the proposal of a pan-European security conference that it had repeatedly been asking for since 1954. NATO member states had examined it on the occasion of the Alliance's 20th anniversary meeting in Washington, and eventually had endorsed the idea at the Brussels NATO Council in December 1969.[5]

Although the Atlantic Alliance was already working on preparation for a CSCE, the EC member states decided to proceed with a parallel work on this issue. It was not simply aimed at involving Ireland, which was not a member of the Atlantic Alliance, in a close coordination on CSCE. This could, in fact, have been realized via classic diplomatic channels. The EC coordination on the CSCE was aimed at promoting the role of Western Europe as stated at The Hague and was based on substantial rationales.

Basically, although Western allies shared some premises and objectives as for the dialogue with the East, the two sides of the Atlantic differed sensibly as for approaches, interests and goals on several issues. It was a matter of fact that the previous privileged partnership between the United States and the Western European countries was deteriorating with the rise of détente, and with the US beginning to move in the global scenario as a solitary superpower. It was also clear that different economic interests and trade issues were making transatlantic relations increasingly difficult and competitive, and for this reason alone, Western Europe needed to shape more autonomously consistent responses and common positions in order to safeguard its interests.[6] Moreover, the increasing dialogue between the superpowers fostered suspicions and fears about a possible condominium and induced EC member states to protect the Community from being "squeezed by the superpowers".[7]

Two main objectives guided the EC countries in their détente policy. First, the Six had a common peculiar interest to pursue at the CSCE: the recognition of the Community and its competences by the Communist bloc and the safeguard of its future development towards a political union. The EC member states suspected that the Warsaw Pact's call for immutability of frontiers and for a collective system of security could be an attempt to halt the development of the Community towards political – and military – integration. Furthermore, the proposal for economic cooperation, and particularly the reference to the elimination of trade discriminatory practices, appealed directly to EC competences and even to EC existence. The issue gained momentum as the Common Commercial Policy had to be implemented by 1 January 1973, entitling the EC to exclusively negotiate and sign commercial treaties.

Secondly, the Western European governments had a common view on what détente had to bring about. Given the exclusive role of NATO in guaranteeing defence and security, the Six looked at détente as an opportunity to change the political scenario in Europe. In the short and mid term, détente had to improve the daily life of all European citizens and promote wider human contacts and mutual knowledge, whatever the regimes and the military alliances. After twenty-five years of peace in Europe, public opinions felt that the Cold War style was outdated and claimed a meaningful change in tones and deeds. The EC member states aimed at improving relations with the East, widening economic and cultural exchanges, starting a mutual advantageous cooperation in several fields. In the long run, they thought that this effective dialogue and the interdependence between the two halves of the Continent could overcome Moscow's mistrust and so ease the process of liberalization of Communist regimes and allow a certain degree of autonomy of Eastern European countries. Hence, Western European governments' détente had in itself a dynamic and revolutionary charge that could not be compatible with the global strategy of the superpowers, whose dialogue at the time seemed to strengthen their interest in the perpetuation of the status quo.

These rationales met the approval of the candidate states, which had been increasingly involved in the political cooperation. They became full members of the EPC before formal admission to the EC: Britain joined the Political Committee in February 1972, while Ireland, Denmark and Norway joined in May.[8] The British in particular contributed actively to EPC debates and constantly advocated "a Europe able to speak with one voice".[9]

The pan-European conference offered the ideal framework to realize these goals. Furthermore, a close coordination of the EC member states' Eastern policy provided a means to make the Federal Republic's Neue Ostpolitik part of a wider Western approach. This was not least to satisfy those partners who feared Bonn's possible swerves towards neutrality – e.g. the British government – and those who wished to contain the Federal Republic's increasing political power and share economic benefits, such as the French.[10] So it was that the promotion of détente in Europe became the first, and the main, task of the EPC. The EC member states confirmed it at the Paris Summit of 1972, when they affirmed their determination to pursue, particularly on the occasion of the CSCE, their policy of détente and peace, and the establishment of a lasting and broader economic and human cooperation with the East European countries.[11]

The EC member states scrupulously set up the EPC for dealing with every possible aspect of what was to be a common policy on détente and CSCE. Not only did they establish ad hoc mechanisms and working bodies to study the issues and formulate proposals and tactics for the conference. They also set procedures to realize a close coordination of EC members within NATO, in order to safeguard their interests and promote their proposals and points of view. And finally, they set up a precise and complete discipline aimed at effectively speaking with a single voice at the CSCE negotiations. No aspects of the CSCE adventure were left aside in the EPC détente policy.

The EPC Mechanism for the CSCE

Between February and May 1971 two special working groups were set up with the aim of dealing with CSCE issues.[12] National senior officials with expertise on NATO or Eastern Europe formed the Sub-committee on CSCE, which had to investigate all aspects of the conference likely to interest the Community from a political point of view. The Sub-committee on CSCE met for the first time on 1 March to set the agenda and assign tasks to the national delegations. It selected five main topics to examine: the attitude of the Soviet Union, its allies and that of the neutral European countries towards the Community (assigned to Germany), possible Eastern European countries' initiatives at the CSCE (Italy), possible EC initiatives on economic matters (Belgium), CSCE duration and follow-up (France), and the role of the Community at the CSCE (Netherlands).

As CSCE economic issues were likely to affect EC competence, it was necessary to involve the Commission in the elaboration of economic proposals. A few months later, the foreign ministers therefore established the Ad Hoc Group on CSCE, in which Commission officials participated together with national delegates.[13] The ministers also stated that the Commission could participate in the meetings of the other EPC Committees only when issues of economic cooperation were examined. They excluded the Commission from intervening in the decision process on other subjects. The opposition of the French government, neatly expressed by Foreign Minister Maurice Schumann stressing the qualitative difference between national political directors and Commission officials, prevented any merging between the EPC and the EC institutions.[14] CSCE studies then developed intensively within EPC Committees and produced very detailed analyzes on Soviet and Western goals, counter-proposals and proper tactics of negotiation.[15]

Coordination within NATO was part of the EPC mechanism for the CSCE. In fact, eight EPC member states were also members of the Atlantic Alliance: France, the Federal Republic of Germany, Italy, Belgium, Holland, Luxembourg, Britain and Denmark. Since the Alliance had answered to the Warsaw Pact appeal for the CSCE and was collectively preparing for the negotiations, some coordination was necessary. In May 1972 the EPC governments decided to create the Group of the Eight at the NATO Economic Committee, which convened before NATO meetings to harmonize positions and present common proposals. This arrangement would also allow the Europeans to better express the interests of the EC. In fact, the proposals of the NATO Economic Committee related to subjects of EC competences, and several important divergences had emerged between EC proposals and NATO recommendations. The latter were generally lukewarm on offers towards Eastern countries, whereas the EC member states aimed at realizing an active cooperation among the CSCE participating states. Furthermore, NATO proposals did not refer to the competence of the EC or to its existence.

This was a severe omission that could either lead to misunderstandings or provide a useful cavil to the Soviet policy of non-recognition.[16] In the autumn of 1972, on the eve of the preparatory phase of the CSCE, also the political sub-group of the eight EC member states at NATO was established. It worked in close coordination with the EPC Sub-committee on CSCE and provided an efficient means of harmonizing national positions. Moreover, the EC member states adopted specific rules and means by which to communicate the EPC documents to allies. The permanent representative of the member state holding the chair of the EC Presidency would give Allies information about ongoing studies, but not on the schedule and agenda of the EPC Committees, which were an internal question and had to be kept secret. As a result of this systematic organization, the EC member states were able to table detailed drafts and documents and to speak with a single voice. However, this close coordination caused some uneasiness to NATO allies, for EC member delegates were not much inclined to amend proposals that EPC committees had worked out.[17]

The EPC member states also refused to set a formal NATO coordination at the CSCE. The Western European governments thought that the CSCE was not and should not become a bloc-to-bloc negotiation. To present NATO-labelled proposals might risk alienating the neutral countries and strengthening discipline within the Communist bloc. The EPC governments preferred an informal arrangement, according to which a national delegation would present the proposal at the CSCE and the other NATO delegations would individually support it.[18] For EPC member states there was a difference between coordination and consultation. They thought it important and useful to keep a broad consultation within NATO throughout the CSCE, independently from agreement on common positions. Coordination, instead, meant the alignment of national positions and actions, and hence could only involve governments that already shared a strong and complex legacy, i.e. the governments of the EC.

Finally, the EC member states set up procedures of coordination to be followed at the CSCE. During the Multilateral Preparatory Talks (MPT) the Sub-committee and the Ad Hoc Group on CSCE were on permanent session and supervised the negotiations. If recommendations implied an important change of the position of the Nine or of EC policies, the delegates prepared ad hoc reports on which the governments decided before giving definitive instructions to the CSCE delegations.[19] As for the second stage of the CSCE – the very negotiations in Geneva – the French government proposed to leave a certain degree of individual initiative to national delegations, without affecting the common position.[20] As usual, France aimed at preserving at least a facade of autonomy. However, the EC partners were inflexible on keeping the coordination as close as possible. As a matter of fact, throughout the Geneva phase of the CSCE the Nine were even more aligned and organized for speaking with a single voice. The two committees on the CSCE worked on permanent session and the nine delegations in Geneva met daily to agree on the tactics. The delegation of the member state in chair of the EC Presidency provided the link between the EPC committees in Brussels and the delegations to the CSCE. The Sub-committee and the Ad Hoc Group usually worked out the proposals from national papers and contributions, and submitted the final texts for approval to the Political Committee, or the capitals, before sending them to the CSCE delegations. Fundamental political questions were analyzed by the COREPER. If the latter's opinion diverged from that of the Political Committee, the foreign ministers took the final decision, being both members of the EC Council and members of the EPC.

EPC Goals at the CSCE

In dealing with the East, and the CSCE more specifically, the EPC governments were careful in striking the right balance between caution and flexibility. On the one hand, they aimed at maintaining Western cohesion and solidarity, on which their security chiefly depended, and at avoiding unjustified euphoria in public opinion in the West that could make it difficult to pass military budget. Moreover, they wanted to make it clear that the East-West dialogue was to develop at the same time as, and without prejudice towards, the process of integration of Western Europe. In accordance with the decision of the EC foreign ministers, the aims of the EPC in the CSCE forum were to cooperate actively on détente in order to show that the EC constituted a serious partner, assess clearly EC competences on specific subjects (i.e. the commercial policy), and protect the process of Western European integration from Soviet threats and interference.[21] On the other hand, the EC countries did not neglect the opportunities that the CSCE offered for improving the situation in Europe and for trying to induce – prudently – changes in the Soviet bloc. In particular, the Western European governments aimed at making clear that they did not accept the Brezhnev doctrine and that relations between states were to be based on principles incompatible with it. Furthermore, the Western European countries wanted to promote freer movement of peoples, ideas and information, and pointed out that progress in these matters would foster cooperation in the economic and other fields that the Soviets professed to want. In all these fields, the EC members were seeking not ephemeral declarations, but agreements on practical measures of East-West cooperation.[22]

Security Issues

The main issue of the West was to frustrate Soviet objectives without appearing to sabotage détente and the CSCE itself. It was a matter of determining how hard a line to take with the Soviets, how far the West should go in spelling out what it saw as the real dangers to European security: the Soviet politico-military domination of Eastern Europe, the Brezhnev doctrine, and Soviet attempts to induce subversion in the Western European countries.

There was a general agreement that the conference should issue a declaration on principles guiding relations among the participating states. From the point of view of the Western European governments, this declaration was to be fully in accordance with international law, and was not to create a sort of regional law in Europe. Consequently, they did not want the declaration to be legally binding, or to be subject to any forms of ratification. In order to realize genuine and lasting improvement in East-West relations, it was not necessary to elaborate new principles, or to change the existing juridical order. It was rather useful to achieve a unique standard of interpretation and application of existing and well-known principles of international law, according to the spirit and the wording of the UN Charter. Above all, it was to be clearly affirmed that these principles were to be applied to relations among all states, whatever the political, social and economic system, the ideological affiliation and the belonging to alliances. The phrasing of the Warsaw Pact proposal on the renunciation of the use of force was formulated so as to suggest justification or endorsement of the Brezhnev doctrine. It stated that the CSCE declarations were not to affect in any case the obligations of the participating states deriving from bilateral or multilateral treaties and agreements. On the contrary, the whole Western definition of principles – non-use of force, territorial integrity, political independence, and peoples' self-determination – was conceived so as to delegitimize the Brezhnev doctrine. The Soviet acceptance of the applicability of principles to relations between all participating states was considered as a sine qua non: in case of refusal, Western European countries would not subscribe any declaration on principles.[23]

The Western European countries could not accept the formulation of the principle of inviolability of existing frontiers. Not only did it shut the doors to the reunification of Germany, but it also seriously affected the process of Western European integration towards a possible political union. It was of fundamental importance not to leave room for ambiguity in view of the fact that the CSCE could neither provide a substitute of a peace treaty, nor neglect the possibility of peaceful changes of borders according to international law and by agreements of the parts involved.

Apart from defensive provisions, Western European countries introduced in their proposal on principles an essential element of Western democratic culture and philosophy: the principle of respect of human rights and fundamental freedoms. Reversing Soviet priorities, upon which détente was first and foremost a question of relations among states and could only later relate to individuals, the Western European governments argued that wider human contacts were as important as economic cooperation and disarmament measures in fostering the relaxation of tension between the blocs and promoting peace and security.[24] This argument was the key point of the EPC conception of détente. One might say that all EC governments shared and endorsed the basic rationales of the Federal Republic's Neue Ostpolitik.

Cooperation in Economics and other Fields

In May 1971, the Political Committee settled the principles guiding the attitude of the EC member states on trade issues and economic cooperation at the CSCE and, more generally, in the East-West dialogue. The member states were to develop their commercial relations and economic cooperation with the Eastern countries in respect of their EC obligations. Prior to this, the development of such relations and cooperation was not to slow or prejudice the development of the Community. The EC member states excluded any option of buying recognition. The Community did not depend on recognition by third countries, and this was a matter of fact with which the Communist countries had to come to terms. Notwithstanding Soviet hostility, it was evident that Moscow also looked for a new relationship with the Western European states in order to gain economic advantages in the form of industrial and consumer goods supplies, cooperation in energy and natural resources, access to Western financial credits and technology to modernise its economy.[25] So did the Eastern European countries, which had adopted a more realistic attitude and, in some cases, a de facto recognition of the Community. Poland, for instance, had established contacts aiming at an agreement on cotton textiles. Bulgaria, Hungary, Poland and Romania had entered into technical agreements with the Commission on aspects of agricultural trade. And Romania had formally approached the Community to request a beneficiary status in the EC scheme of generalized preferences.[26] The recognition of the Community was on the way, but the Soviet Union wanted to lead the process. Secret contacts between the secretary of COMECON and the European Commission had in fact been taking place since 1972 and always on Soviet request.[27] The Kremlin aimed at EC-COMECON relations that could help preserve a strong control over its allies. The Community, on the contrary, preferred bilateral dealings with individual countries, for COMECON had not the same competences, and the Nine did not want to help the Soviet Union strengthen its control over Eastern Europe.[28]

The CSCE seemed to be the right occasion for improving the relations with the Communist countries, and the Nine studied how to get the best out of it. The optimum was to select some subjects of EC competence likely to appeal to the Eastern countries, match their interests and lead them to a more pragmatic attitude. An appealing and balanced offer on cooperation, and an open-minded and forthcoming attitude to the Eastern countries, both within and outside the context of CSCE, could persuade them that the Community was neither a danger nor a threat, but a convenient partner to cooperate and trade with.[29] The Ad Hoc Group listed the offers that the Community could propose at the CSCE to meet some of the Communist countries' concerns: formal application of the Most Favoured Nation clause, adjustments on quota restrictions, lowering of the customs duties, and credits from the European Investments Bank. As the Nine had chosen not to make unilateral concessions, their proposal was based on the concept of reciprocity. The Eastern European countries had to contribute to the removal of obstacles to East-West trade. More specifically, they were to introduce greater price rationality, facilitate business contacts, provide additional information on import and export plans, put an end to arbitrary changes in trade flows and improve administrative, fiscal and legal conditions for Western private firms operating with the East.

With regard to cooperation in the energy field – mostly oil and natural gas – the Communist countries could earn indispensable credits, investments and technology, while the EC states could reduce their dependency on Arab suppliers. Aiming at a wider circulation of goods and persons, the EC member states also looked favourably at cooperation in transports.

While the Eastern European governments advocated the realization of big infrastructure projects, the EC countries aimed at the reduction of existing barriers and proposed coordinated political action to rationalize and harmonize national procedures.[30]

In addition to elaborating economic proposals, the Nine decided to give the Community full visibility at the conference. At the Copenhagen meeting in September 1973, the EC foreign ministers decided to openly involve Commission representatives in the CSCE delegation of the member state in chair of the EC Presidency. As clearly stated at the beginning of the second stage in Geneva, Commission officials would "express the points of view of the Community to the extent required by the EC competence and procedures". According to EPC decisions, the delegations to the CSCE had to make crystal clear that the offer was on behalf of the EC and that implementation would depend on agreement with it.[31]

Freer Movement of People, Ideas and Information

The Nine also agreed on proposals and tactics to promote their idea of détente. The huge, detailed amount of proposals they tabled at the CSCE to this aim related to what came to be known as Basket III. Actually, the EC-Nine introduced similar provisions in the proposals on Basket II – cooperation on economics, science and technology. The intention of the Nine was "to see the question of freer movement permeate every aspect of the Conference".[32] The emphasis on human rights and humanitarian measures, and also on the dissemination of information and ideas, was justified in terms of a "people first" approach to détente: East-West agreement was to bring about concrete benefits to individuals, in their private and professional lives.

As a general principle, the Soviets could have some difficulty in accepting the freer movement of people as a matter of negotiation at the CSCE. Indeed, they had accepted "contacts among people" as an appropriate goal of a CSCE in the 1971 Pompidou-Brezhnev declaration. Similarly, the Danish-Soviet Communiqué of 5 December 1971 stated that the CSCE should promote, inter alia, "the contacts between human beings, which are one of the preconditions for the mutual trust upon which a lasting peace in Europe must be based". The Western Europeans thought it possible to engage the Soviets in a serious discussion by introducing specific proposals with reasonable argumentation and avoiding to the extent possible unnecessary polemics.

The FRG presented the most cautious position. Concerned with achieving results in its Eastern policy, Bonn did not want to give the Soviets any reasons for intervening à la Prague 1968. German Foreign Minister Walter Scheel even proposed to include the freer movement issue in the list of principles guiding relations among the participating states, instead of proposing a specific point on the CSCE agenda.[33]

The French government invited allies not to expect great results on this topic, but left no doubt on the importance it gave to human contacts proposals. Paris thought that the best way to act was to present sober proposals that might induce gradual improvement of the existing situation. At the MPT, the French suggested, it was advisable to present the issue in such moderate terms as to make it difficult for the Communist countries to reject or dispute the proposal. The debate would therefore occur during the conference itself.[34]

The British government gave much relevance to the freer movement question and wanted the CSCE to debate practical measures of improving the quality of life of European citizens. For this reason, the British did not want to engage in an ideological wrangle with the Communist delegations, and fully supported the French point of view on tactics and phrasing.[35]

The Dutch government presented the hardest approach to the subject, and tried to exploit the American support within NATO for a tougher uncompromising position. After a long and harsh debate on the issue, the Dutch delegates had to reconcile with the EPC common position. The French formula prevailed, stating that the CSCE was "to bring about closer, more open and freer relationships between all people in Europe; to stimulate a wider flow of information and of ideas". The sober definition "human contacts" substituted the bolder "freer movement" phrasing.[36] It is important to state clearly that, according to archival sources, Western European governments' action on the promotion of freer circulation of people, information and culture was not meant to dismantle the Communist regimes or to engender revolutions within the Eastern European countries, for such an attempt would probably cause Soviet intervention. The question was to accept the divide of the continent in order to make the iron curtain more porous and let peoples of Europe know and meet each other. The Western European ministers did believe that, in the long run, such contacts would spread the contagion of liberties, but they assumed, and hoped, that the change would be peaceful and develop from within the socialist bloc, first of all from a change of mind in the Soviet leadership.[37]

Conclusion: A Successful Performance and a Lasting Habit

The performance of the EPC at the CSCE was certainly successful. First, the EC-Nine were able to gain the recognition of the Community – even if it was de facto – and secure its future development from external interference.[38] The specific mention of the possibility to change frontiers "in accordance with international law, by peaceful means, and by agreement" unlocked the way both for German reunification and Western European political union.[39]

In addition, the Nine proved to be united when expressing their voice on non-EC topics. In 1972 it became clear that the United States would not engage in a leading role and had no intention to press for the freer movement proposals. Moreover, as negotiations went by, the US government increasingly showed signs of impatience to bring the conference to an end as much as the Soviets did. This attitude could only disappoint the Nine, which realized that it was up to them to lead the fight on Basket III. The Nine stuck to their requests. They resisted all Soviet attempts to introduce references to national laws and customs in order to escape Basket III provisions. The Western European delegates slowed down the work of the other commissions to prevent negotiations in Basket III from falling behind. They also refused to agree to a top-level final phase until concrete results had been reached on human contacts and they even threatened not to convene the third phase if the Soviets kept refusing to make concessions.[40] They eventually reached their aims. Principle VII on human rights and fundamental freedoms featured in the Decalogue as well as Principle VIII on peoples' self-determination, both asserting a clear rejection of the Brezhnev Doctrine and the primacy of individuals. Furthermore, concrete measures were adopted to realize a freer movement of people, information and ideas, with no reference to consistency with national laws. Basket III provisions may seem nothing more than words, but lack of compliance with the Final Act would be under everybody's scrutiny, thanks to the Soviet desideratum for a solemn signature ceremony. The Final Act was meant to be a locus standi for those citizens, within and outside the Communist countries, who wanted to promote reforms and the normalization of human contacts in Europe. The East-West dialogue had brought about agreements on the core issues of the Continent. It had as well to improve peoples' living conditions. That was the Europeans' détente.

Finally, business-like negotiation on Basket II – cooperation in the fields of economy, industry, science and technology and others – engendered a promising atmosphere and settled the guidelines for future negotiations with the Communist countries, in which representatives of the EC Commission would participate.

Detailed preparation, excellent and timely coordination throughout the conference, careful tactics and tough style of negotiation were the elements of the Nine's successful action.

The Soviet leadership was surprised and deeply impressed by the performance of the Nine. At the end of May 1973, Willy Brandt sent a secret note to the president of the EC Commission, giving his impressions on a recent meeting with Brezhnev. What impressed the chancellor most was that Brezhnev no longer used the term "Common Market", but that he referred to the "European Community". Furthermore, the Soviet leader asked whether the Soviet officials, when negotiating with the German firms, would have to go to Brussels. In Brandt's opinion, the Soviets had started to realize the concrete consequences of the EC common commercial policy. He did not believe this could have immediate consequences, but he noticed that a revision process had started in the Kremlin about attitudes towards the Community.[41]

The EC member states made détente and cooperation with the East a permanent task of their political cooperation.[42] To this aim, they set up within the EPC the Group of Experts on Eastern Europe, which had to study Eastern countries' possible reaction towards the integration process, contingent and potential.[43] After its report, the Nine charged the Commission with elaborating an offer on commercial negotiations to the COMECON states, which was presented in November 1974.[44] The member states decided to keep the Group of Experts on work as a forum of reflection and analysis over EC-East relations. On 10 September 1975 the Venice European Council decided to carry on the political cooperation and speak with one voice on issues related to the Final Act and CSCE follow-up meetings.[45] The Nine also acted unanimously within the Economic Commission for Europe (ECE), where they took the leadership of the Western group, as much as they did during the CSCE. Last, but not least, the political cooperation notably increased among the member states' embassies in Eastern countries.

Unlike the superpowers' détente, the dialogue and cooperation between the two halves of the Continent did not experience a crisis after Helsinki, but grew more intense and diversified. Many events suggest that the Nine had no intention to affect détente and its benefits for the sake of the global competition of the two superpowers. For example, Moscow's unwillingness to implement the Final Act provisions on human contacts and its repressive policy towards dissidents led the US delegation to the CSCE follow-up meeting in Belgrade (1977) to protest loudly and hamper any possibility of dialogue. Although the European allies shared such criticisms, they associated to the neutral and Communist countries in blaming the American attitude. It was evident that two years after Helsinki, where they had been the most active and intransigent negotiators on human contacts issues, Western European governments considered it more convenient not to create tensions with the Communist bloc that could endanger détente and prevent the cooperation from going further.

When the Soviet Union invaded Afghanistan, the Western European governments did not back the American embargo. On the contrary, the EC countries' exports to the USSR increased. Western Europe traded heavy machinery and precision equipments for Russian raw materials, particularly oil.[46] By 1982 US trade with the Soviet Union reached just $2.5 billion, a tiny fraction of Western Europe's $41 billion business with Moscow. Even more significant was the Siberian gas pipeline affair. In 1980 French, German and Italian governments began negotiations with the Kremlin for a 3,000-mile natural gas pipeline from eastern Siberia to Western Europe. The European states agreed on the financing of the mammoth project, and obtained the possibility to pay for the gas in their own currencies, thereby bypassing the unstable dollar.

When General Jaruzelski imposed martial law on Poland in December 1981, the EC-10 foreign ministers' joint declaration on 4 January 1982 condemned Moscow for placing "serious external pressure" on Poland, but it stopped short of assigning any direct role to the Soviets. Chancellor Schmidt and Foreign Minister Genscher of the FRG were very active in contesting the US sanctions and in finding alternative and more sensible solutions.

All these examples suggest that the EPC approach to détente and the CSCE – the strategy of fostering mutual advantageous cooperation and interdependence – lasted after Helsinki and helped the European states to preserve détente in the Continent and overcome the Cold War division of Europe.

Notes

1. This article is based upon sources from the following archives: Historical Archives of the European Union, Florence (EUHA), the EU Council Archive, Brussels (EUCA), National Archives, London (NA), Archives du Ministère des Affaires étrangères, Paris (AMAE), United States' National Archives and Record Administration (NARA) and Nixon Presidential Materials Project (NPM), College Park, MD, and Gerald Ford Presidential Library, Ann Arbor, MI (FPL).
2. See *Journal of European Integration History*, vol. 9, no. 2 (2003).
3. EUHA, FMM 37, *The Hague Communiqué*.
4. EUHA, FMM 37, "Rapporto dei Ministri degli Affari Esteri ai Capi di Stato o di Governo degli Stati membri delle Comunità Europee, 20 luglio 1970 e adottato definitivamente il 27 ottobre 1970".
5. *NATO Declaration on European Security*, Brussels, 5 December 1969. In accepting the idea of a security conference, NATO member states settled some preliminary conditions for convening the conference: a successful conclusion of the *Ostpolitik* treaties, a satisfying quadripartite agreement on Berlin and the start of negotiations on force reductions in Europe (MBFR).
6. NA, FCO 28/1684, Tel. from FCO to Sir E. Peck (UKDEL NATO), London, 12 May 1972.
7. NA, FCO 41/1061, Tel. from Sir E. Peck (UKDEL NATO) to Mr Tickell (WOD), Brussels, 29 February 1972; NPM, NSC Country Files, box 679, folder 2 (1 of 2), Tel. no. 30644 from AmEmbassy Paris to SecState Washington, "The French view of US-Soviet *Détente*", 29 November 1973.
8. EUHA, FMM 52, "Relations avec les pays de l'Est (séance du 20 mars 1972)".
9. AMAE, Série Europe 1971 – juin 1976, Sous-série: Organismes Internationaux et Grandes Questions Internationales; Dossier No.2925: CSCE – novembre-décembre 1972. Tél. no.5464/70 de AmbaFRA Londres, "CSCE – Préliminaires d'Helsinki", le 19 décembre 1972; Tel. No.441 from Mr Hildyard (UKMIS Geneva) to Sir A. Douglas-Home, "Meeting of Political Directors: CSCE/EEC", London, 14 February 1972, Document no. 50 in *Documents on British Policy Overseas, Series III*, Volume II, *The Conference on Security and Cooperation in Europe 1972-75*. London, The Stationery Office 1997.
10. NPM, NSC Country Files, box 677, folder 2 (1 of 3), NSC paper, "France in 1971"; NPM, NSC Country Files, box 678, folder 1 (1 of 3), Memorandum for Kissinger, "Georges Pompidou and France's role in world affairs", 18 January 1972. See, for example, Wolfgang Wagner, "Basic requirements and consequences of the Ostpolitik", *The Atlantic Community Quarterly*, vol. 9, no. 1 (spring 1971). For a complete and detailed analysis of the relations between the two countries, see Georges-Henri Soutou, *L'alliance incertaine. Les rapports politico-stratégiques franco-allemandes 1954-96* (Paris 1996).
11. EUHA, FMM 59, Final declaration of the Paris Summit, 20 October 1972.
12. AMAE, série: Europe 1944-70, sous-série: Organismes Internationaux et Grandes

Questions Internationales 1966-70, dossier 2031, MAE, "Echanges de vues sur la CSE à la réunion ministérielle de Munich le 19 novembre (coop. Politique)".

13   EUHA, FMM 37, Commission, SEC(71) 2362: "Problèmes de la CSCE. Initiatives possibles des Communautés Européennes".

14   EUHA, FMM 37, Commission, Compte rendu sommaire, "Discours de M. Schumann à la Commission Politique du PE", Bruxelles, le 16 juin 1971.

15   EUHA, FMM 36, "Rapport du Comité politique sur la CSCE", Rome, 4 novembre 1971; Commission, SEC(72) 3304 final, "Conférence sur la Sécurité et la Coopération en Europe. Proposition pour une position des Communautés Européennes (Principes politiques)", and Commission, SEC(72) 3304 final/2, "Conférence sur la Sécurité et la Coopération en Europe. Proposition pour une position des Communautés Européennes (Volét coopération)", Bruxelles 9 octobre 1972.

16   EUHA, KM 47, Commission, SEC(72) 2052, "Remarques au sujet de certains documents préparés par le secrétariat général du Conseil Atlantique pour le Comité économique de ce Conseil", Bruxelles, le 7 juin 1972.

17   AMAE, série: Europe 1971 – juin 1976, sous-série: Organismes Internationaux et Grandes Questions Internationales, Dossier 2925, Tél. No. 787/793, "Discussion au sein de l'Alliance Atlantique sur l'o.d.j. de la CSCE et les mandats des commissions", Copenhague, le 17 novembre 1972; NA, FCO 41/1055, Tel. no. 361 from FCO to UKDEL NATO, "CSCE", London, 16 November 1972.

18   AMAE, série: Europe 1944-70, sous-série: Organismes Internationaux et Grandes Questions Internationales 1966-1970, Dossier 2031, Lettre collective n. 33/EU du MAE, "Conversations avec les Américaines sur la sécurité européenne", Paris, le 13 avril 1970.

19   AMAE, série: Europe 1971-juin 1976, sous-série: Communautés Européennes, Dossier 3819, Coop.pol.eu., RM(73) 3 P, "Rapport du Président du Comité Politique aux Ministres", le 12 mars 1973.

20   AMAE, série: Europe 1971-juin 1976, sous-série: Communautés Européennes, Dossier 3819, Circulaire no.416 du MAE, "Comité Politique des Neuf. Helsinki – 5-6 juillet – CSCE", Paris, le 10 juillet 1973.

21   EUHA, FMM 36, "Réunion des Ministres des Affaires étrangères à Munich, 19 novembre 1970".

22   AMAE, série: Europe 1971-76, sous-série: Organismes Internationaux et Grandes Questions Internationales, Dossier 2900, Conseil de l'Atlantique du Nord, Document C-M(71) 75, "Les tendences enregistrées en Union Soviétique et en Europe de l'Est – Leurs incidences dans le domaine politique", Bruxelles, le 29 novembre 1971.

23   AMAE, série: Europe 1971-juin 1976, sous-série: Organismes Internationaux et Grandes Questions Internationales, Dossier 2921, DELFRA au Conseil de l'Atlantique du Nord, "Travaux du Comité politique à niveau élevé – Doctrine Brejnev", Bruxelles, le 1er avril 1971.

24   NARA, RG 59, Telegram n. 4325 from US Mission NATO to Dept. of State, 24 August 1972.

25 AMAE, série: Europe 1944-70, sous-série: Organismes Internationaux et Grandes Questions Internationales 1966-70, Dossier 2034, Tél. no. 500-502, "Lien établi par M. Kossyguin entre la réunion de la CSE et le développement de la coopération économique", Moscou, le 21 janvier 1970.

26 EUHA, FMM 36, "Rapport du Comité Politique consacré à la Conférence sur la Sécurité et la Coopération en Europe", Paris Ministerial Meeting, 13-14 May 1971, EUHA, EN 1996, UK Draft Paper: "Relations between the EEC, CMEA and their respective member countries, including the attitude of the Eastern countries to European integration", 1972.

27 Angela Romano, "Behind closed doors. Contacts between EEC and CMEA in the early 70s", in Carla Meneguzzi Rostagni (ed.), *The Helsinki Process: A Historical Reappraisal* (Padova 2005), 107-122.

28 EUHA, FMM 36, Réunion des Ministres des Affaires étrangères: "Discussion sur la CSCE", Paris, le 14 mai 1971.

29 EUHA, FMM 37, Commission, SEC(71) 2362, "Problèmes de la CSCE. Initiatives possibles des Communautés Européennes"; EUHA, FMM 53, British contribution to Ministerial meeting of candidate states and the Commission, "External Relations and Responsibility of the Community", 20 March 1972.

30 EUHA, FMM 36, Commission, SEC(72) 3304 final/2, "Conférence sur la sécurité et la coopération en Europe. Propositions pour une position des Communautés Européennes (Volét Coopération)", Bruxelles, 9 octobre 1972.

31 EUHA, KM 48, COM SEC(73) 3280, "Présence de la Commission pendant la 2ème phase de la CSCE", Bruxelles, le 13 septembre 1973.

32 NA, FCO 30/1251, Record of the Anglo-Swedish Discussions on the CSCE, London, 24 August 1972.

33 Letter from Mr Tickell (WOD) to Sir G. Millard (Stockholm), "Conference on European Security (CSCE): Coordination with the neutral countries", FCO, 6 June 1972, Document no. 10 in *Documents on British Policy Overseas, Series III*, Volume II.

34 AMAE, série: Europe 1971-juin 1976, sous-série: Organismes Internationaux et Grandes Questions Internationales, Dossier 2923, le Ministre à M. l'Amb. de France repr. Permanent de la France auprès du Conseil de l'Atlantique du Nord, "A/S: Discussion au Conseil atlantique sur le Chapitre de l'o.d.j. de la CSCE consacré à la coopération culturelle et aux contacts entre les hommes", Paris, le 10 avril 1972.

35 NA, CAB 133/429, Record of the Brandt-Heath meeting on April 21, 1972, "Conference on European Security".

36 Communiqué of NATO Ministerial Meeting, Brussels, 8 December 1972.

37 Memorandum of Conversation, "Visit of the Prime Minister to Paris 19-21 May 1971" File: CAB 133/422. National Archives, London, UK.

38 Angela Romano, "The Nine and the Conference of Helsinki: a challenging game with the Soviets", in Jan Van der Harst (ed.), *Beyond the Customs Union: The European Community's Quest for Completion, Deepening and Enlargement, 1969-1975* (Brussels 2007), 83-104.

39 *Final Act*, Principle I.
40 AMAE, série: Europe 1971-juin 1976, sous-série: Communautés Européennes, Dossier 3819, "Rapport du Président du Sous-comité CSCE sur les problèmes à résoudre", Bruxelles, le 8 avril 1974; NPM, NSC Country Files, box 708, folder 2, Tel. No. 3226 from US Mission Geneva to Secretary of State, "CSCE: Proposed EC-Nine Demarche to Soviets on Possible Adjournment of Phase II", 22 May 1974; Minute from Walden to Tickell, "CSCE: Human contacts", FCO, 16 April 1973, Document no. 31 in *Documents on British Policy Overseas, Series III*, Volume II.
41 EUHA, EN 1287, Lettre de Willy Brandt à Emile Noël, Bonn le 24 mai 1973.
42 AMAE, série: Europe 1971-juin 1976, sous-série: Communautés Européennes, Dossier 3799, Note du MAE pour M. Arnaud: "D'une politique commune à l'égard des Pays de l'Est", Paris, le 5 février 1974.
43 AMAE, série: Europe 1971-juin 1976, sous-série: Communautés Européennes, Dossier 3799, MAE, Circulaire No.112: "Comité politique des 6/7 février – Rapport du groupe des Pays de l'Est", Paris, le 11 février 1974.
44 AMAE, série: Europe 1971-juin 1976, sous-série: Communautés Européennes, Dossier 3799, Tél. No. 3986-99, DELFRA: "Conseil des 14-15 octobre 1974 – Relations avec les Pays à commerce d'état: préparation de l'offre communautaire de négociations commerciales", Bruxelles, le 18 octobre 1974.
45 EUCA, File 6544, Extrait du Journal Officiel des Communautés Européennes n°194/128, en date du 9/75 – Parlement Européen, PV de la séance du 24 septembre 1975.
46 Robert S. Jordan (ed.), *Europe and the Superpowers: Essays on European International Politics* (London 1991), 129-131.

Bridging the Gap between East and West

The N+N as Catalysts of the CSCE Process, 1972-1983

Thomas Fischer

The recently awakened historical interest in the Conference on Security and Cooperation in Europe (CSCE) has shed new light on the role of the neutral and non-aligned states (N+N) in European Cold War history.[1] The emerging Helsinki Process in the 1970s for a first time provided these states with the possibility to actively participate and engage in a multilateral process dealing with the core issues of European security.[2] During the original CSCE conference leading to the Helsinki Final Act in 1975 the N+N developed a remarkable dual role as *negotiators* (actively contributing to the discussions on the content of the agenda, e.g. Confidence Building Measures, peaceful settlement mechanisms, human rights, follow-up) and *intermediaries* (catalysts of the negotiation process by performing administrative tasks and seeking for compromises).

However, the changing international setting towards the end of the decade also left its mark on the N+N. In a renewed Cold War atmosphere the room to manoeuvre narrowed considerably for the N+N, and their role in the first follow-up meeting to Helsinki in Belgrade in 1977/78 was mainly reduced to mediating between the blocs and trying to keep the Helsinki process alive. This function became even more important at the second CSCE follow-up meeting in Madrid during the years 1980-1983, where only the stopping of the clocks at the end of the pre-conference on 10 November 1980 could prevent the talks from total failure before they had even started. At several points in the course of the Madrid meeting, the negotiations completely stalled over international events (Afghanistan, martial law in Poland) and all heads would turn towards the N+N in expectation that they would "do something". According to various contemporary witnesses the lifeline of the Helsinki process in the early 1980s depended more than ever on the mediating role of the N+N.[3]

This chapter will exclusively focus on the role of the N+N states as *intermediaries* and *catalysts* of the CSCE process. For this reason, individually and commonly sponsored proposals by these states concerning the content of the talks are only analyzed where they deal with matters related to the procedural side of the conference (work organization and administration, follow-up) or where they were seeking for compromise between East and West. Well-known initiatives such as the Swiss project for a peaceful settlement mechanism, the Nordic and Austrian promotion of CBM, as well as the Yugoslav proposal on minority rights are therefore excluded from the scope of this study.

In the first part of this chapter, I will show how the neutral and non-aligned states established their role and influence in procedural matters and in bringing about a first major compromise between the blocs during the original CSCE talks in Helsinki and Geneva in the years 1972 to 1975. In the second part, the influence of the N+N states as promoters of the first follow-up conference in Belgrade 1977/78 is analyzed, while the third part scrutinizes their importance for the continuation of the Helsinki process during the difficult years of the Madrid meeting from 1980 to 1983. Using new multi-archival material and extensive oral history gathered in the course of a three-year research project on the neutral and non-aligned states in the CSCE,[4] the chapter ultimately tries to assess the long-term meaning of the neutrals' engagement for the CSCE follow-up mechanism and their intermediary services between East and West in an atmosphere of renewed Cold War in Europe in the late 1970s and early 1980s.[5]

The Original CSCE 1972-1975

It is well known that neutral Finland through its CSCE initiative of 5 May 1969 has been instrumental in making the originally Soviet idea of an all-European security conference an acceptable concept to East *and* West in the early 1970s.[6] The four European neutrals (Austria, Finland, Sweden and Switzerland) subsequently in bilateral talks during this pre-conference phase widely agreed that the role of a catalyst would most likely fall to them in the CSCE, and that they should make the broadest use of the forum to strengthen their image and role as mediators in the big power game.[7]

Securing a Strong Position in the Talks

When the Multilateral Preparatory Talks (MPT) began at the Dipoli Conference Centre in the Helsinki suburban area of Otaniemi on 22 November

1972, the neutrals immediately undertook a number of concerted efforts and interventions to manifest their role and to secure their future influence in the talks.[8] The basis for their prominent role at the opening of the conference was laid by the general adoption of two important basic principles for the European security talks: 1) All states would participate in sovereign and equal rights; 2) Decisions at the conference could only be taken by consensus.[9] The smaller delegations with their active involvement in the first meetings about procedural matters made sure that these principles were respected and that the CSCE would not just become another military alliance affair in the European Cold War.

After the Finnish hosts had designated their State Secretary Richard Tötterman as president and Ambassador Jaakko Iloniemi as permanent vice president of the talks (to be elected), Romania vigorously protested against the arrangement in the opening session of the MPT and demanded a daily rotating chairmanship with president and vice president coming from different countries. The Swiss, who shared the Romanian discomfort about the Finnish tandem, which very much resembled a permanent conference secretariat, proposed a compromise with a permanent Finnish president but a rotating vice-chair. The Swedish Ambassador Göran Ryding sitting next to his Swiss colleague supported this scenario, and the Austrians in turn emphatically backed a subsequent Romanian amendment to apply the principle of rotation of the chair in future working groups. In this way, the Swiss, in close coordination with the Romanian delegation and together with the help of the skilfully placed interventions of the Swedish and Austrian delegates, were able to secure the influence of the smaller delegations in procedural matters at this early stage of the conference.[10]

A further development helped to promote the neutral states' position as catalysts of the negotiations in Dipoli when it came to the so-called "operation basket" during the discussion of the future conference agenda. In the course of December 1972 a great number of proposals were formally or informally put forward by the participating delegations. The delegations had agreed on a three-stage conference as a "working hypothesis" on 12 December 1972, with an opening stage I at the end of the Dipoli-talks on the level of foreign ministers, followed by stage II, where a final document would be negotiated by the diplomatic delegations, which would then be signed in a closing conference by the heads of states and governments in stage III. This final stage, it was later decided, should be held in Helsinki again.

By the end of 1972 the delicate task of grouping all proposals under a definite agenda had yet to be tackled. Considerable differences between East and West were still to be overcome.¹¹ When the talks in Dipoli resumed after the Christmas break on 15 January 1973, the delegations began to definitively lay out the proposals for the agenda and terms of reference for future committees of the conference. While the copyright for the much applauded creation of four "baskets" as a means to group the diverse agenda items without prejudicing the importance of any single subject is still disputed,¹² it is clear that the Austrian and Swiss delegation were among the main actors when it came to elaborating and organizing the conference agenda.

As documents from the German Foreign Ministry Archives illustrate, the Austrian delegate Helmut Liedermann had already proposed on 11 December 1972 that the Finnish Chairman Richard Tötterman draw up a "list" to which ambassadors could add their agenda suggestions. One day later, the Swiss Ambassador Samuel Campiche "seized the Dutch and Austrian proposals of previous sessions" and suggested to group the agenda items into four main "chapters" ("political problem", "follow-up and Mediterranean", "economic cooperation", "human contacts").¹³ On 17 January 1973 the Swiss delegate re-invoked his country's proposition of 12 December that "all representatives of the participating states without exception nor restriction of any kind and based on the principle of equality should submit to the agenda the points they wished to see discussed, this [procedure] stipulating a vast exchange of ideas."¹⁴ The very next day Swiss Ambassador Samuel Campiche in his intervention seems to have coined the term "baskets" in the discussion on the agenda.¹⁵ It was then the Austrian delegate who (in close coordination with the British delegate) formally suggested using baskets marked with numbers at the plenary session of the MPT on 23 January to proceed with the agenda setting.¹⁶ The Swiss were meanwhile encouraged by the European Community members to prepare a catalogue of proposals so far submitted to the agenda and the terms of reference.¹⁷

In the end, it was Spain which formally suggested on 24 January 1973 that Switzerland should be asked to prepare the synopsis of all the documents collected into a compendium. Switzerland accepted this task and presented its compendium as a working paper on 29 January. The document of nearly thirty pages grouped the proposals into four numbered baskets, dealing with: I) political and security matters; II) economic and related issues; III) human contacts, culture and information; IV) follow-up to the conference.¹⁸ In conclusion, the neutrals, particularly Austria and Switzerland, clearly gained influence and a higher profile during the talks in Dipoli through their initiatives to establish a conference agenda by using and expanding the concept of baskets. But even more importantly, they contributed decisively to creating a framework that would allow for the negotiation of a final document of the CSCE signed two years later in Helsinki.

Coordinating the Agenda

During the subsequent preparation of the so-called "Helsinki blue book" summarizing the recommendations of the Dipoli talks, the neutrals developed further influence through an important administrative task in the coordination of these negotiations. After a three-week break in February 1973, France had proposed the creation of a working group of all delegations to speed up the work on the conference agenda. The Soviet Union instead demanded the formation of four such groups, one for each basket.[19] The compromise consisted in the establishment of a single working group dealing with the four baskets one after the other, starting with Basket I. The working group began its consultations on 1 March 1973 (applying the principle of a rotating chairmanship according to the Austrian proposition of November 1972), but the set-up with a working group embracing all delegations negotiating in six languages immediately proved to be too cumbersome. Therefore, the Swiss delegate on the second day proposed the creation of smaller informal working groups for the further drafting of documents. Following the Swiss proposal, each of these so-called Mini-Groups would consist only of a very limited number of delegates in order to make them more manageable and to accelerate the task of drafting texts for the final recommendations.

Despite initial resistance from the EC countries, the Mini-Groups would soon become an effective instrument. As informal working groups they were not subject to the formal rules of procedures and the principle of rotation of the chair. Instead, the three neutral states Austria, Sweden and Switzerland were assigned the task of coordinating the work of the Mini-Groups on a constant basis. The Swiss were to become coordinator of a first informal group on the problems of political security, a second Mini-Group on confidence-building measures was soon afterwards entrusted to a Swedish coordinator, and Austria performed similar functions in the drafting of a text for Basket II. This task not only won the neutrals wide support and acceptance as catalysts of the talks but also prepared the ground for the future N+N cooperation in the Geneva phase of the conference and in the subsequent Helsinki process.[20] After the Mini-Groups had helped the working group to proceed with Basket I and II issues, the working group finally began to draft a mandate for Basket III in April 1973. In this final round of negotiations in Dipoli from late April to early June the neutrals – now for the first time together with non-aligned Yugoslavia – were again the driving force.

After the CSCE negotiations had moved to Geneva in September 1973 for stage II of the conference, the Soviet position on Basket III (namely on human contacts and the information issue) clamped down again. They were trying to get back control over the concessions made to the West in previous deliberations. For the first time a situation arose where the great powers would only confide in the neutrals to unblock the discussions. The Swiss delegate Edouard Brunner, who had won a reputation for successfully co-ordinating the first Mini-Group in Dipoli, in a first attempt at the end of October 1973 instigated the creation of informal working groups similar to those in Helsinki to start work on the texts for the final document. In view of the sensitivities of East and West concerning Basket III this work should be considered only "pre-drafting". When his proposal found no support with the bloc members, Brunner, a few weeks later, demanded a repetition of "operation basket" (starting with an inventory and catalogue) for Basket III.[21]

This time the work should not be entrusted to a single coordinator, but be organized by four delegations, each responsible for one of the four sub-chapters of Basket III (human contacts, culture, information, education). The Swiss had proposed two neutral states (Austria for human contacts, Sweden for education) as well as a Western country (France for information) and an Eastern bloc member (GDR for culture) for the tasks, while the Swiss delegation would overlook the whole operation. The idea was generally welcomed but the West specifically disapproved of the GDR taking responsibility for the sub-chapter culture. But if the GDR was not integrated, then the participation of France had to be dropped as well. In the end it came down to the four neutrals again to fill out the coordinating function; Austria and Sweden kept their original assignments, Switzerland took over the information chapter and Finland – now devoid of its self-restrained position as host during the MPT – the culture issues. This important role assignment for the neutrals in the coordination of the drafting sub-commissions of Basket III continued throughout the Geneva phase.[22] By consistently mediating in informal meetings between Eastern and Western representatives on their delegations' premises in the building of the European Free Trade Association just opposite the CSCE conference venue in Geneva, the neutrals in the end became the official sponsors of most texts concerning Basket III of the Helsinki Final Act.[23]

The N+N Package Deal in the Summer of 1974

A particular problem arose when the negotiations on the preamble of Basket III started in early spring 1974. At that point the so far separate discussions on the different baskets had to be accorded with regard to the catalogue of CSCE principles that in the meantime had been established in Basket I.[24] In this discussion the Soviets once more tried to get back what they had conceded in the negotiations on the respect of individual human rights in Basket III by giving the principle of non-interference in internal politics priority over these provisions. The Western Europeans on the other side were fiercely fighting not to let the battle for Basket III become a Pyrrhus-victory. As a result, the CSCE negotiations almost completely stalled for several weeks. This situation led to what is normally referred to as *the* moment of glory for the N+N states during the Geneva phase of the negotiations in their role as intermediaries and lifeline of the conference.

After several weeks of political haggling in early summer it was a package deal promoted by the neutral and non-aligned states in July 1974 that broke the deadlock between East and West and opened the way for a final round of negotiations, which ultimately led to the signing of the Final Act the year after. The neutrals later took much pride in bringing about this compromise, and the deal added to their reputation as "honest brokers" and their future standing as accepted "go-betweens" in the conference. It is interesting, however, to take a closer look at the origins and the evolution of the package deal operation of summer 1974, since it clearly illustrates the conditions and restrictions under which the N+N were able to mediate between East and West in the European security talks.

Generally, the story goes that the neutral compromise of July 1974 was inspired by a first compromise formula proposed on the preamble to Basket III by Finland on 4 June in Geneva.[25] The Finnish head of delegation, Ambassador Jaakko Iloniemi, in an interview with the author confirmed that he sometime in May 1974 got instructions from Helsinki to propose a compromise, but as he remembers the first text conveyed to him by his Foreign Ministry was so obviously in favour of the Soviet side that it would have no chance of finding acceptance in the West. He therefore cabled back to Helsinki to get different instructions, which then led to a useful first draft for a compromise that could be worked upon and presented by the N+N as a group proposal in July to give it more legitimacy and lever.[26] Documents of the Finnish Foreign Ministry Archives and the memoirs of former Foreign Minister Kalevi Sorsa make it clear that the Finnish initiative was indeed a Soviet inspired move to get the conference out of the limbo.[27] However, what is even more surprising is the revelation that the deal did not originate from Moscow alone but sprang from direct superpower talks on the highest level between US Foreign Minister Henry Kissinger and his Soviet counterpart Andrei Gromyko outside the CSCE in early May.[28]

As a document from the US National Archives shows, Kissinger and Gromyko had already agreed on a compromise deal in the CSCE when they met on 7 May 1974 for talks at the Presidential Palace in Nicosia, Cyprus, in the context of the problems in the Eastern Mediterranean.[29] At that point, the two superpowers had obviously come to the conclusion that it was now time to come to an end of the negotiations and close the European security talks with a final document. However, Kissinger knew that his Western European allies would never accept the necessary horse-trading with the East if proposed by the US at that stage of the conference. Gromyko stood under similar restrictions from the Moscow bureaucracy and within the Warsaw Pact alliance. Hence, the two men drew up a scenario, where Gromyko would suggest the Finns to take the initiative and propose a compromise along the lines already agreed beforehand by the superpowers:[30]

> Kissinger: On European matters? First, let's talk about the European Security Conference. As I understand it, what is holding up agreement on Basket III is the notion of what country should advance it. I understand it will be Country X, say Finland. We will accept whatever solution Country X proposes but we do not want to propose it.
>
> Gromyko: Do you have any idea?
>
> Kissinger: We think perhaps Finland.
>
> (…)
>
> Gromyko: All right, maybe Finland, maybe Finland. Somebody should approach them.
>
> (…)
>
> Kissinger: We have one other tactical problem with Basket III, Mr. Foreign Minister. When Kovalev talked with Sonnenfeldt and Hartmann [Soviet and US delegates at the CSCE], he adopted the tactic somewhat borrowed from our Geneva discussion – to start with a proposal somewhat less favourable than the position

we agreed on, and then the Soviet Union would make concessions. But if we choose Country X, we would have to give them more or less the same language.

Gromyko: Yes.

Kissinger: If the Soviet Union were to do it, we would play it like the Berlin negotiations, and move slowly towards it.

(…)

Gromyko: What do you think?

Kissinger: Our idea is maybe you should approach Finland. But let me check in Washington how to proceed. It is a bureaucratic problem. I will let you know by the end of the week. Through [the Soviet Ambassador in Washington Anatoly] Dobrynin.

Gromyko: Or your Ambassador [in Moscow].

Kissinger: (…) Let me sum up our understanding: that Country X will be Finland, that you will approach it, and we will support it. We may not come right out and say we support it, but you will understand. We do not want to appear to be pressuring our allies.

And thus the game was played… The solution forwarded by the N+N package deal denied a specific reference to the principle of non-interference in the preamble of Basket III – as claimed by the Eastern side; but on 11 June it proposed a general reference in the Basket III preamble to the *whole* catalogue of principles of the CSCE. At the same time the West agreed to include an additional sentence to principle I (sovereignty) stating: "The participating States respect each other's right to choose and develop its political, social, economic and cultural systems as well *as its right to determine its laws and regulations.*"[31] To counter this concession again another sentence concerning national laws and regulations was drafted for principle X (fulfilment of obligations under international law): "In exercising their sovereign rights, including the right to determine their laws and regulations, *they will conform with their legal obligations under international law*; they will furthermore pay due regard to and implement the provisions of the final document(s) of the CSCE."³² With this addition the provisions of Basket III would not only be carried out with respect to the principles of national sovereignty and non-intervention in internal affairs (as advocated by the Soviets), but also in keeping with the principles of respect for human rights and fundamental freedoms, and fulfilment of international obligations (as demanded by the West). Thus both sides saved face and had reason to believe that Basket III could not be interpreted in a one-sided fashion. The package deal was provisionally registered on 26 July 1974 to be adopted definitely once the last operative parts of the Helsinki final document had been deliberated by consensus.³³

The American delegate John J. Maresca describes how the neutrals proceeded in June and July to bring forward the package on the principles and Basket III:

> To lay the groundwork, neutral delegates first contacted key delegations privately, then formulated their proposal. They presented a first draft to separate, informal gatherings of Eastern, Western, and independent delegations, then sought to improve on their draft to make it fully acceptable. Both East and West moved reluctantly.³⁴

According to Renk, the neutrals had put the alliance members under additional pressure to adopt the strategic trading between Baskets I and III by threatening to suspend their coordinating activities in Basket III if they would not move. The N+N were thus able to use their administrative influence to foster compromise on the substance of the talks.³⁵ But as the document cited above shows, the neutrals mainly became an important player in finding a way out of the conference impasse in spring/summer 1974 because the superpowers needed a third actor to transform their general wish to close the CSCE negotiations with a compromise acceptable to all sides.

More generally speaking, any compromise was easier to accept publicly for the military alliance leaders if it came from a group of neutral small states than from a bloc member. The limited possibilities of the N+N to catalyze the negotiations *on their own initiative* became clear only a few weeks later. After the summer break when the CSCE reconvened in September 1974, the quarrel over the final provisions of Basket III resurfaced. Throughout September and October the Soviets stonewalled again on a central issue in the Third Committee. The neutrals, and according to a British source namely the Swiss diplomat Brunner, were soon "toying with the idea of a [second] package deal with Basket III."³⁶ However, the Soviets, this time, clearly discouraged such an effort.³⁷ This later episode illustrates the restricted room for the N+N to actively manoeuvre the conference when no compromise by West *and* East was wished for.

Commitment to the Follow-up

Besides their important contribution to catalyzing the CSCE negotiations by performing administrative tasks for the conference and acting as intermediaries between East and West, the neutral and non-aligned states were also instrumental on a third level: Until spring 1974 the conference had clarified much of the details concerning Baskets I–III but had hardly started any discussion on Basket IV, that is, how to proceed with the talks once the original conference would have accomplished its aim of establishing a final document. So far only a Czechoslovak proposal on that question had been officially deposited. At this point the neutral and non-aligned states began to strongly advocate the clarification of the terms for a follow-up mechanism of the CSCE.³⁸

The original Soviet proposal to create a permanent consultative committee dealing with the follow-up had always been refused by the West, which did not want the institutionalization of the conference to avoid a blockade of such a permanent organ similar to the situation in the UN Security Council. The Czechoslovak proposal of 18 October 1973 had already tempered down the Soviet proposition by demanding the creation of a consultative committee that would not deliberate on a permanent basis but only *each time its members deemed it necessary*. The West, however, was still displaying a "wait-and-see" attitude and first wanted to conclude the final document of the Geneva talks; only after that would they be ready to enter the discussion about the form of a follow-up. A possible next conference was not yet envisaged for the next three years by the Western states. This position was officially represented by a Danish proposal of 26 April 1974 propagating a testing phase after the signing of the Helsinki Final Act in order to verify the compliance with the provisions of the document. Only after successful "probation" should a follow-up of the CSCE be agreed to by the West.

The Yugoslavs had already tried to revive the debate on the follow-up with a proposal of 28 March 1974,³⁹ which – based on the Czechoslovak position – stipulated the establishment of a "continuing committee" for the follow-up, yet demanded that the committee meet *at least once a year*. The committee should consist of representatives of all participating states and would have the task of verifying, coordinating and enlarging the Helsinki cooperation.

Eventually, it would also decide on the convening of a new conference. A Finnish proposal of 7 June 1974 was drafted along the same lines, but in addition required that a first follow-up meeting should be convened no later than twelve months after the conclusion of stage three of the original conference.[40] At that time the other neutrals also started to support the idea of a follow-up.[41] With the most important Basket III provisions secured, a possible succession of the Geneva-Helsinki talks in their eyes was no longer in danger of becoming a one-way street favouring the East. On the contrary, the follow-up to the CSCE would allow the West to exert a certain influence in the Eastern part of Europe, which could in turn enlarge the Eastern European states' room to manoeuvre with regard to the Soviet Union. At the same time a clearly defined follow-up would allow the neutral and non-aligned states to keep their influence established during the Geneva negotiations on the multilateral level of European security talks, as a British source observed:

> The neutral and non-aligned countries would like to be sure of being able to maintain their active role in the multilateral process of détente after the CSCE. For this reason they want to have an institutional follow-up in the form of a permanent East-West Forum since this would enable them to play the role they will have played at the CSCE and would to a certain degree shield them from the attempts by the USSR to pressurise them.[42]

However, until early 1975 the discussion in Geneva on the follow-up bogged down and opposing attitudes in East and West prevailed. The Swiss head of delegation had predicted already in 1974 that "the follow-up would become subject of the final big 'deal', which would be brokered in the very last nights before the conclusion of the Geneva negotiations under the impression of ultimate nervousness."[43]

On 16 April 1975 Yugoslavia and Finland called an informal meeting of the N+N together with Poland, Romania, Norway, Spain, Great Britain and Canada to discuss the progress of the working group on the follow-up. The Swedes and the Finns had previously tried to break up the Danish proposal by minimizing the waiting period for a next follow-up conference, and now the Swiss delegate Brunner once more tried to advance things by proposing a small informal working group that should investigate the hardliners' positions.[44] The Swiss further tried to mediate between the Danish and the Finnish drafts by informally circulating a compromise proposal on 14 May, which envisaged the establishment of at least a certain periodicity of future meetings. However, the proposal was still met with resistance.[45]

By that time, the discussion on the follow-up had become an almost religious debate between East and West. Partly because of this "unholy alliance" of the big powers, the N+N were unable to advance their position of "periodicity but no institutionalisation" as a basic formula for the follow-up.[46] On the other hand, rivalries within the N+N group – notably between Finland and Yugoslavia over the question where to hold a first follow-up meeting[47] – impeded a commonly sponsored proposal on the issue. The N+N were put to a further test, when Malta, during the very final round of negotiations in Geneva, almost totally obstructed the conclusion of the final document with its demand to give the non-participating Mediterranean states more influence in the future CSCE meetings. This incident clearly reverberated negatively on the ability of the N+N to broker a compromise in the working group on the follow-up.[48]

Thus Bindschedler's prediction held true and the text that was finally registered in the chapter on the follow-up of the conference was a typical CSCE compromise between Eastern and Western demands. It clearly indicated that the reticent view on institutionalization held by Western countries had prevailed over the more ambitious views held by the N+N. At least an opening date for a preparatory meeting to the first follow-up meeting in Belgrade was set for 15 June 1977, which was then to decide on the date, duration, agenda and other modalities for the conference itself. The only institutional link between successive meetings of the Belgrade type made in the Final Act was the following sentence: "This meeting will define the appropriate modalities for the holding of other meetings which could include further similar meetings and the possibility of a new Conference."[49]

Despite the fact that the N+N states did not achieve an ultimate breakthrough on the follow-up question in the Helsinki Final Act, it was during this phase of the CSCE negotiations that the neutrals "through a process of the appetite growing as one eats, and through exchanges of ideas among themselves"[50] became increasingly convinced that the follow-up was in their very own interest as well as in that of Europe as a whole. This was of considerable importance when it came to defining their role for the first follow-up meeting in Belgrade in 1977/78.

Belgrade 1977/78

The first follow-up meeting in Belgrade would become an important precedent for regular CSCE gatherings – as envisaged by the N+N in the Geneva negotiations, at which the implementation of the Helsinki Final Act's provisions would be examined and new proposals discussed. Yet, as the debate on the follow-up mechanism in Geneva had shown, the continuation of the Helsinki process was anything else than guaranteed at the time of the opening of the Belgrade talks. While the N+N were in favour of an elaborate continuation mechanism, they had also come to realize during the negotiations in Geneva that their individual proposals and requests had few chances of success unless they were able to form a strong consensus among each other. Consequently, the neutrals and non-aligned started a closer coordination in anticipation of the Belgrade meeting immediately after the closing of the Helsinki ceremony. In fact, Geneva and the Helsinki summit had raised rather high hopes with the N+N that they would be able to take on a new role in the follow-up meeting, focusing more on their potential as negotiators than on their function as go-betweens for the two blocs.[51]

Disappointed Hopes for a New Role

However, when the thirty-five states met again in Belgrade between 15 June and 5 August 1977 to prepare the follow-up conference, the N+N soon realized that the overall atmosphere had changed. The unhappy omen of totally disrupted relations between Moscow and Washington was looming over the talks. Little was left of the spirit of the superpower détente of the early 1970s. Soviet military interventions in Africa, the end of the "Kissinger era" in US foreign policy, followed by a rhetorically more aggressive human rights policy by the new government of President Jimmy Carter, and a first stalemate in strategic arms limitation talks (SALT) were all hampering a positive development of US-Soviet relations by 1977.

The US so far had considered the CSCE a sidekick of its foreign policy activities. Now they decided that this forum would provide the perfect ground to test the Soviets. President Carter made the Belgrade review conference a top priority and wished for a rigid examination of human rights standards in the East. The USSR in return criticised US foreign policy for its interference in internal Eastern affairs and was anxious to keep the Belgrade meeting as brief and its final recommendations as non-committal as possible. Questions regarding human rights should be excluded and only military aspects and economic cooperation discussed. Given the prevailing circumstances none of the more than one hundred proposals that had been prepared by the various delegations for the Belgrade meeting was endorsed by all participating states and no substantial document was issued in the end. The conference turned instead into a fierce battle of words between the superpowers over the implementation of the Helsinki provisions with regard to human rights.[52]

Under these circumstances the hopes of the N+N states for an enhanced role as contributors to the Helsinki process were bitterly disappointed. Against their own intent, the N+N were once more restricted to the role of mediators between the two military alliances.[53] Already at the preparatory meeting in the summer of 1977 it was only thanks to their efforts that a compromise on the procedure of the upcoming conference could be established and the official talks could finally be opened on 4 October.[54] In bilateral contacts of the Swiss with the Americans in Washington at the end of August 1977, the "active and useful role"[55] played by the N+N during the preceding weeks in Belgrade was appreciatively lauded by the US side, giving a clear indication that the Americans further counted on the N+N as helpful intermediaries for the anticipated debate with the East at the upcoming main conference in Belgrade. Indeed, throughout the following months the N+N could never fully develop their potential role as originators of new initiatives to the conference, but had to concentrate constantly on limiting the damage caused by the dispute between Washington and Moscow.[56]

During the first phase of the conference – which lasted from October to November 1977 and was dedicated to the debate on the implementation of the Helsinki Final Act provisions in the participating states – the N+N took up a firm critical position towards the Eastern states, similar to that of the Western states. Contrary to the latter, however, the neutral and non-aligned formulated their criticism in a more conciliatory way by renouncing to blame individual governments.[57] Instead, they tried a "constructive" criticism by using the following phase of the talks to introduce and establish new standards to the final document of the Belgrade meeting. A first result of this ambition was the provision of a four-page long document in December 1977 summing up the N+N proposals as a basis for the plenary talks on the concluding document, which would start after the Christmas break.[58] Despite the optimism displayed in a report of the Swiss delegate Hans-Jörg Renk of January 1978 – stating that so far the N+N indeed had been able to play a role beyond their traditional intermediary activities and that it should be possible for them to become the "motor" of the talks in Belgrade[59] – these expectations would be disappointed during the second phase of the conference.

A Soviet draft for a final document presented at the opening of phase two in January 1978 simply omitted *any* of the proposals previously made by the other delegations, be they Western, neutral and non-aligned or Eastern![60]

In reaction the N+N, on 1 February 1978, tried to impose the basis for a final document with a comprehensive catalogue of *all* substantial provisions proposed so far.[61] In the attempt to save the substance of the talks, the conference once more resorted to smaller working groups coordinated by the four neutral states and Yugoslavia. They were to deal with the most disputed aspects of the different proposals.[62] This attempt by the N+N to broker a final document based on their own position paper, however, failed dearly. Its failure was mainly owed to the fact that the informal "non-paper"[63] of the N+N in many aspects did not represent a balanced intermediary position between East and West but was rather a reflection of their own ideas on the most disputed issues of the conference, which were often close to the Western position.[64] The "westward" character of the N+N paper is also evident from the fact that on 16 February it was a French proposal that tried to find a compromise between this document and the Soviet paper![65] Yet, the French initiative was to no avail either.[66]

The Soviet Union simply declined a discussion of any substantial precisions of the Helsinki Final Act in the remaining weeks of the negotiations and in the end stopped its participation in the working groups. No individual proposal was able to achieve consensus. Apparently some of the members of the N+N group at the very end would have been ready to abandon a large portion of the substance of their proposal to achieve a compromise between East and West. Yet, this only led to a dispute within the group in the final days of the conference.[67]

The text of the final recommendations was ultimately negotiated bilaterally between East and West and in essence merely repeated the basic assumptions of the Helsinki document. The only important point all participating states on the day of the closing of the Belgrade meeting on 9 March 1978 agreed upon was the convening of another follow-up meeting to be scheduled for 1980 in Madrid.[68] Despite their intensified preparation and stronger cohesion within the group during most of the Belgrade talks, the N+N were neither successful in their intermediary function nor in working towards a substantial final document.

Keeping the Process Alive

Considering the difficult state of affairs in world politics, it was already an achievement that the Helsinki process was kept alive at all – an achievement the N+N could at least claim some credit for. Already during the preparatory conference to the Belgrade meeting, the N+N had made clear that the CSCE follow-up was to be not only precisely defined, but from the very outset conceived it as an automatic and self-sustained development over many years, covering an unlimited number of meetings. At that early stage of the Belgrade talks they had resisted all attempts to play down the importance or the time-perspective of the follow-up process.[69] Yet, in the pared-down version of the concluding document of the Belgrade meeting of 8 March 1978 the periodicity of the follow-up meetings was dropped from the text:

> In conformity with the relevant provisions of the Final Act and with their resolve to continue the multilateral process initiated by the CSCE, the participating States will hold further meetings among their representatives. The second of these meetings will be held in Madrid commencing Tuesday 11 November 1980 [70]

As Leo Mates writes, during the last days of the Belgrade meeting the expectations of the N+N countries had reached the lowest ebb and already agreement on an opening date for the next follow-up conference and the notion of "further meetings" were considered a success:

> They [the N+N] stopped thinking of the Belgrade meeting as a step forward. They were now interested only in saving it as a possible bridge from the sombre present to the hopefully brighter future. It was essential to secure the undisturbed flow of the follow-up process, to secure a meeting in Madrid.[71]

These hopes expressed by the N+N reflected their continued belief in the CSCE and were a sign of their determination to further work for this process despite their disappointment with the big powers in Belgrade.

Madrid 1980-83

When the preparatory talks for the second follow-up conference in Madrid opened on 9 September 1980, the overall situation was by no means easier than two years before in Belgrade. On the contrary, since 1978 the process of détente between East and West had further degenerated. The Soviet intervention in Afghanistan on Christmas Day 1979 was just the most visible sign of this deterioration. After Carter had suspended the ratification of the SALT-II agreement in congress in the summer of 1980 and plans for a nuclear rearmament of NATO in Europe were made public, American-Soviet relations had reached a virtual nadir. Mutual distrust and a general perception of a renewed Cold War dominated the atmosphere. Given these general circumstances and with the Belgrade experience in mind it was clear that the N+N role in Madrid would be mainly restricted to mediating between East and West.

Providing a Way out of the Limbo of the Preparatory Meeting

While the West in the preparatory meeting for Madrid again demanded a broad debate on the implementation of the Helsinki Final Act (notably to criticise the Soviet intervention in Afghanistan and the disrespect for human rights standards in Eastern Europe), the East openly threatened to walk out of the talks if this discussion was not limited to an absolute minimum. A total failure of the follow-up meeting was therefore imminent before it had even started, and "as usual in such CSCE situations all eyes would turn to the neutrals"[72] to find a way out of the stalemate. As the Swiss delegate Petar Troendle reported, "the Soviet delegation treated us separately and the US and other Western States claimed to be in dire need of an initiative from the neutrals to at least unblock the preparatory meeting."[73]

While the Swiss delegation at that point had instructions from Berne to stay firm in line with the West on the issue of the implementation debate,[74] Sweden on 8 November declared its readiness to present an individually sponsored informal paper to help the discussion out of the deadlock – after the other neutral delegations in Madrid had stated their basic support for the initiative.[75] However, despite the intensive activities by a number of delegations trying to build a consensus on the Swedish proposal no solution was found until 10 November.[76] Only the stopping of the clock on this final day of the preparatory talks a few minutes before midnight prevented the second follow-up meeting from a premature break-up and gave the delegates some extra time to establish a working programme for the conference.

During the night of 10 to 11 November 1980 the Austrian delegation circulated a new compromise text on the agenda and timetable,[77] and the Spanish foreign minister explored with the US, Luxemburg, Netherlands and Soviet delegation every possibility of agreement. Yet, the Soviet head of delegation Yuri Dubinin repeatedly recalled previously made concessions in the course of this process so that the head of the American delegation told the press on 11 November that prospects for a conference were bleak. In the end the Western delegations did not allow this scenario to go on forever, and on the evening of 11 November decided to abandon the fiction of the stopped clock to allow the Spanish government the opportunity of opening the main meeting on the date that had officially been set two years earlier.⁷⁸

The foreign ministers of the participating states had come to the Spanish capital to officially open the talks of the second CSCE follow-up meeting. But they had to do so without any pre-defined agenda, and the conference still desperately needed a way out of the limbo. The Spanish Foreign Minister Felipe Gonzalez opened the Madrid meeting twenty minutes before midnight on 11 November, and announced that at 12 p.m. a working group under Spanish chairmanship including the Soviet Union, USA, Norway, West and East Germany as well as neutral Switzerland and Austria would start to push forward discussions on the agenda for the meeting and that the next plenary session would begin at 11 a.m. the following day.⁷⁹

Meanwhile numerous informal negotiations on a possible compromise had taken place between official sessions. The NATO and Warsaw Pact caucuses had settled down in separate parts of the congress building and sent out "messengers", making use of the Swiss delegation as go-between, who in turn acted as a link to the group of neutral and non-aligned states.⁸⁰ Building on these services, the Swiss head of delegation Edouard Brunner and his Austrian counterpart, Franz Ceska, in an N+N group meeting in the afternoon of 12 November decided to force the two blocs to accept a compromise stipulated by the N+N. By 13 November East and West had come relatively close to agreement in the working group but still demanded certain omissions and amendments. While the Western wishes were finally included in a slightly alleviated form, the Eastern demands were consciously ignored when the N+N presented their ultimate proposal for an agenda to the conference that same day.⁸¹

To highlight the dramatic situation, Brunner and Ceska decided that their compromise paper should be explained to the public by the foreign ministers of the N+N countries present in Madrid in a press conference as a "last offer" to both sides.⁸² If this take-it-or-leave-it option was not agreed upon, the conference would have to be postponed for another year. After three days of lingering, this diplomatic manoeuvre by the N+N finally worked according to plan and on 14 November the talks in Madrid could get started properly.⁸³

According to the N+N compromise, which was officially registered as CSCE/RM 2, the debate on the implementation of the Helsinki Final Act provisions was to be limited to the six weeks before the Christmas break, whereas the rest of the time should be dedicated to the discussion of new proposals. More precisely, the implementation debate was to last until 19

December and was to be followed by the examination of new proposals in the new year until 11 February. The subsequent redaction of a final document should take no longer than until 5 March 1981.⁸⁴

Mediating between East and West

While the situation between East and West was already strained during the initial weeks of the debate in Madrid due to the Soviet invasion in Afghanistan, the situation turned from bad to worse over Christmas 1980. Not a single day would pass without mentioning the Afghanistan issue when the talks re-opened in Madrid, and, additionally, the crisis in Poland began to take centre stage in early 1981. The frontlines between East and West became ever more inflexible in the CSCE discussions. Irreconcilable opinions at that time were hindering any progress, notably with regard to the debated issues of Confidence Building Measures (CBM) and a possible CSCE conference on Disarmament in Europe as proposed by the Swedish government. The neutral and non-aligned states in the general debate mainly sided with the West in their accusation of Soviet policy, while Moscow could only count on the unconditional support of a very limited number of allies – namely the GDR and CSSR.⁸⁵

It was the Austrian Foreign Minister Willibald Pahr who tried to unblock the situation with a personal initiative. On 24 February 1981 Pahr invited the governments of Sweden, Yugoslavia and Switzerland to consider a common initiative of the N+N countries to save the conference from failure.⁸⁶ CBM and the project of a Conference on Disarmament in Europe, his argument went, were a common interest of their states, and without further progress on the central issue of disarmament the USSR would never be ready to compromise on human rights issues and the free flow of information as demanded by the West. While the Swedish and Yugoslav Ambassadors to Vienna concurred with Pahr's view, the Swiss Ambassador Iselin took a more sceptic stance. The rather negative attitude of the Swiss Foreign Ministry resulted from the conviction that *first* the Soviets had to re-establish trust by complying with the (human rights) standards of the Helsinki Final Act. Only then should the other delegations consider give-and-take in the talks on a Conference on Disarmament. As the head of the Swiss CSCE delegation Brunner stressed, this was not a general unwillingness of the Swiss delegation to work out compromises, but at that stage a Conference on Disarmament in Europe would simply lead nowhere in his opinion.⁸⁷

Despite these differing views, the Swiss Ambassador in talks with Pahr in

Vienna declared his country's readiness to participate in a secret meeting of the four foreign ministers of Sweden, Austria, Yugoslavia and Switzerland in March to further discuss the issue of mediating between East and West in Madrid. The Swiss Foreign Minister Pierre Aubert, Iselin stated, had already taken on other obligations for the proposed date of 14 and 15 March, however, and would therefore be replaced by Ambassador Brunner in the talks.[88] According to Brunner himself the differences between the four neutral and non-aligned states on how to proceed in Madrid were overcome in this secret gathering and a common strategy was envisaged to bring the conference forward with a new proposal by the N+N.[89]

This proposal was presented on 31 March 1981 by the N+N (without Malta) as a first basis for the closure of the conference. The informal *nonpaper* summed up the points that had already found consent among the participating states and ignored all proposals known to be strictly resisted by either East or West. On the basis of this paper, it was then possible to form five informal contact groups, each coordinated by a member of the N+N, to continue negotiations after the Easter break on the outstanding issues, which were: Amendment of the catalogue of principles (Finland), disarmament and CBM (Sweden), economic relations (Yugoslavia), follow-up and preamble (Switzerland), and human contacts (Austria).[90]

Despite the success of the Austrian initiative to break the deadlock, the conference was soon to fall into another lull in the summer of 1981. Again negotiations stalled over questions of the implementation of human rights standards and the free flow of information, CBM parameters and the CSCE disarmament conference.[91] In July the Swiss delegate Brunner reported from Madrid that both sides wished for a longer break of the conference – until November of that year – to explore new compromises and had asked the N+N to introduce a proposal for adjournment accordingly.[92] While the conference officially took recess for a long summer break, the delegations of Austria, Finland, Switzerland and Yugoslavia in the following weeks further tried to find a solution in informal bilateral contacts with the bloc states.[93] Since these efforts led to nothing, the N+N in early October invited three delegations, of each East and West, to informal talks on their premises in Madrid "to sketch in the furthest limits of each side's willingness to compromise in order to define what was politically feasible."[94]

In fact, the Swiss head of delegation Brunner had received positive signals from the Soviet side in bilateral talks in Moscow on 13 and 14 October to continue the mediating efforts of the N+N. The Soviet Deputy Foreign Minister Leonid Ilichev had also asked Brunner to transmit a message to the US delegate Max Kampelman confirming the basic Soviet will to sign a concluding document of the CSCE negotiations.[95] Having conveyed the message to the American delegate the very next day Brunner remembers a secretly held meeting between Kampelman and Ilichev in Madrid soon after to discuss things face to face.[96]

After the summer break the general atmosphere in Madrid had improved somewhat, not the least because Western fears that the Soviet Union would intervene in Poland had not materialized. According to Zielinski it was now the Austrian delegation which took the lead in sounding out Warsaw Pact and NATO countries on the most disputed issues. In November the Austrians presented a new draft for a closing document of the Madrid talks in a synthesis of Eastern and Western positions.[97] The proposal was first tabled for discussion within the N+N group, which considered the chances of acceptance to be real and was ready to give it the status of an official N+N proposal.[98] The time for compromise for a first time seemed ripe in early December 1981.

Yet, when the Austrian paper was officially presented to the conference on 16 December 1981 and was registered as CSCE/RM/39, international events had toppled the N+N agenda once more. On 13 December General Jaruzelski imposed martial law in Poland and a few days later everything fell to pieces again in Madrid. Under the impression of world-wide protests against the situation in Poland, Ilichev on 17 December officially withdrew previous Soviet support for CSCE/RM/39 and the conference had to recess again over the Christmas break without result. When the meeting in Madrid re-opened on 9 February 1982, most Western and neutral states refused to resume the talks until the violations of the Helsinki Final Act in Poland had been rectified. Following a proposal launched by the Swiss Foreign Minister Aubert on 10 February in his official address to the Madrid meeting,[99] the French and Austrian delegations officially demanded to adjourn the CSCE negotiations until the international situation had cooled down to a level where discussions between East and West would become possible again.[100] On 12 March the conference finally decided to break for eight months and agreed to reconvene on 9 November 1982.[101]

Bridge-builders for a Final Compromise

Once more the N+N tried to make use of the break to find a procedural solution that would help the conference out of the gridlock: On 28 and 29 August 1982 the foreign ministers of the nine N+N states met in Stockholm, where they decided to prepare a second draft for a final document based on their December 1981 proposal.[102] In a first step they intended to forward the talks in Madrid after re-opening by resorting to the instrument of informal Mini-Groups, which should deal with the unresolved issues one after the other. Until Christmas 1982 the informal work in these Mini-Groups – once again coordinated by the N+N – had reached a point where the heads of delegations of the N+N were ready to discuss final tactics to officially table their new proposal. In a separate group meeting in Berne at the end of January 1983 they agreed that now either a quick ending would have to be found to the negotiations based on their proposal or they would cease their mediating efforts and the conference would have to be interrupted for several years. According to Sizoo and Jurrjens their initiative was generally greeted with enthusiasm in East and West,[103] and when the CSCE delegates were re-convoked to Madrid for 8 February, the neutral and non-aligned states were optimistic that this would be the very last phase of a conference that had already "lasted too long".[104]

On 15 March 1983 the N+N proposal for a final document was officially introduced to the conference and registered as CSCE/RM/39revised. Six of fourteen additional Western demands to the original N+N proposal had been included in the compromise paper while the most disputed of these points, which the Soviets had threatened to veto, were omitted.[105] With an appeal initiated by the Finnish Prime Minister Mauno Koivisto, some of the heads of government of the N+N states a few weeks later on 18 April tried to gain agreement on their proposal from the bloc states. In a letter to the conference they declared that the N+N did not only consider their proposal a basis for further negotiations but a "last attempt" from their side to bring the conference to a meaningful end. This initiative, however, again spurred dissent within the N+N group, a dissent that had already appeared during the early phase of the conference. Switzerland and Liechtenstein were not ready to sign the letter. The Koivisto initiative was suspected to be a Moscow inspired move and the manoeuvre was considered a one-sided attempt to pressure the NATO countries into a compromise that clearly favoured the East. Instead, Switzerland and Liechtenstein at that point sided with the US position that declared the N+N document a fairly good basis – albeit not yet the final version – for a last round of negotiations.[106]

The East in an expected change of strategy accepted CSCE/RM/39revised on 6 May 1983 on the condition that no changes at all would be made – thereby putting pressure on the Western and the N+N states to sign this paper in its current form as a final document. But the West and the dissenting N+N countries still insisted on at least four amendments (on a specific wording, on the prohibition of radio jamming, on calling a meeting of experts on human contacts, and on clarification of the mandate for a European Disarmament Conference). The Soviet delegation, however, showed no inclination to re-open negotiations on any of these amendments and the stalemate in Madrid lasted for another two months.[107]

In a very last attempt to cut the Gordian knot, the Swiss delegate Brunner together with the newly elected Spanish prime minister and host of the talks, Felipe Gonzalez, in May 1983 tried to formulate another draft for the final document, once more seeking for compromise between the Western and the Eastern positions. On 17 June Gonzalez presented the thirty-five delegations his proposal as an ultimate compromise and called upon all participating states to come to a conclusion of the meeting. The "deal" prepared by Brunner and Gonzalez on the basis of RM/39rev. envisaged a renunciation of the Western demand on radio jamming (so far an American "must") in return for Eastern agreement to an expert reunion on human contacts to be held in Berne. To smooth the way for Moscow into this compromise without loss of face, the plan for an expert level meeting was not mentioned in the final Madrid document but in a separate annex to it. In addition, the proposal contained a fixed date and place for the opening of the disarmament conference in Stockholm in 1984. On the basis of this document a last minute failure of the conference could ultimately be prevented by July 1983.[108]

The Soviet Union had initially refused the Gonzalez compromise, claiming the original N+N paper of 15 March was the utmost they were ready to agree to, but the West after internal consultation concurred with the amendments on 24 June. Finally the East gave in as well, and on 15 July agreement by all major powers to the Gonzalez-proposal was reached.[109] The six weeks it would still take until the signing of the final document in September 1983 were solely owed to the fact that Malta tried to blackmail the conference into acceptance of its demand for a future CSCE meeting on security and cooperation in the Mediterranean. The manoeuvre failed when the other delegations after some time signalled the Maltese that if they continued their obstruction, the conference would be resolved and reconvened the next day with thirty-four states, leaving Malta out completely.[110] From 7 to 9 September the representatives of all thirty-five states finally met for the signing ceremony of the concluding document for the Madrid meeting.[111]

Conclusions

By analyzing the role of the N+N in the original CSCE conference and in the first two follow-up meetings in Belgrade and Madrid, it becomes evident that the N+N were mainly important to East and West in their position as go-betweens and catalysts of the CSCE process. Whenever the talks at the conference would stall, all heads turned towards the N+N in expectation that they would "do something". Despite their hopes for a certain role change in Belgrade (emphasizing the role as initiators and negotiators of their own proposals rather than the position as "honest brokers"), the N+N soon had to realize that their role at the CSCE was mainly decided by the state of relations between the two military alliances in East and West. Within that limited field of manoeuvre the N+N consistently performed important services as bridge-builders for new ideas and as mediators of compromises to bring the talks forward and save the follow-up of the process. This was most obvious in the early 1980s in a tense atmosphere of renewed Cold War.

In this period the N+N were providing the Helsinki process with a much-needed lifeline guaranteeing the continuation of the exercise through their mediatory services. With the benefit of hindsight this function was particularly important when assessing the long-term effect of the so-called Helsinki networks on the ending of the Cold War. Without the continuity of the official CSCE process in form of the follow-up meetings of Belgrade and Madrid these political movements would have lacked the necessary platform and media attention to stage their demands with regard to a change in the political system of the East. Notably the Swiss and Austrian heads of delegation, Edouard Brunner and Franz Ceska, repeatedly acted as "lubricants" for the stuttering motor of the negotiations in this crucial period and saved the talks from disruption more than once until the international atmosphere in the mid-1980s changed to a more favourable situation for direct talks between East and West.

The N+N as a group was by no means a homogeneous circle in this process. They were rather a loose coalition of states with similar interests, which were acting individually or on group level depending on the issues and positions at stake. Regarding its mediating function, there existed a certain "natural" division of labour within the group, notably among the four neutral states: the Finns usually reflected the Soviet position with high accuracy and the Swiss were considered the best informed on the Western camp, while the Austrians and Swedes played arbiters between these positions. This pre-figuration of the conference structure often helped in finding acceptable solutions for all sides, but as this study shows it also provoked dissent within the N+N over how to proceed every now and then.

The firm and consistent commitment of the whole N+N group to the CSCE follow-up in combination with their readiness to accept the intermediary position, when the bloc powers were seeking for compromise, provided the conference with very important services that only this group of states could perform. It is probably in this role at the CSCE that the N+N contributed most to the overcoming of the Cold War in Europe in the long run.

Notes

1   The CSCE was in fact the only time in Cold War history that the neutral and non-aligned states defined their positions as a unified group actor within a multilateral framework. The N+N group consisted of the following nine countries: Austria, Finland, Sweden, Switzerland, Yugoslavia, Malta, Cyprus, San Marino, and Liechtenstein.

2   Thomas Fischer, *The Birth of the N+N: Austrian and Swiss Foreign Policy in the CSCE, 1969-1975* (paper first presented to the conference "30 Years Since the Helsinki Final Act", Rüschlikon/Zurich, Switzerland, 8-10 September 2005), published as a non-topical essay in Günter Bischof and Fritz Plasser (eds), *The Changing Austrian Voter*, Contemporary Austrian Studies, vol. XVI (New Brunswick 2008), 228-258.

3   See statements on panel 4 of the Oral History Conference in Vienna, February 2007: "The Historical Experience of the Neutral and Non-Aligned States in the CSCE", Oral History Workshop, Austrian Institute for International Affairs, Vienna, Austria, 22/23 February 2007. Available from <http://www.php.isn.ethz.ch/conferences/previous/Vienna_2007.cfm?nav1=2&nav2=1>.

4   The project was based at the Austrian Institute for International Affairs, Vienna, and funded by the "Jubiläumsfonds der Österreichischen Nationalbank" (project no. 11435). Its results have been published in Thomas Fischer, *Neutral Power in the CSCE: The N+N States and the Making of the Helsinki Accords 1975* (Baden-Baden 2003).

5   This article is mainly based on materials from the Swiss Federal Archive in Berne, where the author had full access to all CSCE-relevant documents of the period 1969 to 1983, as well as from the British National Archive in Kew/London for the period 1972 to 1975. Further documentary evidence included in this contribution is from the Finnish Foreign Ministry Archives in Helsinki, the National Archives in Washington, and the Austrian Foreign Ministry. Oral history information used is mainly from the Oral History Workshop "The Historical Experience of the Neutral and Non-Aligned States in the CSCE", organized by the Austrian Institute for

International Affairs in Vienna on 22/23 February 2007 (available from <www.php.isn.ethz ch>).

6   On the details of this initiative see Thomas Fischer, "'A mustard seed grew into a bushy tree': The Finnish CSCE-initiative of 5 May 1969", *Cold War History Journal*, vol. 9, no. 2 (May 2009), 177-201.

7   Fischer, *The Birth of the N+N*, 12.

8   Cf. Hans-Jörg Renk, *Der Weg der Schweiz nach Helsinki: Der Beitrag der schweizerischen Diplomatie zum Zustandekommen der Konferenz über Sicherheit und Zusammenarbeit in Europa (KSZE), 1972-1975* (Berne, Stuttgart and Vienna 1996), 37-43; Luigi Vittorio Ferraris (ed.), *Report on a Negotiation: Helsinki – Geneva – Helsinki 1972-1975* (Alphen aan den Rijn 1979), 10.

9   On the specifics of the consensus principle see Ulf Lindell, *Modern Multilateral Negotiation: The Consensus Rule and Its Implications in International Conferences* (Lund 1988).

10 Renk, *Der Weg der Schweiz nach Helsinki*, 37-43; Cf. Ferraris, *Report on a Negotiation*, 10. The Swiss-Swedish collaboration again proved successful when they accomplished the agreement in a four-week Christmas break (from 15 December 1972 to 15 January 1973) in a concerted effort against Soviet resistance. Renk, *Der Weg der Schweiz nach Helsinki*, 50f.; Ferraris, *Report on a Negotiation*, 13.

11 The East wanted to avoid the formulation of detailed mandates for the topics already on the agenda at the MPT, while the West strongly opposed the Eastern demand for a permanent body of the conference in form of a political consultative committee.

12 According to articles of the Austrian head of delegation, Helmut Liedermann, it was his idea to group several diverse subjects on the agenda under the term "baskets", but the Swiss diplomat Hans-Jörg Renk claims that the copyright for the basket concept belongs to the Swiss Ambassador to Finland, Samuel Campiche, who first introduced the term to the discussion on 18 January 1973. Indeed this seems to be the moment most contemporary witnesses remember as the birth of the basket concept. According to Renk, Campiche had explained the concept of using "baskets like a housewife to separate the laundry of different colours" in order to organize the agenda; each country could add all the points it wanted to a non-enumerative list. Following this exercise, one could start grouping similar proposals together. Renk, *Der Weg der Schweiz nach Helsinki,* 57f.; see also Renk's foreword to Campiche's memoirs: Pierre Friederich and Hans-Jörg Renk, Préface to Samuel Campiche, *Marée du soir: carnets* (Vevey 2001), 10; Cf. "The Historical Experience of the Neutral and Non-Aligned States in the CSCE", Oral History Workshop, Austrian Institute for International Affairs, Vienna, Austria, 22/23 February 2007, Summary Notes Day 1 & 2; Oral history session of the International Conference in Rüschlikon/Zürich, 8-10 September 2005 "At the Roots of the European Security System: Thirty Years Since the Helsinki Final Act"; For Liedermann's allegation, see Helmut Liedermann, "Die Konferenz über Sicherheit und Zusammenarbeit in Europa aus österreichischer Sicht," in Herbert Schambeck (ed.), *Kirche und Staat: Fritz Eckert zum 65. Geburtstag* (Berlin 1976), 555-577; Helmut Liedermann, "Österreichs Rolle

beim Zustandekommen der KSZE," in Oliver Rathkolb, Otto M. Maschke, and Stefan August Lütgenau (eds), *Mit anderen Augen gesehen: Internationale Perzeptionen Österreichs 1955-2000* (vienna, Cologne and Weimar 2002), 487-506, here 495; Liedermann in an interview with the author stated that he had instigated "sometime in November 1972" to draw up a list of baskets ("ein Verzeichnis von Körben anlegen"): Interview with Helmut Liedermann, Vienna, 16 January 2007; According to Sizoo and Jurrjens the Dutch delegate, the late Jhr. B.E. Quarles van Ufford, had told his friends that he in fact had used the word "basket" first – but in its French form: "He had seen in his mind's eye four baskets standing on the platform and cried out: 'On jette toutes les propositions dans un panier'. Later on the French word in use became 'corbeille' instead of 'panier.'" Jan Sizoo and Rudolf Th. Jurrjens, *CSCE Decision-Making: The Madrid Experience* (The Hague, Boston and Lancaster 1984), 73, note 2. This version of the origin of the "basket" term is also evoked by Ferraris, *Report on a Negotiation*, 13.

13   CSCE Delegation reports no. 25 and 29, 11 and 12 December 1972. Documents cited in Christian Nünlist, "What Role for a Small Neutral State in East-West Détente? New Perspectives on Switzerland's Role in the CSCE, 1969-1975" (paper presented at the International Conference in Rüschlikon/Zurich, 8-10 September 2005 "At the Roots of the European Security System: Thirty Years Since the Helsinki Final Act"), here 22.

14   Schweizerisches Bundesarchiv, Bern (hereafter BAr), Personal Papers Ambassador Rudolf Bindschedler (hereafter HA Bindschedler), E 2814, 1989/159, 10: cable no. 19, Helsinki, 17 January 1973.

15   See n. 11.

16   Minutes from Mr. Tickell on CSCE Preparatory Talks, 25 January, 1973, in *Documents on British Policy Overseas, Series III, Volume II, The Conference on Security and Cooperation in Europe, 1972-1975*, 89, n. 7; Akten zur Auswärtigen Politik der Bundesrepublik Deutschland (hereafter AAPBD), Bd. 1 (1973) 24, fn. 3: Fernschreiben Nr. 114 von Botschafter Krapf, Brüssel (NATO), an das Auswärtige Amt, 26. Januar 1973.

17   The National Archive, London (hereafter TNA), FCO 41/1286: Telegram by Mr. Elliott (Helsinki) on CSCE Preparatory Talks, 24 January 1973; Cf. Ferraris, *Report on a Negotiation*, 16.

18   TNA, FCO 41/1289: Working paper, Swiss Embassy, 29 January 1973. A revised version of this paper was officially registered as document CESC/HC/27/Rev.1 on 9 February 1973: TNA, FCO 41/1289: Working Paper Submitted by Switzerland, 9 February 1973; Cf. Ferraris, *Report on a Negotiation*, 16; Renk, *Der Weg der Schweiz nach Helsinki*, 58f.

19   On the following see Renk, *Der Weg der Schweiz nach Helsinki*, 60f.; Ferraris, *Report on a Negotiation*, 19-29.

20   Finland was not yet in the scope of an N+N cooperation since it totally restrained itself during the MPT to its role as host of the talks.

21   Renk, *Der Weg der Schweiz nach Helsinki*, 128.

22 Early proofs of the neutrals' coordinating activities in Committee III can be found in a number of British documents from Geneva: Telegram Mr. Hildyard (UKMIS Geneva) to Sir A. Douglas-Home, Geneva, 2 February 1974; Telegram Mr. Hildyard (UKMIS Geneva) to Sir A. Douglas-Home, Geneva, 7 February 1974; Minute from Mr. Tickell on CSCE: Basket III, FCO, 15 March 1974, in *The Conference on Security and Cooperation in Europe*, Documents nos. 63, 65, and 68; Cf. *Le role de la Suisse à la CSCE: Témoignage de l'Ambassadeur Edouard Brunner*, Recueilli par le Professeur Victor-Yves Ghebali, Genève, 5 août 2002, 25. Available from <www.isn.ethz.ch/osce/networking/secondary_literature/coc/Interview_Amb_Brunner.PDF>.

23 Renk, *Der Weg der Schweiz nach Helsinki*, 129f.; Cf. Liedermann, "Österreichs Rolle beim Zustandekommen der KSZE," 499; Helmut Liedermann, "Von Helsinki über Belgrad nach Madrid: Die Konferenz über Sicherheit und Zusammenarbeit in Europa," in Peter Fischer, Heribert Franz Köck, and Alfred Verdross (eds), *Völkerrecht und Philosophie: Internationale Festschrift für Stephan Verosta zum 70. Geburtstag* (Berlin 1980), 427-444, here 432; Interview with Helmut Liedermann, Vienna, 16 January 2007.

24 The catalogue of principles comprised the following 10 elements: 1) Sovereign equality, respect for the rights inherent in sovereignty; 2) Refraining from the threat or use of force; 3) Inviolability of frontiers; 4) Territorial integrity of States; 5) Peaceful settlement of disputes; 6) Non-intervention in internal affairs; 7) Respect for human rights and fundamental freedoms, including the freedom of thought, conscience, religion or belief; 8) Equal rights and self-determination of peoples; 9) Cooperation among States; 10) Fulfilment in good faith of obligations under international law.

25 Ferraris, *Report on a Negotiation*, 129. The Finnish proposal of 4 June envisaged a compromise formula on the principle of non-intervention, stating that "*every participating State respects the political, economic and cultural foundations of the other participating States, including their right to establish their own legislative systems and regulations.*" Minute from Mr. Fall to Mr. Tickell, CSCE, 17 June 1974, in *The Conference on Security and Cooperation in Europe*, Document No. 86. The Finnish proposal, however, was not acceptable to the Western countries at that time.

26 Interview with Jaakko Iloniemi, Helsinki, 16 May 2006. See also Iloniemi's comment on the origin of the Finnish compromise proposal in panel 3 of the Oral History roundtable held in Vienna in February 2007: "The Historical Experience of the Neutral and Non-Aligned States in the CSCE", Oral History Workshop, Austrian Institute for International Affairs, Vienna, 22/23 February 2007, Summary Notes Day 2, 18.

27 Cf. Kalevi Sorsa, *Kansankoti Ja Punamulta: Politiikan Kuvioita 1972-1976* (Helsinki 2003), 79f.

28 Indeed Iloniemi himself in talks with the Soviet delegate Mendelevich in Geneva on 24 April 1974 seems to have inspired the use of Finland as a go-between for the superpowers when he had stressed the importance of a compromise and uttered the idea that Finland could attempt a mediation between East and West. Ulkoasiain-

ministeriö arkisto (Finnish Foreign Ministry Archive, Helsinki, hereafter UMA), 7 B, Kansio 7, Telegram no. 321 from Iloniemi (Geneva), 24 April 1974.

29 National Archives, Washington, NSC: HAK Office, Box 71, Folder 4: Memorandum of Conversation between Henry Kissinger and Andrei Gromyko, Nicosia, 7 Mai 1974, in *The Road to Helsinki: The Early Steps to the CSCE. Selected Documents from the National Archives, the Gerald Ford Library, and the National Security Archive*, A CWIHP document reader compiled by Hedwig Giusto, Mircea Munteanu, and Christian Ostermann for the International CSCE History Conference in Florence, Italy, 29-30 September 2003.

30 This version of the story is also invoked by the French CSCE-diplomat Jacques Andréani, *La piège: Helsinki et la chute du communisme* (Paris 2005), 74f. See also the statement of Finnish diplomat Markku Reimaa in panel 3 of day two of the Oral History roundtable held in Vienna in February 2007: "The Historical Experience of the Neutral and Non-Aligned States in the CSCE", Oral History Workshop, Austrian Institute for International Affairs, Vienna, 22/23 February 2007, Summary Notes Day 2, 17.

31 BAr, HA Bindschedler, E 2814, 1993/210, 3: Proposal by the Delegations of Austria, Cyprus, Finland, Liechtenstein, Malta, Sweden, Switzerland and Yugoslavia, 11 June 1974. Emphasis added.

32 Ibid. Emphasis added. The proposal is also quoted in Renk, *Der Weg der Schweiz nach Helsinki*, 134; Cf. Sizoo and Jurrjens, *CSCE Decision-Making*, 183.

33 BAr, E 2001 (E) 1987/78, 191: "Package deal", Rapport pour la période du 22 avril – 26 juillet 1974 (2ème phase CSCE – Genève), Berne, le 26 juillet 1974; Cf. Ferraris, *Report on a Negotiation*, 128-131.

34 John J. Maresca, *To Helsinki: The Conference on Security and Cooperation in Europe, 1973-1975* (Durham, NC and London 1987), 126-128, quote 126.

35 Renk, *Der Weg der Schweiz nach Helsinki*, 135.

36 Telegram "CSCE: State of Play", Mr. Hildyard (UKMIS Geneva) to Mr. Callaghan, 20 September 1974, in *The Conference on Security and Cooperation in Europe*, Document No. 97.

37 Telegram "Basket III Sub-Committees," Mr. Hildyard (UKMIS Geneva) to Mr. Callaghan, 19 October 1974, in *The Conference on Security and Cooperation in Europe*, Document No. 101; TNA, FCO 28/2456: "CSCE: State of Play", Mr. Hildyard (UKMIS Geneva) to FCO, 26 October 1974; Cf. Maresca, *To Helsinki*, 107f.

38 On the following see Renk, *Der Weg der Schweiz nach Helsinki*, 152-159; Cf. Ljubivoje Acimovic, *Problems of Security and Cooperation in Europe* (Alphen aan den Rijn 1981), 270-283.

39 BAr, HA Bindschedler, E 2814, 1993/210, 7: "Projet de résolution: Suites à la Conférence sur la sécurité et la coopération en Europe", Proposition presentée par la délégation de la Yougoslavie, Genève, 28 mars 1974 (CSCE/CC/WG/IV/1).

40 BAr, Private Papers Rudolf Bindschedler (hereafter NL Bindschedler), J I.223, 1000/1318, 35: "Die 'Folgen' der Konferenz", Memorandum Rudolf Bindschedler, Genf, 13. Dezember 1974.

41 On the initial hesitance of notably Switzerland see Renk, *Der Weg der Schweiz nach Helsinki*, 153. Cf. Renk's statement in panel 3 of the Oral History roundtable held in Vienna in February 2007: "The Historical Experience of the Neutral and Non-Aligned States in the CSCE", Oral History Workshop, Austrian Institute for International Affairs, Vienna, 22/23 February 2007, Summary Notes Day 2, 20.

42 TNA, FCO 41/1762: "Follow-up to the CSCE", Memorandum UKMIS Geneva, 26 February 1975.

43 Quote from Renk, *Der Weg der Schweiz nach Helsinki*, 155.

44 TNA, FCO 41/1763: Note for the Record (A. Carter), Follow-Up: Meeting on 16 April 1975.

45 TNA, FCO 41/1764: CSCE: Follow-Up, Letter M. O. D. B. Alexander (UKMIS Geneva) to R. A. Burns (FCO, East European & Soviet Division), Geneva, 16 May 1975; CSCE: Follow-Up, Letter R. A. Burns to M. O. D. B. Alexander (UKMIS Geneva), London, 19 May 1975.

46 TNA, FCO 41/1764: Note for the Record (M. A. Savill), CSCE: Follow-Up: Group of 13 Meeting at the Swiss Delegation on 12 June 1975.

47 See the opening statements on panel 4 of the Oral History roundtable held in Vienna in February 2007: "The Historical Experience of the Neutral and Non-Aligned States in the CSCE", Oral History Workshop, Austrian Institute for International Affairs, Vienna, 22/23 February 2007, Summary Notes Day 2, 22f.

48 Renk, *Der Weg der Schweiz nach Helsinki*, 157.

49 Quoted in Sizoo and Jurrjens, *CSCE Decision-Making*, 55.

50 Maresca, *To Helsinki*, 202.

51 The four neutrals met alone for a first time in Helsinki in April 1976, and in Vienna on 22/23 November 1976. In Belgrade on 31 January/1 February 1977 they were joined by the non-aligned, and on 9/10 May 1977 they met alone again in Berne. Fischer, *Die Grenzen der Neutralität*, 210-213; Cf. Michael Zielinski, *Die neutralen und blockfreien Staaten und ihre Rolle im KSZE-Prozess* (Baden-Baden 1990), 241. For the neutral gatherings in Helsinki on 29 and 30 April 1976, and in Belgrade on 22 and 23 November 1976, see the reports of the Swiss Foreign Ministry: BAr, E 2200.48 (-), 1992/148, 12: KSZE-Treffen der vier Neutralen in Helsinki, Bericht Politische Direktion, Bot. Anton Hegner, Bern, 10. Mai 1976; KSZE-Treffen der vier Neutralen in Wien, Bericht Politische Direktion, Bot. Anton Hegner, Bern, 6. Dezember 1976; On the ambition and expectation of a role change for the N+N in the preparation for Belgrade see also Ljubivoje Acimovic, "Das Belgrader KSZE-Folgetreffen: Eine Betrachtung aus jugoslawischer Sicht," in *Das Belgrader KSZE-Folgetreffen: Der Fortgang des Entspannungsprozesses in Europa*, in Hermann Volle and Wolfgang Wagner (eds), Beiträgen und Dokumenten aus dem Europa-Archiv (Bonn 1978), 23-42, here 38.

52 Fischer, *Die Grenzen der Neutralität*, 200-202.

53 Ibid., 214

54 Again it had been the N+N who, in June and July, had provided acceptable compromise proposals on the agenda and the organization of the conference. Victor-

Yves Ghébali, *La diplomatie de la détente: La CSCE, 1973-1989* (Brussels 1989), 22f.; Zielinski, *Die neutralen und blockfreien Staaten und ihre Rolle im KSZE-Prozess*, 243.

55 BAr, E 2001 (E) 1988/16, 213: Telegramm Botschafter Hohl (Washington) an EPD, 31. August 1977.

56 Fischer, *Die Grenzen der Neutralität*, 217-221.

57 Otmar Höll, "Kleinstaaten im Entspannungsprozess: Am Beispiel der neutralen und nichtpaktgebundenen Staaten in der KSZE," *Österreichische Zeitschrift für Politikwissenschaft*, 3 (1986), 293-310, here 297; Leo Mates, "The Neutral and Nonaligned Countries," in Nils Andrén and Karl E. Birnbaum (eds), *Belgrade and Beyond: The CSCE Process in Perspective* (Alphen aan den Rijn and Rockville, MD 1980), 51-63, here 55.

58 The document was registered on 7 December 1977 as CSCE/BM/65; A German version of the document is reprinted in Volle and Wagner (eds), *Das Belgrader KSZE-Folgetreffen*, 146-148; Cf. Fischer, *Die Grenzen der Neutralität*, 217f.; Zielinski, *Die neutralen und blockfreien Staaten und ihre Rolle im KSZE-Prozess*, 244.

59 BAr, E 2001 (E) 1988/16, 214: Botschafter Renk an EPD, 10. Januar 1978.

60 Per Fischer, "Das Ergebnis von Belgrad: Das KSZE-Folgetreffen in seiner Bedeutung für den Entspannungsprozess," in Volle and Wagner (eds), *Das Belgrader KSZE-Folgetreffen*, 23-33, here 27.

61 An account of the common efforts of the N+N in Belgrade is given in a report by the Swiss diplomat Daniel Woker: BAr, E 2001 (E) 1988/16, 215: Die Mitarbeit der Schweiz in der Gruppe der neutralen und nichtpaktgebundenen Staaten im Rahmen der KSZE, Bericht Daniel Woker, Februar 1978.

62 The Swiss delegation was in charge of the principles, Yugoslavia of the military questions, Finland of economic issues, Austria of human rights and Sweden of the follow-up. Zielinski, *Die neutralen und blockfreien Staaten und ihre Rolle im KSZE-Prozess*, 244f.

63 A German version of the non-paper of 1 February 1978 can be found in Volle and Wagner (eds), *Das Belgrader KSZE-Folgetreffen*, 148f.

64 BAr, E 2001 (E) 1988/16, 215: Die Mitarbeit der Schweiz in der Gruppe der neutralen und nichtpaktgebundenen Staaten im Rahmen der KSZE, Bericht Daniel Woker, Februar 1978, 5f.

65 Registered as CSCE/BM/73. Reprinted in Volle and Wagner (eds), *Das Belgrader KSZE-Folgetreffen*, 150-157.

66 Fischer, *Die Grenzen der Neutralität*, 220.

67 Zielinski, *Die neutralen und blockfreien Staaten und ihre Rolle im KSZE-Prozess*, 245; Ian MacDonald, "'Neutral Bid Fails', Report by RFE correspondent, Belgrade, February 27, 1978," in Vojtech Mastny, *Helsinki, Human Rights, and European Security: Analysis and Documentation* (Durham, NC 1986), 177.

68 In the meantime the participating states were hoping to at least advance some of the issues in the context of expert-level reunions (on the question of a Swiss project for the peaceful settlement of disputes in October 1978 in Berne, on the Mediterranean

cooperation in February 1979 in Malta, and in a forum on scientific cooperation in 1980 in Hamburg).

69 Mates, "The Neutral and Nonaligned Countries", 53.
70 Concluding Document of the Belgrade meeting 1977 (8 March 1978). Reprinted in Andrén and Birnbaum (eds), *Belgrade and Beyond*, 161-163; as well as in Mastny (ed.), *Helsinki, Human Rights, and European Security*, 350-352.
71 Mates, "The Neutral and Nonaligned Countries", 62.
72 BAr, E 2010 (A) 1991/17, 249: Telegram Troendle (Madrid) an Politische Direktion EDA, 8. November 1980.
73 Ibid.
74 On differing opinions between the neutral states regarding the preparatory conference see also Ambassador Ceska's statement in panel 4 of "The Historical Experience of the Neutral and Non-Aligned States in the CSCE", Oral History Workshop, Austrian Institute for International Affairs, Vienna, Austria, 22/23 February 2007, Summary Notes Day 2, 26.
75 Fischer, *Die Grenzen der Neutralität*, 292f.
76 Apparently the Swiss delegate Petar Troendle behind the scenes played an important role as go-between in these negotiations. Michael Gehler, *Österreichs Aussenpolitik der Zweiten Republik: Von der alliierten Besatzung bis zum Europa des 21. Jahrhunderts*, Bd. 1 (Innsbruck, Vienna and Bozen 2005), 454; Cf. Zielinski, *Die neutralen und blockfreien Staaten und ihre Rolle im KSZE-Prozess*, 252.
77 See the diplomatic report by the Austrian head of delegation Franz Ceska reprinted in Gehler, *Österreichs Aussenpolitik der Zweiten Republik*, 454-457, here 454.
78 On the episode of "The Stopped Clock" see Sizoo and Jurrjens, *CSCE Decision-Making*, 194-196; and the diplomatic report in Gehler, *Österreichs Aussenpolitik der Zweiten Republimk*, 455.
79 Sizoo and Jurrjens, *CSCE Decision-Making*, 196f.
80 Ibid.
81 BAr, E 2010 (A) 1991/17, 249: CSCE: Historique de ces derniers jours, Telegramm Brunner (Madrid) an Bundesrat Aubert, 15. November 1980; Gehler, *Österreichs Aussenpolitik der Zweiten Republik*, 456; Ceska in an interview with the author recalled the crucial collaboration between himself and Brunner in these last days of the pre-conference for Madrid. Interview with Franz Ceska, Vienna, 2 August 2005.
82 The four N+N foreign ministers present in Madrid were those of Austria, Sweden, Yugoslavia and Cyprus, whereas four other members of the group (Switzerland, Liechtenstein, San Marino and Malta), which were not represented on this level, would give the paper its full official support. Finland abstained from the initiative, because the Finnish Foreign Ministry considered that the proposed commitments to the follow-up after Madrid were too weak in the document. See statement of the Finnish head of delegation Markku Reimaa on panel 3 of "The Historical Experience of the Neutral and Non-Aligned States in the CSCE", Oral History Workshop,

Austrian Institute for International Affairs, Vienna, Austria, 22/23 February 2007, Summary Notes Day 2, 17.

83 BAr, E 2010 (A) 1991/17, 249: CSCE: Historique de ces derniers jours, Telegramm Brunner (Madrid) an Bundesrat Aubert, 15. November 1980; BAr, E 2010 (A) 1991/17, 249: Brief Botschafter Iselin (Wien) an Bundesrat Aubert, 28. November 1980; Gehler, *Österreichs Aussenpolitik der Zweiten Republik*, 456; Cf. Fischer, *Die Grenzen der Neutralität*, 294-296; Zielinski, *Die neutralen und blockfreien Staaten und ihre Rolle im KSZE-Prozess*, 251f.; Höll, "Kleinstaaten im Entspannungsprozess," 297f.

84 The final date of conclusion of the conference was left open deliberately by the N+N proposal to make sure the follow-up to Madrid was guaranteed. A German version of the concluding document of the preparatory meeting of 14 November 1980 is reprinted in *Das Madrider KSZE-Folgetreffen: Der Fortgang des KSZE-Prozesses in Europa*, in Hermann Volle and Wolfgang Wagner (eds), Beiträgen und Dokumenten aus dem Europa-Archiv (Bonn 1984), 126-131.

85 BAr, E 2023 (A) 1991/39, 122: KSZE-Folgetreffen in Madrid, Zwischenbericht Brunner, 14. Januar 1981.

86 BAr, E 2010 (A) 1991/17, 251: KSZE-Konferenz in Madrid: N+N-Initiative, Bericht Botschafter Iselin (Wien) an Bundesrat Aubert, Botschafter Brunner und KSZE-Delegation in Madrid, 25. Februar 1981.

87 BAr, E 2010 (A) 1991/17, 251: Telegramm Brunner (Bern) an schweizerische Botschaft Berlin (DDR), 2. März 1981.

88 BAr, E 2010 (A) 1991/17, 251: KSZE-Konferenz in Madrid: N+N-Initiative, Bericht Botschafter Iselin (Wien) an Bundesrat Aubert, Botschafter Brunner und KSZE-Delegation in Madrid, 25. Februar 1981.

89 Interview with Edouard Brunner, Berne, 15 January 2003.

90 Fischer, *Die Grenzen der Neutralität*, 297-299; Zielinski, *Die neutralen und blockfreien Staaten und ihre Rolle im KSZE-Prozess*, 253.

91 On the details of the discussion see Fischer, *Die Grenzen der Neutralität*, 299.

92 At first the Austrian delegation resisted such an initiative within the N+N group, since they still believed in the possibility to find a solution for the current blockade of the talks. BAr, E 2010 (A) 1991/17, 252: Anruf Botschafter Brunner aus Madrid, Aktennotiz Staatssekretär Probst z.H. Bundesrat Aubert, 21. Juli 1981.

93 Fischer, *Die Grenzen der Neutralität*, 300.

94 Sizoo and Jurrjens, *CSCE Decision-Making*, 161; Cf. Zielinski, *Die neutralen und blockfreien Staaten und ihre Rolle im KSZE-Prozess*, 254; Leo Mates, "Von Helsinki nach Madrid und zurück: Der KSZE-Prozess im Schatten der Ost-West-Beziehungen," in Volle and Wagner (eds), *Das Madrider KSZE-Folgetreffen*, 59f.

95 Fischer, *Die Grenzen der Neutralität*, 300f.

96 Interview with Edouard Brunner, Berne, 15 January 2003. Brunner's bilateral talks with the Soviet and US head of delegation in mid-October 1981 are also conveyed in more general terms in an unpublished Master's thesis: Jacqueline Béatrice Moeri, *Die Rolle der Schweiz in der N+N-Gruppe der KSZE während der Madrider Folgekonfer-*

enz (Hochschule St.Gallen für Wirtschafts- und Sozialwissenschaften, Diplomarbeit 1984), 89.

97 Zielinski, *Die neutralen und blockfreien Staaten und ihre Rolle im KSZE-Prozess*, 254f.

98 According to Ceska, a first draft for a comprehensive document had been prepared on his request by Ursula Plassnik, a young diplomatic member of the Austrian delegation to Madrid, during the summer break. It was then presented to the N–N states in September 1981. See statement of Ambassador Ceska in panel 4 of "The Historical Experience of the Neutral and Non-Aligned States in the CSCE", Oral History Workshop, Austrian Institute for International Affairs, Vienna, Austria, 22/23 February 2007, Summary Notes Day 2, 27.

99 Moeri, *Die Rolle der Schweiz in der N+N-Gruppe der KSZE während der Madrider Folgekonferenz*, 90f. Foreign Minister Aubert and Ambassador Brunner explained the reasons for another adjournment of the Madrid meeting to the Committee for External Affairs of the Swiss national parliament on 18 February 1982. On this occasion they also stated that the Swiss proposal for adjournment had been pre-decided in an informal N+N meeting: BAr, E 2850.1 (-) 1991/234, 12, Personal Papers Pierre Aubert (hereafter HA Aubert): Sitzungsprotokoll der Kommission für auswärtige Angelegenheiten des Nationalrates, Bern, 18. Februar 1982.

100 Fischer, *Die Grenzen der Neutralität*, 302; Cf. Zielinski, *Die neutralen und blockfreien Staaten und ihre Rolle im KSZE-Prozess*, 255; Höll, "Kleinstaaten im Entspannungsprozess," 299; Mates, "Von Helsinki nach Madrid und zurück," 60.

101 Again the N+N had been instrumental behind the scenes in bringing about consensus on the decision to adjourn the conference for some months. For a detailed discussion of the issue of recess for the conference in 1982 see Sizoo and Jurrjens, *CSCE Decision-Making*, 197-208, on the N+N negotiating a compromise behind the scenes, 208.

102 BAr, E 2010 (A) 1995/313, 6: KSZE – Rückblick und Ausblick, Kommission für auswärtige Angelegenheiten des Nationalrates, Teilprotokoll der Sitzung vom 14. Februar 1983.

103 Sizoo and Jurrjens, *CSCE Decision-Making*, 239f.

104 BAr, E 2010 (A) 1995/313, 6: KSZE – Rückblick und Ausblick, Kommission für auswärtige Angelegenheiten des Nationalrates, Teilprotokoll der Sitzung vom 14. Februar 1983; Cf. Fischer, *Die Grenzen der Neutralität*, 374f.; Moeri, *Die Rolle der Schweiz in der N+N-Gruppe der KSZE während der Madrider Folgekonferenz*, 93f.

105 Zielinski, *Die neutralen und blockfreien Staaten und ihre Rolle im KSZE-Prozess*, 256.

106 Moeri, *Die Rolle der Schweiz in der N+N-Gruppe der KSZE während der Madrider Folgekonferenz*, 94-96. The Swiss had supported the N+N proposal from the beginning only with reservation and now distanced themselves from it ever more. The main reason for the Swiss denial of support to the N+N letter of 18 April 1983 was the fact that their own proposal for an expert meeting on human contacts was

skipped from the N+N draft for the final document, since it would stand no chance of acceptance with the East. Fischer, *Die Grenzen der Neutralität*, 375f.

107 In addition, Romania and Malta had both filed amendments, which were acceptable to no one. Sizoo and Jurrjens, *CSCE Decision-Making*, 240f.

108 Edouard Brunner, "Das KSZE-Folgetreffen von Madrid aus der Sicht der neutralen Schweiz," in Volle and Wagner (eds), *Das Madrider KSZE-Folgetreffen*, 79-84, here 83; Cf. Fischer, *Die Grenzen der Neutralität*, 376; Moeri, *Die Rolle der Schweiz in der N+N-Gruppe der KSZE während der Madrider Folgekonferenz*, 98.

109 BAr, E 2850.1 (-) 1991/28, Personal Papers Pierre Aubert: CSCE, Rapport de la delegation Suisse, Bericht Aubert zu Handen des Gesamtbundesrates, 12. August 1983.

110 Interview with Edouard Brunner, Berne, 15 January 2003; *Le role de la Suisse à la CSCE: Témoignage de l'Ambassadeur Edouard Brunner*, 41f.; Zielinski, *Die neutralen und blockfreien Staaten und ihre Rolle im KSZE-Prozess*, 256f.; Fischer, *Die Grenzen der Neutralität*, 376f.; On the "Malta phase" specifically, see Sizoo and Jurrjens, *CSCE Decision-Making*, 242-244; and Moeri, *Die Rolle der Schweiz in der N+N-Gruppe der KSZE während der Madrider Folgekonferenz*, 99f.

111 A German version of the final documents of the CSCE follow-up meeting in Madrid of 6 September 1983 is reprinted in Volle and Wagner (eds), *Das Madrider KSZE-Folgetreffen*, 181-198.

The Rise of the Helsinki Network

"A Sort of Lifeline" for Eastern Europe

Sarah B. Snyder

The 1975 Helsinki Final Act's human rights principle, human contacts provisions, and follow-up mechanism spurred an explosion of dissident activity in Eastern Europe, eventually leading to the development of a transnational network committed to reform in Eastern Europe and the Soviet Union.[1] In the years after the Helsinki Final Act was signed, those committed to its implementation succeeded in unifying and supporting Helsinki activism, advancing a human rights agenda on an international stage, offering incentives for change in Eastern Europe, and facilitating the transition to a new Europe at the end of the Cold War.[2]

The text of the Helsinki Final Act contained elements that stimulated and facilitated the development of a transnational network devoted to the accord's fulfillment. Principle Seven, which committed Helsinki Final Act signatories to respect "human rights and fundamental freedoms, including the freedom of thought, conscience, religion or belief," offered Soviet and Eastern European opposition figures important leverage in their protests against communist regimes.[3] In addition, by consenting to the Helsinki Final Act, states pledged to facilitate human contacts such as family reunifications, bi-national marriages, and travel, providing other grounds for activists to press their governments to liberalize. Furthermore, the inclusion of Principle Seven and the human contacts provisions in the Helsinki Final Act meant that these rights were now under the purview of international relations, supplying justification for external observers to question the Soviet Union and Eastern European countries on their human rights practices.

The Helsinki Final Act's follow-up mechanism, which set a meeting to assess compliance in Belgrade in 1977, was similarly significant to the network's development. The promise to evaluate Helsinki implementation in two years time prompted the establishment of groups to monitor adherence to the accord; these groups ultimately became the core of a transnational advocacy network.[4] Unlike the 1948 Universal Declaration of Human Rights and other international attempts to elevate the importance of human rights, the Helsinki Final Act was uniquely formulated to give rise to a transnational network because the terms of the agreement established that the CSCE states could exchange views on the implementation of the Helsinki Final Act. This meant that internal matters such as human rights abuses would now be subject to international diplomacy.[5] In the intervening years, the Helsinki Final Act inspired a range of people inside and outside government to develop formal and informal mechanisms to monitor Helsinki implementation. Importantly, the first review meeting in Belgrade led to a second; a whole series of meetings followed, fostering links among Helsinki advocates and locating human rights advocacy on the international diplomatic agenda.

In order to understand how human rights activism developed in response to the Helsinki Final Act and went on to shape Soviet and Eastern European attitudes towards human rights advocacy, it is necessary to examine the components, agenda, and tactics of this transnational network. The network operated through the intertwined efforts of dissidents, human rights activists, and Western politicians and diplomats to champion human rights and East-West contacts in the Soviet Union and Eastern Europe. As a result, human rights became an important element of Cold War diplomacy. This chapter analyzes the development of what I see as the three essential components of the transnational network: the establishment of the United States Commission on Security and Cooperation in Europe, the formation of international human rights groups, and an increasing American role in the CSCE follow-up meetings.

Shortly after the signing of the Helsinki Final Act in August 1975, United States Representative Millicent Fenwick (R-NJ) traveled with a Congressional delegation to the Soviet Union and returned determined to enhance the United States role in protecting human rights. Fenwick described meeting Soviet dissidents and refuseniks "in heartbreaking meetings, in small shabby flats and hotel rooms" and hearing "the cries of all these desperate people."[6] Yet, she viewed Soviet citizens as "hopeful" that the Helsinki Final Act would improve their political and social rights.[7] In her memoirs, Fenwick notes how important Soviet dissidents viewed international recognition as "a sort of lifeline."[8] Fenwick was inspired by her encounters in the Soviet Union to take action, describing her trip as "a somewhat distant and theoretical exercise in international diplomacy" that "became a dramatically present and personal issue."[9]

Fenwick returned to the United States convinced of the importance of creating a formal body to monitor Helsinki implementation, especially related to human contacts: "The trip made a lasting impression on many of us who realized, after talking for many hours with dissidents and Soviet citizens wanting to emigrate, that the hopes of these people had been pinned to the implementation of the Helsinki Accord which had been signed just before our arrival."[10] Fenwick proposed a joint legislative and executive commission to examine compliance with the Helsinki Final Act and to press for greater international implementation.[11]

The result of her efforts, the Commission on Security and Cooperation in Europe, became a strong advocate for United States activism on human rights and an essential part of the transnational Helsinki network. For many years, the Commission was the most comprehensive source on Helsinki compliance in the United States and it served as an informal clearinghouse for research related to Helsinki.[12] Commissioners and their staff highlighted Helsinki violations through hearings, publications, and press releases. The Commission frequently served as a conduit for information from nongovernmental organizations (NGOs) to United States policymakers, and it used its unique position to exert influence on American policy. As such, it played a critical role, connecting different activists and policymakers across interests and national lines. Through their efforts to press for Helsinki compliance, members of the Commission succeeded in making the Helsinki process a more potent international force for change.

The early establishment of the Commission offered an outlet for the Eastern monitoring groups, which would emerge shortly thereafter, and their research on violations of the Helsinki Final Act. As one of the first bodies to undertake Helsinki monitoring, the Commission facilitated the development of a network of groups and individuals committed to the implementation of the Helsinki Final Act and heightened the influence of the Helsinki process over time. Once established, it fostered a transnational network of Helsinki activists and gave a voice to their grievances through its hearings, reports, and advocacy. The Commission relied heavily on documents and reports from Eastern Europe, at times invited exiled dissidents to testify, and ultimately championed these Helsinki monitors. The significance of the Commission rests in its connections with a broader Helsinki community, and the influence it was able to bear on the implementation of Helsinki obligations and the broader protection of human rights.

At the same time Fenwick established the Commission, human rights activists in the Soviet Union, prompted by publication of the Helsinki Final Act in Soviet newspapers, began organizing efforts to ensure compliance with the agreement. Representative and Commission member Robert F.

Drinan, a Democrat from Massachusetts, describes Jewish refusenik Anatoly Shcharansky and human rights activist Andrei Sakharov as "amazed but jubilant" to read the full text of the act in a Soviet newspaper.[13] Ludmilla Alekseeva, Moscow Helsinki Group founding member and later its representative in the West, further reported, "Soviet citizens, reading the text of the Final Act in the papers, were stunned by the humanitarian articles; it was the first they had heard of any kind of international obligations in the human rights field of their government."[14] Prompted by the publication of the Helsinki Final Act, dissidents in the Soviet Union debated how they could pursue its implementation. Shcharansky had the idea to form an international movement of seminars and discussions on human rights. In his conception, the groups would start in the West first, at Soviet activists' invitation, and then a Soviet group would be formed. Instead, dissident Yuri Orlov changed the objective to the creation of a Helsinki-focused group in Moscow with well-known dissidents. Orlov wanted the group to monitor the positive and negative sides of Soviet Helsinki implementation. Shcharansky responded to Orlov's new proposal, "This is far more risky than what I had suggested, but since I am the one who got you thinking about it, there is nothing I can do but join."[15] Orlov's initiative led to the establishment of the Public Group to Promote Fulfillment of the Helsinki Accords in the USSR, which was formed on 13 May 1976, by eleven prominent Soviet dissidents and popularly known in the West as the Moscow Helsinki Group or the Moscow Helsinki Watch Group. The group included activists with a range of agendas but a common goal of monitoring Helsinki implementation. In Alekseeva's words, the Helsinki process enabled the "unification of the human rights movement with religious and national movements" because all were working towards rights outlined in the Helsinki Final Act, proof of which could be seen in the composition of the Moscow Helsinki Group – Jewish refuseniks, ethnic nationalists, and human rights activists.[16]

Groups such as the Moscow Helsinki Group served as an essential conduit of evidence of Eastern human rights abuses. They exposed Eastern practices, often succeeding in focusing international attention on a particularly troubling case. The Moscow Helsinki Group drafted reports on a range of abuses such as repression of Helsinki monitors and forced psychiatric treatment as well as accounts of struggles for rights not yet granted under the Soviet system: freedom of conscience, national self-determination, and freedom of movement and residence within the USSR.[17] Initially, the Moscow Helsinki Group made thirty-five copies of each document and sent them by registered mail to the thirty-four foreign embassies in Moscow affiliated with the CSCE and directly to Soviet leader Leonid Brezhnev. As that proved ineffective due to Soviet postal interference, varied methods were used to deliver Moscow Helsinki Group documents to foreign embassies, including through Western news correspondents.[18]

Furthermore, the Moscow Helsinki Group offered an important connection between dissidents in Moscow and concerned people around the world. The group immediately sought to join a broader network of those dedicated to Helsinki implementation by sending its reports to Western NGOs.[19] Although there were not always formal links between human rights groups in the Soviet Union, the Helsinki Final Act served as their common foundation. In Ludmilla Alekseeva's view, the agreement produced a "collective phenomenon of Soviet dissent." The development of grass-roots monitoring groups first expanded within the Soviet Union to Lithuania, Armenia, Georgia, and Ukraine, with the establishment of such groups as the Christian Committee for the Defence of Believers' Rights in the USSR; the Working Commission to Investigate the Use of Psychiatry for Political Purposes; and the Ukrainian Public Group of Assistance to Implementation of the Helsinki Agreements in the USSR.[20] In the wake of the Moscow Helsinki Group's establishment, monitoring efforts extended beyond the USSR, spreading to Poland and Czechoslovakia, among others. Some of the most prominent new groups in Poland were the Polish Workers' Defence Committee, created in the spring of 1976, and the Movement for the Defence of Human and Civil Rights (ROPCiO), which focused on Helsinki monitoring. Later, Charter 77 would develop as a group of loosely affiliated activists in Czechoslovakia committed to dialogue with the government on increasing human rights protections, and in April 1978, the Committee for the Defence of the Unjustly Prosecuted (VONS) was established to monitor judicial actions and more directly challenge the Czechoslovak regime. These activist groups generally utilized similar non-violent tactics: working within their Constitutions and calling on governments to honor obligations to international agreements; and they faced the same punishments: expulsion and loss of citizenship, long prison terms, or harassment, to name a few.

The myriad of international responses to the Helsinki Final Act represented the beginning of the development of a transnational Helsinki network. In time, the broader transnational Helsinki network, of which Moscow Helsinki Group members were key parties, was able to effect implementation of the Helsinki Final Act, secure improved observance of human rights, and fundamentally shift Eastern European politics and society. The establishment of the Moscow Helsinki Group and the Commission within a month of each other raised the international profile of the Helsinki agreement and ensured that Helsinki compliance would remain in the forefront of East-West relations.

The 1977 Belgrade meeting was a critical turning point in the rising influence of the Helsinki network as it focused international attention on Helsinki compliance and provided a forum for the development of transnational links among those committed to Helsinki implementation. Eastern European dissidence increased as the Belgrade meeting approached, with activists realizing that the meeting was an opportunity to highlight their plight and grievances to the international community.[21] The Helsinki Final Act and the Belgrade meeting enabled Eastern dissidents to petition outside observers, an important fact given how unresponsive domestic governments were. As Soviet dissident Valery Chalidze said, "During the past few years, Soviet dissidents have almost given up appealing to their own government, preferring to try world public opinion, international human rights organizations and other governments that have dealings with the Soviet government. We have no other recourse if Moscow is unwilling to listen to us."[22] As such, when the Soviet leadership gave no indication that it was listening in the years immediately following the signing of the Helsinki Final Act, international connections among those monitoring Helsinki implementation increased.

The Belgrade meeting offered the first opportunity to evaluate Helsinki adherence publicly, and thus it spurred considerable output from Helsinki monitoring groups.[23] Many critics of Eastern practices utilized Moscow Helsinki Group documents to support their condemnations, marking the beginning of a productive collaboration between NGOs and CSCE delegations.[24] Each monitoring group, therefore, worked to document violations of the Helsinki Final Act and distributed their research to sympathetic CSCE delegates.[25] During the course of the negotiations, United States Ambassador to the Belgrade Follow-up Meeting Arthur J. Goldberg and other CSCE diplomats drew upon documentation provided by Eastern monitoring groups and the Commission.[26]

Goldberg, an outspoken American jurist, was appointed to head the United States delegation by President Jimmy Carter as part of his commitment to making human rights a centerpiece of his foreign policy. After his election to the presidency, Jimmy Carter raised the American profile within the CSCE such that the United States was the most forthright advocate of Helsinki compliance at the 1977-1978 Belgrade Follow-up Meeting. Goldberg's outspokenness at the meeting ensured a rigorous review of Helsinki compliance. Without United States leadership, the Belgrade meeting could have offered Eastern states the opportunity to tout their efforts at Helsinki implementation with little dissent. Instead, Goldberg challenged international diplomatic norms by "naming names" and citing individual cases in his speeches.[27] In particular, Western delegations successfully raised the international profile of Helsinki monitors at Belgrade; NSC staffer Robert P. Hunter argued that "virtually nobody had heard of the Orlov Group before Belgrade began" whereas afterward the plight of Helsinki monitors was well known.[28] Goldberg's tactics represented a shift in international diplomacy but ultimately strengthened the Helsinki process by imbuing the follow-up meetings with real repercussions. Through their complementary efforts, Helsinki monitoring groups and CSCE diplomats such as Goldberg established a standard whereby those who flaunted their Helsinki obligations would be publicly humiliated in an international forum.

Because Goldberg's diplomacy required heavily documented briefs to support his charges of Eastern human rights abuses, his tenure as ambassador strengthened links among the Commission, which acted as an international clearinghouse for Helsinki information, Eastern monitoring groups, and United States diplomats. To this end, Goldberg suggested in the aftermath of Belgrade that the transnational network would benefit from a United States-based monitoring group made up of private citizens. His idea became Helsinki Watch, the most prominent Western NGO devoted to Helsinki monitoring. Helsinki Watch's establishment proved critical because as Eastern repression of Helsinki activists escalated, Western NGOs were needed to lead the monitoring effort.

The Commission and Helsinki Watch worked together closely in the subsequent years. According to Commission Staff Director R. Spencer Oliver, the two bodies communicated almost weekly, coordinated hearings, and were in near agreement about questions such as the United States approach to the Madrid CSCE Review Meeting. In Oliver's view, Helsinki Watch was a strong ally to the Commission, in particular as it shaped United States public opinion in support of pressing for Eastern compliance with the Helsinki Final Act.[29]

By the opening of the Madrid meeting in 1980, Helsinki monitoring groups had proliferated in both the East and the West and, importantly, had developed networks of supporters more extensive and better coordinated than at Belgrade. Helsinki Watch Executive Director Jeri Laber describes the opening of the Madrid meeting as a "circus" because so many groups had emerged to participate. For human rights activists, the review meetings enabled an exchange of information – the opportunity to disseminate their work more widely and to influence international and domestic public opinion. At Madrid, an informal network of dissidents, human rights activists, and members of ethnic groups with varying degrees of connection to one another attempted to influence CSCE delegates to adopt their agendas. According to political scientist H. Gordon Skilling, the activities of the press, public opinion, and human rights activists created an "Alice in Wonderland atmosphere" at Madrid.[30] NGOs used Madrid to coordinate lobbying efforts and to provide delegations with first-hand research on the situation in Eastern Europe.[31]

By 1981 Helsinki Watch had decided that it needed to move beyond its strategy of collecting information and begin conducting its own research into human rights practices of the countries it was monitoring. Thus, in the fall of 1981, Laber embarked on a solo research trip to Czechoslovakia, Poland, Hungary, and Yugoslavia. At the end of her 25-day trip, Laber stopped in Madrid, where United States CSCE ambassador Max Kampelman arranged a luncheon with fourteen North Atlantic Treaty Organization and Neutral and Non-Aligned ambassadors to the ongoing review meeting. To her surprise, as she reported her findings, she realized she was educating the ambassadors about the situation in these countries: "I realized that many of them were focusing for the first time on the personal tragedies caused by human rights violations. Their response led me to believe that in the future they would raise human rights issues more vociferously with the Eastern bloc delegates at the conference."[32] Her experience offers evidence of the influential connections between NGOs and CSCE diplomats that continued to develop at Madrid, as activists and NGOs convinced CSCE delegates and domestic political leaders to press for Helsinki compliance.

Eastern Helsinki monitors also tried to influence the Madrid meeting, although government repression made such efforts more difficult. Those activists who were prohibited from traveling to Madrid raised their concerns through a range of activities, including issuing open letters and conducting hunger strikes to protest human rights abuses in their countries. For example, in conjunction with an appeal by his wife Irina Valitova-Orlova to Madrid diplomats, imprisoned Moscow Helsinki Group leader Yuri Orlov declared a two-day hunger strike on 15 May 1980 to press for amnesty for all political prisoners. In a similar plea, prisoners from Mirov, Czechoslovakia, wrote to the Madrid conference in January 1981 declaring that, contrary to what Czechoslovak representatives were saying, they had been sentenced because they "raised the question of violations of human rights." In addition, three Charter 77 signatories wrote to the Madrid delegates to encourage a commission to study the conditions of imprisonment of political prisoners.[33]

Faced with a profusion of groups trying to advance their objectives at Madrid, Helsinki Watch recognized that forming connections between likeminded groups across CSCE states could facilitate more effective human rights advocacy. As such, Helsinki Watch initiated the formation of the International Helsinki Federation for Human Rights, or the IHF as it was called, which proved to be a significant development in the Helsinki process. The IHF served as a formal umbrella for Western, neutral, and Eastern national Helsinki committees.[34] For the myriad of monitoring groups spread across CSCE countries, the IHF created an easier means to connect with one another while establishing a central organization to better guide the overarching network.[35]

The establishment of the IHF marked a transition to a more formal Helsinki coalition, enabling Helsinki advocates to pursue joint strategies and tactics, which heightened their effectiveness.[36] First, greater consultation prevented duplicative efforts. Second, the ability to compose an international delegation or to speak with a united, international voice heightened the IHF's influence with political leaders. Third, locating the IHF's headquarters in Vienna created greater physical proximity between human rights activists and the countries they monitored.

At the same time that Western activists were succeeding in improved organization and coordination efforts, Eastern monitoring groups were declining in influence, as NGOs such as the Moscow Helsinki Group had been severely depleted in strength and numbers by arrest, exile, and imprisonment. The Moscow Helsinki Group officially suspended its activities on 6 September 1982, announcing: "The Moscow Helsinki Group has been put into condition where further work is impossible… Under these conditions the group … has to cease its work."[37] Although the group decided to disband, the years of the Madrid meeting were nonetheless highly productive for Helsinki monitoring efforts overall. Furthermore, despite the formal end to the Moscow Helsinki Group, its influence on the movement for reform in the Soviet Union and Helsinki activism more broadly extended throughout the final years of the Cold War.[38]

Faced with ongoing Eastern non-compliance with the Helsinki Final Act, many Western diplomats transitioned from highlighting abuses and negotiating new non-binding agreements to pressing Eastern governments to demonstrate progress towards existing commitments. The United States, for example, pushed the Soviets to take meaningful steps on human rights and hoped for resolution of divided spouse cases, increased emigration, and the release of Helsinki monitors and other prominent political prisoners.[39] Eastern progress on human rights during and soon after Madrid was minimal but established a pattern that accelerated with later meetings, where making new commitments on human rights and humanitarian issues was insufficient and as demonstrating progress on compliance became essential.[40]

Those groups and individuals that made up the Helsinki coalition worked tirelessly over the subsequent years at CSCE review meetings and outside the formal CSCE negotiations to influence Western and Eastern governments. Their ultimate success came in the context of new leadership and efforts at reform in the Soviet Union, which finally led to some acquiescence of the Soviets to respect human rights. By the end of 1988 there were significant improvements in the Soviet human rights situation: 600 political prisoners had been released, emigration had swelled to 80,000, and jamming had ended.

The influence of transnational Helsinki activism can be further seen in the events that shaped the end of communism across Central and Eastern Europe. In the aftermath of the Vienna Meeting, Helsinki monitors, long persecuted by Eastern regimes and championed by supporters in the West, led grass-roots movements in pursuit of human rights and freedoms that fueled change across Europe. Governing in a new atmosphere without a security guarantee from the Soviet Union, Eastern European leaders acceded to their population's demands, many of which were tied explicitly to Helsinki principles.

The broader Helsinki network's activism throughout this period influenced the scope and pace of change, contributing to the collapse of communism in Eastern Europe, the breakup of the Soviet Union, and the end of the Cold War. Initially, the rise of Helsinki monitoring groups in the Soviet Union and Eastern Europe precipitated a wide range of government repression including harassment, forced exile, and imprisonment. Yet transnational activism persisted, and by the time Mikhail Gorbachev became Soviet general secretary in 1985, Soviet progress on human rights had become a prerequisite to Gorbachev attracting Western support for his policy agenda.

Notes

1. The Helsinki Final Act was the culmination of three years of negotiations by representatives of thirty-five European and North American countries at the Conference on Security and Cooperation in Europe (CSCE) and contained principles to govern East-West interactions in Europe. In addition to reaching an agreement on the inviolability of frontiers, which was the original impetus for the Soviet desire to hold the conference, the Helsinki Final Act committed the CSCE states to respect human rights and facilitate human contacts across East-West borders.

2. A number of scholars have written about the influence of non-governmental organizations (NGOs) and on the evolution of Soviet policymaking in this period and my work builds upon their ideas. Historian Akira Iriye has described the development of a human rights network as fostering the growth of civil society in the Soviet bloc. In his work, political scientist Robert D. English explores changing Soviet ideas about political and human values, the transformation of which political scientist Daniel C. Thomas argues was due to what he calls the "Helsinki effect." Thomas contends that the establishment of human rights as a "formal norm" transformed Soviet bloc states and East-West relations. My work complements Thomas' in a number of ways. We agree that in the wake of the signing of the Helsinki Final Act, transnational monitoring efforts developed that ultimately influenced the end of the Cold War. Our different methodologies, however, have led us to emphasize different actors and organizations' influence within the Helsinki network. Furthermore, Thomas attributes greater significance to the role of international norms whereas I regard pressure exerted in bilateral and multilateral forums to be more important. Akira Iriye, *Global Community: The Role of International Organizations in the Making of the Contemporary World* (Berkeley 2002); Robert D. English, *Russia and the Idea of the West: Gorbachev, Intellectuals and the End of the Cold War* (New York 2000); and Daniel C. Thomas, *The Helsinki Effect: International Norms, Human Rights, and the Demise of Communism* (Princeton 2001), 258.

3. The Helsinki Final Act, <www.osce.org/documents/mcs/1975/08/4044_en.pdf> (accessed 17 May 2006). The use of the term human rights is guided by the definition outlined in the 30 articles of the 1948 United Nations Universal Declaration of Human Rights, and upon which the Helsinki Final Act was based.

4. Transnational advocacy networks are bound together by a commitment to shared values, as was the case with the Helsinki network. Margaret Keck and Kathryn Sikkink, *Activists Beyond Borders: Advocacy Networks in International Politics* (Ithaca 1998), 1.

5. Elizabeth Borgwardt has argued that the 1941 Atlantic Charter should be considered the first international declaration on human rights, but as its purpose was conceived differently, its successor the Universal Declaration is a more appropriate point of comparison. Elizabeth Borgwardt, *A New Deal for the World* (Cambridge, MA 2005), 1-11.

6. Fenwick also talks about being inspired to propose the Commission after meeting

a woman with a "desperate expression" as a result of her husband's detention. News Release, "Impressions of the Trip to Russia," 11 September 1975, Folder 33, Box 7, Travel Series, Carl Albert Collection, Carl Albert Center Congressional Archives, University of Oklahoma, Norman, Oklahoma; and Millicent Fenwick, *Speaking Up* (New York 1982), 161. The term refusenik referred to those, usually Jewish, who had been denied permission to emigrate. Amy Schapiro, *Millicent Fenwick: Her Way* (New Brunswick 2003), 169; and Reminiscences of Millicent Fenwick (1988), on pages 404-411 in the Columbia University Oral History Research Office Collection, New York.

7   Testimony, 4 May 1976, Folder 1, Box 181, Millicent Fenwick Papers, Rutgers University, New Brunswick, New Jersey.

8   Fenwick, *Speaking Up*, 161.

9   Ibid.

10   Millicent Fenwick, 17 May 1976, *Congressional Record*, Folder 1, Box 181, Fenwick Papers.

11   Newsletter, "Impressions of the Trip to Russia," 11 September 1975, Folder 33, Box 7, Travel Series, Carl Albert Collection. Her emphasis on human rights throughout her legislative career led some to term her the "Republican Roosevelt," clearly referencing Eleanor, not Franklin or Teddy. Schapiro, *Millicent Fenwick*, 169.

12   In addition, the Commission received and translated many *samizdat* documents and forwarded them to other CSCE states and interested groups. *Samizdat* can be translated as "self-published" and refers to documents such as banned literature or reports of abuses that were produced and distributed clandestinely. Commission on Security and Cooperation in Europe, "A Thematic Survey of the Documents of the Moscow Helsinki Groups," 12 May 1981.

13   Robert F. Drinan, *The Mobilization of Shame: A World View of Human Rights* (New Haven 2001), 73. Anatoli Shcharansky changed his name to Natan Sharansky when he emigrated to Israel. I have chosen to use the original spelling of his name when writing about his activism in the Soviet Union.

14   Ludmilla Alexeyeva, *Soviet Dissent: Contemporary Movements for National, Religious, and Human Rights* (Middletown, CT 1985), 336. I have chosen to use the anglicized version under which she published in the United States only in the notes. Discussion of Alekseeva's role in the main text will use the proper transliteration of her name.

15   I have used Moscow Helsinki Group throughout this chapter. The founding members were Yuri Orlov, Ludmilla Alekseeva, Alexander Korchak, Malva Landa, Vitaly Rubin, Anatoly Shcharansky, Yelena Bonner, Aleksandr Ginsburg, Anatoly Marchenko, Pyortr Grigorenko, and Mikhail Bernshtam. *Arkihiv Samizdata* 2542, May 1976, Box 84, Published Samizdat, Samizdat Archives, Records of Radio Free Europe/Radio Liberty Research Institute, Open Society Archives, Central European University, Budapest, Hungary; Paul Goldberg, *The Final Act: The Dramatic, Revealing Story of the Moscow Helsinki Watch Group* (New York 1988), 35-37, 39; and Yuri

Orlov, *Dangerous Thoughts: Memoirs of a Russian Life*, Thomas P. Whitney, trans. (New York 1991), 188-189.

16   Alexeyeva, *Soviet Dissent*, 345-346; and 25 March 1980, in Vojtech Mastny (ed.), *Helsinki, Human Rights, and European Security: Analysis and Documentation* (Durham 1986), 143-152.

17   Commission on Security and Cooperation in Europe, "A Thematic Survey of the Documents of the Moscow Helsinki Groups," 12 May 1981.

18   Ibid.; and Goldberg, *The Final Act*, 57.

19   Joshua Rubenstein, *Soviet Dissidents: Their Struggle for Human Rights*, 2nd ed. (Boston 1985), 221.

20   As evidence of the informal links between these Helsinki groups, the Lithuanian Helsinki group formally announced in itself a press conference in Moscow on 27 November 1976 in Orlov's apartment. In the same vein, Sharansky writes about spending time in Chistopol Prison with Victoras Piatkus, leader of the Lithuanian Moscow Helsinki Group. Goldberg, *The Final Act*, 132; and Natan Sharansky, *Fear No Evil* (New York 1988), 246.

21   Statement, Tad Szulc, 24 February 1977, Folder 17, Box 274, Fenwick Papers.

22   Valery Chalidze, "Human Rights: A Policy of Honor," *Wall Street Journal* (8 April 1977). Links between different components of the Helsinki network developed due to what scholars of social movements and transnational activism have called a "boomerang" pattern. The "boomerang" effect describes the method by which domestic actors, confronted with obstacles to influencing their own governments, identify external actors who can raise their concerns internationally and exert pressure more effectively on the state. When internal, domestic activism is ineffective, individuals or groups seek out external advocates who can champion their cause more effectively. At his 1978 trial, Orlov noted that the Moscow Helsinki Group appealed to foreign governments because "approaching our own government through the governments of other nations was more effective than a direct approach." Keck and Sikkink, *Activists Beyond Borders*, 12; and Robert Horvath, *The Legacy of Soviet Dissent: Dissidents, Democratization and Radical Nationalism in Russia* (New York 2005), 63.

23   For example, Charter 77 published 150 books and many periodicals as well as distributed 1,000 *samizdat* materials, all to spread information about human rights violations to politicians, delegates, and the public. News Release, 24 October 1979, Press Releases, Box 2442, Dante Fascell Papers, University of Miami, Coral Gables, Florida.

24   The Moscow Helsinki Group produced 26 documents and drafted 195 reports, statements, and letters to inform those at the Belgrade meeting about the human rights situation in the Soviet Union. Robert Kennedy Eichhorn, *The Helsinki Accords and Their Effect on the Cold War* (M.A. Thesis, California State University, Fullerton, 1995), 193, 213; Commission on Security and Cooperation in Europe, "A Thematic Survey of the Documents of the Moscow Helsinki Groups," 12 May 1981; "Belgrade – Getting Down to Squaring the Circle," 1 December 1977, Western Cooperation:

General, 1975-79, Box 60, Subject Files Relating to the bloc, East European Research and Analysis Department, Records of Radio Free Europe/Radio Liberty Research Institute, Open Society Archives; and Dante B. Fascell, "The Helsinki Accord: A Case Study," *Annals of the American Academy of Political and Social Science* 442 (1979), 76.

25 Political scientists Margaret Keck and Kathryn Sikkink have extensively studied transnational advocacy networks and identified different methods by which networks gain support for their agenda, including what they term "information politics," which includes the collection and distribution of relevant information. Information politics was clearly an effective strategy for monitoring groups in Eastern Europe who sought supporters of their campaigns for Helsinki implementation. Keck and Sikkink, *Activists Beyond Borders*, 16. This proliferation of activity, however, sparked a corresponding wave of repression; even the specter of the Belgrade meeting did not inhibit Soviet plans to crack down on domestic dissidents. "USSR Weekly Review," 26 January 1978, CIA Records Search Tool (CREST), National Archives, College Park, Maryland; and William E. Griffith, "East-West Détente in Europe," in Frans A. M. Alting von Geseau (ed.), *Uncertain Détente* (Alphen aan den Rijn 1979), 12.

26 Keck and Sikkink also outline the utility of "leverage politics," or using an influential figure to champion the network's agenda when it has less influence, which was an essential element of the Helsinki network's methods. Such a method relied upon Western diplomats and political leaders to advance their agenda, pressing for greater observance of human rights and the release and emigration of Helsinki activists. Keck and Sikkink, *Activists Beyond Borders,* 16.

27 William Korey, *The Promises We Keep: Human Rights, the Helsinki Process and American Foreign Policy* (New York 1993), xxv.

28 Press Briefing Transcript, 2 February 1978, IT 5 1/1/78-12/31/78, IT – 1, White House Central Files, Jimmy Carter Library, Atlanta, Georgia.

29 R. Spencer Oliver Interview, 26 February 2008.

30 Jeri Laber, *The Courage of Strangers: Coming of Age with the Human Rights Movement* (New York 2002), 120-121; Korey, *The Promises We Keep*, xxvi; Xinyuan Dai, *Compliance Without Carrots or Sticks: How International Institutions Influence National Policies* (Ph.D. Dissertation, University of Chicago, 2000), 146, 186, 191; and H. Gordon Skilling, "The Madrid Follow-up" in Robert Spencer (ed.), *Canada and the Conference on Security and Co-operation in Europe* (Toronto 1984), 317.

31 By the Madrid meeting, the Moscow Helsinki Group had drafted 149 documents. Commission on Security and Cooperation in Europe, "A Thematic Survey of the Documents of the Moscow Helsinki Groups," 12 May 1981.

32 Laber, *The Courage of Strangers*, 132-133, 162, 198-199.

33 *Arkihiv Samizdata* 4133, 5 September 1980, Helsinki: Madrid, 1980-1980, Box 1116, Old Code Subject Files, Soviet Red Archives, Records of Radio Free Europe/Radio Liberty Research Institute, Open Society Archives; Valitova-Orlov to Kampelman, Box 13, Max M. Kampelman Papers, Minnesota Historical Society, St. Paul, Min-

nesota; Orlov, *Dangerous Thoughts*, 234, 242-244; Mastny, *Helsinki, Human Rights, and European Security*, 196; and H. Gordon Skilling, "The Madrid Follow-up", 320. The *Arkihiv Samizdata* files of the Radio Free Europe/Radio Liberty Research Institute contain many similar appeals such as one from Soviet dissidents announcing a hunger strike to coincide with the beginning of a new session at Madrid. *Arkihiv Samizdata* 4854, 8 February 1983, Helsinki: Madrid, 1982-1983, Old Code Subject Files, Soviet Red Archives, Records of Radio Free Europe/Radio Liberty Research Institute, Open Society Archives.

34 When it was first formed, the IHF was made up of Helsinki Committees from France, Norway, the Netherlands, the United States, with groups developing quickly in Austria, Belgium, Canada, and Sweden. Initially it was deemed too dangerous for groups in Eastern Europe or Turkey to join officially. Later the IHF came to include groups from Czechoslovakia, Denmark, the Federal Republic of Germany, Italy, Poland, Switzerland, United Kingdom, Soviet Union, and Yugoslavia, among others.

35 The IHF announced its establishment at a press conference in Madrid on 9 November 1982. Gerald Nagler, who formed a Swedish Helsinki Committee soon after the Italy conference, offered to chair the IHF in Vienna on a part-time, voluntary basis. Laber, *The Courage of Strangers*, 198-199.

36 Sanjeev Khagram, James V. Riker, and Kathryn Sikkink, "From Santiago to Seattle: Transnational Advocacy Groups Restructuring World Politics," in Sanjeev Khagram, James V. Riker, and Kathryn Sikkink (eds), *Restructuring World Politics: Transnational Social Movements, Networks, and Norms* (Minneapolis 2002), 7.

37 Goldberg, *The Final Act*, 278; and Laber, *The Courage of Strangers*, 182-183.

38 Horvath, *The Legacy of Soviet Dissent*, 1.

39 Memorandum, Kampelman to Burt, 18 January 1983, Box 14, Kampelman Papers.

40 Through the use of "accountability politics" leaders are held responsible for upholding policies to which they have committed themselves. Reliance on "accountability politics" by Helsinki activists can be seen throughout the Helsinki process, but especially during the reviews of implementation that occurred at the CSCE review meetings. Those devoted to fulfillment of the Helsinki Final Act repeatedly pressed Eastern European and Soviet leaders to uphold their commitments. Keck and Sikkink, *Activists Beyond Borders*, 16.

Transatlantic Relations, Human Rights, and Power Politics

Gregory F. Domber

On 13 December 1981, the Polish United Workers' Party (PZPR) leader General Wojciech Jaruzelski declared martial law, utilized deadly force to break strikes by coal miners, and arrested and interned thousands of members of the Solidarnosc Trade Union. In reaction, on 23 December President Ronald Reagan imposed economic and political sanctions against Poland. In contrast to Washington, America's West European allies took a much less charged stand, with some even expressing relief at the declaration of martial law. In the historiography of the 1980s, the American response to events in Poland is viewed both as a break in good relations between the Western allies and as a break in East-West relations, with the United States utilizing traditional power politics over Europe's preference to continue détente and cooperation. In the most recent and comprehensive study of the 1980-1981 Polish crisis, Helene Sjursen argues that the US decision to move away from détente was to blame for the break within the Western alliance: "Seeing the protection of human rights as a national mission, the United States pursued this goal according to the premise of power politics, with little regard for the views of its West European allies or collective procedures for weighing up the different goals and norms involved."[1]

Economic sanctions, political restrictions, and tough rhetoric about Poland were an undeniable sign of the Reagan administration's confrontational strategy and illustrative of the so-called Second Cold War. Moreover, the Reagan administration's unilateral decision to impose sanctions on oil and gas equipment meant to block the construction of a natural gas pipeline from Siberia to Western Europe in response to the Polish crisis provides solid evidence for scholars' emphasis on the break in transatlantic relations.[2] However, separating America's ill-fated actions aimed at the Soviet Union from American policies directed specifically at Poland provides a different view of American policy and the relationship between power politics, human rights, and trans-Atlantic relations. In the case of America's Poland strategy, the Reagan administration did not pursue a purely confrontational or disruptive policy. Under pressure from its European allies, the US government restrained its sanctions, showing that the Reagan administration was willing to compromise based on European concerns. With the absence of a coordinated sanctions regime, the United States used human rights norms to forge a more cohesive Western position, at least rhetorically. The Europeans, however, remained timid in the use of power politics, despite moves by the Poles and the Soviets to ignore Western calls for change. By 1986, however, Western European attitudes had shifted to collectively utilize Reagan-style power politics to push the PZPR to declare a final, comprehensive amnesty for political prisoners. Overall, this reevaluation of the Polish case sheds light on the boundaries of American actions during the height of the second Cold War and provides concrete evidence on how trans-Atlantic relations, Western concerns for human rights, and power politics (as opposed to policies of détente) motivated the PZPR to pursue meaningful political change.

Choosing Sanctions Carefully

By all accounts, President Reagan was furious about the declaration of martial law. According to one NSC staff member, the president was "absolutely livid" and allegedly said that "something must be done. We need to hit them hard and save Solidarity."[3] Reagan's anger was equally apparent when he met on 21 December with Polish-American leaders who reported that "'the President was awfully angry' about the events in Poland."[4] This anger was amplified by the president's belief that, "This may be the last chance in our lifetime to see a change in the Soviet empire's colonial policy re[garding] Eastern Europe."[5] In Reagan's view Poland presented a historic opportunity to fight Communism akin to Franklin Roosevelt's decision to lead America into World War II to defeat fascism.[6]

Reagan and his administration's anger and sense of historical purpose led them to take action to punish the Polish government. On 14 December, Deputy Assistant Secretary Jack Scanlan met with the Polish ambassador in Washington to explain that the US was suspending all aid and economic support activities including consideration of $740 million in agricultural aid and $100 million in emergency feed grain sales that had been recently approved.[7] On 23 December, Reagan took his punitive moves further and announced that the United States was halting the renewal of Export-Import Bank insurance credits, suspending all LOT flights to and from the United

States, suspending Poland's rights to fish in American waters, and working with NATO to "increase restrictions on technology trade."[8]

These steps, however, were not the only ones considered. According to internal deliberations, the sanctions announced ranged from "severe" (suspending agricultural aid) to "strong" (postponing fishing rights) to "medium" (suspending LOT flights). "Limited" actions blocking cooperation on joint trade commissions and trade fairs did not merit announcement during prime time, but were exercised quietly. Importantly, the White House kept its strongest options in reserve. The Reagan administration did not immediately take steps to declare Poland in default, to rescind MFN trade status, or to block Poland's entrance into the IMF.[9] Additionally, Washington did not take any immediate unilateral moves affecting multilateral considerations of Poland's massive international debt.

The reaction to martial law was strikingly different in Western Europe. French Foreign Minister Claude Cheysson stated that "the matter remained an 'internal Polish affair that must be handled by the Poles.'"[10] British Foreign Secretary Peter Carrington issued a statement that the British "shall observe a policy of strict non-intervention, and we expect the same of all signatories of the Helsinki Final Act."[11] West German Chancellor Helmut Schmidt took a similar tact explaining that "all the nations that signed the Helsinki declaration on European security should adhere to its non-intervention principle." The West Germans went a step further, releasing a statement that they were following events with "sympathy and concern."[12] By invoking the sovereignty clause of the Helsinki accords, the West Europeans signaled that the Soviets should not intervene militarily in Poland, a major concern at the time; however, they simultaneously acknowledged that martial law was an internal, sovereign matter, implicitly accepting part of Jaruzelski's argument for how and why he declared martial law. These signals showed a clear difference of opinion with the United States.

In the face of this public rift, the Americans lobbied their allies to take a harder line. This included letters on 15 and 16 December from Haig to Cheysson, Carrington, and Genscher outlining American intelligence and thinking about the crisis.[13] On 19 December, Haig pushed them again, stressing the historical importance of their response: "Western inaction at this time will not be forgotten by those who assess the character of our nations and our individual qualities as statesmen in the years to come,"[14] a message seconded by Reagan in personal letters to French President Francois Mitterand, British Prime Minister Margaret Thatcher, and Schmidt a day later.[15] Washington also coordinated with European allies through regular meetings of the North Atlantic Council (NAC), which the State Department viewed "as a stage-setter for possible follow-on consideration of alliance actions as events in Poland unfold."[16] To continue to press for action Assistant Secretary of State Lawrence Eagleburger was dispatched to Rome, Bonn, Paris, and London from 20 to 22 December.[17]

At a 23 December NAC meeting, American efforts to change European policies showed only slight progress and limited consensus. First the British called for action against the Poles and Soviets at the upcoming CSCE meeting in Madrid. The British also reported that the European Community (EC-10) had agreed to suspend shipments of beef to Poland until it could be guaranteed that the food was delivered to the intended recipients. The Danes approved stronger COCOM restrictions. The Italians took the hardest line, flatly stating that they would have trouble continuing their current economic relationship with Poland. The West Germans, however, argued against calling a special ministerial-level NAC meeting, rejected economic punishments, and opposed using CSCE as a forum to present Western disgust about human rights abuses.[18] A week later the United States successfully lobbied through the EC-10 and other groups to allow a ministerial-level NAC meeting, but West Germany remained the key stumbling block keeping NATO from taking a harder stand against the PZPR.[19]

Despite continuing disagreement, Washington hoped to influence West German leaders through previously scheduled bilateral meetings set for 4 and 5 January 1982. As Haig explained to Reagan, "Given the FRG's political, economic, and military weight, we need Germany almost as much as they need us, particularly on an issue such as Poland," adding, "dealing with Schmidt is difficult and frustrating.... On Poland, Schmidt is moving towards our position ... and your meeting provides a good chance to bring him further along."[20] By even internal American accounts, however, both Reagan and Haig's meetings with Schmidt completely failed to create consensus on Poland.[21] Negotiations were so tense that Schmidt exclaimed that he would "not be blackmailed" by un-attributed threats in the media about America pulling troops out of Germany.[22]

Having run into this wall, the secretary of state went back to work on drafting an allied declaration for a NAC special session set for 11 January. Prior to Schmidt's visit, State hoped that the NAC meeting would allow Washington "to pry loose some Allied sanctions against Poland ... [and] to create a common overall policy for the longer haul.... The outcome we want is not a rhetorical declaration but a calm and sober agreed policy."[23] After the meetings, however, Haig approved a severely scaled-back proposal that did not include specific sanctions or political actions. State only planned to push for language which was supportive of their position and which only committed the allies to "do nothing to weaken the effects of" American sanctions.[24]

At the NAC special session, the United States followed their plan, pursuing only strong statements (not specific actions) and pushing for an agreement not to interfere with individual ally's sanctions.[25] In the final communiqué, NATO publicly condemned martial law, deplored Soviet pressure on the Poles, mentioned the "significance of the measures already announced by President Reagan," and pledged "not to undermine the effect of each other's measures." In a nod to growing agreement that something needed to be done, NATO took the mild steps of suspending possible new credits to Poland, delaying consideration of rescheduling Poland's debt, and insuring that humanitarian aid reached the people (as opposed to the government). But the Allies did not take any immediately punitive steps.[26] Haig left Brussels trying to put a positive spin on the outcome: "I consider today's meeting to be a solid success for the alliance.... We sought a common near-and-long-term strategy to help the Polish people, and today the alliance produced one."[27]

Polish Debt

Even in the face of continuing West German efforts to scuttle American pressure against the PZPR, the Reagan administration continued to defer to West European concerns. Most notably, in January 1982 the White House decided to pay Poland's outstanding debts rather than declare the Communist government in default. By December 1981, Poland had accrued roughly $26 billion in debt to the West. Of this, $3.15 billion (14 percent) came from the United States.[28] In April 1981, the United States and other Western governments, who conducted negotiations through an ad-hoc group known as the Paris Club, agreed to reschedule ninety percent of Poland's debt for 1981. To deal with their debt to private Western lenders, the PZPR signed an agreement on 4 December 1981, to reschedule $2.4 billion in debt principal with the London Club (the ad-hoc group that negotiated agreements for private bankers) and pay $500 million in interest by the end of 1981. However, in the wake of martial law, Polish officials announced that they could not even make this reduced payment, bringing the question of default front and centre.[29]

The Reagan administration immediately understood that debt repayment and rescheduling agreements offered the West its strongest point of leverage against the PZPR. Ideological members of the cabinet, particularly Secretary of Defense Caspar Weinberger and UN Ambassador Jeanne Kirkpatrick, believed that the United States should push the Polish economy towards complete collapse by declaring default. This would completely cut them out of consideration for any new private or public loans. Also, if the government declared default, private bankers could do the same, after which the private banks could legally seize Polish assets.[30] On the other side of the debate, more pragmatic voices in the State Department calculated that even with the economy in shambles, Polish exports could pay for all necessary Western imports, but Warsaw did not have enough hard currency to cover its debt payments as well. In their estimation, economic leverage after 13 December came from "continuing trade relationships; debt service relief, both public and private; and access to new credits, both public and private." This leverage would be weakened if the Poles declared a unilateral moratorium on debt repayment. Thus, in the State Department's view, it was in the US government's best interests for public and private bankers *not* to declare default.[31]

American sensitivity to European concerns also played an important part in this debate. Poland owed most of its debt to West Europeans. Default would cause Poland's debt to be devalued, leading to widespread budget and financial difficulties for European banks. The problem was particularly acute for West German lenders because they held the largest portion of debt. The State Department and Haig privately expressed concern about the negative effects that a unilateral American government decision that hurt European bankers would have on allied cohesion at a point when relations were already strained. In the final report, advocates for default acquiesced to more pragmatic arguments by the State Department.[32]

On 31 January, the Reagan administration announced it would pay $71 million to US banks to cover past due payments. In return American banks agreed not to call for Poland to repay its loans in full, ending the default debate. The White House argued that this was only a temporary arrangement until Warsaw could pay its debts, but as the *Washington Post* reported this led to a much larger commitment: "For fiscal 1982, the total exposure on guaranteed loans comes to $308 million, and in the next two fiscal years, the total owed to the banks and guaranteed by the CCC comes to $613 million."[33] In a domestic American atmosphere obsessed with deficit spending, this was a difficult message to swallow. On 3 February, the *Wall Street Journal* editorial page condemned the decision, arguing that Washington was "slipping into tacit collaboration with martial law by making it easier for the Soviet bloc to finance repression."³⁴ Public uncertainty increased after it surfaced that Washington's decision protected West German bankers whose government had done so much to sabotage American sanctions.³⁵ On Capitol Hill Senator Daniel Patrick Moynihan convened hearings of the Senate Appropriations Committee and criticized the administration's inability to apply meaningful pressure on "either the military junta in Warsaw or its masters in Moscow."³⁶ AFL-CIO President Lane Kirkland also attacked the decision, arguing: "In effect, President Reagan told the Soviets to disregard his tough talk. He announced that the United States would not use the most potent economic weapon at our disposal in defense of Solidarity."³⁷ In the face of public pressure from all political angles, the Reagan administration continued to side with West European concerns and pursued a prudent policy not to force default.

Human Rights, CSCE, and Consensus

In its campaign to push for sanctions against Poland, Washington consistently invoked human rights abuses and commitments made to protect them in the Helsinki Final Act. In his 17 December speech Reagan declared the arrest and imprisonment of thousands of union leaders and intellectuals a "gross violation of the Helsinki pact," and on 23 December he explained, "The Polish Government has trampled underfoot solemn commitments to the UN Charter and the Helsinki accords."³⁸ In the NAC, US Ambassador to NATO William Bennet, Jr. focused his criticism on the "clear and gross violation of the Helsinki Final Act."³⁹ On 29 December, Reagan privately called for a special meeting of the CSCE in early January because events in Poland "clearly run counter to the obligations assumed by the Soviet Union and the Polish government under the Helsinki Final Act and for that reason cannot be ignored by other CSCE signatories."⁴⁰

At the same time, the US government launched a publicity campaign "to keep the media pot boiling" to "create a great moral wave" against events in Poland.⁴¹ Public protests arose nearly spontaneously on 13 December, with crowds gathering outside Polish embassies in Paris, Vienna, London, Brussels, Milan, Rome, Lisbon, and Athens.⁴² Larger protest rallies with supporters numbering in the thousands took place a few days later in Paris and Rome, with smaller events throughout the continent.⁴³ In American analysis, this outpouring of emotion showed that the European public was "out in front of government attitudes on the Polish situation." Knowing that European governments would have to respond to this public groundswell, Washington began a publicity campaign to highlight human rights abuses. This included working through the Helsinki/CSCE process, "where we need to energize national Helsinki Watch groups and brand Moscow with violation of the Helsinki Final Act."[44] The campaign culminated in a ninety-minute television programme produced by the US government to express the "indignation of America and other free peoples at the imposition of martial law and repression of human freedoms in Poland."[45] Overtly the programme – titled "Let Poland be Poland" and broadcast around the world at the end of January – was meant to demonstrate Western unity against Polish and Soviet repression; however, given the mainly non-Communist audience it was clearly designed to bolster Western resolve to act as well.

With the NAC special session behind them, the US government turned its attention to CSCE. By mid-January the idea of a special session on Poland had been scrapped, but the White House still saw the planned resumption of ongoing talks in Madrid on 9 February as a focal point to spawn concerted action. Moreover, as human rights conditions worsened, the Allies grew more unified, with even the West Germans coming in line on the need to push political and diplomatic efforts to punish the Poles.[46] By the end of January the White House decided to send Haig to Madrid to vehemently protest human rights abuses under martial law. The Americans asked their allies to send their foreign ministers as well, and after speaking out against the situation in Poland, to work to suspend negotiations. In the State Department's estimate, this tactic would "contribute to Western objectives if it focuses attention on Poland and Soviet responsibilities," and thus "demonstrate that the Allies are united and determined, and reinforce to the East the damaging impact on East-West relations of Poland and other Eastern violations of the Final Act."[47]

In the first full victory for American policy to coordinate action vis-à-vis Poland, the CSCE meeting transpired as Haig and his colleagues had hoped. When talks resumed in Madrid, Haig, Genscher, and other Western foreign ministers took the floor to condemn human rights violations occurring in Poland. In response to harsh criticism from the US delegation, the Polish delegate (who was heading the session by coincidence) in coordination with the Soviet representative used parliamentary procedures to block further speeches for the day by French, British, Italian, and other West European representatives who had planned to speak. This parliamentary move infuriated the European delegates, increasing Western cohesion. As a Canadian delegate reported, "The whole thing has been a fabulous stroke of luck for the West. We came here with Genscher and Haig still disagreeing on key points, and with others equivocal about where they stand. Now the Russians have made everybody so angry through their arbitrary tactics that they're all rallying behind Haig."[48] Tensions remained high and the meeting was eventually suspended until November. The Allies had fully coalesced under the aegis of the Helsinki Final Act and concern about human rights abuses to make strong statements against abuses in Poland. Moreover, they successfully united in actions that led to the suspension of the Madrid meeting, despite earlier fears of causing rifts in East-West relations. The West had finally *acted* together.

Human Rights and Change in Poland

Nonetheless, these concerted statements at Madrid did little to modify PZPR and Soviet policies. In fact, the Poles and the Soviets consistently brushed aside any criticisms of human and workers' rights abuses by invoking claims of sovereignty and non-interference in domestic affairs, also codified in the Helsinki Final Act. References to Polish sovereignty were explicit in many of General Jaruzelski's early justifications for his actions. Soviet leaders also rejected calls for improvements of human rights conditions in Poland and countered that American statements, both before and after the declaration of martial law, constituted interference in Polish and Communist bloc affairs. In a personal letter to Reagan, Soviet General Secretary Leonid Brezhnev rejected the Helsinki Final Act as justification for criticizing martial law, reminding the president that the agreement "stipulates the refraining from any interference in affairs which come under the internal competence of another state."[49] Eighteen months after the declaration of martial law, when US Congressman Clarence Long visited Warsaw in August 1983 and brought up human rights abuses, Jaruzelski berated him with a rambling argument invoking Polish sovereignty. Long became so fed up with the general's explanations that he interrupted him to say that he had to go to the bathroom, only to clash again when he returned.[50] Finally, as many times as the American representative in Warsaw, John Davis, used the Final Act to justify raising human rights concerns, Polish Ministry of Foreign Affairs representatives rejected those concerns as interference in sovereign Polish affairs.[51] In the Polish case, contradictions between two of the principles of the Helsinki agreements created a situation in which what little traction commitment to international human rights norms had on actions within Poland were at best weakened, and at worst nullified. Human and workers' rights abuses continued to occur frequently throughout the first half of the 1980s.

Moreover, the liberalization in Polish behaviour in the years after December 1981 was primarily related to domestic concerns, not international criticism or norms. Solidarnosc leader Lech Walesa was released in November 1982 following a series of meetings between Polish Primate Jozef Glemp and Jaruzelski, evidence of the PZPR's need to make concessions to the domestic Catholic Church to maintain stability.[52] In December 1982, a limited contingent of unthreatening political prisoners was released at the same time that the PZPR took the symbolic step of suspending martial law in order to focus on Poland's economic problems.[53] In spring 1983 the PZPR decided to allow Pope John Paul II to make a pilgrimage that June only after lengthy negotiations with Vatican and Warsaw church representatives confirmed that the Pope would temper his political messages, continuing the Church's traditional role as a stabilizing intermediary between the people and the government.[54] Finally, the decision to lift martial law and declare a limited amnesty for political prisoners on 22 July 1983 was made after legal changes institutionalized many of the government's new powers and because the PZPR needed to further normalize the economy, which had been severely burdened under the restrictions of martial law. Another amnesty was announced on 22 July 1984, but most of the high-interest prisoners released at this point were quickly re-interned. From December 1981 to early 1985, scant concrete evidence has surfaced to indicate direct connections between either domestic or Western criticism of human rights abuses and significant Polish moves towards political or economic liberalization.

Nor is there much evidence that the PZPR was liberalizing in these first years to improve relations with the West. In *The Helsinki Effect*, Daniel Thomas bases his argument that human rights monitoring by Helsinki Watch groups and others "helped restrain the more reactionary elements within the regime" on an unsubstantiated claim that Jaruzelski desired "to rebuild contacts with the West ruptured by martial law."[55] However, a close inspection of Polish records from the period shows that in the weeks and months following martial law, the Polish government insulated itself economically from the West by turning decisively to the East. This included trips abroad requesting increased raw materials and credits from the Soviet Union and other Socialist nations.[56] Jaruzelski also wrote personal pleas to the general secretaries of brotherly parties seeking increased and specific economic support.[57] Most importantly, the PZPR focused its efforts at improving their economy through internal reforms and improved coordination with COM-

ECON.[58] By breaking economically with the West, Poland further decreased Western leverage to promote change. There were no concerted efforts in the first years after December 1981 to improve economic relations with the West, so there was no need to make concessions on human rights.

In contrast to these trends, there are two striking examples of when Western policies directly affected the human rights situation. In May 1983, the NSC embraced a new step-by-step approach to relations with Poland, meaning that sanctions would be used as bargaining chips to be lifted and imposed individually to respond to changes in PZPR behaviour.[59] The step-by-step approach won its greatest victory in 1984 when Davis and Eagleburger negotiated with a PZPR intermediary, Adam Schaff, for the release of eleven high-profile political prisoners in return for removing a few sanctions.[60] Four of the eleven political prisoners were set to go on trial in the summer of 1984, but all eleven were released after only one day of trial as part of a larger political amnesty announced on 22 July 1984. In return, as agreed, the Americans allowed LOT to resume regularly scheduled flights to the United States and announced that scientific-technical exchanges would be restarted.[61]

The greatest victory for Western power politics, however, came in 1986. As the Polish economy continued to stagnate despite reforms and increased cooperation with COMECON, Jaruzelski and his leadership gradually accepted that they could not extricate themselves from continuing decline without Western help. At the heart of this stagnation were debt repayments: they could not continue servicing their immense foreign debt without increasing foreign exports to gain much-needed Western currency; however, to increase foreign exports the Poles needed to gain new Western credits to buy needed technology and raw materials in the West.[62] New credits had been suspended following martial law, and with Poland's economy still in shambles from domestic political turmoil few businesses were looking to invest without guarantees on their investments from Western governments. To get out of this macro-economic Catch 22, the PZPR rewrote regulations regarding joint enterprises with Western investors. The PZPR simultaneously worked, beginning in 1985, to reinvigorate relations with Western Europe, most notably Italy, West Germany, France, and the United Kingdom. This initiative included numerous lower-level visits by West European officials to Poland and culminated with Jaruzelski's meeting with French President Mitterand in December 1985, the general's first visit to a Western capital since the declaration of martial law.[63] In July 1986, Poland even began exploratory talks with the EEC on a bilateral trade agreement.[64]

Poland's hopes for economic gains, however, became entwined with human rights concerns. In early 1986, the PZPR hinted that it was considering another amnesty for political prisoners. In response the American deputy chief of mission in Warsaw offered general statements in line with the standing step-by-step policy and suggested the possibility of ending sanctions if *all* political prisoners were released.[65] More importantly, on 30 July the EEC (led by Great Britain) sent a demarche explaining that if the expected amnesty was not complete and full Western European countries would summarily end all of the political and economic deals then under consideration. In effect, Poland would lose all of the gains it had made in the previous eighteen months, returning to square one in its push to gain new Western credits.[66] In the face of this united Western front, the PZPR acquiesced.[67] Six weeks after a partial political amnesty was announced on 22 July 1986, the PZPR released all remaining political prisoners. For the first time since December 1981, all of Poland's dissidents were free. This move also signaled a new relationship between the PZPR and the Solidarnosc-led opposition: political prisoners were never incarcerated for long periods again. The West had finally succeeded in decisively defending human rights in Poland.

Human Rights, CSCE, and Power Politics

In the historiography on Poland in the 1980s, most analyzes focus on tensions within the Western bloc following the declaration of martial law, blaming the break on the Reagan administration's unilateral policies. This analysis is correct when looking at American attempts to impose sanctions on the Soviet Union after the declaration of martial law, but it obscures a much more flexible American approach on actions against Poland. Washington went out of its way through diplomatic correspondence, NATO meetings, special ministerial sessions, bilateral contacts, and missions to Europe to create consensus about imposing sanctions on Poland. Despite stubborn, often vitriolic resistance by the West Germans, the White House even took steps to protect European banks rather than punish the Polish government. In their push to create consensus with Western Europe, the United States met with the most success by highlighting human rights abuses and Western commitments in the Helsinki Final Act. Western Europe never imposed as strong sanctions as the United States, but by mobilizing public opinion and policy-makers' concerns about human rights, the White House was able to create at least rhetorical consensus at the Madrid CSCE meeting.

Western consensus on human rights abuses, however, did not lead to immediate change in Poland. Both Warsaw and Moscow refused to accept their obligations to allow for certain freedoms under the Helsinki Final Act; rather they chose to invoke the principle of non-interference encapsulated in the same agreement. What few changes occurred in the human rights situation in Poland between 1981 and 1985 were more linked to domestic concerns than any desire to fulfill international obligations or norms. However, in 1986 West Europeans collectively took steps to exercise power politics – the threat of specific economic sanctions – in the name of human rights, causing significant changes in the Polish government's behaviour. Concerted use of power politics by Western Europe in 1986 (as Reagan had wanted earlier) led to substantive change in the human rights situation in Poland.

Three important lessons come out of this analysis of Western policy towards Poland in the first half of the 1980s. First, when analyzing the Reagan administration it is important to look beyond the president's rhetoric to see how policies were actually pursued over the long term. While Reagan was clearly motivated by ideological commitments, his administration often pursued much more pragmatic policies. This is particularly true when ideological members of his cabinet (neo-conservatives like Weinberger and Kirkpatrick, for example) were outmanoeuvred by more pragmatic voices (usually from the State Department). Second, commitments to human rights made in the Helsinki Final Act provided a useful tool for Americans to pressure Western Europeans to act in defence of human rights. As explained more fully in *The Helsinki Effect*, the signing of the Final Act created a set of international norms that helped galvanize public opinion in the West. Public outcry almost certainly played a role in pushing West European governments to take a harder stance on Poland at the Madrid CSCE meeting. As citizens of electoral democracies, Western Europeans had mechanisms in place to force their governments to respond to public sentiment. Moreover, it is plausible – even likely – that continued public concern about human rights abuses in Poland and activities by Helsinki Watch groups helped to solidify Western resolve that finally led to the EEC threatening punitive sanctions against Poland in summer 1986. In the Polish case, the Helsinki agreements did appear to "entrap" the West Europeans "in a transnational process of political change structured by formal international norms."[68]

Third, a close inspection of the documentary records shows that power politics mattered; they played an essential role in the PZPR's decision to declare a complete and final amnesty in summer 1986. This then calls into question certain arguments about why the Helsinki agreements were effective. Thomas' argument about the Helsinki agreements accelerating social mobilization on both sides of the Iron Curtain remains convincing; however, because his final conclusions are predicated on an argument that denies the role of punitive Western actions, the Polish case calls into question Thomas' findings about Socialist bloc countries being "entrapped" by their agreements regarding international norms of behaviour.[69] Contrary to what Thomas argues, East Europeans' commitment to international norms did not, in themselves, force Communist governments to change their behaviour; they were forced to change by economic and political pressure from the West. Social mobilization behind the Iron Curtain and in the West still mattered, though, because this transnational network created an information-gathering and distribution web that galvanized Western public opinion against human rights abusers, increasing pressure on Western politicians to act to punish countries in the Eastern bloc. So while the mechanism for pressure and entrapment is different, the outcome remains the same.

This view, in turn, supposes an alternate theory for understanding why the Soviets and East Europeans vacillated from relative acceptance of dissidents in the mid-1970s to cracking down heavily on dissidence in the late 1970s and early 1980s: when Western Europe and the United States acted in concert to defend human rights by either threatening or taking punitive action, the Socialist bloc chose to modify its behaviour. When a unified front to utilize sanctions could not be created, the Soviet Union and the East bloc disregarded human rights obligations. Certainly Poland's experience in the 1980s fits this pattern. The West was able to successfully pressure the Soviet Union not to invade Poland in 1980 and 1981 by unanimously threatening dire consequences if troops intervened. However, in the face of a very fractured Western resolve to respond to martial law in December 1981 and early 1982, the PZPR chose not to move decisively to limit human rights abuses. It was only after the West took a united punitive stand that lasting change came for Poland's political prisoners. United Western action in the form of power politics got results on human rights, divided stances did not.

Notes

1. Helene Sjursen, *The United States, Western Europe and the Polish Crisis: International Relations in the Second Cold War* (New York 2003), 137.
2. For the most in-depth study on the pipeline issue and the break it caused in the Western Alliance, see Antony Blinken, *Ally vs. Ally* (New York 1987). Detaching American policy towards Poland from policy towards the Soviet Union is admittedly a bit artificial; however, it provides an interesting analytical lens.
3. Peter Schweizer, *Reagan's War* (New York 2002), 165-166.
4. Bernard Gwertzman, "The President Weighs Steps on Poland," *New York Times* (22 December 1981): A1.
5. As quoted in *Reagan's War*, 166. For Reagan's full diary entry, dated 21 December, see Douglas Brinkley (ed.), *The Reagan Diaries* (New York 2007), 57.
6. Richard Pipes, *Vixi* (New Haven 2004), 171.
7. Cable from Secstate to Amembassy Warsaw, "Polish Government Statement on Situation in Poland; US Suspension of Aid to Warsaw," dated 15 December 1981, National Security Archive (hereafter NSA), Soviet Flashpoints Originals (hereafter SFO), Box 2.
8. "Address to the Nation about Christmas and the Situation in Poland, December 23, 1981," in *Public Papers* (1981), available on the Reagan Library's website: <www.reagan.utexas.edu>.
9. Memorandum for James Nance, "Discussion Paper for NSC Meeting," dated 21 December 1981, NSA, Soviet Flashpoints (hereafter SF), Box 26, 1-22 December 1981. MFN was only rescinded in November 1982 when the PZPR officially declared Solidarność illegal. Similarly, the United States only began blocking Poland's IMF membership later in 1982, when it became clear that martial law would not be lifted quickly.
10. Maureen Johnson, "Deep Concern in the West, Protests at Polish Embassies," *Associated Press* (13 December 1981), accessed via Lexis-Nexis Academic Universe.
11. Mark S. Smith, "International News," *Associated Press* (14 December 1981), accessed via Lexis-Nexis Academic Universe.
12. "International," *United Press International* (14 December 1981), accessed via Lexis-Nexis Academic Universe.
13. See Cable from Secstate to Amembassy Bonn, London, and Paris, "Message from the Secretary," dated 15 December 1981, NSA, SFO, Box 1, and Action Memorandum from Lawrence Eagleburger to the Secretary, "Consultations with the Allies on Poland," dated 18 December 1981, from Malcolm Byrne, Pawel Machcewicz and Christian F. Ostermann (eds), *Poland 1980-1982: Internal Crisis, International Dimensions, A Compendium of Declassified Documents and Chronology of Events* (Washington, D.C. 1997). Copies are available through the National Security Archive.
14. Cable from Secstate to Amembassy Paris, London, and Bonn, "Message for Cheysson, Carrington, and Genscher from the Secretary," dated 19 December 1981, NSA, SFO, Box 2.
15. Cable from Secstate to Amembassy Paris, London, and Bonn, "Message for Mit-

terand, Thatcher, and Schmidt from the President," dated 20 December 1981, NSA, SFO, Box 2.

16 Cable from Secstate to USMission NATO, "Poland: Dec 16 NAC on 'Gray Area' Scenario," NSA, SFO, Box 1.
17 Michael Getler, "U.S. Seeks European Support for Moves Directed at Soviet Union," *Washington Post* (22 December 1981): A12.
18 See Cable from Secstate info to Amembassy Tokyo, "(U) Poland: NAC Discussion December 23," dated 30 December 1981; and Cable from Secstate info to Amembassy Tokyo, "Poland: December 23 NAC Consultations," dated 30 December 1981; both in NSA, SFO, Box 4. At the 30 December NAC meeting, West Germany gave up its restrictions on a special NAC ministerial meeting.
19 The ministerial-level meeting was agreed to at a 30 December meeting of the NAC: Cable from Sesctate to EC Collective, "Secretary's December 28 Luncheon Meeting with EC-10 Ambassadors in Washington," dated 30 December 1981, NSA, SFO, Box 4.
20 Memorandum from Alexander M. Haig to the President, "Visit of Helmut Schmidt, Chancellor of the Federal Republic of Germany, January 5, 1982," dated 31 December 1981, NSA, SF, Box 27, December 1981. See also Haig's memo after meeting with Schmidt: Memorandum from Alexander M. Haig to the President, "Your Meeting with Chancellor Schmidt," dated 5 January 1982, NSA, SF, Box 27, January 1982.
21 "Joint Statement Following a Meeting With Chancellor Helmut Schmidt of the Federal Republic of Germany January 5, 1982," *Public Papers* (1982), available on the Reagan Library's website: <www.reagan.utexas.edu>. For media coverage see Reginald Dale, "Reagan demands 'tangible' allied moves on Poland," *Financial Times* (6 January 1982): A1; as well as Don Oberdorfer, "Haig Silent on Future Sanctions," *Washington Post* (7 January 1982): A1.
22 Memorandum of Conversation, "Secretary Haig's Breakfast Meeting with FRG Chancellor Schmidt," dated 6 January 1982, NSA, SF, Box 27, January 1982.
23 Action Memorandum from Lawrence Eagleburger to the Secretary, "Memorandum for the President on Poland, and Next Steps with the Allies," dated 4 January 1982, NSA, SF, Box 27, January 1982.
24 For the initial text, see: Action Memorandum from H. Allen Holmes to the Secretary, "The Alliance Declaration on Poland," dated 5 January 1982, published in *Poland 1980-1982*. For the approved text, see Action Memorandum from H. Allen Holmes to the Secretary, "Revised NATO Ministerial Declaration," dated 6 January 1982, NSA, SF, Box 27, January 1982.
25 Actual American records of the January 10-12 NAC have not been declassified. These statements are made based on the briefing materials and contingency plans created for Haig's trip. Those records can be found in: NSA, SF, Box 27, January 1982.
26 For the full text of the January 11 NAC Ministerial Communiqué, see the NATO website at <http://www.nato.int/docu/comm/49-95/c820111a.htm>. Poland's debt was already rescheduled for 1981, so delays in the process were not an immediate concern to anyone. Likewise, suspending new credits was presumed to be only temporary and non-binding.

27 James Reston, "Haig's Verbal Success," *New York Times* (January 1982): A23.
28 For this breakdown of Poland's debt, see "Fact Sheet on 12 Poland's Debt" published as part of Senate Appropriations Committee, *Polish Debt Crisis*, 97th Cong., 2nd Session, 1982, 18-19.
29 Information Memorandum from Robert Hormats to the Secretary, "Actions taken in response to your calls from Brussels on Polish Economic Assistance," dated 14 December 1981, NSA, SFO, Box 3, and Cable from Secstate to Amembassy Vienna, "Finance Minister of Debt Service and Emergency Measures," dated 24 December 1981, NSA, SF, Box 26, 23-25 December 1981.
30 Dan Morgan and Robert Kaiser, "Group of Aides Sought Tougher Stand on Poland," *Washington Post* (15 January 1982): A1.
31 Action Memorandum from Robert Hormats and Lawrence Eagleburger to the Secretary, "Western Economic Leverage on Poland and Secure Phone Call to Regan," dated 17 December 1981, NSA, SF, Box 26, 1-22 December 1981.
32 "Report on the Working Group on the Implications of Invoking the Exceptional Circumstances Clause of the 1981 Polish Official Debt Rescheduling Agreement," dated 20 January 1982, NSA, SF, Box 27, January 1982.
33 Dan Morgan, "U.S. tells its Banks Some Polish Debt will be Paid," *Washington Post* (2 February 1982): A11.
34 "Congresses Choice on Poland," *Wall Street Journal* (3 February 1982): 24.
35 Reporting on this topic is too wide to include all references, but for a representative, if mild, sample see Leslie Gelb, "Reprieve on Polish Debt," *New York Times* (3 February 1982): A1, and Paul Lewis, "Role of the Western Banks in Poland's Debt Crisis," *New York Times* (3 February 1982): A10.
36 *Polish Debt Crisis*; Moynihan quoted at 50, Ikle at 7, and Hormats at 40.
37 "AFL-CIO Press Release, 4 February 1982 [re Kirkland statement on Reagan Administrations policy on Polish debt]," dated 4 February 1982, George Meany Memorial Archive, Information Department, CIO, AFL-CIO Press Releases, 1937-1995, Box 48, 48/3.
38 See "President's New Conference, December 17, 1981," and "Address to the Nation about Christmas and the Situation in Poland, December 23, 1981," both in *Public Papers* (1981), available on the Reagan Library's website: <www.reagan.utexas.edu>.
39 Cable from USMission NATO to Secstate, "Poland: NAC Discussion on Allied Public Posture," dated 19 December 1981, NSA, SFO, Box 1.
40 Cable from SecState to All NATO Capitals, "CSCE: Emergency Meeting on Poland," dated NSA, SF, Box 26.
41 Memorandum of Meeting, "U.S. Response to Polish Crisis," dated 22 December 1981, NSA, SF Box 26, 1-22 December 1981.
42 "West Rallies Behind Solidarity," United Press International (13 December 1981), accessed via Lexis-Nexis Academic Universe.
43 Loren Jenkins, "Western Europeans Demonstrate Against Crackdown in Poland," *Washington Post* (14 December 1981): A19; and Michael Getler, "U.S. Seeks Euro-

pean Support for Moves Directed at Soviet Union," *Washington Post* (22 December 1981): A12.

44 Memorandum from Alexander Haig to the President, "Influencing European Attitudes on Poland," dated 26 December 1981, in *Poland 1980-1982*.

45 Cable from SecState to All Diplomatic Posts, "'Let Poland Be Poland' – An Overview," dated 23 February 1982, NSA, SFO, Box 4.

46 Cable from Amembassy Bonn to SecState, "Poland Updating Measures – the FRG (III)," dated 25 January 1982, NSA Originals, Box 4.

47 Cable from SecState to USMission NATO, "CSCE: Guidance for January 27 NAC," dated 27 January 1982, NSA, SFO, Box 4.

48 John Goshko, "East-West Parley Suspended After Poland Assailed," *Washington Post* (10 February 1982): A1.

49 A translation of the Russian version of Brezhnev's letter to Reagan can be found as "Hotline Communication from Leonid Brezhnev to Ronald Reagan regarding Martial Law in Poland, December 25, 1981," in Andrzej Paczkowski and Malcolm Byrne (eds), *From Solidarity to Martial Law* (Budapest 2006), 496-498. The quotes in this paragraph are taken from: Cable from Secstate to Amembassy Moscow and Warsaw, "Brezhnev—Reagan Letter," dated 26 December 1981, NSA, SFO, Box 1.

50 For a summary of Long's visit, see Notatka Informacyjna z pobytu grupy członków Izby Reprezentantów Kongresu USA z Kongresmanem Clarence D. Long'iem w Polsce w dniu 17.08.83 r. [Information Note from the visit of a group from the U.S. House of Representatives with Congressman D. Long to Poland on 17.8.1983], dated 22 August 1983, Polish Ministry of Foreign Affairs Archive (hereafter MSZ), 48/86, W-1, Dep III (1983), AP 220-6-83. For a full transcript of the meeting with Jaruzelski, see Zapis z rozmowy Towarzysza Premiera Gen. W. Jaruzelskiego z grupą kongresmenów amerykańskich w dn. 17.viii.1983 r. [Transcript from Comrade Premier General W. Jaruzelski's conversation with a group of American congressmen on 17.8.1983], dated 17 August 1983, Polish Archive of Modern Records (hereafter AAN), KC PZPR, V/203, 200-228, esp. 211 and 218.

51 In 2003-2004 I completed a review of all files from 1980-1989 in Department III (North America division) at the Ministry of Foreign Affairs Archive in Warsaw. Davis frequently raised human rights concerns, but was consistently rebuffed with complaints that Washington was interfering in sovereign internal affairs. See, for example, Unofficial Translation of 3 November 1983, PRL Government Note [in English], dated 3 November 1983, MSZ, 48/86, W-1, Dep III (1983), AP 22-1-83/B. This fundamental disagreement on the meaning of the Helsinki accords, between concerns for human rights versus the sanctity of national sovereignty, goes back to the origins of the agreement. As Daniel Thomas explains in chapter 2 of his book *The Helsinki Effect* (Princeton 2001), during preliminary talks the Soviet Union and the communist bloc successfully argued to have non-interference in international affairs listed ahead of respect for human rights and fundamental freedoms in the Final Act's declaration of principles. This was done in part to use one principle to deflect the applicability of the second.

52 For correspondence between Glemp and Jaruzelski see records for the 29 June 1982, Politburo meeting in: AAN, Sygn. 1833, Mikr. 3002, 1-16. For information on internal decision making see Mieczyslaw Rakowski, *Dzienniki Polityczne 1981-1983* (Warsaw 2004), 362. For the final decision see Protokoł nr. 56 z posiedzenia Biura Politycznego KC PZPR w dniu 18.xi.1982 [Protocol no. 56 from the proceedings of the PZPR Central Committee Politburo on 18.11.1982], dated 18 November 1982, AAN, KC PZPR, V/182, 217-252.

53 For specific information, see Protokoł nr. 56, 246.

54 See Report, Wytyczne Polityki Wyznaniowej [Current Vatican Policy], dated 4 February 1983, AAN, KC PZPR, V/191, 11-16; Węzłowe Zadania Polityki Zagranicznej PRL w 1983 r. [Vital PRL Foreign Policy Tasks for 1983], dated c. January 1983, AAN, KC PZPR, V/190, 8-27, esp. 17; Untitled report [re Ikonowicz's visit to the Vatican], dated April 1983, AAN, XIA/1417, Korespondencja z członkami BP i Sekretarzami KC PZPR [Correspondence with Politburo Members and PZPR Central Committee Secretaries], 1983, 1-15; Report on the internal situation, Wydzial Informacyjna KC PZPR, dated 23 May 1983, AAN, KC PZPR, V/198, 207-221; as well as published accounts: John Kifner, "Free Prisoners, Pope asks Poland," *New York Times* (30 April 1983): A4; and Rakowski, *Dzienniki 1981-1983*, 460, 494.

55 Thomas, *The Helsinki Effect*, 208.

56 For the Moscow visit, see Pilna Notatka z wizyty w Moskwie Delegacji Partyjno-Państwowej z I Sekretarzem KC PZPR, Prezesem Rady Ministrów tow. Wojciechem Jaruzelskim, w dniach 1-2 marca 1982 r. [Urgent Note from the Visit to Moscow by the Party-Government with First Secretary of the PZPR Central Committee, Head of the Council of Ministers Wojciech Jaruzelski from 1 to 2 March 1982], dated 5 March 1982, AAN, KC PZPR, V/172, 555-561. Other delegations visited Hungary, Yugoslavia, East Germany, and Czechoslovakia.

57 See separate letters in AAN, KC PZPR, XIA/1394, 3-30.

58 For an example of COMECON coordination see Informacja o spotkaniu konsultacyjnym Sekretarzy Komitetów Centralnym oraz Stałych Przedstawicieli krajów członkowskich RWPG w sprawie przygotowań do narady gospodarczej na najwyższym szczeblu [Information about the consultative meetings of the Secretaries of Central Committees as well as standing chairmen from member nations of COMECON on the matter of preparations for economic consultations at the highest level], dated 30 March 1983, AAN, KC PZPR, V/197, 249-253.

59 On 13 May President Reagan signed an NSPG titled "Next Steps on Poland." The text of all of the memoranda mentioned in this paragraph remains classified. The information here is gleaned from withdrawal sheets from Paula Dobriansky's files at the Reagan Library. See the withdrawal sheets for January to May 1983 in Ronald Reagan Presidential Library (hereafter RRPL), Paula Dobriansky Files, Box 90892, Poland Memoranda 1981-1983.

60 Memorandum from Paula Dobriansky to Robert McFarlane, "Poland: Response to Unofficial Emissary Schaff," dated 9 February 1984, RRPL, NSC, European and Soviet Affairs Directorate, Box 91186, Vatican; and Memorandum from Robert

McFarlane to the President, "Poland: Response to Unofficial Emissary Schaff," dated 16 February 1984, PPRL, NSC, European and Soviet Affairs Directorate, Box 91186, Vatican. See also Adam Schaff, *Notatki Kłopotnika* (Warsaw 1995). These eleven political prisoners included four activists linked to KOR (Jacek Kuron, Adam Michnik, Henryk Wujec, and Zbigniew Romaszewski) and seven activists linked to Solidarnosc (Andrzej Gwiazda, Seweryn Jaworski, Marian Jurczyk, Karol Modzielewski, Grzegorz Palce, Andrzej Rozpłochowski, and Jan Rulewski).

61 Statement by Principal Deputy Press Secretary Speakes on United States Sanctions Against Poland, August 3, 1984," *Public Papers of the President* (1984), available on the Reagan Library's website: <www.reagan.utexas.edu>.

62 See Węzłowe Zadania Polityki Zagranicznej PRL w 1986 r. [Vital PRL Foreign Policy Tasks for 1986], dated c. January 1986, AAN, KC PZPR, V/294, 9-31; Informacja o wspołnych przedsięwzięciach z udziałem kapitału obcego w krajach socjalistycznych [Information about cooperative ventures utilizing foreign capital in socialist countries], dated 14 November 1985, AAN, KC PZPR, V/292, 91-96; and Wydział Ekonomiczny Opinia dot.: projektu ustawy o spoółkach z udziałem kapitału zagranicznego [Economic Department: Opinion about the legislation project for companies utilizing international capital], dated 30 December 1985, AAN, KC PZPR, V/292, 109-111.

63 For a full list of visits and a more detailed explanation of the events leading to Poland's decision to release all political prisoners, see Gregory F. Domber, "Rumblings in Eastern Europe: Western Pressure on Poland's Moves toward Democratic Transformation," in Frédéric Bozo, Marie-Pierre Rey, N. Piers Ludlow, and Leopldo Nuti (eds), *Europe and the End of the Cold War* (Oxford 2008).

64 Karen E. Smith, *The Making of EU Foreign Policy* (New York 1999), 58.

65 Notatka z rozmowy z radcą Ambasady USA w Warszawie Davidem Schwartzem [Note from a conversation with US embassy counselor David Swartz], dated 10 July 1986, AAN, KC PZPR, XIA/1422, 292-293.

66 Notatka w sprawie implikacji naszej sytuacji wewnętrznej dla stosunków Polski z państwami Europy Zachodniej [Note concerning the implications of our internal situation for Polish relations with the nations of Western Europe], dated 6 August 1986, AAN, KC PZPR, V/314, 179-187.

67 Propozycje w sprawie rozszerzenia zakresu stosowania ustawy z dnia 17 lipca 1986 r. o szczególnym postępowaniu wobec sprawców niektórych przestępstw [Proposition concerning expanding the law from 17 July 1986 about procedures against criminals], dated 9 September 1986, AAN, KC PZPR, V/316.

68 Thomas, *The Helsinki Effect*, 282.

69 As stated in the preceding paragraph, Thomas' arguments about social mobilization in the West remain convincing. Also, his arguments regarding Gorbachev internalizing international norms about human rights remain consistent with the arguments presented here.

French Support for Eastern European Dissidence, 1968-1989

Approaches and Controversies

Bent Boel

The role of non-governmental organizations in East-West relations during the post-war period has never been a central issue in the literature about France and the Cold War. However, over the years a number of publications have touched on different aspects of this theme. The following article will take a closer look at the grass-roots contacts between French non-State actors and Eastern European dissidents during the period 1968-1989. Its goal is twofold. First, it will identify ten key themes – explicit or implicit propositions – in the existing literature. Second, it will discuss these approaches. Overall it will argue that this is an area where a number of commonly held assumptions need to be revised or nuanced.

"Ending Yalta" was a recurrent goal in French foreign policy during the Cold War. In its Gaullist version, it was to be served by a "détente from above" which would challenge the superpowers by encouraging governments in both Eastern and Western Europe to act as if they were not overly constrained by their alliance allegiances.[1] From the mid-1970s onwards, a veritable cult of Eastern European dissent developed among French leftwing intellectuals. This gave the Yalta-ending discourse another dimension, since the logical implication of such outspoken support for the dissidence seemed to be the establishment of direct, face-to-face contacts with Soviet bloc oppositionists. In the 1980s, such grass-roots attempts to overcome the Iron Curtain – to act as if it did not exist – were dubbed a strategy of "détente from below."[2]

"Détente from below" may actually be understood in several ways. It could be seen very broadly as a strategy aimed at encouraging non-state relations across the Iron Curtain, implying in particular a freer flow of people and information between the two halves of Europe. Such a broad definition was in line with what the architects of the Ostpolitik and the committed Western supporters of the Helsinki Accords were subscribing to.[3] Historically, however, the expression is connected to the so-called non-aligned peace movement in the 1980s, for whom "détente from below" evolved into a proactive strategy of establishing a direct dialogue with independent peace groups in the East, an approach which was bound to produce tensions with the communist regimes. In a Western context, the first version was – at least in principle – uncontroversial, although governments may often have felt more comfortable with state-focused policies. For obvious reasons, Western governments were more wary of a sovereignty-infringing active support for dissidents.

France has a special status when it comes to Western attitudes towards dissidents in Eastern Europe during the Cold War. In no other country were Eastern European dissidents as celebrated as they were in France from the mid-1970s onwards.[4] And in no other country was political support for the independent Polish trade union Solidarnosc as intense as it was in France in the early 1980s.[5] But to what extent was this rhetorical support followed up by practical assistance, that is, to what extent does it really deserve to be considered an example of an implementation of a strategy of détente from below? This article does not purport to downplay the role of pure rhetorical support. Public displays of sympathy in the West (statements, letters, demonstrations, petitions, etc) certainly played an extremely important role both politically and morally for oppositionists in the East. And Western radios decisively contributed to breaking the information monopoly that the communist regimes were striving to uphold.[6] However, it is difficult to get around the fact that much rhetorical support also – and sometimes perhaps primarily – served domestic political purposes. Moreover, virtually everybody in the West – save Moscow-oriented Communist parties and their "fellow travellers" – would, when prompted to voice an opinion, express their condemnation for human rights violations in the East as well as their principled sympathy for the dissidents. The focus of this article will therefore be a narrower one, since it will raise the following question: to what extent was the widespread French sympathy for the dissidents translated into a proactive strategy of "detente from below" involving direct face-to-face contacts with the dissidents?

There is as yet no general study of French support for dissidence in Eastern Europe during the Cold War. There are, however, a number of partial studies. In the following I will argue that in this literature one may identify ten (explicit or implicit) propositions about French support for dissidents. I will present these, and discuss them, in an attempt to shed light on the French role in the "détente from below" during the final years of the Cold War.

I. In the Beginning Was … the Gulag Effect

Nobody disputes that there was an intense debate among French leftwing intellectuals about attitudes towards Soviet bloc communism in the aftermath of the publication of Alexandr Solzhenitsyn's *The Gulag Archipelago* in Paris (in Russian in December 1973, in French in May 1974), nor the fact that after three years of such debate a "cult of the dissidence" had become a key element in French intellectual politics. The level and intensity of many French intellectuals' sentiments about this matter created tensions within the Left, primarily between a number of prominent intellectuals on the one hand, the Communist Party (PCF), but also large segments of the Socialist Party (PS) on the other.[7]

What is disputed, however, is the reason why such an intense debate took place. While some emphasize external factors, others find internal ones to be more important. According to most accounts, French interest in Eastern European dissent is rooted in the "discovery" of the Gulag by French intellectuals, following the publication of Solzhenitsyn's book. Such authors often refer to the so-called "Gulag effect" when discussing the intellectual climate in France during the second half of the 1970s.[8] Sometimes the development of Eastern European dissent in the aftermath of the Helsinki Accords is identified as an additional factor.[9] One way or another, in this view it was the dissidents who woke French intellectuals up and removed the blindfold from their eyes. An alternative approach, however, argues that Eastern European dissidence was instrumentalized by those who disapproved of the alliance concluded in 1972 between the PS and the PCF and felt uneasy about the likely return of the Communists to government for the first time since 1947. Michael Scott Christofferson has argued that rather than a Gulag effect we ought to talk about a Gulag metaphor. The debate about Solzhenitsyn's book – which erupted even before the book had been translated into French – as well as that about the dissidents was in fact a debate about French domestic politics.[10]

Disagreement concerning causality is closely linked to a controversy – with obvious moral implications – about the attitude of the Left towards Soviet-style communism during the years prior to 1974. The "discovery-thesis" builds on the assumption that French leftwing intellectuals had been, at the very least, blind to the horrors of Stalinism and had persisted in their indifference towards the plight of those living under communist rule within the Soviet bloc – even after the crushing of the Hungarian rebellion in 1956 or the Warsaw Pact invasion of Czechoslovakia in 1968. Leftwing blindness could be explained by a number of reasons, including ideological sympathies (among other factors due to the PCF's pervading influence on France's post-war intellectual climate as well as – throughout the 1960s and into the 1970s – a strong thirdworldist orientation in many leftist circles), geopolitical concerns (attachment to East-West détente), electoral considerations (in 1972 François Mitterrand endeavoured to embrace the PCF in order to gain power and in the same process suffocate the rival party on the Left).[11] This thesis has been contested by Christofferson, who argues that the French intellectuals were not indifferent bystanders to the horrors of "really existing socialism" prior to 1974. Neither was the political non-communist Left. As far as the PS was concerned, tactical manoeuvring should not be mistaken for softness on communism.[12]

Dealing with French grass-roots assistance for dissidents in Eastern Europe, it is obviously important to find out when (only after 1974?) and why (due to the "Gulag effect"?) this support started. As for the chronology, Christofferson certainly has a point: a number of initiatives aimed at supporting the dissidents had roots in intellectual commitments going further back than Solzhenitsyn's book. Moreover, quite a few of those intellectuals who were active in supporting dissidents in 1977 had been active before the publication of *The Gulag Archipelago*. On the other hand, continuity among a relatively limited number of French intellectuals engaged in supporting dissidents in the East does not prove overall continuity in attitudes among French intellectuals (or on the French Left in general). As shown by Christofferson himself, the intellectual climate did change in France during the 1970s and a key element in this change was the radically enhanced focus on Eastern European dissidence.[13] Statements that seem to have raised only few eyebrows in the early 1970s had become unacceptable at the end of the decade. In 1975, Mitterrand visited Leonid Brezhnev in Moscow and signed a communiqué praising Soviet socialism.[14] As late as 1976, after a meeting with Janos Kadar in Budapest, he accepted a common communiqué which expressed admiration for progress made in the construction of a socialist society which the Hungarian people had reached under the leadership of the working class and its party.[15] Just a few years later, such statements would seem both ludicrous and embarrassing to anybody outside the narrowing PCF-associated circles. Moreover, a discussion of the Left's attitude should look beyond individuals and investigate the attitudes and role of institutions such as political parties and key media. At that level there certainly is room for arguing that there was both blindness and restraint on various sectors of the Left as far as Soviet-style communism was concerned.[16] Whether Solzhenitsyn-induced or not, a change did occur in the mid-1970s.

But how can one explain the timing? The "Gulag effect"-thesis has some obvious limitations. In particular, information about Soviet misdeeds was available long prior to the publication of Solzhenitsyn's book.[17] Moreover, no similar impact could be noticed in any other country. And indeed: what seems largely missing from the discussions about the French turn towards the dissidence is an international perspective. When one compares France with other Western countries, it appears obvious that there is a high degree of parallelism in the development of attitudes towards dissidence. Lack of interest for dissidents prior to the mid-1970s was not a French peculiarity, it was a widespread Western phenomenon. The same observation could be made concerning the increased interest for dissidents during the second half of the 1970s. However, as far as the latter phenomenon is concerned, it seems pretty clear that French support for the dissidents after the mid-1970s – and the stridency of the French debate – was greater than in any other country. In order to explain this French peculiarity one needs to take into account some specific French factors, that is, the domestic political instrumentalization of the dissidence issue (reflecting the disillusionment of many leftists with Soviet-style communism as well as some intellectuals' post-1972 anxieties over the prospect of the Communists acceding to governmental power).[18] This development should certainly be seen in the light of the fact that among many other things May 68 in France had a clear anti-communist dimension: it was very much a rebellion against the dominance of the PCF in large segments of the Left – and in particular the intellectual Left – throughout the post-war period.

II. Was It Just Empty Rhetorics?

Pierre Hassner once remarked that "the French talk like the Americans but act like the Germans," adding that "the Americans believe in sticks, the Germans in carrots and the French in words."[19] And, arguably, in no other Western country was there as much talk about Eastern European dissidents as in France in the 1970s and 1980s. One may be tempted to conclude that the French love for words about (and in support of) the dissidents masked an absence of concrete support. This was certainly hinted at by the Germans who were grappling for a line of defence as they were subjected to heavy French criticism due to their cautious reactions to the Polish crisis.[20]

The literature about the French and Eastern dissidence largely focuses on the role of the intellectuals, which is hardly surprising. Eastern European dissidence was very much about words, that is, the right to think and speak one's mind. The issue of freedom of expression was always likely to resonate more strongly with intellectuals than with other social groups. However, when it comes to practical assistance and face-to-face contacts with the dissidents, the French actually did do something. Many examples could be given. Only the most obvious and spectacular case will be presented here. Arguably, in no other Western country was popular support for Solidarnosc as intense and active as it was in France, particularly in the aftermath of the declaration of martial law in December 1981.[21] And this support was not just rhetorical, it did lead to active support and face-to-face contacts with Polish oppositionists. The French had contacts with the Poles long before the Gdansk agreements in August 1980. Such contacts can actually be traced back to the late 1950s. French trade unionists were probably the very first to visit the striking workers in Gdansk in August 1980 and hand over money to their representatives. This encounter was followed by a long period of sustained efforts on part of French non-communist trade unions (first of all CFDT, but also unions such as FO and CFTC) to support Solidarnosc politically and practically.[22] While these organizations played an extremely important role, many other groups – religious, humanitarian, etc. – contributed as well. All of these efforts redoubled in intensity in the aftermath of the declaration of martial law. French popular support for Solidarnosc manifested itself in a wide variety of ways: polls, statements, large demonstrations (even in small provincial towns), the acquisition and wearing of Solidarnosc-badges, financial support. Hundreds of trucks left France with different Polish towns as their destination. They would transport humanitarian aid of different kinds: food, medicines, cloths, toys, etc. Such aid was not necessarily apolitical, since it would often be earmarked for political prisoners or their families. Some deliveries would be more clandestine in nature: duplicators, photocopiers, stencils, and ink. The numerous people involved in these activities would collect money, do the packaging, sponsor prisoners and help their families, inform the public, etc.[23] While international comparisons in such a field are obviously difficult, this assistance to Solidarnosc was certainly among the most important organized in the West.[24]

III. An Eastern Europe outside Poland

Much has been written about French support for Solidarnosc. So much so that one could easily be induced into believing that this was the only French support given to the opposition in Eastern Europe. However, the story about French practical assistance to the dissidents is larger than that.

There are good reasons why so much has been written about the Polish case. Poland was number one when it came to French support for opposition in Eastern Europe. This should come as no surprise: the same could be said about practically all other Western countries (West Germany being a special case due to the existence of the GDR). For at least three reasons: ever since 1956 Poland had been the Soviet bloc country with the most active, diverse and semi-tolerated opposition. Moreover, Poland's borders had become relatively permeable. And finally: the establishment of Solidarnosc, the first independent trade union in a Soviet bloc country, was a truly revolutionary event, which titillated the imagination, hopes, and dreams in the West as no other event in Eastern Europe had done since 1945. While this is generally true for Western countries, it is particularly true for the French. Official French speeches often refer to the special relationship existing between France and Poland based on historical, cultural and emotional ties, geopolitical interests as well as personal relations resulting from the Polish migration to France. While there is both myth and truth in this, one ought to add that Poland neatly lent itself to being a metaphor, and Solidarnosc was certainly put to French domestic political uses, as was obvious in the case of the CFDT (see below). The focus in the literature on the Polish issue thus seems well warranted. However, it should not obfuscate the fact that there was also French support for oppositionists in other Soviet bloc countries. There were quite a few contacts with Czechoslovakia,[25] some as well with Soviet dissidents, and a few with the East Germans.[26] Such support is rarely even mentioned in the literature, if so then rather briefly, and it certainly deserves further investigation.

IV. The Key Role of the Anti-Totalitarian Left

Much of the literature dealing with French support for dissidence in Eastern Europe focuses on what in the early 1980s became known as the second Left (or anti-totalitarian Left).[27] Politically speaking, this label referred to those who were hostile to the traditional Jacobin (state-centric) current within the

French Left, emphasizing instead the role of the civil society, the need for decentralization and, more utopically, *autogestion* (self-management). Key institutional components of the second Left were: Michel Rocard's followers within the PS, the trade union CFDT, a number of publications, foremostly the periodical *Esprit*.[28] In addition, a number of prominent intellectuals (often linked to the above-mentioned publications) may be considered as part of that same current.[29]

The fact that the so-called anti-totalitarian Left supported the dissidents is hardly surprising. At the very core of its political identity lay a rejection of anything resembling Soviet-style socialism. While the roots of this anti-Jacobin current within the French Left can be traced far back in history, the libertarian (and anti-PCF) elements of May 68 certainly gave it a strong impetus. During the Prague Spring the left-socialist party PSU led by Rocard was the political party that most enthusiastically showed its sympathy for the Prague Spring reformers. In 1974, Rocard joined the PS and became the key political figure of what would later be labelled the second Left.[30]

The "anti-totalitarian Left" first of all played a role by shaping a political climate more favourable to the dissidents in the East. As far as practical assistance was concerned, the CFDT – the single largest component of the second Left – was a driving force in the movement of solidarity with Solidarnosc.[31] It was the first Western trade union to send a representative to give both moral and financial support to the striking workers in Gdansk in August 1980. During the following months the CFDT became the major French supporter of Solidarnosc. There were exchanges of visits at the top level as well as at the grass-roots level, and cooperation agreements between the two trade unions were concluded. The CFDT endeavoured to provide different forms of assistance, including material deliveries, money, training and advice. After the declaration of martial law on 13 December 1981, it confirmed its position as the major French supporter of Solidarnosc. It did not content itself with strongly worded protests, demonstrations and pressure on the French government to take a tougher stand towards the Jaruzelski regime in Poland. It helped establish (and initially also housed) the Parisian antenna of Solidarnosc. This Solidarnosc committee became very active over the coming years in organizing and channelling aid to Poland. Moreover, throughout the 1980s the CFDT got involved in practical aid, including assistance of a more clandestine nature, to Solidarnosc. This was organized by the Confederation itself as well as by its regional organizations which had established direct contacts and signed cooperative agreements with regional Solidarnosc unions.[32]

When it comes to concrete support for, and face-to-face contacts with, Eastern European dissidents, however, an exclusive focus on the second Left would be grossly misleading. First of all, the efforts of the second Left should not be overstated. While CFDT was a key actor, it almost exclusively dealt with Poland. That choice was understandable: as any trade union it would generally focus on trade union matters, and there was no equivalent to Solidarnosc in any other Soviet bloc country.[33] Other parts of the second Left may have been involved in helping the dissidents, but they were a rather small minority. The political branch of the second Left (Michel Rocard and his followers within the PS) does not seem to have been significantly involved in such practical activities. Rocard himself, though voicing his support emphatically, had no dissident contacts.[34] He became prime minister in 1988 but foreign policy remained firmly in the hands of Mitterrand.

Second, helping the dissidents was not the monopoly of any one group. What is striking about the French face-to-face contacts with Eastern European dissidents is the ideological diversity of those involved in practical assistance. Politically speaking, supporters of the dissidents were to be found across the political board. This was especially true for Poland. Religious (Catholic) groups made an important contribution.[35] In the late 1980s, a few politicians on the political Right got in touch with and helped the dissidents (in particular through the Fonds Européen pour la liberté d'expression, established in late 1987[36]). Even within the PCF there were a few people who had contacts with oppositionists, and in the mid-1970s the PCF as such briefly flirted with Euro-Communism and met with a few Eastern dissidents who had fled to the West.[37] Usually, however, PCF-members with dissident contacts were already marginalized within the party and on their way out.[38] As far as trade unions are concerned, CFDT did play a key role, but other unions which had no affinity with "the Second Left" – in particular FO and CFTC – were very active as well. Even the CGT, or rather elements within the CGT, were occasionally in touch with Eastern European oppositionists.[39] The PS as such could hardly be said to have been heavily involved on the side of Eastern European dissidents. French socialists, however, undoubtedly had sympathy for the Prague Spring. They organized a conference about the Prague Spring in 1972 and on that occasion established contacts with exile dissidents.[40] Further conferences dealing with Soviet bloc socialism were organized in the late 1970s and afterwards. Generally, however, contacts with the dissidents were taken care of by a few committed individuals. The key person, acting as go-between, was Gilles Martinet, a prominent member of the PS. He entertained contacts throughout the 1970s with GDR oppositionists (and participated in solidarity meetings for Rudolf Bahro, Robert Havemann and Wolf Biermann).[41] Jean Pronteau, a former communist who joined the Socialist Party in 1973, entertained close links with Karel Bartosek since the mid-1960s.[42] Mitterrand himself allegedly had an excellent relationship with Jiri Pelikan.[43] A number of French intellectuals also got involved and had Eastern oppositional contacts. While such meetings generally took place on French soil, a few intellectuals had face-to-face contacts with dissidents. A major actor in such contacts was the Jan Hus Foundation (from 1979), which among its collaborators included Jacques Derrida and Jean-Jacques Vernant. PEN Club France also played a role, although it preferred the tools of quiet diplomacy.[44] L'Ecole des hautes études en sciences sociales (originally VIe Section de l'Ecole Pratique des Hautes Etudes, from 1974 EHESS) heavily contributed to establishing contacts between French academics and Eastern European intellectuals after 1956.[45] A few journalists were important in this field as well, among them Bernard Guetta and Amber Bousoglou.[46] One reflection of the French intellectual interest in Eastern European dissidence was the fact that throughout the 1970s and 1980s publishing houses became more and more open to unofficial writers from the East.[47] The translation of such literature into French clearly presupposed clandestine communication channels with Eastern Europe. In addition, there were a number of solidarity groups, exiles and periodicals that had dissidents contacts.

While extremely diverse, those actively assisting the dissidents and crossing the Iron Curtain were always tiny minorities (which often had strong ideological or religious beliefs, and sometimes had a tradition of semi-clandestine activism). This applied to the Solidarnosc-related aid and even more so to assistance given to groups in other Eastern countries. While these small groups could be found across the political board, it remains fairly clear that among those involved in face-to-face contacts the Left dominated. Many of the solidarity groups were established by people oriented towards the Left. A few helpers were to be found within the PS as well as within the left-socialist party PSU. However, a key role, in the publicized as well as in the more clandestine activities, was played by the French Trotskyites. Indeed no French political current focused more on the Soviet bloc oppositionists than did the Trotskyites. While they were divided into many groups, the two major ones in this field were the LCR (French Section of the Fourth International) and the OCI (the so-called Lambertists). For both, supporting oppositionists in the East was a key concern. The OCI was heavily involved in many French groups supporting dissidents in the East and it was also behind a number of courier activities aimed at Eastern Europe.[48] The LCR's emphasis was less on France, and its Soviet bloc-related operations were less publicized than the OCI's, but it was very much involved in clandestine help for Eastern oppositionists. While this activity was to some degree internationally coordinated (within the Fourth International) the LCR was the key player due to the fact that it was the biggest Trotskyite organization in the West after 1968 and also because it had the experience, the Eastern European contacts, the people and the logistics required for such illegal actions.[49]

V. Was the French Independent Peace Movement Really Insignificant?

The French non-aligned peace movement does not loom large in the literature.[50] This is not surprising. While it managed to organize a few impressive demonstrations, overall the French peace movement in the 1980s played a marginal role compared to what happened in a number of other European countries. Its lack of domestic political impact may be explained by a combination of various factors: the so-called Munich complex which had discredited pacifism as the moral equivalent to appeasement of totalitarian dictatorships, anti-communism (the Mouvement pour la Paix was widely perceived to be a communist front organization), nuclear pacifism (the French supported nuclear weapons largely because they believed that it made war less likely), fears of a new Rapallo (i.e., of perceived neutralist tendencies in the West German peace movement), the absence of a tradition for public debate about foreign policy, etc. The lack of domestic political impact is even more striking in the case of the French so-called non-aligned peace movement. The CODENE (Comité pour le Désarmement Nucléaire en Europe) was created in November 1981 in a reaction against the communist dominance of the French peace movement as well as inspired by already existing non-aligned peace groups in Western Europe. The founding moment for such groups was the END Appeal (April 1980) that called on independent peace activists in the East and in the West to build a pan-European alliance across the Cold War divide, opposing authorities in the East as well as in the West.[51] While the CODENE was originally established as a cartel consisting of about thirty different groups (peace groups, religious organizations, environmentalists, etc.), politically generally situated to the left of the Socialist Party, it developed into being a mix of a cartel and a grass-roots movement with about one hundred local groups. Compared to other Western European independent groups, however, the CODENE remained small. Like its Western counterparts, it opposed nuclear missiles both in the East and in the West (including the French ones) and it firmly stated that there could be no peace without respect for human rights in Eastern Europe. Like other non-aligned Western European peace groups it got actively involved both on a bilateral and on a multilateral level in a dialogue with independent groups in Eastern Europe. In Poland it dialogued with the Solidarnosc-associated group of intellectual dissidents organized within the Committee for the Defence of Society (KOS), as well as (from 1985 onwards) with Freedom and Peace (WiP), just as it cooperated with Solidarnosc's antennas in Paris and Brussels. In Czechoslovakia it repeatedly met and cooperated with people from Charter 77. In 1983, the two groups co-authored the first common statement issued by independent peace activists from East and West. The following year, it issued a statement together with the Dutch IKV[52] and Charter 77 and another one together with KOS and the Italian Lega per l'Ambiente. At END's convention in Perugia (July 1984) the CODENE was active among those favouring the establishment of close relations with independent activists in the East, both by co-founding the European Network for East-West dialogue which focused on establishing links with Eastern European dissidents and by issuing a joint declaration together with the Swiss Peace Council, the West German Greens as well as members of Charter 77 and the Hungarian Dialogue Group. CODENE activists often travelled to Eastern Europe (Czechoslovakia, Poland, GDR, Hungary) to meet oppositionists. On several such occasions they were arrested and expelled. In France, they intervened publicly through statements and demonstrations to support dissidents, even in matters not directly connected to peace. Within the European non-aligned peace movement, the CODENE thus belonged to the "radical" group, that is, those who most adamantly favoured establishing close links with the dissidents and opposed contacts with the official Eastern European peace committees. Despite its weakness – and its insignificance in terms of influencing French policies – the CODENE played a disproportionately important role in East-West grass-roots contacts in two ways: it was an important actor within the pan-European network of so-called non-aligned peace activists as well as in the purely French contacts with dissidents.[53] It may have had more non-Solidarnosc dissident contacts than any other French organization in the 1980s.

VI. The Neglected Role of the Solidarity Groups

A number of groups solidarizing themselves with Eastern oppositionists were created throughout the 1970s and 1980s.[54] Nothing much has been written about them, despite the fact that they played an important political role and in a few cases had a significant practical impact.[55] A complete list of these groups would be extremely long. And many of them were short-lived or lacked substance despite grand-sounding names or impressive lists of board members. In quite a few cases these groups may have been front organizations for small – mostly Trotskyite – groups. These groups generally focused on supportive actions within a French context such as organizing demonstrations or meetings, collecting signatures, lobbying politicians before their visits to Eastern countries, issuing public statements or publishing documentation. Some of these groups, however, did get involved in transnational activities, that is, direct support for Eastern oppositionists. One such case was the Comité du 5 janvier pour une Tchécoslovaquie libre et socialiste (established in 1970). As its name indicated, it strongly identified itself with the Prague Spring.[56] While it concentrated on the French context, it also intervened more directly in Czechoslovakia: it launched a campaign to donate toys to the children of political prisoners in Czechoslovakia and had money sent to the prisoners' families. When Zdeněk Mlynář, a prominent oppositional ex-communist, had emigrated from Czechoslovakia, he wrote the Comité du 5 Janvier to thank it for the "moral, political and financial assistance" that it had given the opposition.[57] But the importance of the solidarity groups is most obvious in the post-1980 Polish case, where a number of organizations (Solidarité avec Solidarnosc, Association Solidarité France Pologne and innumerable local groups) played a key role in channelling assistance to Poland before and especially after the declaration of martial law. Though the efforts subsided after 1982, some of them were pursued throughout the 1980s.

VII. Paris as the Capital of Eastern European Dissidence

For many years it has been a common perception in France that this country has a special relationship to Eastern Europe, due to old historical and cultural links, geo-political considerations, movements of immigration and even, in the case of Romania, linguistic closeness. In addition, Paris has traditionally been an important centre for revolutionaries, exiled dissidents or more generally intellectuals from all around the world. Throughout the post-war period many Eastern European intellectuals found a safe haven in Paris and in some cases became actively involved in French intellectual life.[58] This emigrant milieu was far from being a homogeneous group. It comprised divergent views and various traditions which among other things reflected the successive waves of emigration from the East. For example, the non- or anti-communists emigrating in the 1940s or 1950s were often very critical of the reform communists who left after the Warsaw Pact invasion of Czechoslovakia in 1968. However, the presence in France of numerous Eastern exile intellectuals[59] led to the establishment of a number of important exile institutions. In particular, some of the most important Soviet bloc exile publications, or periodicals focusing on Eastern European dissidence, were edited in Paris: *Kontinent* (published by the Russian writer Vladimir Maximov from 1974), *Kultura* (the most important Polish exile publication, edited by Jerzy Giedroyc, with the first issue published in Rome, the following in Paris from 1947[60]), *Svedectvi* (published by Pavel Tigrid from 1956, initially in New York but from 1960 in Paris), *L'Alternative* (published by François Maspero 1979-1985) and its successor *La Nouvelle Alternative* (edited by Karel Bartosek from 1986), *Magyar Füzetek* (a major Hungarian exile publication, published by Pierre Kende in Paris 1978-1989), and *Lettre internationale* (founded by Antonin Liehm and Paul Noirot in 1984).

While some Eastern exiles may have felt ignored and marginalized in French intellectual life for a long period, this certainly changed in the 1970s, as Eastern European dissidence became a key issue for French intellectuals. A seminar organized in 1976 to commemorate the twentieth anniversary of the Polish October and the Hungarian revolution, which was attended among others by Adam Michnik, was a major turning point in that respect. In addition, throughout the 1970s a number of institutions helped create forums where French and exile intellectuals would interact, confront their views, and cooperate.[61] Among these were the periodical *Esprit* (Jean Marie Domenach, editor 1957-1976, and Paul Thibaud, editor 1976-1988[62]), Rencontres européennes,[63] Pierre Hassner's informal East-West group,[64] la Fondation pour une entraide intellectuelle européenne[65] or le Comité international de soutien à la Charte 77.[66]

Eastern European exiles' contribution to assisting the dissidents was crucial. Directly, as their activities were a major component of the overall support for the opposition in the East (in particular, they often provided the channels through which Western support could reach the dissidents). And indirectly, as they helped stimulate Western interest and support. Sometimes Westerners going East would first come to Paris to meet exiles such as Pavel Tigrid and get addresses in Eastern Europe or even money for the dissidents.[67] The more anonymous exiles would also play a key role. For example, a number of Solidarnosc activists who were in France in December 1981 (reflecting the strong Franco-Polish links developed in the aftermath of the establishment of Solidarnosc) decided to stay after the declaration of martial law. Some of them actively helped the Polish opposition, in particular through the Solidarnosc antenna in Paris.[68] Generally, one can observe that many of those involved in supporting the dissidents were somehow connected with the East: either as exiles themselves or through family connections, sometimes marriage. This applied to some of the more prominent intellectuals (e.g., Jacques Derrida and Jacques Le Goff) as well as to many of the lesser known activists.

It is hard to overestimate the contribution of Eastern European exiles in France as far as help for the dissidents is concerned. It could therefore make sense to describe Paris as the capital of Eastern European dissent in the West. On the other hand, this role should not overshadow the fact that major centres of emigrant activity were to be found in countries such as Germany, Austria, Sweden and the UK.

VIII. Was It All about Domestic Politics?

As mentioned above, Michael Scott Christofferson has argued that domestic political considerations played a key role in French support for the dissidence. Other scholars as well have emphasized the role played by domestic political considerations, particularly with regards to the Polish crisis.[69] While domestic political factors were crucial in determining the intensity with which the French followed the situation in the East, and while it may be tempting to emphasize the political instrumentalization of the dissidents, things look somewhat different when we examine the role of individuals and especially when we focus on those involved in face-to-face contacts with the dissidents.

To some degree French support for the dissidents may be explained by domestic considerations. For President Mitterrand and for the French socialist government it was politically beneficial to be seen as supportive of the dissidence. The public outcry in the aftermath of the declaration of martial law in Poland in December 1981 most probably prompted the government to take a tougher stand than it otherwise would have done.[70] Later in the

1980s, meeting with the dissidents became a ritual which was expected by the media and the absence of which might have produced strong protests at home. Likewise, for the second Left, and the CFDT in particular, supporting Solidarnosc was a means to criticize the socialist government, to attack the CGT and to revitalize its own membership. Finally, it may be argued that for the CODENE supporting the dissidents was a way to gain legitimacy for a pacifism that faced an uphill battle in France. All these possible uses, however, are also indications of the strength of pro-dissident feelings in French public opinion at that time (since strongly voiced pro-dissident views were widely perceived as an important – and required – asset in domestic politics).

While supporting the dissidence may have been instrumentalized for domestic political purposes by all three segments of the non-communist Left, it was not mere rhetorics. The so-called first Left was undoubtedly more cautious in its support than the second Left or the CODENE. But the French government followed a rather tough course towards Poland in the aftermath of the declaration of martial law, and in 1988 Mitterrand took two steps which were seen as important by Eastern dissidents: he invited Lech Walesa to visit France and he had his famous breakfast with Vaclav Havel and other Czechoslovak dissidents at the French embassy in Prague. Overall though, the French Socialists did give Realpolitik the highest priority. This was much less true of the second Left and not at all of the CODENE. The second Left, and the CFDT in particular, was extremely active in its practical support of Solidarnosc. While the humanitarian and financial aid to the Poles was publicized, the clandestine assistance obviously was not. The same could be said of the geographically more diverse contacts of the CODENE: while the support, and in some cases the results of the dialogue, was publicized, most assistance and most contacts established by the trade unions and the CODENE never benefitted from any flattering media exposure. Those engaged in these activities were clearly deeply committed to them. The second Left and the CODENE thus shared important values as they defended and in practice helped the dissidents. But the issue of pacifism as well as the respective nature of the two organizations prevented them from achieving a closer cooperation.

In general for the Left (and far Left) supporters of the dissidents, there was necessarily a tactical (and nonetheless genuine) consideration, namely to demonstrate that the Socialism they advocated had nothing to do with what was practised in the East. Soviet-style Socialism was seen – by these people – as a major impediment to further domestic political success. However, part of the aid was clearly non-instrumental in domestic political terms (or if instrumental, then in a rather indirect way). This is most obvious in those cases where it was secret – which much of it was, particularly the one coming from the Trotskyites. Such clandestine assistance on the one hand had only limited PR value; on the other hand, it entailed certain costs (in terms of finances, labour, risks). Some people, while driven by very diverse political beliefs, basically felt that this was the right thing to do.

What is striking in an international context is that the French non-communist Left within a European context was one of the most pro-dissident ones, particularly in the Polish affair. The French Socialists were among those Socialists in Western Europe who were most outspoken in their support of Solidarnosc. As argued above, the CFDT seems to have identified itself more intensively with the struggle of Solidarnosc than any other Western European trade union. And the CODENE was among the most committed supporters of the "detente from below" approach within the non-aligned peace movement.

IX. International Dimensions of the French Assistance to the Dissidence

Most literature referring to French support for the dissidents places such support within a purely national, i.e. French, context. The international context is mainly there for comparative purposes, i.e. to argue that the French were among those who did the most. The properly international dimension of the assistance to the dissidents is rarely elaborated upon.[71] However, French efforts to support the dissidents cannot be comprehended within a purely national context. Such endeavours often had an international source or at least inspiration. Moreover, in some cases they were also coordinated internationally. First of all, developments like the Helsinki Final Act (mainly as mediated through the re-launching of Eastern European dissidence), policies followed by other countries (the US under Jimmy Carter or the Netherlands), and the general turn towards human rights policies (as illustrated by the Helsinki Accords) certainly had an impact. In addition, many of the organizations involved in helping dissidents had international affiliations that played a role – and sometimes a decisive one – for their involvement with the dissidents. French trade unions all had international affiliations (ICFTU, IFCTU, ETUC, etc.) that in different ways associated them with key players in the assistance given to Solidarnosc throughout the 1980s. As far as the PS is concerned, contacts with East European oppositionists were built into its international affiliations. For instance, exiled Eastern European social democratic parties were affiliated with the Socialist International. Moreover, the Czechoslovak socialist exile group, Listy, likewise had links with the European socialists, in particular through its main protagonist, Jiri Pelikan, who was elected on the PSI's list in 1979 and remained part of the Socialist group in the European Parliament, 1979-1989.[72] The role of international affiliations is obvious also in the case of the French section of the Fourth international (LCR) and it was present as well in the case of the Lambertist Trotskyites. Something similar could be said about the French PEN Club, the French section of the Jan Hus Foundation, or the CODENE, the establishment of which was at least in part inspired by the British END Appeal. Beyond the initial inspiration, many activities aimed at helping the dissidents took place within an international framework or were internationally coordinated. This was most visibly the case in the CODENE's activities that would often involve several different non-aligned peace groups. It also applied to a number of Trotskyite activities. In one case, for example, Danish Trotskyites would call on their French comrades for help in Poland.[73] Much French assistance to Poland was channelled via Sweden. And the proximity of Bornholm (a Danish island in the Baltic Sea) to Poland was exploited by French Solidarnosc activists to send balloons with political messages to Poland.

X. Did It Matter?

Finally, as always, one should ask the question: did it really matter? In principle, pro-dissident grass-roots activism could have mattered in the East or in the West. The most important question is of course whether it mattered in the East, that is, for the dissidents (and thereby, presumably, though not everybody would agree on that, for the 1989 revolutions in Eastern Europe). That issue will not be discussed here. Suffice it to say, dissidents at the time certainly found it helpful and encouraging. And as far as Poland is concerned, the wealth of literature existing on the topic (including in Polish) seems an indication of the fact that many do feel that it was important, at least in the Polish case.

In principle, pro-dissident activism or feelings may also have had an impact in another way, i.e. in the West, by influencing official French policies towards Eastern Europe. Considering the very pro-dissident intellectual climate in France throughout the 1980s, it might be tempting to believe that France was uniformly supportive of the dissidents. However, as pointed out by Jacques Almaric, that was very far from being the case.[74] French foreign policy does not have any tradition for taking into account moral or human rights considerations. The markedly "realist" orientation of French foreign policymakers also characterized French policy towards the Soviet bloc. In the 1970s, the French President Valéry Giscard d'Estaing first of all cultivated his relationship with communist leaders such as Leonid Brezhnev and Edward Gierek, while only occasionally practising the so-called quiet diplomacy (i.e. intervening discretely with the regimes in the East to press individual human rights cases).[75] French preference for state-focused policies also manifested itself in the low priority given to French radio transmissions towards Eastern Europe, which were discontinued in 1974.[76] Though this remains to be investigated, French embassies in the East often seem to have ignored dissidents far into the 1980s (there were a number of exceptions, but they may have reflected individual inclinations rather than official policy).[77]

The French Socialists' rhetoric was very pro-dissident in the early 1980s. But to what extent did this attitude influence official policy when the Socialists took over in 1981? Only modestly, one may argue. The electoral victory of Mitterrand was by many perceived as a victory for those who aspired to a more "moral" foreign policy, taking into account the ideological nature of the Soviet Union and the need to support oppositional forces in the East. And de facto, once Mitterrand took over, he decided on a "cure de desintoxication" as far as Franco-Soviet political relations were concerned. When he did visit Moscow in June 1984 he astounded Tchernenko and other Soviet dignitaries by praising Andrei Sakharov in his toast speech in the Kremlin.[78] When Foreign Minister Roland Dumas in 1985 visited Prague, several of his advisers met known critics of the regime.[79] The picture is far from crystal clear, however. In particular, Mitterrand's meeting with General Wojciech Jaruzelski at the Elysée palace in December 1985 stained his "pro-dissident" image. In January 1986, Jean-François Baylet, deputy secretary of foreign affairs in the socialist Fabius-government, went to Warsaw but was instructed to avoid contacts with Solidarnosc and other oppositional forces.[80] At the end of the 1980s,[81] as Mikhail Gorbachev's politics of glasnost and perestroika were implemented and a cautious liberalization took place in Hungary and Poland, the French became more daring. In September 1988, the socialist Foreign Minister Roland Dumas met with dissidents in Prague; and Mitterrand's trips to Czechoslovakia and Bulgaria before the fall of the Wall both followed a similar pattern. Beside the official programme there were meetings with local dissidents.[82] Depending on one's views, it is possible to see these meetings as the real motive to visit reform-shy Eastern bloc countries or as a fig leaf designed to conceal the socialist government's "business as usual" with the dictatorships in the East.

Conclusions

In this article I have discussed ten different propositions about French support for Eastern European dissidents during the late Cold War. One general question has been underlying these discussions: to what extent did the French play a role in the grass-roots contacts between Westerners and Eastern oppositionists during the 1970s and 1980s? In suggesting an answer to this question I will focus on three issues: chronology, actors and French exceptionalism.

Chronology. There was an active French support for dissidents in Eastern Europe throughout the 1970s and 1980s. Initially such activities were limited to small – especially Trotskyite – groups. Later, they became much more widespread. As far as the face-to-face contacts are concerned, the so-called Gulag effect does not seem decisive (if anything, its impact was indirect and delayed). The impact of the Helsinki Accords – or rather, the response of Eastern European dissidents to the Final Act – was in many ways crucial. Repressive measures taken against groups such as KOR in Poland or Charter 77 and VONS in Czechoslovakia led to a mobilization in France and elsewhere in the West. However, events in Poland created a whole new situation. The Gdansk strikes, the ensuing agreements and the establishment of Solidarnosc in Poland in 1980 had a huge impact in France. And the declaration of martial law in December 1981 triggered an impressive outpour of sympathy as well as active French support for Polish oppositionists. The intellectual climate (the "cult of the dissidence") certainly played a key role when it comes to explaining the overwhelming French response to Solidarnosc. As far as face-to-face contacts with Eastern Europe dissidents are concerned, however, the issue is not before or after *The Gulag Archipelago* but before or after Solidarnosc.

Actors. In the 1970s, Trotskyites and Eastern European exiles were key actors in the face-to-face contacts with dissidents. This role did not vanish after 1980, but its relative importance somewhat diminished as many others got involved in the aid. Sociologically this change was reflected in the fact that whereas in the 1970s many among those involved in the Eastern trips may have been students, in the 1980s the social diversity was much greater, involving in particular numerous trade unionists.

French exceptionalism. The French peculiarity is obvious as far as rhetorics are concerned. But in the Polish case French practical assistance was also exceptionally large. While much of the French pro-dissident rhetorics can only be understood when domestic political considerations are taken into account, there is more to it than that: French support was not just empty words. Another important French peculiarity was the important contribution made by exiles as well as by different Trotskyite groups.

In Eastern Europe as well as in France, what is remembered – if anything – of the French assistance to oppositionists is French support for Solidarnosc. In this article I have tried to argue that there is more to remember than that. The French did play a role in the "détente from below". However, this has to some degree been forgotten, or, rather, was never much known in the first place – partly, it may be argued, because of a limited French official and academic interest for "détente from below" activities.[83] And partly because grass-roots contacts across the Iron Curtain by their very nature had to remain discrete.

Notes

1   Maurice Vaïsse, *La grandeur. Politique étrangère du général de Gaulle 1958-1969* (Paris 1998), 419-420; Frédéric Bozo, *Mitterrand, la fin de la guerre froide et l'unification allemande* (Paris 2005), 66.
2   See for example Patrick Burke, "A Transcontinental Movement of Citizens? Strategic Debates in the 1980s Western Peace Movement," in Gerd-Rainer Horn and Padraic Kenney (eds), *Transnational Moments of Change. Europe 1945, 1968, 1989* (Lanham 2004), 189-206; Lawrence S. Wittner, *The Struggle Against the Bomb*, Volume 3, *Toward Nuclear Abolition. A History of the World Nuclear Disarmament Movement 1971 to the Present* (Stanford 2003), 83-85.
3   Sylvia Rohde-Liebenau, *Menschenrechte und internationaler Wandel* (Baden-Baden 1996); Daniel C. Thomas, *The Helsinki Effect. International Norms, Human Rights, and the Demise of Communism* (Princeton 2001); Jacques Andréani, *Le Piège. Helsinki et la chute du communisme* (Paris 2005).
4   François Hourmant, *Le désenchantement des clercs. Figures de l'intellectuel de l'après-Mai 68* (Rennes 1997).
5   Marcin Frybes, "French Enthusiasm for Solidarnosc," *European Review*, vol. 16, no. 1 (2008), 65-73; Seweryn Blumsztajn, *Je rentre au pays* (Paris 1985), 151-152. For a different view see Natalie Bégin, "Kontakte zwischen Gewerkschaften in Ost und

West. Die Auswirkungen von Solidarnosc in Deutschland und Frankreich. Ein Vergleich," *Archiv für Sozialgeschichte*, vol. 45 (2005), 293-324.
6   Jacques Semelin, *La liberté au bout des ondes. Du coup de Prague à la chute du mur de Berlin* (Paris 1997) (see for example p. 267).
7   Hourmant, *Le désenchantement des clercs*, 117; Pierre Grémion, *Paris/Prague. La gauche face au renouveau et à la régression tchécoslovaques, 1968-1978* (Paris 1985), 199-234; Pierre Grémion, "La réception des dissidences à Paris," in Anne-Marie Le Gloannec and Aleksander Smolar (eds), *Entre Kant et Kosovo. Études offertes à Pierre Hassner* (Paris 2003), 377-403; Michael Scott Christofferson, *French Intellectuals Against the Left. The Antitotalitarian Moment of the 1970s* (New York 2004); Ulrike Ackermann, *Sündenfall der Intellektuellen. Ein Deutsch-Französischer Streit von 1945 bis heute* (Stuttgart 2000), 170-171; Friedhelm Boll and Stéphane Sirot, "Deutsche und französische Intellektuelle und der Fall Solschenizyn," in Ilja Mieck and Pierre Guillen (eds), *Deutschland, Frankreich, Russland. Begegnungen und Konfrontationen* (Munich 2000), 323-343; Robert Horvath, "'The Solzhenitsyn Effect': East European Dissidents and the Demise of the Revolutionary Privilege," *Human Rights Quarterly*, vol. 29 (2007), 879-907.
8   Ibid.
9   Anne Dulphy and Christine Manigand, "L'opinion publique française et la problématique des droits de l'homme face au processus d'Helsinki," in Elisabeth du Réau and Christine Manigand (eds), *Vers la réunification de l'Europe? Apports et limites du processus d'Helsinki de 1975 à nos jours* (Paris 2005), 143-165; Pierre Grémion, *Intelligence de l'anticommunisme. Le Congrès pour la liberté de la culture à Paris 1950-1975* (Paris 1995), 609.
10 Christofferson, *French Intellectuals Against the Left*, 89-112.
11 Grémion, *Paris/Prague*, 199-234; David Drake, *Intellectuals and Politics in Post-War France* (New York 2002), 63-96.
12 Christofferson, *French Intellectuals Against the Left*, 91.
13 Ibid., 184.
14 Daniel Vernet, "Mitterrand, l'URSS et la Russie," in Samy Cohen (ed.), *Mitterrand et la sortie de la guerre froide* (Paris 1998), 26.
15 Jacques Rupnik, "La France de Mitterrand et les pays de l'Europe du Centre-Est," in Samy Cohen (ed.), *Mitterrand et la sortie de la guerre froide* (Paris 1998), 210. Concerning the Socialist Party's relationship with the GDR, see Michel Cullin, "Die französischen Sozialisten und die DDR," in Dorothée Röseberg (ed.), *Frankreich und 'Das andere Deutschland'. Analyzen und Zeitzeugnisse* (Tübingen 1999), 35-38.
16 Grémion, "Méprises, résistances, malentendus: la gauche française face au Printemps de Prague," in François Fejtö and Jacques Rupnik (eds), *Le Printemps tchécoslovaque 1968* (Brussels 1999), 222-231; Gilles Martinet, "Les ambiguïtés de la gauche française face au Printemps de Prague," in ibid.; Pierre Daix, "Le Parti communiste français et le Printemps de Prague," in ibid.; Florence Grandsenne, "Les intellectuels français et l'insurrection hongroise de 1956," *Histoire et liberté. Les cahiers d'histoire sociale*, no.

28 (2006), 7-31; Pierre Rigoulot, *Les paupières lourdes. Les Français face au goulag: aveuglements et indignations* (Paris 1991), 9-10.

17 Cécile Vaissie, "Les chèvres, les choux et les canards sauvages. Les ambiguïtés françaises face à la dissidence soviétique," *Communisme*, nos 62-63 (2000), 154; Christian Jelen and Thierry Wolton, *L'Occident des dissidents* (Paris 1979), 115-137.

18 Christofferson, *French Intellectuals Against the Left*, 90.

19 Pierre Hassner, "The View from Paris," in Gordon Lincoln (ed.), *Eroding Empire: Western Relations with Eastern Europe* (Washington 1987), 216.

20 Lawrence D. Orton, "The Western Press and Jaruzelski's War," *East European Quarterly*, vol. 18, no. 3 (September 1984), 279-305; Dieter Bingen, *Die Polenpolitik der Bonner Republik von Adenauer bis Kohl, 1949-1991* (Baden-Baden 1998), 210-211.

21 See, for example, Marcin Kula, "Les réactions françaises au mouvement de 'Solidarité' et à l'introduction de l'état de siège en 1981 en Pologne," in Bernard Michel and Jozef Laptos (eds), *Les relations entre la France et la Pologne au XXe siècle* (Krakow 2002), 205-224; Andrzej Chwalba, "Syndicats français et 'Solidarnosc' dans les années 1980-1990," in Andrzej Chwalba, *Czasy 'Solidarnosci': Francuscy Zwiazkowcy i NSZZ Solidarnosc 1980-1990* (Krakow 1997), 255-262; Marcin Frybes, "Solidarnosc-CFDT. L'expérience d'un dialogue Est-Ouest," *Revue de la CFDT*, no. 3 (September 1997), 9-26; Frybes, "French Enthusiasm for Solidarnosc"; Marie Kolago, *Solidarnosc dans le regard français: l'exemple de la CFDT. Les rapports CFDT-Solidarnosc 1980-1993*, Mémoire présenté pour le DEA Histoire du XXe siècle, IEP de Paris, 2000; Blumsztajn, *Je rentre au pays*, 151-152; Emmanuel Wallon, "Etat de guerre," in Bronislaw Geremek and Marcin Frybes (eds), *Kaléidoscope Franco-Polonais* (Paris 2004), 84-89; Alain Touraine, "Solidarnosc", in ibid., 231-239. For a different view see Bégin, "Kontakte zwischen Gewerkschaften in Ost und West."

22 Frybes, "Solidarnosc-CFDT. L'expérience d'un dialogue Est-Ouest."

23 Frybes, "French Enthusiasm for Solidarnosc"; Kula, "Les réactions françaises."

24 Frybes, "French Enthusiasm for Solidarnosc"; Blumsztajn, *Je rentre au pays*, 151; Idesbald Goddeeris, "Western Trade Unions and Solidarnosc: A Comparison From a Polish Perspective," *The Polish Review*, vol. 52, no. 3 (2007), 305-329 (see p. 312). Some authors argue that the German (humanitarian) assistance was greater than any other (see Wladysslaw Bartoszewski, *Und reiss uns den Hass aus der Seele* [Warsaw 2005], 172-173). One needs to make a distinction between political (rhetorical) support (extremely strong in France), purely humanitarian help (massive in Germany, but also very important in France) and more or less clandestine assistance for the opposition (where the French do seem to have been more active in relationship to Poland than most others).

25 Jean-Yves Potel, *Quand le soleil se couche à l'Est*, Editions de l'Aube (1995), 21-23; Barbara Day, *The Velvet Philosophers* (London 1999), 88-99.

26 Jean-Pierre Hammer, "Begegnungen mit Künstlern und Intellektuellen der DDR. Erinnerungen und Dokumente eines Zeitzeugen," in Röseberg (ed.), *Frankreich und "Das andere Deutschland"*, 609-625; Cullin, "Die französischen Sozialisten und die

DDR"; Ulrich Pfeil, *Die 'anderen' deutsch-französischen Beziehungen. Die DDR und Frankreich 1949-1990* (Cologne 2004), 476-479.

27 Hervé Hamon and Patrick Rotman, *La Deuxième gauche. Histoire intellectuelle et politique de la CFDT* (Paris 1982), 11-12; Paul Thibaud, "Solidarnosc: la solidarité et les malentendus," *Esprit* (October 2005), 157-162; Touraine, "Solidarnosc"; Frybes, "French enthusiasm for Solidarnosc," 66.

28 Goulven Boudic, *Les métamorphoses d'une revue. Esprit 1932-1982* (Rennes 2005).

29 Hourmant, *Le désenchantement*, 147; Ackermann, *Sündenfall der Intellektuellen*, 154-161.

30 Grémion, *Paris/Prague*, 74, 218-219.

31 See above-mentioned publications by Frybes, Chwalba and Kolago.

32 Frybes, "French Enthusiasm for Solidarnosc"; Kula, "Les réactions françaises."

33 There were a few other cases, however, where CFDT did voice support for Eastern European dissidents. Its secretary general, Edmond Maire, was a founding member of the Comité international de soutien à la Charte 77. Moreover, some contacts had been made throughout the years, particularly with Polish oppositional figures, whether in Poland (Tadeusz Mazowiecki in the early 1960s), visiting Paris (Adam Michnik in 1976), or exiles in Paris (Krzysztof Pomian), cf. Bent Boel, "Mai 68, La France et la dissidence en Europe de l'Est, 1968-1989" (forthcoming article).

34 Interview with Rocard, 24 November 2005; Pierre Favier and Michel Martin-Roland (eds), *La décennie Mitterrand, Paris*, vol. 1 (Paris 1990), 450.

35 Frybes, "French Enthusiasm for Solidarnosc"; Kula, "Les réactions françaises."

36 Jean-Marie Vanlerenberghe, "Un précurseur: le Fonds Européen pour la liberté d'expression", 31.1.2005 (see <http://www.colisee.org/article.php?id_article=1675>).

37 Concerning eurocomunism, see Maud Bracke, *Which Socialism, Whose Détente? West European Communism and the Czechoslovak Crisis* (Budapest 2007); Boel, "Mai 68."

38 Boel, "Mai 68."

39 Ibid.

40 Note, Jean Pronteau, Pronteau archives.

41 Pfeil, *Die 'anderen' deutsch-französischen Beziehungen*, 466.

42 Interview with Suzanne Bartosek, 14 November 2007.

43 Gianlorenzo Pacini, "Il socialismo dal volto umano," *Nuova storia contemporanea*, vol. 10, no. 1 (Jan.–Feb. 2006), 117-158 (see p. 151).

44 Nicole Racine, "Le Pen Club international ou la solidarité entre écrivains (1945-1986)," in José Gotovitch and Anne Morelli (eds), *Les Solidarités internationales. Histoire et perspectives* (Brussels 2003), 153-164, (see pp. 156, 159, 162).

45 Jacques Le Goff, *Une vie pour l'histoire* (Paris 1996), 130-133, 158-160.

46 Bernard Guetta and Jean Lacouture, *Le Monde est mon métier* (Grasset 2007); Interview with Bruno Groppo, November 2007.

47 Ioana Popa, "Dépasser l'exil. Degrés de médiation et stratégies de transfert littéraire chez des exilés de l'Europe de l'Est en France," *Genèses*, vol. 38 (March 2000), 5-32; Ioana Popa: "Un transfert littéraire politisé. Circuits de traduction des littératures

d'Europe de l'Est en France, 1947-1989," *Actes de la recherche en sciences sociales*, no. 144 (2002), 55-69.

48 Interview with a former OCI courier, Karel Yon, "Modes de sociabilité et entretien de l'habitus militant. Militer en bandes à l'AJS-OCI dans les années 1970," *Politix*, vol. 18, no. 70 (2005), 137-167, see p. 160; Jeannine Verdès-Leroux, *La foi des vaincus. Les 'révolutionnaires' français de 1945 à 2005* (Paris 2005), 391-393.

49 Interviews with former LCR courriers.

50 However, see Katrin Rücker, "Les gauches française et allemande dans la 'guerre froide' des euromissiles et la course au pacifisme: entre malentendus et 'Sonderweg'," *Revue d'histoire diplomatique*, no. 117 (2003), 35-62; Wittner, *The Struggle Against the Bomb*, 157-159; Christian Mellon, "Peace Organisations in France Today," in Jolyon Howorth and Patricia Chilton (eds), *Defence and Dissent in Contemporary France* (London 1984), 202-216. Jean-François Gribenski, "La contestation anti-missiles des années quatre-vingt: une contestation pacifiste?" (Thèse pour le doctorat de l'Université Paris II, Dec. 1992).

51 Burke, "A Transcontinental Movement of Citizens?"

52 On IKV see Beatrice de Graaf, *Über die Mauer. Die DDR, die niederländischen Kirchen und die Friedensbewegung* (Münster 2007).

53 Interview with Dieter Esche, November 2007.

54 Examples: Le Comité pour le respect des accords d'Helsinki; la Fondation pour l'Entraide intellectuelle européenne; Association des amis de Soljénitsyne; Association internationale pour la liberté et la culture; Comité des psychiatres contre les hôpitaux psychiatriques spéciaux, Comité contre l'utilisation de la psychiatrique a des fins répressives, le Comité International contre la repression, Comité pour la défense des libertés dans les pays se réclamant du socialisme; Comité pour la libération des enfants-otages tchécoslovaques, Comité pour la libération immédiate des emprisonnés politiques dans les pays de l'Europe de l'Est, Comité international des mathématiciens, Comité du 5 janvier pour une Tchécoslovaquie libre et socialiste, Comité Borisov; Comité des physiciens pour la défense de Youri Orlov, Comité de défense d'Anatole Chtcharanskski, Solidarité avec Solidarnosc, Comité Biermann, Comité international de soutien à la Charte 77.

55 Laurent Schwartz, *Un mathématicien aux prises avec le siècle* (Paris 1997), 497-528.

56 On 5 January 1968, Alexander Dubcek replaced Antonin Novotny as the first secretary of the Czechoslovak Communist Party.

57 BPIC archives, Comité du janvier, F pièce 4063 (15), Letter, 26 June 1977, Zdeněk Mlynář to Comité du 5 Janvier.

58 Marcin Kula, "Paris vu par une famille d'historiens polonais," in Zbigniew Naliwajek and Joanna Zurowska (eds), *Le Sacre d'une capitale. Paris vu par les écrivains, les historiens et les voyageurs* (Warsaw 2005), 265-279; Antoine Marès, "Témoignages d'exilés et de réfugiés politiques d'Europe Centrale en France après 1945," *Matériaux pour l'histoire de notre temps*, no. 44 (Oct.–Dec. 1996), 48-54; Jacques Rupnik, "Das Erbe der Charta 77 und die Entstehung einer europäischen Öffentlichkeit," *Transit*, vol. 33 (2007) 97-110; Tony Judt, "Paris and the tribes of Europe," *French Politics and*

Society, vol. 10, no. 2 (spring 1992), 35; Stéphane Dufoix, *Politiques d'exil. Hongrois, Polonais et Tchécoslovaques en France après 1945* (Paris 2002).

59 Krzysztof Pomian, Pierre Kende, Akos Ditroï, Czeslaw Milosz, Milan Kundera, François Fejtö, Constantin Jelenski, Paul Goma, K.S. Karol, Aleksander Smolar, Georges Mink, just to name a few.

60 Ulrich Schmid, "Eine intellektuelle Chronik Polens. Entstehung, Bedeutung und Ende der polnischen Exilzeitschrift 'Kultura,'" *Osteuropa*, vol. 51 (January 2001), 46-57; Rafal Habielski, "'Kultura'. Son programme, son rôle," in Michel and Laptos (eds), *Les relations entre la France et la Pologne au XXe siècle*, 225-236. Grazyna Pomian, "Le rôle politique de l'émigration polonaise en France depuis 1945," *Matériaux pour l'histoire de notre temps*, no. 61 (2001), 62-68; Stefan Meller et Thierry de Montbrial (eds), *Mémoires d'un combat: Kultura 1947-2000* (Paris 2001).

61 Grémion, "La reception des dissidences," 394.

62 Boudic, *Les métamorphoses d'une revue*; Thibaud, "Solidarnosc: la solidarité et les malentendus."

63 Grémion, "La réception des dissidences," 392.

64 Interviews with Pierre Hassner (21 November 2005) and Pierre Grémion (28 November 2005).

65 Grémion, *Intelligence de l'anticommunisme*, 501-509; Nicolas Guilhot, "A Network of influential Friendships: the Fondation pour une Entraide Intellectuelle Europeenne and East-West Cultural Dialogue, 1957-1991," *Minerva*, vol. 44 (2006), 379-409.

66 Hourmant, *Le desenchantement*, 145.

67 This was for instance what a group of Danish environmental activists did in the early 1980s when on their way to Czechoslovakia they made a detour via Paris (interview with Henrik Halkier, April 2006).

68 Blumsztajn, *Je rentre au pays* (Paris 1985).

69 Jean-Christophe Romer and Thomas Schreiber, "La France et l'Europe centrale," *Politique étrangère*, vol. 60, no. 4 (1995), 919.

70 Claude Cheysson's unfortunate initial reaction to the declaration of martial law ("Of course we will do nothing….") may also have contributed to the tough French stand, to avoid any suspicion that the French government was "soft" on Jaruzelski.

71 However, see Grémion, "La réception des dissidences à Paris," 400-401.

72 Francesco Caccamo, *Jiri Pelikán. Un lungo viaggio nell'arcipelago socialista* (Venice 2007).

73 Interview with Danish former Trotskyite couriers.

74 Jacques Almaric, "Les voleurs de la révolution", *Libération* (1 August 2005).

75 Bent Boel, "Statsræson og menneskerettighedspolitik. Frankrig og Østeuropa under den kolde krig," *1066. Tidsskrift for historie*, vol. 4 (2003), 12-19.

76 Semelin, *La liberté au bout des ondes*, 35.

77 See Grémion, "La réception des dissidences à Paris," 401. This issue, however, is disputed and still requires investigation. In particular, the French embassy in Warsaw on a number of occasions seems to have been quite sympathetic vis-à-vis

the opposition after 1980 (interview with Jacques Faure, 23 November 2007, and Jacques Semelin, 26 May 2005).
78 Roland Dumas, *Affaires étrangères, tome 1 (1981-1988)* (Paris 2007), 184.
79 Hassner, "The View from Paris," 217.
80 Ibid., 203.
81 The victory of the right-wing parties at the French elections in March 1986, which allowed the Gaullist leader Jacques Chirac to form a new government, simply confirmed the "normalization" of the Franco-Polish relations. Prime Minister Chirac's views do not seem to have differed much from President Mitterrand's, and policy towards Eastern Europe did not become a subject of conflict during the period of so-called cohabitation (1986-1988).
82 Most famously, in December 1988 Mitterrand had breakfast at the French embassy in Prague with Vaclav Havel and other dissidents. In January 1989 he met the dissident and future president Jelou Jelev. Mitterrand did meet GDR oppositionists when he visited GDR, but that was in December 1989 (cf. Pfeil, *Die 'anderen' deutsch-französischen Beziehungen*, 623).
83 Olivier Mongin, *Face au scepticisme. Les mutations du paysage intellectuel (1976-1998)* (Paris 1998), 325.

Appendix:
From Helsinki to Belgrade

Skjold G. Melibin

At the request of the organizers of the Cold War Conference at the University of Copenhagen, I delivered the intervention printed below about the beginning of the CSCE, "Present at the Creation", which covered my experiences from the opening of the preparatory talks until the beginning of the CSCE proper (Helsinki, November 1972-August 1973). After the conference, I was asked to present my experiences from the first follow-up meeting in the CSCE process (Belgrade, October 1977-March 1978). Hence the following notes, "The Belgrade Meeting 1977-1978 In Memoriam – Super Power Diplomacy to the Rescue".

In the interval between the events described in these two papers, the CSCE and other important international developments took place. As is known the conference concluded with the adoption of a Final Act which would prove to become essential to the efforts and hopes of overcoming the unnatural division of Europe – which was at the heart of the Cold War. But there were many complications and difficulties on the road towards this goal, and in the period between Helsinki and Belgrade they were numerous. First and foremost, there were the vicious arguments between East and West about the right interpretation and implementation of the provisions in the Final Act about the human dimension. Elsewhere, the negotiations on strategic armaments had run into new difficulties: the negotiations on millitary force reductions in Europe were at a standstill, conflicts in Africa found East and West supporting opposing partners, and the world economy was suffering from a critical recession. Many detailed descriptions of this dramatic period are available.

I had the privilege of being head of the Danish delegations to the preparatory talks, to the CSCE itself and to the Belgrade meeting. The two papers which follow thus cover the beginning and the end of my direct preoccupation with the CSCE process. I hope that they provide a useful contribution to an overall picture of this rich and productive period in the history of Europe.

"Present at the Creation"

It has been suggested that the roots of the CSCE stretch as far back as to a proposal presented by Soviet Foreign Minister Molotov in 1954 at the Four-Power conference in Berlin. There is one element of truth in this reflection in so far as it was that proposal which let the "conference cat" out of the bag. The Molotov proposal envisaged a conference which should prepare a collective European security pact. However, it did not carry the day. Above all it held too many obligations which would serve to stagnate the situation in Europe rather than to overcome the East-West division of the continent, and at the end of the day next to nothing survived from the Molotov proposal. But, as is well known, for many years the idea of some kind of a conference on Europe was discussed, both bilaterally and multilaterally, in all kinds of European and transatlantic contexts.

And out of all this came the creation: On 22 November 1972 we met in Helsinki at the initiative of the Finnish Government. And "we" were representatives of thirty-two European countries, the USA and Canada. The objective was to prepare a conference on security and cooperation in Europe. So far, so good. The stage was set. But where was the script?

Nowhere, because none of us had any clear idea of where the process which we were about to initiate would or could lead us. To tell the truth, when we sat down around the mega-triangle table in Dipoli Congress Hall at the University of Helsinki, the question foremost in my mind was: "Now what?" I did not say that aloud to anyone at the time – or later for that matter – but I feel convinced that most of my colleagues must have nourished similar thoughts.

We were to prepare a conference with no precedent and no generally agreed positions fit to build upon – be that in respect to the structure, the agenda or the final outcome of that conference. Of course, there were many political ideas floating around in the muddy waters in the wake of the countless political activities that took place during the preceding decades. But these were ideas pointing in all possible – and some impossible – directions and were certainly not lighthouses in the dark; "floating" is a precise description of these ideas.

The debate that followed was – as is well-known – correspondingly kaleidoscopic, and before long I found myself pondering: why and how on earth did I end up here? Of course I knew the answer to this question. In the late summer of 1972, the permanent under-secretary in the MFA told me that he, together with the minister, had decided that I should be asked to take up the task as chief negotiator both in the preparatory talks to the so much talked about conference on Europe and also during the conference itself. Grammatically it could be perceived as a question, in ministerial terms it was an order.

I mention this because, if the truth must be told, I did not fancy that idea at all. I entered the Foreign Service in 1950 and thus belong to a generation which at that time, in respect to foreign policy, was preoccupied with the wish to create and maintain a new and solid international order – not least in Europe – after the dismal experiences of World War II. An order not based upon words, intentions and promises only, but including a manifest and sufficient military capacity to discourage anyone from even considering the prospect of foul play. In a European context and for a western country, NATO was the ultimate answer to that problem. And we found that answer to be proved true as the Cold War developed over the years to come.

Of course, none of us considered a state of cold war to be a durable solution to the many problems left over from World War II. Every sensible person knew that some kind of détente was necessary, and most of us were looking forward to the day when we could harvest the fruits of efforts to that end. But I was not attracted by the prospect of being a part to these efforts. I foresaw them becoming protracted and tiresome and the result possibly tedious. However, those in power in Denmark were not the least impressed by my preoccupations. So there I was in a corner of the mega-triangle table at Dipoli in Helsinki and like Dickens' Mr Micawber waiting for something to turn up.

And eventually it did: up to and during the second session of the preparatory talks beginning in January 1973 something did turn up. The then nine members of the European Community took an initiative which would become an important factor in the preparation and organization of the conference which was to follow. Based on preparations over several years in NATO and in the European Community, we drew up a comprehensive proposal to a detailed agenda for the conference to be.

This initiative was meant to serve two essential purposes. First, to promote negotiations and provide the preparatory talks with a concrete objective. Second, to demonstrate the effectiveness of the newly established foreign policy cooperation between the EC countries.

The proposal consisted of three main parts: 1) security, 2) economic cooperation, and 3) human contacts and exchange of information – plus a glazing: culture and education. The first two items in this third part of the proposal were intended to open up for the passage of European borders by persons, news and ideas. They were foreseen to be the object of very strong opposition from the Soviet Union and the other Warsaw Pact countries, and several among us feared that the discussion of it might develop into a veritable crisis for a conference and possibly reflect negatively on its sponsor. Therefore, when it came to finding among the EC members someone willing to take up the sponsorship for this proposal, everybody stuck to the old soldiers' doctrine: "never volunteer".

This was the situation when on a gloomy January afternoon the nine were constructively discussing the contents of their proposal, but with everybody staying clear of the question of the sponsorship of part three. Half listening to this discussion, it all of a sudden dawned on me: why not Denmark? When everything was said and done, what could happen in the real world that we would not be able to cope with on a good day? The text corresponded to established Danish views on freer movement of and contacts between people and exchanges of information and ideas across borders. Sponsoring a text like that would be straight down the road in Danish domestic politics. And for a small country it would have the added advantage that as spokesman for an important group of countries on an important subject we would be guaranteed a crucial role in parts of the negotiations at the conference. So, I asked for the floor and after some remarks about this and that I said that Denmark was prepared to assume the sponsorship for part three of our proposal, adding that it would be subject to the final approval of my foreign minister. The effect was perceptible: an entirely new member of the Community! Had the world gone out of order? You could almost hear a pin drop in the room. And at a pause in the meeting I rushed to the telephone and – luckily – got through to the minister who after a very short time of reflecting said, "Yes, of course". Bingo! After a few minutes I informed the meeting accordingly.

Thereby the EC countries could establish a basis for a full discussion of a complete agenda for the conference to be. And for my own part, I, all of a sudden, found my conference assignment to be both interesting and challenging.

The Danish proposal was presented right at the beginning of the resumed preparatory talks in January 1973. I emphasized the qualities of our proposal in respect to both security and cooperation and its importance to the inhabitants of all European countries. Some EC partners, NATO allies and neutrals supported the Danish proposal – and then we waited for the reaction.

It came the next day – not from the Soviet Union, but from Poland, which must somehow have been convinced that a head-on attack on the Danish proposal might yield results. At least the Polish representative did not mince his words in describing the miserable qualities of the Danish proposal.

I answered the day after, and in defending my proposal tried to live up to the eloquence of my Polish colleague. After this a kind of East-West political street brawl developed, and at the end of that the atmosphere in the meeting room was definitely tense. So, in order to take the temperature where it counted, I saw to it that in leaving the room I met the Soviet delegation. And was I surprised! "How are you Ambassador?" Diplomatic small talk, a playful question about the Danish proposal and pornography – but not an unfriendly or unpleasant word. And the Polish representative? He was all alone – left to himself by friend and foe.

This leads me to a reflection about the Soviet delegation. Its leadership consisted of three people: Deputy Foreign Minister Valerian Zorin, head of delegation, and two high ranking officials from the Foreign Ministry in Moscow – a very competent trio, among Western delegates known as "The Marx Brothers". Zorin was a veteran from way back, and in his long career since 1922 in various capacities in the service of the Communist Party and the Soviet state, he had not been known for his liberal approach to political problems. We had therefore expected him to perform as a conservative revolutionary.

But we had a surprise coming. Old times was long ago and as an intelligent man he had read the signs of the new times very clearly. Furthermore, his instructions must have been to be as cooperative as possible, short of compromising essential Soviet interests. This was logical since the Soviet Union wanted a positive outcome of the talks to pave the way for a conference which they wanted very much. This did not make negotiating with Zorin and his lieutenants a picnic, for they were still very astute negotiators, and we did not know their instructions. However, it would explain why they were often difficult but never unpleasant counterparts with whom to negotiate, and also why, in the end, the preparatory talks arrived at very satisfactory solutions to the problems dealt with in the Danish proposal.

There is also something peculiar to emphasize about the other superpower, the USA. The American political position was – not surprisingly – for all practical purposes quasi-identical with that of the EC countries. But once the negotiations got going the Americans, by and large, left the direct negotiations with the Soviets to the EC countries. Why? I do not know for sure, but my guess is this: during the years of preliminary and informal discussions on a possible conference, the Europeans in a number of cases had been pressing the US to be more forthcoming than Washington wanted or considered necessary. And in the end we got our conference. At that point Washington may well have thought: over the years we have had to negotiate with the Soviets on God knows how many different East-West problems. Why not let the Europeans take upon themselves the leading part in this one since they wanted the conference so much? Now let them feel what it is like to be up front dealing on their own with the Russians.

This did not mean that the Americans left the Europeans to their own devices, not at all. They supported us all along the way, but we were the ones mainly responsible for producing the basis for results. Thus the transatlantic cooperation was upheld and in good shape, but the distribution of roles was different than usual in that the main axis in the negotiations went between the EC and the Soviet Union – and that continued during the CSCE itself, and it worked very well.

So much for the beginning, autumn 1972 through spring 1973. What did we expect from the CSCE at that time? I do not remember exactly. But one thing I do know for sure is that the impact of the CSCE on European history in the following fifteen to twenty years went far beyond what even the most optimistic among us had expected. After less than twenty years the unnatural East-West division was swiftly done away with and for all practical purposes by non-violent means. I think it is fair to say that the CSCE was the single most important political factor in this fortunate development.

I have described the hesitations I felt in the beginning when I was told to be Danish chief negotiator at the preparations to the CSCE and at the conference itself. Today, when I look back upon my nearly forty-seven years in the Danish Foreign Service that task was probably the best in all those years. This also serves to confirm the time-honoured principle which is incumbent upon any diplomat: "never ask for a post, never refuse one."

The Belgrade Meeting 1977-1978 In Memoriam: Super Power Diplomacy to the Rescue

It ended as stated in the heading. But it did certainly not begin that way. The first of the follow-up meetings foreseen by the Helsinki Final Act of

August 1975 took place in Belgrade from October 1977 through March 1978. Briefly, the purposes of the follow-up meetings were the following: exchanging views on the implementation of the Final Act and on the development of the process of détente as well as defining the modalities for the holding of other meetings.

As the international situation developed from August 1975 to October 1977, this agenda became sheer dynamite. In the Soviet Union and in other Warsaw Pact countries, dissidents – individuals or in groups – became more active, referring to the principle on human rights and to the provisions on freer movement and exchange of views and ideas across borders in the Final Act. The authorities in these countries considered many of these activities criminal, acting accordingly. The governments in western and neutral countries made clear that such action against dissidents were in contravention of the Final Act and harmful to the efforts to promote détente. The press and other mass media chimed in with similar critical views; the Warsaw Pact countries answered in kind, and the exchange of views on the implementation of the Final Act developed into vehement and ugly quarrels.

Prominent in this course of events was the strong commitment proclaimed by US President Carter to the strict observance of human rights on a global scale. The US delegate Arthur Goldberg stuck meticulously to this line, and the Soviet delegate Yuli Vorontsov answered in as clear terms as they come – the atmosphere at the meeting suffering accordingly. This challenge by the US most probably suited the Soviet Union quite well. To achieve the Helsinki Final Act, the Soviet Union had had to make many concessions to western ideas in the fields of human rights, of freer movements between countries, and of exchanges of information and ideas. The last thing the Soviet Union wanted from the Belgrade meeting were new decisions implying any significant development of these various decisions. A heated discussion with unpleasant recriminations was as good a guarantee as any against constructive results. Therefore, the Soviet delegate threw himself into a fiery exchange of views with anyone, not least the US, who criticized the Soviet performance in respect to compliance with the Final Act.

In a sideshow to this common disturbance, various initiatives crossed the stage and disappeared into oblivion. N+N attempts at bridge building between East and West failed, including the preparation of a comprehensive N+N proposal for a Final Document which, however, in several important respects was not acceptable neither to the western countries, because it only addressed selected parts of the substance of the Helsinki Final Act, nor to the eastern countries – for the opposite reason, that is, it went too far into substance. A Soviet proposal dealt only with substance in limited and very general terms, the Soviet delegate claiming that only texts that were likely to be adopted should be discussed, that is, no more provisions on human rights or human contacts. A Western proposal laid the main stress on precisely these subjects, and at some point the US worked out a proposal along the same lines, but reflecting maximalist positions on the observance of human rights and the promotion of freer movement for people, news and ideas across all frontiers between European countries. All of it leading nowhere. The debate around these various initiatives could easily be used as the basic material for a diplomatic textbook on "How to capsize a conference without really trying".

From 1 January 1978 Denmark took over the Presidency of the EC. As a prudent measure to scan the horizon for possibilities or the lack thereof, I invited my Soviet colleague to a luncheon à deux – a very traditional diplomatic step. The outcome was no puzzle: any notion of substantial decisions emanating from the Belgrade meeting was best forgotten, the sooner the better. In order to keep all options open, however remote, or to appear defaitistic, my report back to the EC and NATO groups was slightly touched up.

But the decisive part of the luncheon discussion and the net outcome were as follows. At some point I said, "Why do we not try to take an open and unbiased negotiation at the conference on the basis of the US proposal, and when we all have had our say, who knows how it will end?" And Vorontsov answered: "I know."

The discussions at the conference had continued a little while into 1978 when the US delegate Arthur Goldberg told me that he had had an idea and that he wanted my reaction because it included me. Representing the Presidency of the EC, I had the following role in his scheme: the US, the Soviet Union and the EC were to agree on a text to be tabled by the EC Presidency. It would be void of any particular substance, but contain provisions which would establish the importance of détente and of the implementation of the provisions of the Final Act. Furthermore, that the discussions at the conference had been useful to the purposes and to the continuation of the process initiated in Helsinki, and in establishing time and place for the next follow-up meeting, the proposal would ensure that the process be kept alive and pursued further. I accepted the idea and recommended it to the other EC countries, who accepted. So did the Soviet Union – I suspect that Vorontsov had heard about the idea before me.

The scheme devised by Goldberg presupposed that once the EC countries, the NATO countries and the Soviet Union (the Warsaw Pact countries) had agreed on a text, these three parties should devise by which means the neutral and non-aligned countries could be convinced to see the merits of what was to become a Danish proposal. To achieve this, Goldberg, Vorontsov and I would consult the neutrals and the non-aligned one by one. Changes proposed by any of them to our joint text would be accepted only if all three of us agreed to do so. This relatively rigid working hypothesis was not very popular among the twelve out of thirty-five participants who did not belong to NATO, the EC or the Warsaw Pact. However, it did work. A peculiar situation arose when the Romanian delegate declared that his country could not accept the text as it was and that he would not submit himself to a tribunal. Therefore, he asked me to present his views as to some modest changes in the text, whereby I was fetched up in the somewhat peculiar situation of having to negotiate with the Soviet Union – and with myself! – on behalf of Romania. But it succeeded.

On 4 March the Danish proposal as outlined above was officially tabled at the conference. A few changes from the original text had been made in order to make allowance for wishes from Austria, Romania and Yugoslavia, and for the holding of a few expert meetings, and there was a – so to say – traditional last minute crisis about a Mediterranean problem to get Malta on board. But everything worked out, the next follow-up meeting was fixed to commence on 11 November 1980 in Madrid and consensus among the thirty-five participants could be registered on 8 March 1978.

Thus the CSCE process was saved and could proceed with the results which followed and culminated around 1990.

Contributors

Oliver Bange holds a Ph.D. in International History from the London School of Economics (1997). He is a Senior Researcher at the Military History Research Institute, German Ministry of Defence, in Potsdam, and responsible for the "GDR in the Warsaw Pact". Until 2008 he coordinated the project "CSCE and the Transformation of Europe" at the University of Mannheim. He is the author of *The EEC Crisis of 1963: Kennedy, Macmillan, de Gaulle and Adenauer in Conflict* (2000) and the editor of *Helsinki 1975 and the Transformation of Europe* (2008). He is currently finishing a major work entitled *Ostpolitik and Détente – The Beginnings, 1966-1969*.

Giovanni Bernardini obtained his Ph.D. in History of International Relations at the University of Florence in 2005 with a dissertation on the relations between the Federal Republic of Germany and the United States of America in the period 1969-1974. He has been a Research Fellow at the University of Padua since 2006. His publications include several articles and essays on West German foreign policy during the 1970s, as well as on the foreign activities of the German Social Democratic Party.

Bent Boel has a Ph.D. in History from the University of Copenhagen and Diplômé de l'Institut d'Etudes Politiques de Paris. He is Associate Professor at the Department of History, International and Social Sciences at Aalborg University. His publications on French contemporary history, European cooperation, transatlantic relations and the Cold War include *The European Productivity Agency and Transatlantic Relations, 1953-1961* (2003).

Gregory F. Domber is Assistant Professor of History at the University of North Florida. He received his Ph.D. with a dissertation entitled "Supporting the Revolution: America, Democracy, and the End of the Cold War in Poland, 1981-1989" from George Washington University in 2007. In 2007-2008 he was a Fellow at Stanford University's Center on Democracy, Development, and the Rule of Law. His current research focuses on democratization and the role of non-governmental organizations in international relations.

Thomas Fischer studied History, Political Sciences, Public and International Law in Zurich and Brussels. He earned his Ph.D. from the University of Zurich in 2003. Since 2004 he has been a Research Affiliate at the Austrian

Institute for International Affairs in Vienna. Since September 2008 he has been a Research Fellow with the International History and Politics Unit at the Graduate Institute of International and Development Studies in Geneva. His fields of interest include the study of neutrality, Cold War international history, conflict management and the policy of good offices. His most recent study, *Neutral Power in the CSCE: The N+N States and the Making of the Helsinki Accords 1975*, will be published in 2009.

Wanda Jarzabek received her Ph.D. at Warsaw University. She is Assistant Professor at the Institute for Political Studies of the Polish Academy of Sciences in Warsaw. Her main research fields are Polish political and social history in the twentieth century and international relations during the Cold War with special focus on the German question. Her publications include *Hope and Reality: Poland and the Conference on Security and Cooperation in Europe, 1964-1989* (2008), *Polska wobec Konferencji Bezpieczeństwa i Współpracy w Europie. Plany i rzeczywistość, 1966-1975r.* (2008) and *PRL w politycznych strukturach Układu Warszawskiego w latach 1955-1980* (2008).

Stephan Kieninger studied Modern History and Political Science at the University of Mannheim where he is currently working on his Ph.D. thesis "U.S. Strategies for Détente, 1969-1977". Most recently, he held a Ph.D. fellowship at the German Historical Institute in Washington, D.C. His first essay on conflicting détente stratagems in Washington is part of the volume *Helsinki 1975 and the Transformation of Europe*, edited by Oliver Bange and Gottfried Niedhart (2008). Together with Oliver Bange he is the editor of a document collection on the GDR's policy towards the CSCE which was published as an E-Dossier by the Cold War International History Project in 2008.

Wilfried Loth is Dr.phil. and Professor of Modern and Contemporary History at the University of Duisburg-Essen. He is Chairman of the European Union Liaison Committee of Historians. His research interests include political Catholicism, the contemporary history of France, the history of European integration, and the history of the Cold War. Recent publications include *Overcoming the Cold War. A History of Détente, 1950-1991* (2002) and (edited with Georges-Henri Soutou) *The Making of Détente. Eastern and Western Europe in the Cold War, 1965-75* (2008).

Skjold G. Mellbin was employed in the Danish Foreign Ministry 1950-1996. From 1981 to 1983 he was Chairman of the government appointed Committee on Security and Defence Policy. He headed the Danish Delegation at the Preparatory Talks to the CSCE 1972-73, the CSCE 1973-75, the CSCE's follow-up meetings in Belgrade 1977-78, at Helsinki in 1992, and at the Stockholm conference 1984-86. He was Danish ambassador in Prague 1974-78, in Athens 1986-90 and in Helsinki 1990-96. From May to November 1995 he was the OSCE's head of mission in Sarajevo.

Angela Romano received her Ph.D. in International History and is currently contract Professor of History of North America at the University of Florence. Her research fields of interest include the external relations of the EC/EU, particularly with the Soviet bloc, transatlantic relations, détente, and the CSCE process. Her most recent publication is *From Détente in Europe to European Détente. How the West shaped the Helsinki CSCE* (2009).

Sarah B. Snyder is the Cassius Marcellus Clay Fellow in the Department of History at Yale University. She received her Ph.D. from Georgetown University in 2006 and specializes in transnational, international, transatlantic and diplomatic history. She is finishing a manuscript analyzing the development of a transnational network devoted to human rights advocacy and its significant contributions to the end of the Cold War.

Poul Villaume is Professor of Contemporary History at the University of Copenhagen. He earned his Dr.phil. degree in 1995 with a dissertation on Danish national security policy 1949-1961 entitled *Allieret med forbehold: Danmark, NATO og den kolde krig*. He is the co-author (with T. Borring Olesen) of volume 5 of "The History of Danish Foreign Policy", *I blokopdelingens tegn, 1945-1972* (2005). He is the author of numerous articles in Danish and international books and journals on Cold War related issues and on Danish, European, and United States foreign policies in the twentieth century.

Odd Arne Westad is Professor of International History at the London School of Economics and Political Science. He has written or edited twelve books on contemporary international history, the most recent of which are *Decisive Encounters: The Chinese Civil War, 1946-1950* (2003) and *The Global Cold War: Third World Interventions and the Making of Our Times* (2005), which won the Bancroft Prize. Professor Westad is a founding editor of the journal *Cold War History*, and, with Professor Melvyn Leffler, the General Editor of the forthcoming three-volume *Cambridge History of the Cold War*.

Select Bibliography

Acimovic, Ljubivoje, *Problems of Security and Cooperation in Europe* (Alphen aan den Rijn: Sijthoff & Noordhoff, 1981).

Alexeyeva, Ludmilla, *Soviet Dissent: Contemporary Movements for National, Religious, and Human Rights* (Middletown, CT: Wesleyan University Press, 1985).

Andrén, Nils and Karl E. Birnbaum (eds), *Belgrade and Beyond: The CSCE Process in Perspective* (Alphen aan den Rijn: Sijthoff & Noordhoff, 1980).

Bange, Oliver and Gottfried Niedhart (eds), *Helsinki 1975 and the Transformation of Europe* (New York and Oxford: Berghahn Books, 2008).

Bange, Oliver, "An Intricate Web – Ostpolitik, the European Security System and German Unification", in Oliver Bange and Gottfried Niedhart (eds), *Helsinki 1975 and the Transformation of Europe* (New York and Oxford: Berghahn Books, 2008).

Bange, Oliver, "Ostpolitik as a Source of Intra-Bloc Tensions", in Mary Ann Heiss and S. Victor Papacosma (eds), *NATO and the Warsaw Pact – Intra-Bloc Conflicts* (Kent, OH: Kent State University Press, 2008).

Bange, Oliver and Stephan Kieninger (eds), *Negotiating one's own demise? The GDR's Foreign Ministry and the CSCE negotiations – plans, preparations, tactics and presumptions* (Mannheim 2008).

Blinken, Antony, *Ally vs. Ally* (New York: Praeger, 1987).

Bluth, Cristian, "Détente and Conventional Arms Control: West German Policy Priorities and the Origins of MBFR", *German Politics*, vol. 8, no. 1 (London: Taylor & Francis, 1999).

Borgwardt, Elizabeth, *A New Deal for the World* (Cambridge, MA: Harvard University Press, 2005).

Borring Olesen, Thorsten and Poul Villaume, *I blokopdelingens tegn 1945-1962, Dansk udenrigspolitiks historie, bd. 5* (Copenhagen: Gyldendal Leksikon, 2005).

Bozo, Frédéric, Marie-Pierre Rey, N. Piers Ludlow and Leopoldo Nuti (eds), *Europe and the End of the Cold War: A Reappraisal* (London: Routledge, 2008).

Brown, Archie, *Seven Years that Changed the World: Perestroika in Perspective* (Oxford and New York: Oxford University Press, 2007).

Bundy, William, *A Tangled Web: The Making of Foreign Policy in the Nixon Presidency* (New York: Tauris, 1998).

Davy, Richard, "Helsinki Myths: Setting the Record Straight on the Final Act of the CSCE, 1975", *Cold War History*, vol. 9, no. 1 (February 2009).

Dobrynin, Anatoly F., *In Confidence: Moscow's Ambassador to Six Cold War Presidents* (Seattle: University of Washington Press, 2001).

Domber, Gregory F., "Rumblings in Eastern Europe: Western Pressure on Poland's Moves toward Democratic Transformation," in Frédéric Bozo, Marie-Pierre Rey, N. Piers Ludlow and Leopldo Nuti (eds), *Europe and the End of the Cold War* (Oxford: Routledge, 2008).

Drinan, Robert F., *The Mobilization of Shame: A World View of Human Rights* (New Haven: Yale University Press, 2001).

Dülffer, Jost, *Europa im Ost-West-Konflikt 1945-1990* (Munich: Oldenbourg, 2004).

English, Robert D., *Russia and the Idea of the West: Gorbachev, Intellectuals and the End of the Cold War* (New York: Columbia University Press, 2000).

Fascell, Dante B., "The Helsinki Accord: A Case Study," *Annals of the American Academy of Political and Social Science* 442 (1979).

Fenwick, Millicent, *Speaking Up* (New York: Harper and Row, 1982).

Ferraris, Luigi Vittorio (ed.), *Report on a Negotiation: Helsinki – Geneva – Helsinki 1972-1975* (Alphen aan den Rijn: Sijthoff & Nordhoff, 1979).

Filitov, Aleksei M., "Problems of Post-War Construction in Soviet Foreign Policy Conceptions during World War II", in Francesca Gori and Silvio Pons (eds), *The Soviet Union and Europe in the Cold War, 1943-53* (Basingstoke: Macmillan, 1996).

Fischer, Thomas, "'A mustard seed grew into a bushy tree': The Finnish CSCE Initiative of 5 May 1969", *Cold War History*, vol. 9, no. 2 (May 2009).

Gaddis, John Lewis, *The Cold War. A New History* (New York and London: Penguin, 2005).

Gaddis, John Lewis, *We Now Know. Rethinking Cold War History* (Oxford and New York: Clarendon Press, 1997).

Gaddis, John Lewis, *The Long Peace: Inquiries into the History of the Cold War* (Oxford and New York: Oxford University Press, 1987).

Giusto, Hedwig, Mircea Munteanu and Christian Ostermann (eds), *The Road to Helsinki: The Early Steps to the CSCE, Selected Documents* (Collection of Documents, distributed for the participants of the International Conference on the CSCE, Florence 2003).

Goldberg, Paul, *The Final Act: The Dramatic, Revealing Story of the Moscow Helsinki Watch Group* (New York: Morrow, 1988).

Goodby, James, *Europe Undivided, The New Logic of Peace in US-Russian Relations* (Washington D.C.: United States Institute of Peace Press, 1998).

Griffith, William E., "East-West Détente in Europe," in Frans A.M. Alting von Geseau (ed.), *Uncertain Détente* (Alphen aan den Rijn: Sijthoff and Noordhoff, 1979).

Hanhimäki, Jussi M., *The Flawed Architect. Henry Kissinger and American Foreign Policy* (Oxford: Oxford University Press, 2004).

Hanhimäki, Jussi M., "Ironies and Turning Points: Détente in Perspective", in Odd Arne Westad (ed.), *Reviewing the Cold War: Approaches, Interpretations, Theory* (London and Porland: Routledge, 2000).

Harrison, Hope M., *Driving the Soviets up the Wall. Soviet-East German Relations, 1953-1961* (Princeton, NJ: Princeton University Press, 2003).

Horvath, Robert, *The Legacy of Soviet Dissent: Dissidents, Democratization and Radical Nationalism in Russia* (New York: RoutledgeCurzon, 2005).

Iriye, Akira, *Global Community: The Role of International Organizations in the Making of the Contemporary World* (Berkeley: University of California Press, 2002).

Jarzabek, Wanda, "Hope and Reality: Poland and the CSCE, 1964-1989", *CWIHP Working Paper # 56* (May 2008).

Jervis, Robert L., *The Logic of Images in International Relations* (Princeton: Princeton University Press, 1970).

Jordan, Robert S. (ed.), *Europe and the Superpowers: Essays on European International Politics* (London: Pinter Publishers, 1991).

Keck, Margaret and Kathryn Sikkink, *Activists Beyond Borders: Advocacy Networks in International Politics* (Ithaca: Cornell University Press, 1998).

Kieninger, Stephan, "Transformation or Status Quo: The Conflict of Stratagems in Washington over the Meaning and Purpose of CSCE and MBFR, 1969-1973", in Oliver Bange and Gottfried Niedhart (eds), *Helsinki 1975 and the Transformation of Europe* (New York and Oxford: Berghahn Books, 2008).

Klitzing, Holger, *The Nemesis of Stability. Henry A. Kissinger's Ambivalent Relationship with Germany* (Trier: Wissenschaftlicher Verlag Trier, 2007).

Kochavi, Noam, "Insights Abandoned, Flexibility Lost: Kissinger, Soviet Jewish Emigration, and the Demise of Détente", *Diplomatic History* 29.3 (2005).

Korey, William, *The Promises We Keep: Human Rights, the Helsinki Process and American Foreign Policy* (New York: Institute for East West Studies, 1993).

Laber, Jeri, *The Courage of Strangers: Coming of Age with the Human Rights Movement* (New York: Public Affairs, 2002).

LaFeber, Walter, *America, Russia and the Cold War, 1945-1972* (New York: McGraw-Hill, 1997).

Lippmann, Walter, *The Cold War. A Study in United States Foreign Policy* (New York: Harper & Brothers, 1947).

Loth, Wilfred (ed.), *Europe, the Cold War and Coexistence, 1953-1965* (London and Portland: Routledge, 2004).

Loth, Wilfried, "The Origins of Stalin's Note of 10 March 1952", *Cold War History*, vol. 4, no. 2 (January 2004).

Loth, Wilfried, *Overcoming the Cold War. A History of Détente, 1950-1991* (Houndsmills and New York: Palgrave Macmillan, 2002).

Loth, Wilfried, "Moscow, Prague and Warsaw: Overcoming the Brezhnev Doctrine", *Cold War History*, vol. 1, no. 2 (January 2001).

Loth, Wilfried, "Germany in the Cold War: Strategies and Decisions", in Odd Arne Westad (ed.), *Reviewing the Cold War: Approaches, Interpretations, Theory* (London and Portland: Routledge, 2000).

Loth, Wilfried, *Stalin's Unwanted Child. The Soviet Union, the German Question and the Founding of the GDR* (London and New York: Palgrave Macmillan, 1998).

Loth, Wilfried and Georges-Henri Soutou (eds), *The Making of Détente. Eastern and Western Europe in the Cold War, 1965-75* (London and New York: Routledge, 2008).

Lundestad, Geir, "The Cold War according to John Lewis Gaddis", *Cold War History*, vol. 6, no. 4 (November 2006).

Maresca, John J., *To Helsinki: The Conference on Security and Cooperation in Europe, 1973-1975* (Durham and London: Duke University Press, 1987).

Mastny, Vojtech, "Superpower Détente: US-Soviet Relations, 1969-1972," in David C. Geyer and Bernd Schaefer (eds), *American Détente and German Ostpolitik, 1969-1972*, special issue of Bulletin of the German Historical Institute (Washington D.C.: German Historical Institute, 2004).

Mastny, Vojtech, *The Cold War and Soviet Insecurity. The Stalin Years* (New York and Oxford: Oxford University Press, 1996).

Mastny, Vojtech (ed.), *Helsinki, Human Rights, and European Security: Analysis and Documentation* (Durham: Duke University Press, 1986).

Mastny, Vojtech and Malcolm Byrne, *A Cardboard Castle? An Inside History of the Warsaw Pact 1955-1991* (Budapest: Central European University Press, 2005).

Mates, Leo, "The Neutral and Nonaligned Countries," in Nils Andrén and Karl E. Birnbaum (eds), *Belgrade and Beyond: The CSCE Process in Perspective* (Alphen aan den Rijn: Sijthoff & Noordhoff, 1980).

Naimark, Norman M., *The Russians in Germany. A History of the Soviet Zone Occupation, 1945-1949* (Cambridge, MA and London: Harvard University Press, 1995).

Naimark, Norman M. and Leonid Gibianskii (eds), *The Establishment of Communist Regimes in Eastern Europe, 1944-1959* (Boulder, CO: Westview Press, 1997).

Nelson, Keith L., *The Making of Détente* (Baltimore: The Johns Hopkins University Press, 1995).

Niedhart, Gottfried, "Peaceful Change of Frontiers as a Crucial Element in the West German Strategy of Transformation", in Oliver Bange and Gottfried Niedhart (eds), *Helsinki 1975 and the Transformation of Europe* (Oxford and New York: Berghahn Books, 2008).

Niedhart, Gottfried, "Ostpolitik: Phases, Short-Term objectives, and Grand Design", in David C. Geyer and Bernd Schaefer (eds), *American Détente and German Ostpolitik 1969-1972*, special issue of Bulletin of the German Historical Institute (Washington D.C.: German Historical Institute, 2004).

Nuti, Leopoldo, "The United States, Italy and the Opening to the Left, 1953-1963", *Journal of Cold War Studies*, vol. 4, no. 3 (2002).

Orlov, Yuri, *Dangerous Thoughts: Memoirs of a Russian Life*, trans. Thomas P. Whitney (New York: William Morrow and Company, 1991).

Ratti, Lucca, "Britain, The German Question and the Transformation of Europe: From Ostpolitik to the Helsinki Conference (1963-1975)", in Oliver Bange and Gottfried Niedhart (eds), *Helsinki 1975 and the Transformation of Europe* (New York and Oxford: Berghahn Books, 2008).

Renk, Hans-Jörg, *Der Weg der Schweiz nach Helsinki: Der Beitrag der schweizerischen Diplomatie zum Zustandekommen der Konferenz über Sicherheit und Zusammenarbeit in Europa (KSZE), 1972-1975* (Bern, Stuttgart and Vienna: Verlag Paul Haupt, 1996).

Romano, Angela, "Behind closed doors. Contacts between EEC and CMEA in the early 70s", in Carla Meneguzzi Rostagni (ed.), *The Helsinki Process: A Historical Reappraisal* (Padova: Cedam, 2005).

Rubenstein, Joshua, *Soviet Dissidents: Their Struggle for Human Rights*, 2nd ed. (Boston: Beacon Press, 1985).

Sarotte, M.E., *Dealing with the Devil: East Germany, Détente, and Ostpolitik, 1969-1973* (Chapel Hill, NC: The University of North Carolina Press, 2000).

Schwartz, Thomas A., *Lyndon Johnson and Europe: In the Shadow of Vietnam* (Cambridge, MA: Harvard University Press, 2003).

Schweizer, Peter, *Reagan's War* (New York: Anchor Books, 2002).

Selvage, Douglas, "The Treaty of Warsaw: The Warsaw Pact Context", in David C. Geyer and Bernd Schaefer (eds), *American Détente and German Ostpolitik, 1969-1972*, special issue of Bulletin of the German Historical Institute (Washington D.C.: German Historical Institute, 2004).

Sharansky, Natan, *Fear No Evil* (New York: Random House, 1988).

Sizoo, Jan and Rudolf Th. Jurrjens, *CSCE Decision-Making: The Madrid Experience* (The Hague, Boston and Lancaster: Martinus Nijhoff Publishers, 1984).

Sjursen, Helene, *The United States, Western Europe and the Polish Crisis: International Relations in the Second Cold War* (New York: Palgrave Macmillan, 2003).

Skilling, Gordon H., "The Madrid Follow-up", in Robert Spencer (ed.), *Canada and the Conference on Security and Co-operation in Europe* (Toronto: Centre for International Studies, University of Toronto, 1984).

Smith, Karen E., *The Making of EU Foreign Policy* (New York: St. Martin's Press, Inc., 1999).

Smyser, William R., *From Yalta to Berlin. The Cold War Struggle over Germany* (New York: St. Martin's Press, 1999).

Soutou, Georges-Henri, *La guerre de Cinquante Ans. Les relations Est-Ouest 1943-1990* (Paris: Fayard, 2001).

Stephanson, Anders, "Liberty or Death: The Cold War as US ideology", in Odd Arne Westad (ed.), *Reviewing the Cold War: Approaches, Interpretations, Theory* (London and Portland: Routledge, 2000).

Stephanson, Anders, "Rethinking Cold War History", *Review of International Studies* 24 (1998).

Sutterlin, James S. and David Klein, *Berlin: From Symbol of Confrontation to Keystone of Stability* (New York: Praeger, 1989).

Thomas, Daniel C., *The Helsinki Effect: International Norms, Human Rights, and the Demise of Communism* (Princeton: Princeton University Press, 2001).

Varsori, Antonio and Elena Clandri (eds), *The Failure of Peace in Europe, 1943-49* (Houndsmills and New York: Palgrave Macmillan, 2002).

Wagner, Wolfgang, "Basic requirements and consequences of the Ostpolitik", *The Atlantic Community Quarterly*, vol. 9, no. 1 (Spring 1971).

Wenger, Andreas, Vojtech Mastny and Christian Nuenlist (eds), *Origins of the European Security System. The Helsinki Process Revisited, 1965-75* (Oxford and New York: Routledge, 2008).

Westad, Odd Arne, *The Global Cold War: Third World Interventions and the Making of Our Times* (Cambridge: Cambridge University Press, 2006).

Westad, Odd Arne, *Decisive Encounters: The Chinese Civil War, 1946-1950* (Stanford: Stanford University Press, 2003).

Westad, Odd Arne (ed.), *Reviewing the Cold War: Approaches, Interpretations, Theory* (London and Portland: Routledge, 2003).

Wilkens, Andreas, *Der unstete Nachbar. Frankreich, die deutsche Ostpolitik und die Berliner Vier-Mächte-Verhandlungen 1969-1974* (Munich: Oldenbourg, 1990).

Zubok, Vladislav M., "The Soviet Union and Détente of the 1970s", *Cold War History*, vol. 8, no. 4 (Special Issue: Détente and Its Legacy) (November 2008).

Zubok, Vladislav M., *A Failed Empire. The Soviet Union in the Cold War from Stalin to Gorbatchev* (Chapel Hill, NC: The University of North Carolina Press, 2007).

Zubok, Vladislav M., "Gorbachev and the End of the Cold War. Perspectives on History and Personality", *Cold War History*, vol. 2, no. 2 (January 2002).

Zubok, Vladislav M., "The Collapse of the Soviet Union. Leadership, Elites, and Legitimacy", in Geir Lundestad (ed.), *The Fall of Great Powers. Peace, Stability and Legitimacy* (Oslo and New York: Aschehoug, 1994).

Zubok, Vladislav M. and Constantin Pleshakov, *Inside the Kremlin's Cold War: From Stalin to Khrushchev* (Cambridge, MA: Harvard University Press, 1996).

Zuzowski, Robert, *Political Dissent and Opposition in Poland. The Workers' Defense Committee "KOR"* (Westport, CN: Praeger, 1992).

INDEX

Adenauer, Konrad, 28
Afghanistan, 13, 27, 137, 143, 159, 160, 162
Alekseeva, Ludmilla, 182-183, 190
Almaric, Jacques, 233
l'Alternative, 228
Andropov, Yuri, 26-27
Appeal for a European Security Conference, *see* Budapest Appeal 1969
Arbatov, Georgi, 29
Armenia, 183
Atlantic Alliance, *see* NATO
Atomic weaponry, 22, 25-26, 37, 39, 159, 225, 226
Austria, 14, 144-148, 160-164, 167, 193, 229, 251

Bahr, Egon, 29, 58, 60, 65, 68, 84-86, 88, 106-107
Bahro, Rudolf, 224
Baker, James, 29
Bartosek, Karel, 224, 228
Baruch, Bernard M., 19
Basic Treaty (GDR-FRG), 69
Baylet, Jean-François, 233
Belgium, 36, 40, 51, 127, 193
Belgrade CSCE Follow-up Meeting (1977-1978), 13-15, 49, 137, 143-144, 155-160, 167, 179-180, 184-185, 243, 245, 247-251
Berlin, 12, 25, 39, 44-45, 59-77, 83, 87-88, 91, 93, 105, 110, 113, 151, 244
Berlin crisis, 105
Biermann, Wolf, 224
Bindschedler, Rudolf, 155
Blech, Klaus, 71, 77
Bock, Siegfried, 69, 70, 74
Bousoglou, Amber, 224
Bowden, Lewis, 104
Brandt, Willy, 9, 12, 58, 60-63, 65-68, 79, 83, 86-89, 91, 93-95, 101-107, 110, 136
Brezhnev Doctrine, 82, 129-130, 135
Brezhnev, Leonid, 22, 26-27, 39, 58-59, 61-62, 64-65, 68-70, 72, 82, 108, 112, 129-130, 133, 135-136, 183, 203, 218
Bridge building, 12, 65, 101-102, 109-111, 113-114, 249
Britain, *see* Great Britain
Brunner, Edouard, 148, 152, 154, 161-164, 166-167
Brzezinski, Zbigniew, 65
Budapest Appeal 1969, 40, 84
Bundestag, FRG, 45, 47, 60, 66, 89, 110, 112

Cargo, William, 103-104
Carstens, Karl, 38
Carter, Jimmy, 10, 14, 156, 159, 184, 231, 249
Ceausescu, Nikolae, 66, 109
Ceska, Franz, 161, 167, 175, 177
CFDT (Democratic Confederation of Labour), France, 220-223, 230-231
CFTC (French Confederation of Christian Workers), France, 220, 223
CGT (General Confederation of Labour), France, 223, 230
Charter 77, Czechoslovakia, 183, 187, 226, 228, 234
Christian Committee for the Defence of Believers' Rights in the Soviet Union, 183
Christofferson, Michael Scott, 217, 229
Churchill, Winston, 28
CMEA, see COMECON
COCOM (Coordinating Committee for Multilateral Export Controls), 42, 198
CODENE (Committee for Nuclear Disarmament in Europe), France, 225-226, 230-232
COMECON (Council for Mutual Economic Assistance), 62, 132, 136, 205
Cominform (Communist Information Bureau), 24
Comité du 5 janvier, France, 227
Comité international de soutien à la Charte 77, France, 228
Commission on Security and Cooperation in Europe, US, 180-181
Common Agricultural Policy (CAP), 123
Common Commercial Policy (CCP), 125, 136
Conference on Security and Cooperation in Europe, see CSCE
Confidence Building Measures (CBM), 144, 162-163
Copenhagen Cold War Conference 2007, 10
COREPER (Comité des Représentants Permanents), European Union, 129
CPSU (Communist Party of the Soviet Union), 25, 27, 58-59, 68
CSCE (Conference on Security and Cooperation in Europe), 10-17, 29-30, 35, 38, 40, 42, 47-51, 57, 69-72, 101-102, 106-108, 109-110, 112-115, 124-137, 143-145, 147-156, 158-168, 180, 183-188, 198, 201-202, 206-207, 243-244, 248, 251, see also ESC
Czechoslovakia, 8, 38, 39, 45, 63, 64, 65, 80, 104, 105, 183, 186, 217, 221, 226, 227, 228, 233, 234

Delimitation policy, 12, 57, 68-69, 71, 77
Denmark, 15, 16, 36, 40, 123, 126, 127, 245, 246, 250
Department of State, U.S., see State Department
Derrida, Jacques, 224, 229
Détente, 7-13, 15-17, 19, 26-29, 35-36, 40-43, 48-51, 57-59, 61-65, 67, 71-72, 79-80, 82-84, 87-89, 91-95, 101-107, 109-110, 114-115, 123-126, 129-131, 133, 135-137, 154, 156, 159, 195-196, 215-216, 218, 231, 235, 245, 249-250
Detente from above, 215
Detente from below, 15, 215, 216, 231, 235

INDEX

Dialogue, 13, 51, 79, 81, 85, 99, 123-126, 129, 131, 135-137, 183, 216, 226, 230
Dialogue Group, Hungary, 226
Dipoli, 144-148, 244-245
Disarmament, 11, 26, 30, 40, 42, 51, 85, 109, 131, 162-163, 166
Dissidents, 10, 15, 137, 180-184, 186, 206, 208, 215-234, 249
Dobrynin, Anatoly, 111, 151
Dölln, meeting in, GDR, 1969, 65-67
Domenach, Jean-Marie, 228
Dubcek, Alexander, 64, 239
Dumas, Roland, 233

Eagleburger, Lawrence, 106, 198, 205
East Germany, *see* German Democratic Republic (GDR)
EEC (European Economic Community) 9, 42, 70, 205, 206, 207
EHESS (L'Ecole des hautes etudes en sciences sociales), France, 224
Eisenhower, Dwight D., 26, 105
Ellsworth, Robert, 93
Embargo, against Soviet Union, 13, 137
END (European Nuclear Disarmament) Appeal, 225-226, 232
EPC (European Political Cooperation), 13, 15, 123, 124, 126-129, 131, 133-137
ESC (European Security Conference), 104, 106, 107-111, 113, *see also* CSCE
Esprit, 222, 228
d'Estaing, Valery Giscard, 233
Euro-Communism, 115, 223
European Security, 11, 16, 40-41, 69, 79-80, 84-95, 102, 104, 106-112, 124, 130, 143-145, 149-150, 154, 197, 244

Fabius, Laurent, 233
Falin, Valentin, 68
Farley, Philip, 109-110
Free Democratic Party (FDP), West Germany, 65, 88-89
Federal Republic of Germany (FRG), 9, 12, 37-42, 44-45, 47, 49, 50, 57, 61-62, 64-65, 68, 71, 79, 83-86, 88, 91-94, 103, 106, 109, 127, 134, 137, 193, 198, 253
Fenwick, Millicent, 180-181
Finland, 14, 144, 148-151, 154-155
Fondation pour une entraide intellectuelle européenne, France, 228
Force ouvrière (FO), France, 220, 223
Ford, Gerald, 114, 122
Fourth International (LCR), *see* Trotskyites
France, 7, 9-10, 15, 36, 80, 87, 110, 127, 129, 147-148, 193, 205, 215-221, 224-230, 233-235
Freer movement of goods, people and ideas, 12, 101, 104, 106-107, 113-114, 129, 133-135, 246, 249-250
French Communist Party, *see* PCF
FRG, *see* Federal Republic of Germany

Gaddis, John Lewis, 20, 32-33, 101-102
GATT (General Agreement on Tariffs and Trade), 42
Gdansk, August 1980, 15, 220, 222, 234
GDR, *see* German Democratic Republic
de Gaulle, Charles, 61, 101, 123
Geneva, 70, 107, 128-129, 133, 144, 147-150, 153-156, 254
Genscher, Hans-Dietrich, 47, 137, 197, 202-203

Georgia, 188
German Democratic Republic (GDR), 8, 11-12, 25, 39, 41, 45, 57-71, 85, 115, 148, 162, 221, 224, 226, 253-254
German "peace note" 1966, 35, 37, 39
Germany, 7-12, 23-24, 26, 30, 36-40, 44-45, 47, 50, 58-68, 70, 72, 79, 82-84, 86, 103, 105, 109-110, 115, 127, 131, 161, 193, 198, 205, 221, 229, 253
Giedroyc, Jerzy, 228
Gierek, Edward, 50, 233
Gilpatric, Roswell, 26
Glasnost, 233
Goldberg, Arthur J., 14-15, 184-185, 249-251
Gomulka doctrine, 11, 40, 53
Gomulka, Wladislaw, 8, 11, 23, 36, 38-41, 52, 53, 66, 240
Gonzalez, Felipe, 161, 166
Gorbachev, Mikhail, 14, 27-29, 188, 233
Görlitz, border treaty of, 1950, 38
Grand Coalition, FRG, 61-62
Great Britain, 9, 23, 36, 51, 87, 114, 123, 126-127, 154, 205, 206
Greece, 9
Gromyko, Andrei, 25, 27, 68, 114, 118, 150-151
Guetta, Bernard, 224
Gulag effect, 217, 218, 219, 234

Hacke, Christian, 51
Hager, Kurt, 67
Hague Summit, 123, 124
Hallstein doctrine, 62, 86
Harmel Report 1967, 99
Hassner, Pierre, 219, 228
Havel, Vaclav, 230
Havemann, Robert, 224
Heinemann, Gustav, 224

Helsinki Final Act, 11, 14-15, 35, 46-48, 70-72, 101, 110, 113-114, 137, 143, 145, 147, 148, 149, 152-158, 160-162, 167, 173, 179-193, 197, 201-203, 206-208, 215, 217, 231, 234, 243-245, 248-249, 247-250
Helsinki Watch, 14, 182, 185-187, 202, 204, 207
Hillenbrand, Martin, 103, 109, 113
Holland, see Netherlands
Honecker, Erich, 11, 57-58, 67-68, 70-77
Human rights, 11, 13-16, 49, 95, 131, 133, 135, 143, 149, 152, 156-157, 160, 162-163, 179-193, 195-199, 201-208, 216, 226, 231, 233, 249-250
Hungary, 8, 23, 25, 39, 132, 186, 226, 228, 233
Hækkerup, Per, 16

IKV (Inter Church Peace Council), the Netherlands, 226
Iloniemi, Jaakko, 145, 149
International Helsinki Federation for Human Rights (IHF), 14, 187
Italy, 7, 9, 87, 105, 127, 193, 205

Jan Hus Foundation, 224, 232
Jaruzelski, Wojciech, 27, 137, 164, 195, 197, 203-205, 222, 233
Jedrychowski, Stefan, 41
Johnson, Lyndon B., 65, 83, 101

Kadar, Janos, 66, 218
Khrushchev, Nikita, 25-26, 105
Kissinger, Henry, 12-13, 16, 81-83, 86-88, 90-94, 101-115, 150-151, 156
Kontinent, 228
KOR (Workers' Defence Committee), Poland, 234

Korving, Bennett, 51
KOS (Committee for the Defence of Society), Poland, 226
Kosygin, Alexei, 62
Kultura, 228

Laber, Jeri, 85, 186
Lambertists (OCI), *see* Trotskyites
Le Goff, Jacques, 229
Lega per l'Ambiente, Italy, 226
Lettre internationale, 228
Liedermann, Helmut, 146
Liehm, Antonin, 228
Lippmann, Walter, 19-20
Listy (Socialist exile group from Czechoslovakia), 232
Lithuania, 183
Longo, Luigi, 24
Luxembourg, 127
Luxembourg Report, 124

Madrid CSCE Follow-up Meeting (1980-1983), 143-144, 158-167, 185-188, 198, 202-203, 207, 251
Magyar Füzetek, 228
Maiskii, Ivan, 23
Martinet, Gilles, 223
Marshall Plan, 24
Martial law, Poland, 14, 137, 143, 164, 195, 196, 197, 199, 200, 202, 203, 204, 205, 206, 208, 220, 222, 227, 229, 230, 234
Maximov, Vladimir, 228
May 1968, 219, 222
MBFR (Mutual and Balanced Force Reductions), 12, 90-93, 95, 102, 106-112, 114

Michnik, Adam, 228
Mielke, Erich, 60, 67, 77
Mitterrand, François, 218, 223-224, 229-230, 233
Mlynar, Zdenek, 227
Molotov, Vyacheslav, 23, 244
Moscow Helsinki Group, 182-184, 186-187
Mouvement pour la Paix, France, 225
Movement for the Defence of Human and Civil Rights (ROPCiO), Poland, 183
Moynihan, Daniel Patrick, 201
Munich Agreement of 1938, 39, 63

N+N (Neutral and Non-Aligned States), 13, 143-144, 149, 153-154, 161-163, 165
Nagy, Imre, 23, 25
NATO (North Atlantic Treaty Organisation), 9-11, 13-14, 16, 44, 69-70, 80-81, 87, 89-93, 95, 101, 103-108, 110-111, 113-114, 124-128, 134, 147-148, 151, 157, 159, 161, 164-165, 179, 182, 187, 197-199, 201, 206, 245-246, 250-251
Netherlands, the, 127, 160, 193, 231
NGOs (non-governmental organisations), 11, 14, 181, 183, 184, 185, 186, 187
Nixon, Richard, 12-13, 58, 79-84, 86-87, 90, 94-95, 101-106, 108, 111-123
Noirot, Paul, 228
Non-Proliferation Treaty (NPT), 63
Norden, Albert, 64, 67, 73, 74
North Atlantic Council, 91, 93, 114, 198
Norway, 123, 126, 154, 161

La Nouvelle Alternative 228
NSDM 162 (National Security Study Memorandum 162), US, 112

Oder-Neisse line, 36-37, 40-42, 45, 52, 53, 63
Olszowski, Stefan, 46
Orlov, Yuri, 182, 185-186
Ostpolitik, 9, 11-12, 35-41, 43, 45, 47, 49-51, 58-67, 88, 90-91, 93-95, 101-106, 110-112, 126, 131, 215

Pahr, Willibald, 162
PCF (French Communist Party), 217-219, 222-223
Peace movement, non-aligned, 216, 225, 226, 231
Peace groups, independent, 216
Pederson, Richard F., 110
Pelikan, Jiri, 224, 232
PEN Club France, 224, 232
Perestroika, 27, 29, 233
Poland, 8, 11, 14-15, 23, 27, 35-37, 39-51, 55, 63, 86, 88, 132, 137, 143, 154, 162, 164, 183, 186, 193, 195-208, 219, 221-223, 226-227, 229-230, 232-234, 247
Polish United Workers' Party (PUWP), 35, 195
Pompidou, Georges, 101, 123, 133
Portugal, 9
Potsdam, 10, 30, 36, 38
Prague Spring of 1968, 19, 27, 40, 105, 222-223, 227
Pronteau, Jean, 224

Quadripartite Agreement on Berlin, 69, 83, 91, 138

Radio Free Europe (Polish Section), 44, 48
Rapacki, Adam, 38, 40, 63
Rapallo, 9, 11, 50, 225
Reagan, Ronald, 10, 14, 28, 195-201, 203, 206-207
Rencontres Européennes, France, 228
Renk, Hans-Jörg, 152, 157
Rocard, Michel, 222-223
Rogers, William, 89-91, 104, 111-114
Romania, 8, 23, 62, 86, 109, 132, 145, 154
Ruete, Hans, 38
Rusk, Dean, 61, 65, 101
Ryding, Göran, 145

Sakharov, Andrei, 182, 233
SALT (Strategic Arms Limitation Talks), 68-69, 90, 94, 114, 156, 159
Samuel Campiche, 146
Sanctions, against Poland, 14, 15, 109, 137, 195, 196, 197, 198, 199, 201, 205, 206, 207, 208
Scheel, Walter, 46, 70, 92, 134
Schmidt, Helmut, 38, 47, 137, 197-198
Schröder, Gerhard, 63
Schumann, Maurice, 107, 110, 127
Security, 10, 16, 20, 29, 40, 42, 67, 69, 72, 90, 92-93, 102-104, 106-110, 112, 130, 143, 150, 153, 180-181
SED (Socialist Unity Party), GDR, 58, 61, 62, 63, 64, 66, 67, 68
Semjonov, Vladimir, 62-63
Shcharansky, Anatoly, 182
Shdanov, Andrei, 23-24
Shevardnaze, Eduard, 29
Socialist International, 232
Socialist Party (PS), France, 217, 224
Socialist Party (PSI), Italy, 232
Sokolak, Henryk, 47

Solidarnosc, 15, 27, 195, 204, 206, 216, 220-224, 226-227, 229-235
Solzhenitsyn, Alexandr, 217-219
Sonnenfeldt, Helmut, 16, 86, 108, 111, 150
Soutou, Georges-Henri, 20-21, 254
Soviet Union, 9, 10, 11, 13, 14, 20-23, 25, 27, 36, 37, 39-43, 45, 50, 61, 62, 64, 65, 68, 70, 80, 81, 84, 87, 89, 94, 101, 102, 104-111, 127, 132, 137, 147, 154, 156, 158, 161, 162, 164, 166, 179-183, 187, 188, 195, 201, 204, 206, 208, 212, 233, 246, 247-251
Spain, 9, 146, 154
SPD (West German Social Democratic Party), 59-62, 64-65, 67-68, 83-84, 88-89, 103
Stalin, Joseph, 21, 23-25, 28, 59, 217
Stalinism, 59, 217
Stasi (State Security Police), GDR, 11, 71-72
State Department, US, 12, 16, 83, 89-90, 94, 101, 102, 103, 104, 107, 109-114, 198, 200, 202, 207
Stoph, Willi, 62, 67
Strauss, Franz Josef, 63, 65
Sub-committee on CSCE, 126-128
Suslov, Mikhail, 27
Svedectvi (Testimony), 228
Sweden, 14, 144, 147-148, 160, 162-163, 168, 193, 229, 232
Swiss Peace Council, 226
Switzerland, 144, 146-148, 161-163, 165, 168, 193

Thomas, Daniel, 15, 189, 204, 212
Tigrid, Pavel 228-229
Töttermann, Richard, 145, 146

Trade Unions, 15, 59, 60, 65, 67, 195, 216, 220-223, 230, 231, 235
Transnational activism, 14, 188, 191
Trotskyites (French), 15, 224, 225, 227, 231, 232, 234, 235

Ulbricht, Walter, 11, 38-39, 57-69, 71, 85
Ukraine, 183
Ukrainian Public Group of Assistance to Implementation of the Helsinki Agreements in the USSR, 183
United Kingdom, *see* Great Britain
United Nations, 10, 30, 40
United States, 8, 10, 12-14, 36, 51, 58, 79-81, 86, 88, 94-95, 104, 105, 108, 110, 114, 125, 135, 180-181, 184-187, 193, 195-201, 205-206, 208
USSR, Union of Soviet Socialist Republics, *see* Soviet Union
Ustinov, Dimitri, 27

Vernant, Jean-Jacques, 224
Vest, George, 111-113
Vienna CSCE Follow-up Meeting (1986-1989), 188
Vietnam, 13
VONS (Committee for the Defence of the Unjustly Prosecuted), Czechoslovakia, 183, 234

Working Commission to Investigate the Use of Psychiatry for Political Purposes, Soviet Union, 183
Walesa, Lech, 204, 230
Warsaw Pact, 84-85, 92-94, 103-106, 124-125, 127, 130, 150, 161, 164, 217, 228, 246, 249, 251
Wehner, Herbert, 62, 65

West Germany, *see* Federal Republic of Germany (FRG)
Westpolitik, 61, 62, 65, 66
Wilson, Harold, 114
Winzer, Otto, 60, 67, 70
World War II, 7, 8, 9, 29, 110, 196, 245

Yalta, 10, 30, 36, 215
Yugoslavia, 148, 154-155, 158, 162-163, 168, 186, 193, 251

Zedong, Mao, 25